Do Housing Allowances Work?

Editors: KATHARINE L. BRADBURY
ANTHONY DOWNS

Do Housing Allowances Work?

Contributors: Garland E. Allen, Jerry J. Fitts, and Evelyn S. Glatt

Harold W. Watts with Felicity Skidmore

Henry J. Aaron

Mahlon R. Straszheim

Peter H. Rossi

Eric A. Hanushek and John M. Quigley

Edwin S. Mills and Arthur Sullivan

David N. Kershaw and Roberton C. Williams, Jr.

John F. Kain

Anthony Downs and Katharine L. Bradbury

The Brookings Institution
Washington, D.C.

Library of Congress Cataloging in Publication data:

Main entry under title:

Do housing allowances work?

(Brookings studies in social experimentation)
Papers and comments presented at a con-
ference at Brookings Institution, November 19,
1979.
Bibliography: p.
Includes index.
Contents: The experimental housing allowance
program / Garland E. Allen, Jerry J. Fitts,
and Evelyn S. Glatt—A critical review of the program
as a social experiment / Harold W. Watts with Felicity
Skidmore—Policy implications: a progress report /
Henry J. Aaron—[etc.]
1. Housing subsidies—United States—Con-
gresses. I. Bradbury, Katharine L., 1946–   .
II. Downs, Anthony. III. Brookings Institution.
IV. Series.
HD7288.83.D6   363.5'8   81-66189
ISBN 0-8157-1052-6   AACR2
ISBN 0-8157-1051-8 (pbk.)

9 8 7 6 5 4 3 2 1

THE BROOKINGS INSTITUTION is an independent organization devoted to nonpartisan research, education, and publication in economics, government, foreign policy, and the social sciences generally. Its principal purposes are to aid in the development of sound public policies and to promote public understanding of issues of national importance.

The Institution was founded on December 8, 1927, to merge the activities of the Institute for Government Research, founded in 1916, the Institute of Economics, founded in 1922, and the Robert Brookings Graduate School of Economics and Government, founded in 1924.

The Board of Trustees is responsible for the general administration of the Institution, while the immediate direction of the policies, program, and staff is vested in the President, assisted by an advisory committee of the officers and staff. The by-laws of the Institution state: "It is the function of the Trustees to make possible the conduct of scientific research, and publication, under the most favorable conditions, and to safeguard the independence of the research staff in the pursuit of their studies and in the publication of the results of such studies. It is not a part of their function to determine, control, or influence the conduct of particular investigations or the conclusions reached."

The President bears final responsibility for the decision to publish a manuscript as a Brookings book. In reaching his judgment on the competence, accuracy, and objectivity of each study, the President is advised by the director of the appropriate research program and weighs the views of a panel of expert outside readers who report to him in confidence on the quality of the work. Publication of a work signifies that it is deemed a competent treatment worthy of public consideration but does not imply endorsement of conclusions or recommendations.

The Institution maintains its position of neutrality on issues of public policy in order to safeguard the intellectual freedom of the staff. Hence interpretations or conclusions in Brookings publications should be understood to be solely those of the authors and should not be attributed to the Institution, to its trustees, officers, or other staff members, or to the organizations that support its research.

Foreword

Arguments about the best way to help poor people improve their housing have been going on for years. They have strongly influenced public policies that involve the annual spending of billions of dollars. Yet because there was little detailed scientific knowledge concerning housing market behavior, certainly not enough to resolve such arguments, Congress in 1970 funded one of the largest social experiments ever undertaken: the Experimental Housing Allowance Program.

The main purposes of the endeavor were to test the practicality and effects of a housing allowance and to learn as much as possible about how housing markets really work. Since 1973 the U.S. Department of Housing and Urban Development has been carrying out experiments for varying lengths of time in twelve cities, and nearly all data from the experiments have now been collected and analyzed.

This volume presents the findings of the experiments and analyzes their most important implications. It results from a conference held at the Brookings Institution in November 1979 that was sponsored by the Department of Housing and Urban Development. At the conference, eight papers were presented by academic housing specialists whom Brookings had commissioned to write about various aspects of the housing allowance experiments. Other experts prepared formal comments on the papers, and the presentation of each paper was followed by a general discussion by the participants. The participants included representatives from the staff that administered the experiments, from the outside contractors that conducted them (the Rand Corporation and Abt Associates), from the Urban Institute team that was engaged to collate the results, and from civil rights, consumer, and other organizations.

In the first paper, which presents background material for the eight conference papers, three members of the staff of the Department of Housing and Urban Development describe the housing experiments and summarize their findings. In the concluding paper, Anthony Downs and Katharine L. Bradbury of the Brookings Economic Studies program review the issues that emerged from the general discussion at the conference.

The editors and authors are grateful for useful comments by members of the staffs of the Department of Housing and Urban Development, the Rand Corporation, Abt Associates, and the Urban Institute, especially for those of Jerry J. Fitts, Ira S. Lowry, and Stephen D. Kennedy. The manuscript was edited by Janet Horwitz and Andrea De La Garza of Editorial Experts, Inc. Its factual content was verified by Thea M. Lee of Brookings under the supervision of Penelope Harpold. Anita G. Whitlock, also of Brookings, circulated the papers and comments and made the conference arrangements with commendable efficiency. The index was prepared by Diana Regenthal.

This is the sixth book in the Brookings series of Studies in Social Experimentation. The series assesses the usefulness of experiments in increasing knowledge about the effects of domestic social policies and programs of the federal government. The research in social experimentation is conducted as part of the Brookings Economic Studies program, which is directed by Joseph A. Pechman.

The research upon which this book is based was supported by a Grant Cooperative Agreement with the U.S. Department of Housing and Urban Development. The views expressed here are solely those of the authors and should not be ascribed to the U.S. Department of Housing and Urban Development, or to the trustees, officers, or other staff members of the Brookings Institution.

BRUCE K. MAC LAURY
President

June 1981
Washington, D.C.

Contents

Tables

Contents

Figure

David N. Kershaw and Roberton C. Williams, Jr.

GARLAND E. ALLEN

JERRY J. FITTS

EVELYN S. GLATT

The Experimental Housing Allowance Program

Housing allowances are payments made directly to eligible households to help them pay the costs of living in housing of their choice. Such payments can vary, depending on (1) what income limits or other household characteristics are used to establish eligibility; (2) whether or not households receiving payments are required to live in housing that meets specific quality standards and, if so, the nature of those standards; and (3) the method used to compute the size of the payment received by each household. Many forms of housing allowance are thus possible; only a small number were tested in the Experimental Housing Allowance Program.

With the eligibility standards used, only low-income families—about 20 percent of all U.S. households—were eligible. Under the program, an eligible family selected a place to live from the existing housing stock. If the unit met the housing requirements established for the program, the family received a monthly housing allowance, the size of which depended on the program's benefit formula. The basic version of the formula provided a payment equal to the cost of standard housing less 25 percent of the family's income. The cost of standard housing established for the program varied by region of the country and by number of bedrooms required for the family size. Although a family could pay more or less than the program cost standard, in general it needed to pay only 25 percent of its in-

Portions of this chapter appeared in U.S. Department of Housing and Urban Development, *The Experimental Housing Allowance Program: Conclusions, the 1980 Report* (Government Printing Office, 1980).

1

come for standard housing, with the allowance payment bridging the gap between the family's contribution and the cost of standard housing.

Housing allowances contrast sharply with the majority of government-supported housing programs for low-income families. Before the Experimental Housing Allowance Program, these programs were usually directed at the production or supply of housing, with the subsidy permanently linked to housing units, not to families. As long as families remained eligible and lived in these particular units, subsidy benefits were passed on in the form of below-market rents.

The Housing Act of 1937 proclaimed the goal of decent, safe, and sanitary dwellings for low-income families. During the four decades that followed, various program approaches for meeting that policy goal have been debated.[1] The topic of housing allowances in particular has appeared in policy debates at least four or five times since 1937. In the middle and late 1940s, position papers and testimony for and against housing allowances were presented during the Taft subcommittee hearings as well as during the discussions that led to the adoption of the Housing Act of 1949.

Until the Housing and Urban Development Act of 1965 was implemented, however, no housing policy had incorporated the concept of housing allowances into its design. The Housing and Urban Development Act of 1965 introduced two new programs—the rent supplement program and the section 23 leased existing housing program. The rent supplement program granted income-related subsidies to tenants of privately owned housing units. Under section 23, the government leased modest standard housing at market prices and then subleased these units to low-income households. The main differences between these two housing programs and housing allowances are that under the 1965 Act households did not receive subsidies directly, and the subsidies were tied to housing units rather than to individual households.

Over the years, many arguments were made for and against the housing allowance approach. Critics of housing allowances argued that giving low-income families cash earmarked for housing would cause housing prices to rise substantially. Some viewed low-income renters as captives of their landlords and believed that landlords would raise the rents of program recipients by the amounts of their allowances. Others argued that the program's housing standards would create an inflationary competition

---

1. U.S. Department of Housing and Urban Development, *Experimental Housing Allowance Program: A 1979 Report of Findings* (GPO, 1979), p. 1.

for acceptable dwellings, as those living in substandard housing sought to qualify for assistance.

Because housing allowance payments would not usually be large enough to induce recipients to purchase or rent newly constructed units, some critics concluded that the program would not increase the supply of acceptable dwellings. They believed that homeowners and landlords would be unwilling or unable to improve substandard dwellings and that recipients would avoid such dwellings, even when improved, because of the neighborhoods in which they were located. Other critics argued that administering an allowance program would be organizationally complex. And some felt that it would be difficult to limit the scale of such a program.

Proponents of housing allowances often stressed the issue of cost, arguing that using the existing housing stock in a housing allowance program is much less expensive than providing low-income families with newly constructed housing. Because families receiving housing allowances would live in units comparable to those of families just above the income limits, they also viewed the program as more equitable than one that would provide low-income families with new units that ineligible higher-income families could not afford. They further argued that an allowance program encourages more maintenance and thus helps to preserve the enormous investment in the existing housing stock.[2]

To elicit some empirical evidence about the concept, Congress directed the Department of Housing and Urban Development (HUD) to establish the Experimental Housing Allowance Program. This mandate was expressed in title V, section 504, of the 1970 Housing and Urban Development Act. It authorized $20 million for the program, called for its completion by the end of fiscal year 1973, limited the program to rental housing, and specified the payment formula. In 1974 section 504 was amended to reflect the program design described below.

Analysis of the many issues raised about housing allowances defined three basic sets of questions. (1) How do families respond to housing allowances? (2) How are housing markets affected by allowances? And (3) how might a housing allowance program be administered and what are its administrative costs?

2. For a more detailed discussion of the history of housing allowances, see David B. Carlson and John D. Heinberg, *How Housing Allowances Work: Integrated Findings from the Experimental Housing Allowance Program* (Washington, D.C.: Urban Institute, 1978), pp. 49–51.

Early in the design process it was concluded that three different though interrelated experiments were necessary. Given the questions raised by the allowance approach, the designers felt that the results from experimentation would be confounded if more than one set of questions was tested in a single experiment or location.

The Demand Experiment

The program's demand experiment focused on how families respond to housing allowances. Some of the specific questions it addressed were as follows:

• Who participates and how are participation rates affected by program features such as payment levels?

• Does a housing allowance program cause participants to move to new locations?

• What portion of the allowance payment is used for housing?

• Does the quality of housing improve for participating households?

• What are the major differences in household responses between a payment program constrained by housing requirements and a program not so constrained, such as welfare payments?

• How do housing allowances compare with other housing programs in terms of participation, housing quality attained, locational choices, and costs?

Design Overview[3]

Answers to these questions obviously depend partly on program rules, so the design systematically varied payment levels, housing requirements, and payment formulas to learn how outcomes would differ. The specific variations tested are described below.

Since changes occur in the absence of any program, it was not sufficient to measure the locational, expenditure, and quantity changes families make when receiving housing allowances. To isolate the effects attributable solely to the housing allowances, the demand experiment included data on similar families (controls) that did not receive such payments. The difference between the changes in housing conditions of control

3. Abt Associates, *Experimental Design and Analysis Plan of the Demand Experiment* (Cambridge, Mass.: Abt, August 1973).

families and those receiving housing allowances represents the *induced* effects of the program. The demand experiment design also included a comparison of the effects on similar families of receiving welfare payments (unconstrained by any housing requirements) and housing allowances.

The demand experiment was conducted over a three-year period in two metropolitan areas: Pittsburgh, Pennsylvania, and Allegheny County, which encompasses it; and Phoenix, Arizona, along with surrounding Maricopa County. These sites were selected from among thirty-one standard metropolitan statistical areas by using a set of criteria that included vacancy rate and size of housing market area as key selection factors. Given the objectives of the experiment, both sites chosen had to be sufficiently large to prevent the allowances to experimental households from having any significant inflationary effect on market rents. Both sites had populations in excess of 500,000 and vacancy rates of about 6 percent in 1970. The other factors in the set of criteria reflected differences of interest to policy makers. Pittsburgh is a slowly growing, older city with a large black population; Phoenix is a rapidly growing, newer city with a large Hispanic population.

In each of these housing markets, about 50,000 families were surveyed. Representative samples of families eligible by income were selected to participate in the various groups discussed above. Between the two sites, approximately 950 control families were selected, and about 2,500 families were enrolled in either constrained or unconstrained payment plans.

Variations Tested

Through combinations of payment formulas and housing requirements, seventeen experimental plans were tested. Two payment formulas were used. The *housing gap formula,* described above, can be expressed as $P = C - bY$, where P is the allowance payment; C is the cost of standard housing established for the program; b is the rate at which the allowance is reduced as household income increases (or the implicit tax rate); and Y is net family income. Under the *percent of rent formula,* the payment (P) is a percentage of the family's rent, $P = aR$, where R is the rent and a is the fraction of the rent paid by the allowance. This formula was included primarily for analytical reasons. From it demand functions were estimated that describe the way in which incomes, expenditures on housing, and prices of housing and of other goods are related. Such estimated functions were used to simulate responses to a variety of programs not directly tested in the demand experiment. Together with the estimates of supply response, they can also be used to simulate the change in market prices and housing expenditures resulting from shifts in demand or costs.

In combination with the primary payment formula (housing gap), four approaches to housing requirements were tested. Based on American Public Health Association criteria, a set of minimum housing standards was developed as the principal approach.[4] Considerable care was exercised in arriving at these standards. They include fifteen major categories of physical attributes that, when taken together, define a decent, safe, and sanitary housing unit (see table 1 for a list of the categories), plus an occupancy standard limiting occupants to two per acceptable bedroom. A second approach, the unconstrained plan, required participants to meet no housing standards. The two other housing requirements tested, high minimum rent and low minimum rent, were included as possible surrogates for physical standards. In these plans, payments were made, regardless of the physical quality of the dwelling, if a household's rent was at or above a required minimum.

How the variations in payment formula and housing requirements combine in the seventeen plans is summarized in table 2. The costs of standard housing used in the housing gap formula are shown in table 3.

Data Base

In this experiment the following methodology was developed to identify a sample of households representative of the eligible population at each site.[5] From a screening interview of about 50,000 households in each site, those who initially appeared to be eligible were randomly assigned to one of the seventeen treatment plans or to the control group.[6] Those assigned were interviewed to obtain baseline information.[7] In these interviews, administered to about 4,000 households in each site, detailed information was obtained on income, current housing conditions, expenditures and preferences, and household demographics. On the basis of data from

4. Helen E. Bakeman, Carol Ann Dalto, and Charles S. White, Sr., "Draft Report on Minimum Standards Requirements in the Housing Allowance Demand Experiment" (Abt, February 1979).
5. Abt Associates, *Experimental Design.*
6. Abt Associates, "Screener Survey Interview," March 1973.
7. Abt Associates, "Baseline Survey Interview," April 1973.

Table 1. Components of Minimum Standards for the Demand Experiment

1. *Complete plumbing:* Private toilet facilities, a shower or tub with hot and cold running water, and a washbasin with hot and cold running water will be present and in working condition.

2. *Complete kitchen facilities:* A cooking stove or range, refrigerator, and kitchen sink with hot and cold running water will be present and in working condition.

3. *Living room, bathroom, kitchen presence:* A living room, bathroom, and kitchen will be present. (This represents the dwelling unit "core," which corresponds to an efficiency unit.)

4. *Light fixtures:* A ceiling or wall-type fixture will be present and working in the bathroom and kitchen.

5. *Electrical:* At least one electric outlet will be present and operable in both the living room and the kitchen. A working wall switch, pull-chain light switch, or additional electrical outlet will be present in the living room.[a]

6. *Heating equipment:* Units with no heating equipment, with unvented room heaters that burn gas, oil, or kerosene, or that are heated mainly with portable electric room heaters will be unacceptable.

7. *Adequate exits:* There will be at least two exits from the dwelling unit leading to safe and open space at ground level (for multifamily building only). Effective November 1973 (retroactive to program inception), this requirement was modified to permit override on a case-by-case basis where it appears that fire safety is met despite lack of a second exit.

8. *Room structure:* Ceiling structure or wall structure for all rooms must not be in condition requiring replacement (such as severe buckling or leaning).

9. *Room surface:* Ceiling surface or wall surface for all rooms must not be in condition requiring replacement (such as surface material that is loose, contains large holes, or is severely damaged).

10. *Ceiling height:* Living room, bathroom, and kitchen ceilings must be 7 feet (or higher) in at least one-half of the room area.[a]

11. *Floor structure:* Floor structure for all rooms must not be in condition requiring replacement (such as large holes or missing parts).

12. *Floor surface:* Floor surface for all rooms must not be in condition requiring replacement (such as large holes or missing parts).

13. *Roof structure:* The roof structure must be firm.

14. *Exterior walls:* The exterior wall structure or exterior wall surface must not need replacement. (For structure, this would include such conditions as severe leaning, buckling, or sagging, and for surface, conditions such as excessive cracks or holes.)

15. *Light/ventilation:* The unit will have a 10 percent ratio of window area to floor area and at least one openable window in the living room, bathroom, and kitchen or the equivalent in the case of properly vented kitchens and/or bathrooms.[a]

Source: Joseph Friedman and Daniel Weinberg, "Draft Report on the Demand for Rental Housing: Evidence from a Percent of Rent Housing Allowance" (Cambridge, Mass.: Abt Associates, September 1978), p. A-31.

a. This housing standard is applied to bedrooms in determining the number of adequate bedrooms for the program occupancy standard.

Table 2. Demand Experiment Sample Sizes at Time of Enrollment and Two Years Later, by Allowance Plan[a]

		Housing requirement [b]			
		Minimum standards	Minimum rent		No requirement
b value	C level		Low = 0.7C*	High = 0.9C*	
0.15	C*	121 (81)	. . .	. . .	. . .
0.25	1.2C*	91 (63)	85 (58)	88 (60)	. . .
0.25	C*	133 (77)	132 (89)	145 (88)	145 (103)
0.25	0.8C*	128 (82)	124 (79)	137 (78)	. . .
0.35	C*	137 (75)	. . .	. . .	. . .

Addendum:

a value	Percent of rent plan[b]
0.60	66 (49)
0.50	235 (190)
0.40	265 (179)
0.30	258 (176)
0.20	176 (111)

Source: Stephen D. Kennedy, *Final Report of the Housing Allowance Demand Experiment* (Abt, May 14, 1980), pp. A-19, A-20.

a. Housing gap: $P = C - bY$, where C is a multiple of C^*; b = rate at which the allowance decreases as income increases; C^* = cost of standard housing (varied by family size and also by site); C = basic payment level to a family with no income; and Y = adjusted income. Percent of rent: $P = aR$. Controls: 959 (603 two years after enrollment).

b. Numbers in parentheses are at two years after enrollment.

these interviews, eligible families were later offered enrollment in the program. In each site about 1,250 families were enrolled in one of the experimental plans and another 400 to 500 families joined the control group.

Household report forms[8] were completed by all enrollee and control households at the time of enrollment and monthly thereafter. These reports tracked changes in rent, income, household composition, and so forth. Supplements to these reports, which provided the same kind of data but in greater detail, were obtained annually.

Trained housing inspectors completed housing evaluation forms,[9] which provided extensive information on the housing quality of every dwelling unit occupied by enrollees and controls. These inspections were made at enrollment, each year thereafter, and whenever an enrolled or control household moved.

8. Abt Associates, "Initial Household Report Form" and "Household Report Form," April 1973.

9. Abt Associates, "Housing Evaluation Form," April 1973.

Table 3. Estimated Cost of Standard Housing Used in Payment Formula of Demand Experiment, 1972, 1973, and 1975

| Number of bedrooms | Size of household | Estimated market rents (dollars)[a] | | | |
| | | Pittsburgh | | Phoenix | |
		October 1972	March 1975	March 1973	March 1975
0	1	105	115	125	135
1	2	120	130	155	165
2	3–4	140	150	180	190
3	5–6	160	170	220	235
4	7 or more	190	205	265	280

Source: U.S. Department of Housing and Urban Development, *Experimental Housing Allowance Program: A 1979 Report of Findings* (GPO, 1979), p. 100.

a. Estimated monthly cost of shelter and utilities for a dwelling of the indicated size that meets specified quality standards. Standard costs were initially derived from estimates by local panels of experts and subsequently increased to reflect measured inflation. The effective date of each schedule is shown in the table.

Enrolled households and controls were interviewed periodically, at intervals of six, twelve, and twenty-four months after enrollment.[10] From these interviews, information was obtained on such subjects as housing and neighborhood preferences and satisfaction, search and moving behavior, and views about the allowance program.

Exit interviews[11] were conducted for a sample of households that either refused to enroll or enrolled and later terminated. The households were interviewed to gather information on the reasons for their behavior.

In both demand experiment sites, information on program participation, location, housing quality, costs, and participant satisfaction and preferences was collected on the public housing, section 23 leased housing, and section 236 interest subsidy housing programs for comparison with a housing allowance program.[12]

Field Operations[13]

After completion of the design, screening interviews, baseline surveys, establishment of site organizations, and training of site personnel, enroll-

10. Abt Associates, "First Periodic Interview," September 1973; "Second Periodic Interview," April 1974; "Third Periodic Interview," January 1975.

11. Abt Associates, "Exit Interview," August 1973.

12. Abt Associates, "Program Comparisons Interview," August 1975.

13. Abt Associates, *Site Operating Procedures Handbook of the Demand Experiment* (Abt, April 2, 1973).

Table 4. Demand Experiment Operations, 1973–77

			Recipient households after two years		
Site	Operating time	Enrollment[a]	Number	Average adjusted income (dollars)[b]	Average monthly payment (dollars)
Pittsburgh	April 1973– February 1977	1,211	736	5,000	61
Phoenix	May 1973– February 1977	1,255	569	5,100	78

Source: HUD, *A 1979 Report of Findings*, p. 99.
a. Does not include control households in each site.
b. Gross annual income minus federal and state income taxes, social security taxes, medical expenses, and so forth.

ment began in the spring of 1973. The first ten months of operations concentrated on enrollments, and families then received payments for three years; the site operations therefore extended over a four-year period.

To avoid confusion between participants' reactions to the experimental offers and their adjustment to the phaseout of the experiment, analysis of household responses is based on data collected from households during their first two years in the experiment. During their last experimental year, households were helped to enter other subsidized housing programs for two more years of assistance.

Table 4 shows that almost 2,500 households were initially enrolled in both sites, and that about half were receiving payments after two years.[14] The average payment was about $69 a month.

The Supply Experiment

The purpose of the supply experiment was to determine the effects of housing allowances on housing markets. Among the specific questions this experiment was designed to address are the following:

• When all eligible families are offered the opportunity to receive housing allowances, will landlords, developers, homeowners, mortgage lend-

14. For a detailed summary of demand experiment household responses, see Joseph Friedman and Daniel Weinberg, "Draft Report on Housing Consumption Under a Constrained Income Transfer: Evidence from a Housing Gap Housing Allowance" (Abt, April 1979); and Friedman and Weinberg, "Draft Report on the Demand for Rental Housing: Evidence from a Percent of Rent Housing Allowance" (Abt, September 1978).

ers, real estate brokers, and others accommodate the recipients in their attempts to improve their housing conditions? Or, as some predicted, will the price of housing simply increase without a corresponding improvement in housing?

• To what extent will housing allowances stimulate repairs, substantial rehabilitation, or the construction of new units?

• As housing allowance recipients attempt to increase their housing consumption by moving, what neighborhoods will they seek and which ones will they succeed in entering? What is the impact on the neighborhoods they leave and enter? Will families move from the central city to the suburbs?

Design Overview[15]

While some of the specific questions of the supply experiment were similar to those of the demand experiment, a different approach was required to answer these questions. In the supply experiment, enrollment was open to all eligible families in two metropolitan housing markets. The supply experiment is the first housing program for low-income families to have open enrollment.

Eligible households—homeowners and renters—were offered what was believed to be a likely housing allowance plan, were such a program adopted for the entire nation. A housing gap payment schedule was used. The amount of the allowance payment equaled the difference between the cost of modest standard housing, which varied with family size and region of the country, and 25 percent of the family's preallowance income. These payments were made only to those households that either lived in or moved to units that met the program's housing standards. These standards are similar to those in the demand experiment and were based on the American Public Health Association criteria and local housing codes of the supply experiment sites.

Considerable care was exercised in selecting the two housing markets for the supply experiment: Brown County, Wisconsin, whose central city is Green Bay; and St. Joseph County, Indiana, whose central city is South Bend. All of the nation's standard metropolitan statistical areas were considered in the selection process. The housing markets chosen had to differ in certain ways, yet be typical of a substantial portion of markets through-

15. Ira S. Lowry, ed., *General Design Report: First Draft* (Santa Monica: Rand Corp., May 1973).

out the nation.[16] Brown County has a rapidly growing urban center, a relatively tight housing market, a good housing stock, and a very small minority population. St. Joseph County has a declining central city with a deteriorating housing stock, a minority population of average size but growing, and an excess supply of central city housing.

Data Base

The housing allowance program was monitored primarily through periodic analyses of administrative records.[17] The records include enrollment applications, verification and reverification of household eligibility, histories of allowance payments, and housing evaluations of dwelling units. These records provide considerable information on the characteristics of applicants and enrollees, their housing conditions and expenditures at the time of enrollment, and subsequent changes in income, household composition, housing characteristics, and housing expenditures. The records also provide useful data on applicants who were declared ineligible and on those who were declared eligible but who finally declined to participate.

Although administrative records of the allowance program do measure its market stimulus, data on the market response come primarily from an annual cycle of field surveys of owners and occupants of a stratified random sample of marketwide residential properties. Hereafter "sample" refers to this marketwide sample. At each site a panel of approximately 3,300 dwelling units was tracked by means of surveys administered at baseline and for three years thereafter. Several specific surveys were included.

Each property in the sample was examined in the field to record its physical characteristics and the general characteristics of the immediate neighborhood. The survey instrument was designed to detect alterations or improvements, changes in the physical condition or use of the property, and changes in the neighborhood. This survey was administered at baseline and three years later.

Interviews with the landlord of every rental property in the sample were carried out annually. The sample interviews recorded the landlords' rental

16. Jeanne E. Goedert, *Generalizing from the Experimental Housing Allowance Program: An Assessment of Site Characteristics,* 229-0 (Urban Institute, June 1978).
17. Housing Allowance Office, Inc., *Housing Allowance Office Handbook,* November 1974.

revenues and outlays for building maintenance and operation during the preceding year, including a detailed account of repairs and improvements and their costs. Also acquired were data on mortgage financing, property ownership and management, property and tenant characteristics, landlord-tenant relations, and plans for the property. Finally, the interviews elicited the landlords' impressions of the program and how it affected them.

For rental properties in the sample, annual interviews with the current occupants were conducted; on large properties the housing units were sampled. This survey collected information on the interior features and conditions of the housing unit and on contract rent and other housing expenses. Data were also collected on family composition and characteristics, income, education, and occupation. The interview for homeowners in the sample covered similar topics but also asked detailed questions on mortgage financing and housing expenses similar to those addressed to landlords.

In addition to observing the immediate environs of each property in the sample, data were gathered on larger neighborhoods at each site. Detailed information on land use, access to public facilities, amenities, and the condition of housing and streets or other public areas in each neighborhood was gathered at baseline and was updated three years later.

Periodic surveys of the activities and policies of market intermediaries were undertaken at each site. Included among the market intermediaries were mortgage lenders, real estate brokers, insurance firms, and home improvement contractors.

The systematic surveys were supplemented at each site by a resident observer, who gathered informal information about community events, activities, and attitudes that might affect the housing allowance program. The observer's reports help to interpret survey findings and flag issues that warrant additional research.

Field Operations

Enrollment in the experiment began in mid-1974 in Brown County and in late 1974 in St. Joseph County. In each site, the operations were designed to extend over ten years. It was felt that ten years of allowance payments were needed to give eligible households, landlords, and market intermediaries a sense that the experiment was permanent—that is, similar in duration to a real housing program—making their responses to the ex-

Table 5. Status of the Supply Experiment in January 1980

| | Recipient households in January 1980 | | |
Housing tenure by site	Number	Average adjusted income (dollars)[a]	Average monthly payment (dollars)
Brown County, Wisconsin[b]			
Renters	2,676	4,113	93
Homeowners	1,104	4,947	78
All households	3,780	4,357	89
St. Joseph County, Indiana[b]			
Renters	2,521	2,827	114
Homeowners	3,371	4,040	85
All households	5,892	3,521	97

Source: HUD, *Experimental Housing Allowance Program: Conclusions, the 1980 Report* (GPO, 1980), p. 88.

a. Gross annual income minus deductions for dependents, medical expenses, and so forth.

b. The operating period for Brown County is June 1974 to June 1984; for St. Joseph County, December 1974 to December 1984. These periods include the five-year experimental period and a five-year additional commitment of allowance payments to eligible participating families.

periment similar to their responses to a real program. For analysis, however, it was felt that only the first five years of data collection were necessary to measure their responses.

Table 5 shows the number of recipient households, their average income, and their average monthly payment. The costs of standard housing used for payment calculation are shown in table 6.

The Administrative Agency Experiment

The objective of the administrative agency experiment was to gather information about the administration and costs of delivering housing allowances. The design and analysis, therefore, focused on those administrative functions considered to be of major importance for the administration, management, and operation of a national housing allowance program.

Design Overview

The experiment consisted of experimental allowance programs administered by several different types of public agencies and an independent evaluation by a research firm. The research firm and all agencies performed their roles under contract to and in consultation with HUD.

The design provided for natural rather than systematic variations in administrative procedures. Agencies were encouraged to develop their own procedures for administering the allowance program within a set of broad guidelines developed by HUD. An approach that would systematically vary the procedures used by agencies was rejected, in part because no adequate theoretical or empirical basis existed for identifying the most important types. Furthermore, HUD wanted to understand the extent to which local administrative procedures required detailed federal specification to ensure the effective implementation of an allowance program and to learn about innovative practices that might emerge from the procedural choices made by the agencies. Left to their own devices, would agencies choose procedures appropriate to their situation and appropriate for meeting the goals of the program? HUD believed that systematic design variations might have precluded valuable learning from locally developed models.

The administrative agency experiment was implemented as if it were a typical housing program. Eight agencies, which potentially could administer a national housing allowance program, were selected to operate the experiment. They consisted of two public housing authorities, two county agencies, two state community development agencies, and two welfare agencies.[18] The agencies were required to submit, for HUD approval, an operating plan that specified their approach to and organizational structure for performing required administrative functions. The program guidelines were set forth in an operating manual.[19] The required functions included making eligible households aware of the program (outreach); selecting and screening applicants; certifying income; inspecting housing units; making payments to families; providing housing market information; assisting families in their search for housing and in dealings with landlords; informing families of their equal opportunity rights; and providing legal assistance in discrimination cases. Although the functions were required, the approaches were selected by the individual agencies.

18. The eight agencies are the Salem, Oregon, Housing Authority; Tulsa, Oklahoma, Housing Authority; San Bernardino, California, County Board of Supervisors; Jacksonville, Florida, Department of Housing and Urban Development; Commonwealth of Massachusetts Department of Community Affairs; State of Illinois Department of Local Government Affairs; Social Services Board of North Dakota; and Durham County, North Carolina, Department of Social Services.

19. Abt Associates, *Agency Program Manual* (Abt, March 1973).

Table 6. Estimated Cost of Standard Housing Used in Payment Formula of Supply Experiment, 1974–80

		Estimated market rents (dollars)[a]									
		Brown County					St. Joseph County				
Number of bedrooms	Size of household	June 1974	April 1976	May 1977	May 1978	July 1979	Dec. 1974	Sept. 1976	Sept. 1977	Jan. 1979	Jan. 1980
0	1	100	125	130	140	155	100	115	120	130	155
1	2	125	145	155	170	180	125	140	150	160	175
2	3–4	155	175	185	200	220	145	160	175	190	200
3	5–6	170	195	205	235	255	160	175	185	195	235
4 or more	7 or more	190	210	220	265	280	170	185	190	205	260

Source: HUD, Conclusions, the 1980 Report, p. 89.
a. Estimated monthly cost of shelter and utilities for a dwelling of the indicated size that meets specified quality standards. Standard costs were initially estimated from pre-program field surveys of rental dwellings in each site; they were subsequently increased to reflect measured inflation, nearly all of which was in fuel and utility prices. The effective date of each schedule is shown in the table: the measurement dates were several months earlier: September 1973, January 1976, January 1977, March 1978, and January 1979 for Brown County; and August 1974, July 1976, August 1977, and August 1979 for St. Joseph County.

Once agreement on the operating plan was reached, agency administration was monitored by HUD through its central and field offices in much the same way that HUD monitors its ongoing programs.

In the eight agencies, the number of households to which payments could be made was limited to 900 in six cases, 500 in one case, and 400 in another. The payment formula was similar to the one used in the supply experiment and to one of the housing gap types in the demand experiment: the difference between the cost of modest standard housing and 25 percent of the family's preallowance income. Payments were made only to families that either lived in or moved to units that met the program's housing standards.

The agencies provided operating and financial data on forms designed by the evaluation contractor to ensure data comparability across the eight sites. Operating forms, which provided basic data on each household at successive stages in the program, included a household application form, verification-of-income form, housing evaluation form, and termination form. From them, data were collected on household eligibility, household demographic characteristics, how the household satisfied the requirement to receive payments, and reasons for terminating participation in the program. Agency management reports provided financial, scheduling, and planning data. They included information on flows of participants each month and costs and staff time expended for each function during the month.

Description of the Evaluation[20]

The evaluation contractor had no role in designing or conducting the experimental program operations. The contractor obtained the agency forms and collected additional data designed to evaluate agency operations. Data collected by the evaluation contractor included on-site observers' reports, interviews with a sample of participants at each site, and housing quality evaluations of a sample of dwelling units.

At each site an observer spent a year and a half recording the procedures and experiences of the agency. The observer's mission was to observe the agency as a whole. In particular, the observer prepared a monthly log recording performance of various administrative functions, chronologies of program events, interviews with agency staff, and several

20. Abt Associates, *Evaluation Manual of the Administrative Agency Experiment* (Abt, December 1972).

case studies following the experience of individual households in the program.

Interviews with a sample of participating households were conducted at each site at enrollment, after six months of payments, and sixteen months after enrollment.[21] These interviews collected information on the households' attitudes toward the agency administration and their satisfaction with the program.

Trained housing inspectors completed housing evaluation forms, which provided extensive information on the quality of the dwelling units of the same households sampled for periodic interviews.[22] Information was collected at the same intervals specified for the periodic interviews.

A sample of households that had either refused to enroll or had enrolled and later terminated were interviewed to gather information on their reasons for doing so.[23]

Data collected by agencies and the evaluator were analyzed in two ways: (1) descriptive case studies of individual agencies, and (2) analysis by functions across the agencies. The case studies and functional analyses were considered complementary. The case studies characterized each site as a whole and analyzed interactions that occurred in the program, among the operating functions, the households involved, and the program management. The functional analyses characterized each function in general and examined the variations in function performance and circumstances across sites.

Field Operations

The enrollment period lasted for seven months at each site. The initial enrollment was completed at the last site in May 1974. In Jacksonville, where the number of participants was significantly lower than anticipated, the enrollment period was reopened to determine whether changes in agency operations could achieve different results. Through its second enrollment period, completed in July 1975, the agency was able to obtain the number of participants to reach its target.

During its experimental phase, the administrative agency experiment was designed to provide two years of allowance payments. Families re-

21. Abt Associates, "First Participant Survey of the AAE," January 1973; "Second Participant Survey of the AAE," June 1974; "Third Participant Survey of the AAE," September 1974.
22. Abt Associates, "Housing Evaluation Form of the AAE," March 1973.
23. Abt Associates, "Former Participant Survey of the AAE," January 1973.

Table 7. Status of the Administrative Agency Experiment after the First Year of Operation

		Recipient households[a]		
Site	Operating time period	Number	Average adjusted income (dollars)[b]	Average monthly payment (dollars)
Bismarck, North Dakota	July 1973–April 1976	367	3,000	72
Durham, North Carolina	July 1973–April 1976	483	2,400	74
Jacksonville, Florida	April 1973–July 1977[c]			
	First enrollment	300	2,000	86
	Second enrollment	541	3,200	74
Peoria, Illinois	April 1973–February 1976	835	3,700	85
Salem, Oregon	March 1973–January 1976	870	2,800	84
San Bernardino, California	March 1973–March 1976	776	2,900	84
Springfield, Massachusetts	April 1973–February 1976	861	3,000	89
Tulsa, Oklahoma	August 1973–May 1976	825	2,700	72

Source: HUD, *A 1979 Report of Findings*, p. 96.

a. This represents steady-state operations—when the experiment was fully operating and before households were phased into other housing programs.

b. Gross annual income minus deductions for dependents, medical expenses, and so forth.

c. The operating period in Jacksonville was longer than at other locations because enrollment was reopened.

ceiving housing allowances in the experiment received an additional commitment from HUD of assistance under other subsidized housing programs, primarily section 23 leased existing housing. This commitment ran for three years after the experimental phase ended and was conditional on family eligibility for these programs. The eight state and local agencies involved in the experiment transferred their responsibilities to local agencies, which administered programs for recipient families during the three-year follow-up period.

In all, nearly 6,000 households received payments. At the time the experiment was fully operational, the average annual adjusted income of participating families was slightly under $3,000 and their average monthly housing allowance payment was about $80, as shown in table 7. The estimated market rents for adequate housing are shown in table 8.

Table 8. Estimated Monthly Market Rents for Adequate Housing During First Year of Operation of the Administrative Agency Experiment

Dollars

Site	*Number of bedrooms (size of household)*					
	0 *(1)*	*1* *(2)*	*2* *(3–4)*	*3* *(5–6)*	*4* *(7–8)*	*5 or more* *(9 or more)*
Bismarck	90	120	155	195	230	230
Durham	100	115	145	175	190	190
Jacksonville	120	140	165	210	240	265
Peoria	100	130	155	195	225	235
Salem	100	125	155	195	225	240
San Bernardino	95	125	150	190	225	225
Springfield	110	125	155	185	220	240
Tulsa	90	115	145	170	210	210

Source: HUD, *Conclusions, the 1980 Report,* p. 95.

Summary of the Program Design

Tables 9 and 10 on pages 22 to 24 show the principal program design elements of each component of the Experimental Housing Allowance Program and the income eligibility limits by site. For simplicity of presentation and comparison, table 9 refers to the part of the demand experiment in which the payment formula and housing requirement are most like those used in the supply and administrative agency experiments.

Findings from the Program[24]

When the program began in early 1972, not much information was available about the housing conditions of low-income families or about the effect of the housing programs designed to serve them. The Experimental Housing Allowance Program was the first major attempt to subject a housing program concept to systematic testing. The program followed families for up to five years and measured their housing changes in response to different types of assistance. It examined housing markets in a similar manner.

24. For a more detailed discussion of findings, see HUD, *A 1979 Report of Findings;* and HUD, *Conclusions, the 1980 Report.* See also the other papers in this volume.

Experimental operations are now complete. The findings presented below draw on all the experiments to provide an overview of what has been learned.

Housing Conditions of Low-Income Households[25]

The incomes of approximately 20 percent of all U.S. households make them eligible for a housing allowance program. When the Experimental Housing Allowance Program began, the majority of these eligible households lived in housing that the program considered substandard. Judged against the quality standards adopted for the program, the range was from 49 percent of eligible homeowners in the supply experiment sites to 73 percent of eligible renters in the demand experiment sites. Furthermore, 44 percent of the preprogram housing units of representative renters in the demand experiment were judged to be severely substandard.

Besides living in substandard units, many low-income households have high rent burdens. More than one-fourth of the eligible renter households in the demand experiment sites spent over 40 percent of their total disposable income for housing; more than two-thirds spent over 25 percent. For the poorest—those below the poverty level—the situation was even worse. About one-fifth of all such households in Pittsburgh and Phoenix not only lived in severely substandard housing but also spent over 40 percent of their disposable income for that housing.

Enrollment in the Program[26]

Enrollment, the first stage of participation in the program, provides evidence of the eligible population's interest in the program.

In the supply experiment, where the program was made available to all who were eligible, about half of the eligible renters and 30 percent of the

25. See James L. McDowell, *Housing Allowances and Housing Improvement: Early Findings,* Rand/N-1198-HUD (Rand Corp., September 1979); Bakeman, Dalto, and White, *Minimum Standards Requirements;* and David W. Budding, "Draft Report on Housing Deprivation Among Enrollees in the Housing Allowance Demand Experiment" (Abt, November 1978).

26. See Stephen D. Kennedy and Jean MacMillan, "Draft Report on Participation Under Alternative Housing Allowance Programs: Evidence from the Housing Allowance Demand Experiment" (Abt, October 1979); Bruce W. Lamar and Ira S. Lowry, *Client Responses to Housing Requirements: The First Two Years,* Rand/WN-9814-HUD (Rand Corp., February 1979); and the paper by Mahlon R. Straszheim in this volume.

Table 9. Principal Program Design Elements in the Experimental Housing Allowance Program

Design element	Demand experiment	Supply experiment	Administrative agency experiment
Administrative organization	Run by Abt Associates, Inc.	Run by Housing Allowance Office, Inc., established by Rand Corporation	8 public agencies (2 each of 4 types)
Evaluative organization	Abt Associates, Inc.	Rand Corporation	Abt Associates, Inc.
Duration of experiment	3 years	10 years	2 years
Number of sites	2	2	8
Scale of program	Approximately 1,250 households and 500 control households at each site	Open enrollment (9,700 households by January 1980); no control households	400–900 households at each site; no control households
Payment formula	Center of design: housing gap formula $(P = C - bY)$; other variations tested	Housing gap formula	Housing gap formula
Household contribution rate (b)	Center of design: $b = 0.25$; other variations tested	$b = 0.25$	$b = 0.25$

Income definition (Y)	Gross income minus federal, state, and social security taxes; less $300 annually per earner for work-related expenses; and other specific deductions	Gross income minus $300 exemption per dependent and each secondary wage earner; 5% standard deduction (10% for elderly); and other specific deductions	Gross income minus $300 exemption per dependent and each secondary wage earner; 5% standard deduction (10% for elderly); and other specific deductions
Technique for estimating rent for adequate housing (C^*)	Center of design: panel of experts (percent variations of this estimate also tested)	Rent survey and panel of experts	Panel of experts
Rent definition	Either gross rent or contract rent plus formula-based allowance for utilities paid by household	Either gross rent or contract rent plus formula-based allowance for utilities paid by household	Either gross rent or contract rent plus formula-based allowance for utilities paid by household
Housing requirements (form of earmarking)	Center of design: minimum standards; other variations tested	Minimum standards	Minimum standards
Household unit eligibility	Households of 2 or more related individuals; elderly, disabled, or handicapped single persons	Households of 2 or more related individuals; single persons	Households of 2 or more related individuals; elderly, disabled, or handicapped single persons
Tenure eligibility	Renters	Homeowners and renters	Renters
Nonmonetary assistance	Housing information and equal opportunity support provided	Housing information and equal opportunity support provided	Housing information and equal opportunity support provided

Table 10. Maximum Net Annual Income Limits for Eligibility by Household Size for Each Site in the First Year of Operation

Dollars

Site, by program	Size of household					
	1	*2*	*3-4*	*5-6*	*7-8*	*9 or more*
Demand experiment (1973)						
Phoenix	6,000	7,450	8,650	10,600	12,750	12,750
Pittsburgh	5,050	5,800	6,750	7,770	9,150	9,150
Supply experiment (1974)						
Brown County	4,320	5,520	6,960	7,680	8,640	10,080
St. Joseph County	4,320	5,520	6,480	7,200	7,680	7,680
Administrative agency experiment (1973)						
Bismarck	4,400	5,200	7,000	7,800	8,500	9,000
Durham	4,800	5,500	6,900	7,500	8,000	8,500
Jacksonville	4,800	5,520	6,250	6,750	7,050	7,300
Peoria	4,800	6,200	7,300	8,300	9,200	9,900
Salem	3,600	4,800	6,200	7,500	8,300	8,900
San Bernardino	3,600	5,050	6,250	7,450	8,200	8,750
Springfield	4,800	5,500	6,900	8,000	8,600	9,100
Tulsa[a]	3,360	4,560	6,000	7,200	7,600	8,000

Source: HUD, *Conclusions, the 1980 Report*, p. 99.
a. These figures apply to the period after October 15, 1974.

eligible homeowners had enrolled after four years. On the other hand, when eligible households were approached individually in their homes and invited to enroll, as was the case for renters in the demand experiment, around three-fourths accepted the enrollment offer. The supply experiment approach to enrollment comes closest to those of other programs serving lower-income populations. The Experimental Housing Allowance Program shows that the enrollment of all those eligible is not likely.

Among eligible households, enrollment rates vary with household composition, race, and income. Households headed by single persons, either elderly or single parents, are much more likely to enroll than those composed of couples. Minority households enroll at a greater rate than nonminority households. Those with the lowest incomes are more likely to enroll than those close to the top income limits of the program. The enrollment rates of renters are significantly higher than those of homeowners, in part because single heads of households, minorities, and those with very low incomes tend to be renters.

Qualifying for Allowance Payments[27]

The second stage of participation in the program was to qualify for payments.[28] Households that did not have to meet any housing requirements qualified for payments as soon as they were enrolled. For them, as for all those eligible for an income-maintenance type of program, enrollment is the only step required for participation. The same holds true for households that have to meet housing requirements but already live in acceptable housing; they can qualify for allowance payments without altering their housing situation. But households that are not living in acceptable housing must repair their units or move to qualify for payments.

The Effect of Housing Standards on Participation

Comparison of the three groups of households highlights the dramatic effect of housing standards requirements on participation in the program. Households that did not have to meet housing requirements participated at rates 100 to 160 percent higher than households that did have to meet housing requirements in the demand experiment. In Pittsburgh only 30 percent and in Phoenix 45 percent of those whose dwellings initially failed later qualified for payments. In the supply experiment, where the housing quality standards were less stringent, about three-fourths of the families whose dwellings initially failed eventually qualified for payments.

More stringent housing requirements not only reduced participation but also affected the composition of the group receiving allowance payments. Minorities and large households, for example, participated less often because they were less likely to meet the housing requirements when they enrolled. The same was true for poorer households. The poorer the quality of the dwelling unit, the less likely the household occupying it was

27. Ibid.
28. In the rest of this discussion of findings, the term "participation" will refer to households qualifying for and receiving payments.

to participate. Thus the quality of the housing stock in a locality interacted with the dampening effect of housing requirements to reduce participation rates. If allowance payments were not tied to housing standards, participation rates were higher, but about two-thirds of the households receiving payments did not live in standard housing.

Payment Level Effects on Participation

Allowance payment levels bear a strong relationship to participation. Higher payments clearly increased participation, although some households still did not participate even when they were entitled to a relatively large payment. For example, at an average monthly payment level of $43, about one-fourth of the renters who had to meet housing requirements participated; at double that payment, twice as many participated.[29] In this example, then, it takes four times as much in total program costs to double participation.

Reasons for Nonparticipation

Those who enrolled and then terminated their enrollment gave the following as reasons: too much effort for too little money; lack of interest in taking money from the government; expectation of more money; no desire to move or improve their units just to receive more money; too much checking up on the families; too many procedures; too many forms; and unwillingness to have their units inspected.

Those who remained enrolled but never met the housing requirements gave the following as reasons: they did not feel they would find a unit they liked as much as their present one; their present unit was close to schools, work, relatives, or friends; they did not want to leave the neighborhood; and they did not feel the allowance payment was large enough to pay for a unit they would like better. In all, one-third of these households never searched for another unit. And of these, over 70 percent consistently said they were satisfied with their present unit and neighborhood.

The experience of similar participating households suggests that many nonparticipants could have found a unit that met housing requirements, could have paid a higher rent from the allowances they would have received, and would have had at least $480 a year of allowance dollars left

29. HUD, *Conclusions, the 1980 Report*, p. 10.

over, which could have been spent for other purposes. Apparently, therefore, the reasons given for nonparticipation outweigh the attractions of additional money and a unit meeting the program's housing requirements.

Use of the Allowance Payment[30]

The entire allowance payment was used for the benefit of the eligible household. It could be used in two ways: first, to reduce what were found to be very high rent burdens, where the dwelling unit itself already met the housing requirements; and second, to improve the quality of housing, either from inadequate to adequate or from adequate to higher quality. It is also possible for allowances simultaneously to reduce the rent burden and improve the housing quality. In the demand experiment, on average, one-fourth of the allowance payment was used to obtain better housing. Most of the allowance payment was used to decrease the high housing-cost burden; it was, in effect, spent on goods and services other than housing.

Allowance payments do induce households to live in standard housing. All the households receiving payments in the experiment with housing requirements had to occupy standard housing. However, when payments were not tied to housing standards, approximately two-thirds of the recipients did not live in standard housing. To ensure that recipient households live in acceptable housing, payments must be tied to housing standards.

All the households in the program tended to minimize additional expenditures on housing. Households that did not have to meet the program's housing requirements increased their expenditures for housing by 2 to 5 percent when their incomes increased by 10 percent. The expenditures of households that had to meet the program's housing requirements depended on the housing they occupied at the time they enrolled. For those that already lived in standard housing, the expenditure pattern was much like that of households that did not have to meet the requirements. On the other hand, their housing quality outcome was quite different, since they occupied standard housing.

Many households had to improve their housing conditions to qualify for allowance payments. Those that eventually qualified usually moved; the median expenditure for housing for those that moved increased by

30. See Friedman and Weinberg, "Draft Report on Housing Consumption," and the paper by Eric A. Hanushek and John M. Quigley in this volume.

24 percent in Phoenix and 8 percent in Pittsburgh, and all occupied standard housing. Therefore, a program requirement tied to housing quality does induce increased housing expenditures as well as improve housing, especially for those whose preallowance housing does not meet housing standards.

It is not surprising that low-income households are inclined to minimize their housing expenditures. Among households receiving payments in the housing allowance experiments, preprogram rent burdens averaged about 40 percent of gross income. If housing allowances are counted strictly as payments to reduce housing expenditures rather than as additions to income, they typically reduce rent burdens to about 25 percent of income. However, the recipient is likely to view the allowance as an addition to income rather than as an offset to rent. For example, a renter with an annual gross income of $4,000 and an annual rent payment of $1,600 incurs a rent burden of 40 percent. If the same renter receives an allowance payment of $1,000 a year and views it as an addition to income, the rent burden is reduced to 32 percent of the new total income of $5,000, holding housing expenditures constant. But if housing expenditures increase, as they did for those who improved their housing conditions, the rent burden as a portion of total income will be higher than 32 percent. Thus few enrollees were anxious to increase their housing expenditures beyond the amount clearly needed to meet program requirements.

Mobility and Choice of Location[31]

Allowances did not induce much more mobility than otherwise would have occurred. At most, mobility increased 7 percentage points for all households and 10 percentage points for those whose initial housing did not meet the standards. All movers, whether they received a payment or not, chose slightly better neighborhoods with fewer low-income residents, less crime, less litter, more public services, and better transportation.

31. See Jean MacMillan, "Draft Report on Mobility in the Housing Allowance Demand Experiment" (Abt, June 1978); Avis Vidal, "Draft Report on the Search Behavior of Black Households in Pittsburgh in the Housing Allowance Demand Experiment" (Abt, July 1978); Reilly Atkinson, William Hamilton, and Dowell Myers, "Draft Report on Economic and Racial/Ethnic Concentration in the Housing Allowance Demand Experiment" (Abt, January 1979); Kevin F. McCarthy, *Housing Search and Mobility*, R-2451-HUD (Rand Corp., September 1979); and the paper by Peter H. Rossi in this volume.

Housing Market Effects[32]

Before the Experimental Housing Allowance Program, a major question about a full-scale housing allowance program was whether it might lead to substantially higher housing prices without a corresponding improvement in housing. Another question was how much such a program would stimulate housing repairs, substantial rehabilitation, and new construction.

The supply experiment has operated open-enrollment allowance programs in two sites for more than five years. There is no evidence in either site of program-induced rent increases beyond those needed to pay for housing improvements. Allowances have not stimulated new construction or major rehabilitation.

The program has been responsible for modest improvements to many homes. To date, about 11,000 dwellings in Brown and St. Joseph counties have been repaired by, or at the request of, enrollees seeking to qualify for allowance payments. These repaired dwellings amount to about 8 percent of all dwellings in these sites. Because many of the defects—especially the health and safety hazards—were easily remedied and because homeowners, landlords, renters, and friends provided nearly all the labor, cash outlays averaged only $60.

Homeowners increased their voluntary maintenance activity when they received allowances. Annual reinspections of all units also turned up new housing defects. These were usually corrected so that the household could remain in the program.

Housing Allowance Program Costs[33]

There are two primary components in the total cost of a housing allowance program: payments to households and costs of local administration of the program.

It is estimated that approximately 8 million homeowners and 9.5 million renters would be eligible for a housing allowance program like the supply experiment. Based on data from the Experimental Housing Allowance Program, we estimate that 50 percent of the renters (4.8 million)

32. See Rand Corporation, *Fourth Annual Report of the Housing Assistance Supply Experiment* (Rand, May 1978), and the paper by Edwin S. Mills and Arthur Sullivan in this volume.
33. See Carlson and Heinberg, *How Housing Allowances Work.*

and 30 percent of the homeowners (2.4 million) would receive payments if a national program were implemented. Annual payments would amount to about $1.7 billion for homeowners and $4.0 billion for renters, for a total of $5.7 billion in 1976 dollars.

Administrative costs estimated from the program are about $250 annually for each recipient household. Total costs for providing allowances to homeowners would be $2.3 billion ($1.7 billion for payments plus $0.6 billion for administration) and for renters $5.1 billion ($4.0 billion for payments plus $1.1 billion for administration). The total program would cost about $7.4 billion annually.[34]

Some Program Comparisons[35]

In the course of testing the program, some data were collected at the same time on 116 public housing and section 236 rental housing construction projects in Pittsburgh and Phoenix. These demand experiment sites were selected because they allowed comparisons with representative samples of low-income populations not served by any federal housing program.

The comparisons show that the allowance program serves minority, elderly, and large households at rates comparable to or somewhat below the rates at which they are represented in the eligible population. By contrast, in public housing programs, minority and elderly households are overrepresented. In both sites, for example, minorities are served in public housing at double their rates in the income-eligible population. Allowance households, like families eligible by income who are not served by any program, live in neighborhoods that have lower concentrations of minorities and low-income people than public housing.

Benefits for both types of programs were measured in two ways: the market value of the rental unit, derived from measures of its quality and neighborhood characteristics; and the income benefit accruing to the household in additional disposable income resulting from the rent subsidy received. The public housing and allowance programs provided vir-

---

34. Ibid., p. 47.

35. See Stephen Mayo and others, "Draft Report on Housing Allowances and Other Rental Housing Assistance Programs—A Comparison Based on the Housing Allowance Demand Experiment," pt. 1: "Participation, Housing Consumption, Location, and Satisfaction," and pt. 2: "Costs and Efficiency" (Abt, 1979).

tually identical benefits: about 70 percent of the total benefit was additional disposable income and about 30 percent accrued in the form of better housing, that is, housing with a rental market value higher than that of the housing occupied by comparable households not receiving aid. The section 236 benefit pattern was similar.

To make valid comparisons, costs for the construction programs (built over time) were adjusted to a common base year—in this case 1975. From combined site averages for the public housing and section 236 programs, annual costs per unit were found to be about 80 percent greater than the cost of a housing allowance unit ($3,856 versus $2,115). The difference is explained, in part, by the sharply rising costs associated with new construction. For example, a new construction unit would have cost about 14 percent more than a housing allowance unit in 1965. By 1975 the differential had increased to 82 percent. During the same decade, while construction costs increased 104 percent and interest rates increased 68 percent, the rents of existing units increased by only 42 percent.

HAROLD W. WATTS

with Felicity Skidmore

A Critical Review
of the Program
as a Social Experiment

The Experimental Housing Allowance Program is a set of four loosely coordinated components initiated by the Department of Housing and Urban Development (HUD) at a certain time and with specific (not necessarily harmonious) aims regarding the evaluation of an innovative approach to housing policy. This paper discusses how and how well these components were designed to serve the purposes that HUD had in mind, and more generally how the analysis and data produced by the program reflect on the value of experimentation for choosing and implementing economic and social policies.

The Components of the Program

Broadly outlined, the program's components are, first, the housing allowance demand experiment, which was designed to measure the demand response of a dispersed sample of households in two cities (Pittsburgh, Pennsylvania, and Phoenix, Arizona) to a variety of housing allowance treatments. This part of the program was similar in design and

I am grateful for the assistance of Fred Sturm, who sorted and sifted through many documents and reports to distill the design issues and resolutions. Manuscript typing was ably handled at Columbia by Lillemor Engberg and at Mathematica Policy Research by Carol Szul. I was also helped substantially by the comments on an early draft received from Marc Bendick, Jr., Katharine L. Bradbury, Anthony Downs, Jerry J. Fitts, and Ira S. Lowry. They are in no way responsible for the conclusions.

concept to the various income maintenance experiments. It was comple-
mented by the housing assistance supply experiment, which was intended
to estimate the responsiveness of the supply of housing to an increase in
demand generated by a universal allowance program. This part of the
program provided a "saturation" treatment in two metropolitan areas
(Green Bay, Wisconsin, and South Bend, Indiana)—that is, a uniform
housing allowance program available to all residents who met specified
eligibility rules. Between these two components, then, both sides of the
housing market were accounted for; together they were expected to provide an improved empirical basis for forecasting the total effects of a
housing allowance on price levels and quantity adjustments in housing
markets.

While the demand and supply experiments concentrated their attention
on the microeconomics of households and housing suppliers, a third component, the administrative agency experiment, explored the behavior of
public agencies that might be considered as possible administrative entities for carrying out a full-scale national housing allowance program.[1]
This segment focused on an aspect of policy formulation that has somewhat belatedly become recognized as very important—that of ensuring
that the expressed intent of the program can be carried out, with reasonable fidelity and at predictable costs, by the agency assigned administrative responsibility.

The fourth component—the integrated analysis—was to combine the
evidence from the three field tests with more general knowledge and
judgment as needed to maximize the usefulness of the new data and experience for forecasting the consequences and costs of alternative housing
allowance programs. A major part of this effort was directed toward
securing comparability and coordination of the measurements across the
field experiments. Another major objective was the development of a
model of housing markets that could simulate the operation of various
market interventions based on full application of the knowledge gained
from the experiments.

The Experimental Housing Allowance program was easily the most
comprehensive and ambitious effort so far attempted to evaluate a potential new policy. It was directed toward learning vital information about the
behavior of consumers, producers, and administrative agencies. It recognized the need to integrate the new findings with existing knowledge to

1. For a detailed description of the design and data collection of the three program components, see the paper by Garland E. Allen, Jerry J. Fitts, and Evelyn S.
Glatt in this volume.

provide an array of conditional benefit and cost forecasts that could guide the design of a national housing allowance program and inform the political debate necessary to legislate it.

How well has the performance so far fulfilled the expectations and hopes for this ambitious effort? How sturdy would the policy analysis presented to Congress and the public be if there were an enthusiastic effort on the part of HUD to enact a housing allowance? Conversely, can the evidence produced by the Experimental Housing Allowance Program provide a firm basis for rejecting a housing allowance as an inferior or clearly dominated approach to solving any (or every) one of the variously perceived problems in the area of housing?

No policy is ever likely to be so uniformly dominant that behavioral research and analytic conclusions eliminate the role of values and preferences in the debate about social policy. (Anything as attractive as that would surely have been discovered and introduced on more primitive grounds.) What can be hoped for is a progressive narrowing of the grounds for dispute, as forecasts of the costs and consequences of alternative policies become ever more precise, until the remaining grounds for argument lie in the realm of values and priorities attached to known outcomes.

It seems clear that for the specific task of designing a workable housing allowance and arguing, both pro and con, the comparative merits of the allowance approach, the Experimental Housing Allowance Program has been a help. While there is still a long way to go before the costs and benefits of different housing policies can be confidently projected, the range of disputation over technically answerable issues has been narrowed by the program in many important ways. Moreover, the program has added qualitatively different data to the inventory of evidence that promises substantial future dividends in understanding how housing markets work. But the design of the program also exhibits important gaps and weaknesses that must be considered, both for lessons about social experimentation in general and for the qualifications that are required for the interpretation of the findings.

The Demand Experiment

The design for examining housing demand behavior borrowed heavily from the conceptual and methodological approaches used in the income maintenance experiments. Samples of low-income households were drawn in two sites. The sample households were first randomly assigned to one of several types of treatment, including a null or control treatment, and then to more specific treatment cells. The behavior of interest—in this case housing expenditure and characteristics of occupied housing—was measured by a longitudinal survey and through the administrative records of the housing allowances. Income and substitution (or price) elasticities characterizing the response of low-income households to price or conditional income subsidies were sought as a basis for projecting the impact of national policies involving such subsidies on the level and distribution of housing resources. The Experimental Housing Allowance Program has all these features in common with the income maintenance experiments.

The treatments followed two models (not counting the informational treatment given to a segment of the control group that was otherwise unsubsidized): the housing gap and the percent of rent approaches. The housing gap treatment is essentially an income subsidy conditioned on both income level and occupancy of a satisfactory level of housing. For households that qualify for benefits ex ante the treatment, the primary change is an increase in disposable income and a consequent reduction in the rent burden measured as a fraction of disposable income. The percent of rent plan is a simple price subsidy. Sample households assigned to this type of plan were given benefits equal to a fixed fraction of their expenditure on rent.

These two main treatment categories provided a basis for estimating the effect of both conditional income augmentation and price variation on household decisions about housing. In the conventional language of demand theory, the design provides for exogenous variation that can be used to estimate both income and price (or substitution) effects based on longitudinal observation of households before and after treatment or on the contemporaneous differentials in price or income circumstances induced by the treatments.

The housing gap plan was generally regarded as suitable for full-scale implementation. The percent of rent plan, in contrast, was introduced mainly as a means of getting more reliable estimates of price elasticities than are available from nonexperimental data. There were, for example, no limitations on income levels built into the percent of rent plans (although the stratified assignment of sample households to these plans effectively enforced a limit on preexperimental income). A price subsidy for rental housing embodied in a national policy, however, would be almost certain to vary the subsidy rate with income level or limit eligibility to certain low-income groups as in current public housing.

The final element of experimental variation was in the criteria used for defining the housing standard. As a point of reference, one plan applied no requirements at all, which makes the allowance equivalent to a negative income tax program with a relatively low tax rate. Two alternative substantive housing standards were introduced. One required a recipient to spend a certain minimum on housing; here two alternative minimum levels were tried. The other approach used more conventional, detailed specifications of features required for a housing unit to be qualified as standard.

The application of housing standards, which earmarks the benefit, distinguishes the housing gap plan from an unrestricted income-conditioned cash transfer. The nature of the earmarking differs, however, according to the form in which the standards are applied. The conventional standards, which must be assessed by some form of inspection, are formally independent of the rent. Since payments are made in cash, there is no effective earmarking for households that initially occupied standard housing.[2] The existence of the standards would have a restrictive effect only if the housing became substandard or if the household decided to move.

The minimum rent standards had an effect very similar to the operation of the food stamp program before the minimum purchase requirement was abolished. A benefit was paid only to households making total rent payments equal to a certain percentage of the average cost of standard housing. The only difference between this and the food stamp program is that the issuing of special purpose coupons ("funny money") is avoided.[3]

The Supply Experiment

The supply experiment was a "saturation" experiment, providing the equivalent of a single, full-blown housing gap program to all eligible households in a particular geographical area. The housing standard en-

2. If a household found an extraordinary bargain in the form of standard housing that cost less than the benefit, the benefit would be reduced to equal the housing expenditure.
3. All experimental households, whatever their subsidy plan, received some nonfinancial services, which included basic information about the experiment, about housing markets, and about laws (in particular, equal opportunity issues). These features were not varied among enrolled families, but an effort was made to assess their independent effect by providing such services to only part of the control group. Subsequent discussion will be limited to the design and findings relevant for the financial benefits provided by the various plans.

forced was of the conventional inspection-against-checklist variety. The checklist was not, however, identical to the one used in the demand experiment; it was somewhat less stringent and conformity typically required only a minor modification. About 30 percent of a sample of housing units were, for example, not classified the same way by experienced raters from the two experimental sites.[4]

A major difference between the supply experiment treatment and the analogous treatment in the demand experiment was that the former enrolled homeowners as well as renters. The supply experiment thus included a more comprehensive segment of the low-income housing market and enabled its beneficiaries to move back and forth between owning and renting without losing benefit-eligibility status. The supply experiment also afforded a longer horizon for benefit payments (ten years instead of the three years for the demand experiment). Since primary interest was focused on the behavior of housing suppliers and homeowners, it was felt, plausibly, that modifications of housing structures requiring substantial capital investment could not be expected from an increase in demand known to be of temporary origin. Two sites were selected for saturation to provide examples of both a relatively tight but expanding market with a small minority population (Green Bay) and a looser or even stagnant market with a large minority population in the central city surrounded by suburbs populated almost entirely by whites (South Bend). The main emphasis was on gathering data on how homeowners respond to the conditional income subsidy and how landlords respond to the increased capacity of tenants (and potential tenants) to pay for standard housing.

The Administrative Agency Experiment

This experiment was mainly concerned with ascertaining the capacities of alternative agencies for initiating and administering a housing allowance program. The sample included eight agencies, which were required to administer a housing gap type of allowance like the one applied in the supply experiment, but that applied only to renters and provided benefits for a maximum of two years (although efforts were authorized to shift participants to other programs or even extend support to avoid hardship at termination). The stimulus was a set of rules and regulations specify-

4. Joseph J. Valenza, *Program Housing Standards in the Experimental Housing Allowance Program: Analyzing Differences in the Demand and Supply Experiments,* 216-30 (Washington, D.C.: Urban Institute, July 1977), p. x.

ing the required features of a housing allowance. These rules left a substantial amount of discretion to the agencies in the methods used to perform the various functions. The agencies were directed to provide open enrollment for eligible households, though this was restricted to a specified maximum at any one time. Thus the treatment, regarded as the fraction of potentially eligible households to be enrolled, varied among the sites according to the size of the eligible population.

Data on costs, administrative practices and innovations, unforeseen problems, and the outcomes for recipients were collected. But except for the systematic selection of four different types of agencies—public housing authorities, county agencies, community development agencies, and welfare agencies—there was no systematic variation of procedure or objective.

The Evaluation Spectrum and Where the Program Components Fit

The issue here is where on the spectrum of evaluative activities the three field components of the Experimental Housing Allowance Program fit and whether they are well-placed on that spectrum for answering the policy questions they were designed to address.

Evaluative activities, as I define them, are all efforts to find answers to questions of the form "What would happen to (   ) if (   )?" The first pair of parentheses contains one or more variable outcomes or responses, and the second pair specifies the conditions under which one or more variable inputs or stimuli are to be manipulated. The spectrum over which the activities range starts at the extreme of the elaborate and highly stylized laboratory experiment and extends to the barely purposeful grope. It is important to stress that one end of the spectrum cannot be judged superior to the other in any absolute sense, nor can the position on the spectrum be correlated with the potential for adding to knowledge. The most informative evaluation approach depends on the level of knowledge that already exists about causes of the outcomes of interest and on whether one can specify a relatively narrow set of causes and outcomes of the evaluation.

The "ultra-experiment" at one end of the spectrum is one in which all the causal influences are known, measurable, and manipulable, and the outcome is measurable with a high degree of precision. Under such conditions all but one or a few causal factors can be held constant in a suit-

ably designed laboratory and the remaining factor or factors can be
varied while the outcome is carefully observed. In this situation there is
no need for randomization because there are no unknown or uncontrolled
influences. Statistical procedures for analyzing the data produced are of
minor importance as well, except in finding economical summary descriptions of the outcome(s) or in assessing the precision of measurements taken in repeated trials with a less-than-perfect measuring device.

Along the midsection of the spectrum lie the so-called social experiments and demonstrations. They differ from the ultra-experiment in several ways. First and most obviously—although this is more a consequence
of other differences than a distinction in its own right—they involve the
behavior of human beings, or organized groups of them, interacting with
the institutions, rules, and conventions that characterize a society. It is
clearly impossible to reproduce several fully articulated societies or even
one within the walls of a laboratory; but even if a laboratory society were
possible, the notion that the behavior in question can be reduced to components that can be examined in isolation from "real life" situations is
viewed with suspicion. The causal structure is not known and seems to be
much more complex in the case, say, of housing expenditure or labor supply than the rate of oxidation of iron or the germination of a dandelion
seed.

Randomization and Systematic Variation

Where these social evaluation efforts lie on the spectrum with respect
to analytic rigor depends on the extent to which they use the most powerful tool in social experimentation—randomization. Randomization provides a way to isolate partial relationships. If a sample of relevant units—
persons, households, firms, or agencies—can be selected and randomly
assigned to treatments that exogenously vary one or more supposed causal
factors to a measured (or describable) extent, the observed difference in
behavior can be attributed to the difference in treatment. One of these
treatment alternatives frequently is a null treatment—that is, a subset of
units is randomly assigned to a control group that, by definition, receives
no treatment. Controlled variation among randomized groups, however,
does not *require* a null treatment.

Randomized assignment to varying treatments provides a basis for
estimating a partial relationship that is conditional on the coincident con-

figuration of all other influences that are at least stochastically identical for all groups being compared.

The demand experiment is an example of this type of evaluation technique and clearly deserves the appellation "social experiment." Price and income subsidies and earmarking rules were varied among treatments, and the expenditure and consumption behaviors of households randomly assigned to those treatments were measured as the outcome variables.

Although randomization is a relatively powerful method for exploring partial relationships, the demand experiment shows that it is not a full substitute for knowing what the relevant influences are when all the circumstances are held stochastically constant. A partial relation well established in the social and economic environment of one time and place may be misleading if relevant factors in the randomized portmanteaux are different at other times and places. The demand experiment was introduced in only two sites, each offering different levels of market tightness, different minority structures, different climates, and many other differences that may or may not affect the demand behavior of households. The partial relations estimated at the two sites cannot be directly generalized to other locations without adding further knowledge or assumptions about how other variables affect the partial relation and how those variables are distributed in the more general set of locations. The alternative of drawing a random sample from the whole universe (that is, the household population of the United States) makes the "one place" conform to the objective of generalization and hence includes correlates of location in the randomization process. But this strategy is much more expensive, both in treatment administration and in data collection. The resulting wider range of variation in the stochastically controlled variables that are not measured (or even recognized) in the behavioral model will also add to the imprecision of results for any given sample size. And even if interspatial generalization is secured by more complete randomization, the problem of intertemporal generalizations remains. Unless an experiment lasts a long time and the time-varying circumstances are drawn from a stationary process, the randomization device will not help to ensure that experimentally estimated relationships will be reliable guides for forming policy that will be effective at a different time.

All of this indicates that the most powerful approach available in social experimentation must rely on some additional knowledge or assumptions to provide information about the effects of policy. For example, in the case

of the human response to an index finger coming into unexpected contact
with a conductive surface at 150°C, the unrepresentativeness of the time
or place where experimental data are collected is not of special concern.
But this is because some (mostly implicit) theory fosters the belief that
the correlates of time and place have little to do with such an involuntary
response. Most would accept that experimentally estimated parameters
of muscular and vocal responses to such pain are "portable" within fairly
broad limits. Responses to income and price subsidies are not so obviously invariant.

The best that one can do without such firm understanding is to resort
to any understanding, however uncertain, about the most promising factors that may mediate the partial relations and use that to guide the
sampling and other design features toward achieving the largest gains in
precision and generalizability. Then samples, or sites, should be selected
to provide enough variation to permit testing and estimating the strength
of the mediating influences so that generalizations can be made over time
and space. Where one is neither completely in control of all relevant factors nor completely ignorant about the forces that influence behavior,
there is no simple rule of optimality that insists on full randomization or
a self-representing sample of the universe. There is, in short, no "uni-
versally most powerful design" for estimating the partial response to experimental variation of some causal factor in cases where other causal
factors mediate those responses and also vary over time and space. The
decision to pursue further knowledge about housing demand through a
controlled experiment that used a randomly selected sample of households and a systematically varied set of housing-related treatments was, in
my judgment, well taken. The decision to go to only two sites is somewhat
more debatable, but as the preceding discussion suggests, I do not think
that adding more sites would have significantly increased the knowledge
gained from the experiment.

Saturation

Next along the spectrum come what I call the quasi experiments or
field demonstrations. The supply experiment fits this general category—
again justifiably so, in my view—because the knowledge sought was in
the nature of a complete market outcome. A demonstration involves a
part of the stimulus provided by a "real" social policy that is impossible
to simulate in an experimental design making use of random assignment

to systematically varied treatments—namely, the equal treatment of equals. Equal treatment may alter the information available to eligible households, adaptive responses may be contagious, and finally a real policy will exhibit outcomes resulting from general equilibrium adjustment that may well be consistent with the estimated partial relationships but will have different individual outcomes because of indirect or feedback influences on variables held "constant" in the randomized experiment. In the case of housing markets, the most obvious source of general equilibrium modifications comes from the response of housing supply mechanisms to the subsidy-induced change in demand. Interest in this more complete outcome leads in to what have been called "saturation experiments." The primary observational unit is a whole market and a uniform treatment is applied to all units in that market.

The supply experiment followed this approach and saturated two sites with a uniform housing subsidy treatment. Such an approach, however, led to additional problems of design, since for aggregated responses the sample consisted of only two and there was no control group with which to compare them.[5]

It is easy (and important) to ask, "What happens to (1) housing prices, (2) rehabilitation, maintenance, and construction, (3) interneighborhood migration, and so forth, if every household is eligible for the same income-conditioned housing subsidy?" Specifying a powerful experimental design for answering these questions is harder. The problem is that since the treatment is applied to a whole market, the element of control required to attribute observed responses to differently manipulated treatments is now harder to achieve through randomization. Such control would take a random selection from some population of markets assigned to receive the treatment with another solution being observed only for comparison. The number of housing markets needed to get control via randomization is clearly too large for serious consideration of this approach. The two sites that were saturated with a full entitlement program cost approximately $40 million each—a representative sample of sites allocated between treatment and control groups could easily have cost more than $1 billion.

5. The possibility still exists of exploiting the HUD annual housing survey. While the variables measured by the survey are very limited in comparison to the measurements made in the supply experiment, useful contrasts could be derived. It should be noted in this connection that the supply experiment's panel of residential properties is similar in design to the annual housing survey.

One alternative for pursuing the housing supply issue would have been to find matched pairs of sites, one of each pair to receive the treatment and the other to be as similar as possible to the first except for the absence of the housing allowance program. This approach clearly depends on the strength of the prior knowledge used to decide which characteristics of the sites are important determinants of the outcomes and which are not. If only a few spatially varying influences need to be controlled, there is some chance of finding suitable pairings. But if everything matters, there is little hope of finding close matches, and the approach is no improvement on full or uninformed randomization.

The supply experiment did not, however, choose this approach. Its claim to being an experiment is thus even more tenuous because its evaluation approach depends on projections or extrapolations from the experience of the recent past and on general economic conditions. The main chance for detecting experimental response in quasi experiments of this sort depends on a stimulus that produces discontinuity from the recent past or from model-based projections sufficient to unmistakably identify the response. In this part of the program, as has been mentioned, the primary interest was in the responsiveness of the supply mechanisms to increased demand. Hence the opportunity to observe the supply mechanisms in the process of adjusting to a new equilibrium depended on a large enough increase in demand for the relatively crude indicators of change to detect and chronicle the adjustment process. Aside from this rather weak basis for isolating the consequences of the exogenous experimental stimulus, the supply experiment is perhaps best regarded as a demonstration or field trial of a new social policy.

As I have tried to make clear, the intellectual respectability of an experiment relative to a demonstration should not be presumed to favor the experiment. Demonstrations certainly have a longer history and appear to be able to answer some kinds of questions better than experiments. One does not have to set up a full experimental program to find out whether an airplane will fly or whether a particular social program innovation can be operated in any community without being blown out of the water. Unforeseen complications or bugs can be discovered this way and feasible corrections can be devised on the spot. Comparisons with performance norms can be carried out for such things as percentage of eligible households enrolling, success of enrolled households in finding housing meeting program standards, and so forth. A demonstration or field test is perfectly satisfactory for determining whether a program is sufficient for attaining specified objectives.

The supply experiment thus has little claim to the title, but it has many of the properties of an excellent demonstration. The major question is the defensibility of the enormous extra cost of saturating two sites with a special subsidy program, when the major objective and achievement was to develop a rich set of longitudinal observations on the operation of housing markets with particular emphasis on supply mechanisms. A wide variety of information was collected, both from the program activity itself and through surveys of homeowners, renters, and landlords. But for the most part these activities could have been carried out just as well in one or more sites that were not receiving an experimental stimulus. Much can be learned by observing how consumers and owners and other institutional actors in housing markets behave in changing circumstances, and since circumstances are always changing, equally careful design of a longitudinal study would provide valuable evidence. An exogenous change in demand induced by a particular program is in no way a necessary part of that study.

The defense that can be made for the original saturation decision is that the main and most urgent objective of the supply experiment as originally conceived was to deal with the recurrent criticism that supply would not respond to an increase in low-income housing expenditures and that the subsidies would all be absorbed in higher rents.[6] Thus a substantial amount of effort and forethought was given to providing a large enough jolt of extra housing expenditure to allow observation of the various housing supply responses in action without at the same time delivering such a shock to local markets that spectacular (even if temporary) price increases would be inevitable even if housing supplies were reasonably responsive. Control of the intensity of outreach, advertisement, and enrollment capacities provided a basis for controlling the size of the shock.

As it turned out, the increase in demand was relatively minor and absorbed without apparent trace in both supply experiment sites. But it is still important, if some of the features of the design are to be understood, to remember that a main objective of the supply experiment was to pro-

6. Admittedly, investigators from the Rand Corporation, the contractor for the supply experiment, did not necessarily share the predominant concern about price volatility or overestimate the impact on demand of the treatments specified.

vide evidence on the responsiveness of supply mechanisms, usually expressed as concern that higher prices would absorb all of any increment to housing expenditure.

What is now left to place on the spectrum is the administrative agency experiment. Clearly this part of the program has the makings, in principle, of a social experiment in my sense of the term. A given treatment in the form of a mandate to operate a particular kind of program serving a specified number of households was administered to eight administrative agencies. These agencies consisted of four pairs, each pair representing a different category of agency; thus comparisons were possible among the four different types with two replications of each type. The question being asked is in the classic form, "What will happen to enrollment, outreach, image of the program, and so forth, if this agency administers a housing allowance program or that agency administers it?" One might wish for a higher level of replication to provide more precision in any differences that occur; nevertheless, the basic design appears to fit the stereotypical mold fairly well.

Unsystematic Variation

In this case, however, the design did not live up to its potential. The experiment was not well designed to find the answers to specified questions. The treatment was not systematically varied among agencies, nor was it identical. It lapsed into a situation where the agencies were allowed wide discretion in setting most of the program's provisions and delivery mechanisms. Both the prior knowledge and the questions to which answers are wanted are sufficiently precise to make it possible to conceive and design a properly defined social experiment that would provide carefully balanced and controlled comparisons of administrative alternatives in various settings (as the paper by Kershaw and Williams in this volume attests). But this was not the case. The administrative agency experiment did, however, demonstrate that the program could be operated by existing agencies rather than by a new agency such as the ones set up expressly to operate the programs in the supply experiment sites. It also demonstrated that an allowance program was feasible in an expanded range of city sizes and types. But neither the design nor the findings can be said to justify the budget allotted to it in the name of experimentation. The agency experiment will not be discussed further in this paper. It is admirably and exhaustively treated by Kershaw and Williams.

This leaves the barely purposeful "grope" anchoring the other end of the evaluation spectrum, examples of which cannot be found in the Experimental Housing Allowance Program. The Federal Reserve System may be moving in to provide a current example of this approach, however. Again, one must not derogate groping as a means of finding something out. In the absence of theory, or at least theory that seems to be working, groping may be the best approach that can be designed. It is certainly better than anxious hand-wringing. In the scheme developed here, the degree of experimental rigor is more a result of the existing state of knowledge and of the ability to define measures of, or devise manipulations for, relevant variables than it is an unfettered choice of whether to be rigorous or not.

The Outcomes of the Program

The Demand Experiment

The demand experiment has generally accomplished its objectives if these are interpreted as measuring the responses of a given set of households operating in markets with a given housing stock or, more properly, a rate of change in that stock unaffected by experimentally induced changes in demand. A variety of treatments extended to a preselected sample of renters yielded a significant amount of variation in income and price subsidies and in the kind of housing standards required for support.

Participation (maintaining or obtaining residency in standard housing) is a major issue for evaluation of housing allowances. Such participation is clearly related to the stringency of the housing standards and the size of the subsidy. If the standards are set low enough so that nearly every housing unit meets them, the improvement in housing from the income subsidy of a housing gap treatment comes in the form of reduced rent–income ratios (that is, a larger share of disposable income is available for other uses), or, depending on the income elasticity of housing demand, it may lead to upgrading within the category of standard housing. If, on the other hand, more stringent standards are applied—and in the demand experiment approximately three-quarters of the dwelling units were found to be substandard in the initial examination (partly because of faults in the unit itself and partly because of overcrowding)— some remedial action must be taken if the households are to qualify for benefits. This may involve moving to different quarters, modifying the unit to meet the existing standards, or decreasing the number of inhabitants.

The stringency of standards distinguishes a housing allowance program from a general-purpose income-maintenance transfer program, and the participation rate that results is central to any assessment of the costs and benefits. If most inhabitants of substandard housing take immediate action to qualify for the benefits, the resulting high participation rate implies that a substantial improvement in housing as measured by those standards has taken place and that the cost is close to that of a similarly scaled negative tax. If, however, large numbers of households remain in their substandard dwellings—because the financial benefits are low, the financial and psychic costs of moving or improving are high, or for other idiosyncratic reasons—the effect on the actual housing situation of the sampled households will be more limited and correspondingly less public expenditure will be made in the form of income subsidies.

It was found that, at the rates of subsidization offered in the experiments, substantial numbers of households declined to take advantage of the benefits. The expected higher participation rates of those offered higher benefits were observed; similarly, the higher the cost of possible remedial actions, the lower was the rate of participation. Those who moved or took other steps to qualify for benefits showed the expected larger increases in housing expenditure. Even with the minimum rent form of standards, some households declined to increase their expenditure on rent to the standard even though the required extra payment would have been smaller than the allowance payment. Overall, the effects on housing expenditures were relatively small—about 15 percent even for families that decided to participate. Patterns of expenditure changes followed the same and generally sensible patterns shown for participation —namely, larger benefits tended to induce larger changes in expenditure, both those required by the standards and the voluntary ones based on higher real incomes.

In the language of welfare economics, a high participation rate and consequent substantial changes in housing arrangements induced by the "coercive" provisions of the program also signify substantial "deadweight loss" of general welfare—people are induced away from preferred actions by the conditional benefit. The fractional levels of participation observed in the experiments may imply, however, that the deadweight loss is relatively small in that the households for whom participation would require substantial departures from preferred consumption patterns simply refuse to participate. The other side of the same coin, of course, is that equity questions are raised—is it fair that households facing equal budgetary hardship are selectively aided according to their taste for housing?

Whatever the merits of these issues, the demand experiment has furnished a much firmer basis for predicting how many and which sorts of households will maintain or secure standard housing if they are offered financial benefits of different amounts for doing so. Similarly, the percent of rent treatments have added precision to notions of the price elasticity of housing demand. The large effective price changes induced by these treatments led to relatively strong substitution effects. While differences were observed in the price elasticities across the two sites, it is evident at least that the treatments were successful in bringing about observable changes in both places and that the resulting data provide a fertile source of evidence for continuing analysis of response to price changes.

The Supply Experiment

The most important outcome of the supply experiment was that the size of the increase in demand was very small and that consequently there was little opportunity to observe the response of the various supply mechanisms to such a stimulus. This can be regarded as a finding of the first importance in that it provides assurance that market mechanisms can accommodate the changes induced by a housing allowance program without precipitous price changes or other disturbances. It can also be regarded as a failure in design in that it does not provide the expected opportunity for gaining more precise and detailed understanding of how housing markets or submarkets respond to major changes in demand. The approved design was well executed by the contractor; effective and efficient administrative arrangements were made for publicizing the program, processing applications, dispensing the benefits, and carrying out an elaborate data-gathering effort that included both direct observations at the administrative level and interview information from surveys of households and landlords.

Because the stimulus to the market mechanisms was relatively small, the analysis of the valuable data produced will depend largely on the sort of spontaneous variation that would be present in any extensive longitudinal observation in a site without an experimental program. Given the shortage of data of this kind, new insights into the workings of housing markets should be gained that will be valuable for a wide range of potential policy formulation and evaluation. Indeed, the theories of short-run response developed by Rydell are excellent examples of such use of longitudinal data.[7]

It could be argued that the design should have allowed for adjustments in the level of benefits, the tax rate, or the housing standards during the course of the experiment to assure a readily identifiable supply response. As suggested earlier, however, such a procedure would have made the experimental treatment resemble a feasible public policy less and less. Hence, any gain in experimental action would have exacted a cost in the relevance to policy of the undertaking. In my view, the finding that markets and consumers are well able to accommodate the sort of change induced by a full-scale housing allowance is sufficiently important to justify the administration of a fixed program throughout, given the widespread concern expressed before the experiment began.

A Major Gap in the Conception of the Housing Adjustment Process

The deliberate similarity between the demand experiment and the income maintenance experiments has already been mentioned. The notion to be developed in this section is that a deeper and more inadvertent similarity was imposed, which has limited the way the findings can be interpreted. This is the concentration in both cases on the longitudinal study of a fixed sample of households. The problem with this strategy is that, although it may capture most of the total response when labor supply is the object of the study, it will neglect a major part of the dynamics of response in housing demand. A sample drawn from a given population of low-income households at any one time will include a large proportion of the active or potential labor suppliers whose choices would be affected by an income subsidy or negative income tax. When an experimental program is introduced, longitudinal observation of adult behavior in those households includes most of the response that can be expected, at least in the short or medium run. Since the first negative income tax experiments were designed, the analytic problems connected with household dissolution have become more evident, whether such dissolution is

7. C. Peter Rydell, *Shortrun Response of Housing Markets to Demand Shifts,* R-2453-HUD (Santa Monica: Rand Corp., September 1979).

affected by the experimental treatment or not. But in the case of labor supply, at least, the subject of interest is largely independent of household composition. One can also follow the principal earners of an initially sampled household and continue to observe their labor supply behavior. This is because, at least to a good first approximation, labor supply decisions are made by an individual. Housing decisions, in contrast, are based on a group of individuals banded together as a household or spending unit. Collectively, they constitute the entity that occupies the housing, and when one or more of them leave, the remaining household is essentially a different one and the departing members must either form new households or augment the membership of, and essentially change, others.

A Michigan longitudinal panel study found that over a six-year period (1968–74) 7 to 8 percent of the households that included a married couple experienced a divorce and that these rates have been rising. While a large fraction of divorced persons remarried within the period (29 percent of women and 44 percent of men), such splits do expand the number of households for some period of time. But more important are the departures of older children. Most children leave home between the ages of eighteen and twenty-five, some to form new married households, some to live alone, and others to enter into communal or roommate arrangements. Of children between the ages of ten and eighteen living at home in 1968, 28 percent had left to marry by 1973, and another 10 percent had become household heads. Of the smaller number who were still at home and aged between nineteen and twenty-nine in 1968, only 17 percent were still at home five years later. The general churning around is indicated by the statistic that only a third of the children under ten in 1968 experienced no family change in five years.[8]

These changes in household composition have been found to be sensitive to economic forces and to public policies, and one must expect price and income subsidies related to housing to be of prime importance when considering the establishment of a new household or changing one's household affiliation in some other way.

It is useful in examining this issue to think of the way a population is distributed among an array of households as a highly dynamic process. An individual household grouping, conceived narrowly as a fixed set of

8. See Greg J. Duncan and James N. Morgan, eds., *Five Thousand American Families—Patterns of Economic Progress*, vol. 4: *Family Composition Change and Other Analyses of the First Seven Years of the Panel Study of Income Dynamics* (University of Michigan, Institute for Social Research, 1976), pp. 5–6.

individuals who change only by growing older, is an ephemeral concept. The total number of households formed out of a given population is highly variable and surely responds in part to economic forces. Given the roughly one-to-one correspondence between the number of households and the number of occupied housing units, how much of the process of change in the demand for housing units can be observed by following a fixed sample of households that ignores the effects of household formation and dissolution? The strategy of following a preexisting set of households or their principal remnants after departures seems to me to miss a critical part of the way in which adjustment in the expenditures on or consumption of housing takes place.

Another unfortunate limitation on generalizability comes from the concentration in the demand experiment on rental markets. Analysts of cross-sectional data tend to think of renters as a more or less fixed and predetermined category of households. After all, the total fraction of the population living in rented quarters changes relatively slowly. However, for many, renting is only a necessary step on the way to buying a home. In terms of a lifetime plan to accumulate the capital required for homeownership, a major part of the response to an income subsidy beyond what is necessary to qualify for such benefits may be observed as a shorter period of renting. Similarly, in the case of the percent of rent treatments, the large changes in price and substitution rates might well be expected to make tenancy much more attractive than homeownership if the treatments were likely to last anything like a lifetime. One would not, however, expect temporary price breaks to produce major changes in a lifetime plan to own a home—here again, some part of the response to benefits could be expected in the form of an earlier change to homeownership.

The importance of tenure change is also shown in the Michigan data for the same period. Of family units having the same head in 1973 as in 1968, the 1968 wife as head, or a single female head who married, only 23 percent were renters in 1967. More than a third of these (8.8 percent) had become owners by 1973, and the percentage change in housing costs was 1.5 times the percentage change in income for the group with the same head throughout the period. By contrast, the renters who moved to different rental dwellings during the same period incurred housing cost changes proportional to income changes.[9]

9. James Morgan and Sandra J. Newman, "Changes in Housing Costs, 1968 to 1974," in Duncan and Morgan, eds., *Five Thousand American Families,* vol. 4, pp. 219–56.

More generally, there are other kinds of housing expenditures besides those related to a household's principal dwelling—second and vacation homes, hotels, and dormitories or other institutional accommodations. Most of these assume more importance as components of a total shelter budget at higher levels of income, and so little is lost by ignoring them in assessing the impact of an income-tested program for low-income people. But the same is not true of the processes of household change. Clearly, crowding is one way low-income households economize on shelter costs, and the privacy and autonomy that a separate dwelling provides appears to be a need of fairly high priority to those who can afford it. Consequently, the interpretation of income and price elasticities estimated on the basis of the kinds of samples used in the demand experiment must be extremely careful. These should more properly be described as income and price elasticities for households that do not change much in composition and have not yet made the transition from renter to owner. This is a fairly narrow group and falls far short of accounting for all or even a majority of the sources of response to changes in income distribution or housing prices.

Carrying out a more satisfactory analysis in the demand experiment by examining the contrasts in household changes between the control and experimental groups is still possible. So far, however, only the changes in expenditure, residence, or repair have been recognized as adjustments in housing demand. Changes in the number or types of persons housed should be included as another way to adjust the quantity or quality of housing for a household.

Potentially, the supply experiment, largely because of its saturation design with a relatively long horizon and the inclusion of homeowners, is in a better position to assess a more comprehensive array of household adjustments to the changes induced by housing allowances. All households in the area can avail themselves of the benefits, and the availability of such benefits can be anticipated by persons who are contemplating forming new households. And the supply experiment, by including homeowners as well as renters, offers the opportunity to observe the effects of the transition from owning to renting. Finally, the duration is longer, and this may encourage more households to participate.

Unfortunately, the habits of cross-sectional analysts show up most strongly in a research paper produced by the supply experiment, which aims at estimating the income elasticities of housing demand.[10] With no

10. John E. Mulford, *Income Elasticity of Housing Demand*, R-2449-HUD (Rand Corp., July 1979).

mention or apparent awareness of the qualifications mentioned here, this major report displays estimates based on a given set of originally sampled households that maintained essentially the same membership and not only did not change from owning to renting during the three-year period of observation but made no change in residence at all. The paper does not base the estimates on changes during the period, but rather on interhousehold comparisons of the usual cross-sectional kind. This procedure has traditionally been justified by the argument that a cross section of households is randomly distributed around long-run equilibrium values at each level of income. It is clear that here again the implicit model is based on the notion that household composition is a predetermined, if not totally fixed, characteristic. By carrying out separate analyses for owners and renters, the paper earns another qualification because of its implicit assumption that the owner-renter choice is also fixed or relatively independent of the forces that determine expenditures within each category. Hence, while a more comprehensive distribution of housing adjustments might be explored within the supply experiment, no such effort has been undertaken to date.

This criticism of the design cannot be offered as an "I told you so" complaint. Issues relating to household formation were not discussed when the experiments were designed, though I and others had ample opportunity to raise them. I believe that analysts who work with longitudinal data are becoming more aware of the analytic problems related to household change, and all are aware of the importance for policy of the family or marital stability aspect of the more general problem. But with the benefit of hindsight, it seems evident that the dynamics of household formation is at the very heart of the matter when one considers the demand for "household containers," or housing. The difficulty of getting a better grasp of that process is formidable, but it seems unfortunate that a concerted effort to comprehend the most central part of housing demand was not made in this program.

But how could the experiment have been designed to capture more of the adjustment in housing demand to price and income subsidies? The household formation problem is a difficult one, particularly in a scattered treatment design such as the demand experiment. One possibility would be to entitle all sample household members over fourteen years of age to housing allowances at the rate assigned to their initial household. This entitlement would be valid for any other household the person might become a member of during the experimental period. The problem is that such a procedure would give a bonus to sample members for forming new households or combining with others that would not exist (in the same form) in a real program. The longitudinal survey would also have to be carefully designed to follow the housing status of all original household members. It would be possible to confirm or refute the notion that subsidies related to housing have an effect on the household formation process, but it probably would be impossible to infer much about the quantitative effect of a real program because of the artificial attractiveness as household members of the scattered persons entitled to allowances.

The effect of a saturation experiment or demonstration such as the supply experiment on the household formation process should be more normal, particularly if the entitlements last for as long as ten years. Again a careful longitudinal design would be necessary to monitor the new household affiliation of persons who left originally sampled households. Also, the entire population would have to be sampled because some (possibly temporary) low-income households are formed from members of high-income units. Here again, the lack of a basis for comparison would be a problem. It would be necessary to have studied the household formation (and dissolution) process in the experimental sites before the introduction of housing allowances and to carry out a concurrent survey of a population in a "matched" site without allowances. If a great deal was known about the household formation process, that knowledge could be used to project expected patterns and hence identify changes that could be attributed to the allowance program. But the economics of household formation and evolution has not been highly developed, and confident projections of this kind cannot yet be made.

Another source of demand from new households in a given market comes from net migration. In a full national program, housing allowances would probably have little, if any, effect on migration. But in evaluating the effect on a single city the consequences of the differential advantage provided by a housing allowance program would have to be considered. This might argue for ruling that after a certain date migrants into the city would be ineligible for the program, although this would increase the complexity (and artificiality) of the demonstration. The entitlements for current residents who considered migrating, perhaps while forming a new household, might also be made portable to simulate the full effect of a national program. Otherwise, the allowances would form an artificial obstacle to mobility. Alternatively, one can simply ignore the whole migra-

tion process as an object of study and recognize that net migration is likely
to be artificially increased by the introduction of a demonstration program
in a few selected cities. Some indication of the strength of this influence
could have been secured in the demand experiment if all members of
selected households were eligible only for nonportable allowances. The
out-migration patterns of the people receiving "treatment" could then be
compared with those in the "control" panel.

For examining the effect on tenure change a number of changes in
design should be considered. First, making homeowners as well as renters
eligible for allowances has an effect on the long-run attractiveness of renting versus owning. If only renters are eligible, fewer persons will form
their long-run plans around the eventual purchase of a home. But if
owners are eligible as well, no one has to give up the "income supple-
mentation policy" by becoming an owner. In the demand experiment,
some part of the treatments (in the housing gap segment only) should
have been made applicable to owned housing for renters who become
owners. The initial sample could have included only renters if the switch
from owning to renting was relatively rare or of less interest. But varying
this feature would have been valuable for examining changes in the balance of long-run tenure choice.

But even if the long-run strategy continues to be directed toward
ownership, the effect of housing allowances—whether limited to renters
or not—may be, in part, expressed in a shorter period of renting. The
pattern of a young couple deciding to "rough it" for a time to hasten the
advent of owning their own home seems plausible, at least on the basis
of casual observation. To examine this phenomenon, the duration of an
experiment could be extended so that more such transitions would be
observed, but this would add greatly to both costs and delay. A less costly
alternative would be more complete observation of household expenditure patterns and wealth accumulation. Because the transition to ownership usually entails a down payment and frequently an increase in durable
goods (such as range, refrigerator, washer, more or better cars for longer
commutes), it should be possible to detect differences in spending and
accumulation behavior that are related to more advanced schedules for
home purchase. Expenditure surveys for long-lived panels are difficult
and expensive but would provide a more timely indicator of this possible
effect of housing allowances on housing demand. Such observations could
be supplemented by "softer" queries about long-run plans and expectations regarding housing, fertility, and so forth.

If a significant part of the housing response to a housing allowance does operate through the long-run mechanism of whether and when one makes the transition to ownership, then more serious questions about the length of the experiment must be raised. Such effects appear to operate mainly through the basic (unearmarked) income effect on households that meet the standards for participation. A temporary increase in income is more likely to be saved, on the permanent income hypothesis, even if the accumulation of liquid wealth for the purchase of a home is not part of the household's plan.

Earmarking through housing standards would force higher current expenditure on housing by any participating household that had to move or make repairs to qualify, and this would reduce the resources that could be accumulated for homeownership. Attention to this issue would place more emphasis on the comparison with unearmarked transfers, either from the fully controlled variant in a demand type of experiment or from using contrasts with the income maintenance experiments.

Other Possible Criticisms

Should Housing Standards Criteria Have Been More Varied?

The housing standards used to qualify households for benefits are the only mechanism that differentiates housing allowances (using the gap formula) from a simple negative income tax. The argument has been made that, for this reason, more attention should have been given to varying these standards. As it stands, two types of standards, the conventional lists of physical and occupancy minima and fixed expenditure minima, were used, each at two levels of stringency.[11] These could have been elaborated by varying the stringency still more widely or by devising other standards. More attention could have been paid to occupancy and use patterns or to neighborhood characteristics and less to the condition of wall surfaces and so forth. In design trade-offs, more elaboration of one kind usually means less of another. It could be said that the demand experiment placed the most emphasis on variation in the size and structure of the "bribe" offered for meeting a given few housing standards,

11. Only one conventional list of standards was applied in the demand experiment, but the supply experiment used a less stringent list. Also, one cell applied no housing standards, thus providing a de facto negative income tax with a housing allowance label.

when it could have increased the alternative standards offered at about the same cost. The consequences of the alternative standards for participation rates, and for the housing choices made by participants, could then have been compared.

But major problems exist in specifying standards that can be uniformly and efficiently enforced once one gets beyond basic physical characteristics. Also, there are no obvious ways of scaling or measuring the dimensions of stringency—dimensions in which different *types* of standards have not even been identified. Consequently, the array of standards, once defined, would have to be analyzed one by one rather than as part of a continuum. While it seems to me that a good case can be made, in principle, for more experimentation with standards, it is far from clear just what standards could have been tried or how they could have been administered in a precisely measured way. Given the results obtained in the experiments, it seems doubtful that some alternative standard could have been found that would, for a certain bribe, have led a large number of eligible households to drastically alter their housing choices. It appears, with the variations used in the supply and demand experiments, that tougher standards reduce participation and induce only a small adjustment in the housing expenditures of participants—you can buy only so much cooperation with a given bribe. Conceivably the standards used are a long way from the "efficiency frontier" and a different set or type would get a lot more net improvement in housing through either more participants or more improvement per participant. I know of no promising alternatives and feel that it would be premature to use an experiment as costly as this one to engage in a blind search. The limited variations in standards that were applied in the experiments certainly deserve careful analysis of their effect both on the efficiency of the policy for meeting housing standards and on the equity implications of the bribe payments. But I do not believe there were feasible alternative standards that differed enough from the ones used to justify a different orientation of the experimental program.

Should the Supply Experiment Have Paid More Attention to Demand Issues?

It will be recalled that the "measurement of market effects was the core of the housing allowance supply experiment research charter."[12] Since it

---

12. Rand Corporation, *Fifth Annual Report of the Housing Assistance Supply Experiment,* R-2434-HUD (Rand, June 1979), p. xi.

was found that there were no discernible market effects, the research plan connected with the supply experiment was reconsidered and redirected toward the study of the dynamics of participation and eligibility, clearly issues on the demand side.[13] Just as clearly, these are issues that can be examined in a different environment from the demand experiment. The critical difference is that in the supply experiment sites the same housing gap allowance plan was made available to all eligible households—new, old, or incipient—rather than to a selected and scattered sample of experimental households. How might the experiment have been shaped differently if these concerns had been included in the core of the original research charter?

The most important modification would have been to assure greater comparability between the demand and supply experiments in the micro-data collected from households so that the effects of saturation as opposed to individual entitlement on issues of participation and eligibility could have been studied. This would have argued for a longitudinal sample of households comparable to the experimental and control panels drawn and followed by the demand experiment. The coverage of such a panel perhaps should have been expanded to sample from the entire range of households rather than being limited to the low-income strata, although there would still be a strong argument for sampling lower strata at a higher rate.

Greater concern with the demand issues might also have led to consideration of whether entitlement should have been defined differently at the two sites; that is, with one site restricted to renters. This would have yielded more directly comparable contrasts in treatment between the scattered sample (demand) site and the saturation (supply) site restricted to renters. It would also have contrasted the two saturation sites on the consequences of entitling homeowners as well as renters to program participation. As it stands, the consequences of allowing homeowners to participate cannot be separated from the effects of saturation. Of course, if this plan had been followed, it would have been impossible to get a clear contrast between the relatively tight and expanding housing market of Green Bay and the stagnant market in the inner city of South Bend. Since no major impact on the market was found in either site, this concern certainly seems less urgent now than it was at the time. Alternatively, the addition of a third saturation site could have been considered, at the cost of another $40 million. It seems to me that a third site limited to renters

---

13. Administrative issues were also given more emphasis in the revised plan.

would have been at least as valuable as either of the existing sites, which afford the contrasts between tight and loose markets.

In the design of a longitudinal household sample, both sites should have included households regardless of their current tenure status. Such a sample, which covered the full universe of incomes, perhaps stratified, would have contained a subsample that could have been identified to provide full comparability with the specifications for the demand panel.

There was, in fact, the embryo of the kind of survey that would be helpful in pursuing demand issues in the supply sites—the comparability panel, which focused only on rental households, further truncated to represent the eligible and near-eligible households on the basis of income. Through some combination of poor sample design by the Urban Institute and lack of appreciation by the Rand Corporation of the potential importance of this survey, the resulting data have not been deemed worthy of further analysis by either party. This survey should have concentrated on the processes of household formation and tenure transition, followed all offshoots or fragments of the originally sampled households, and possibly devised a means of sampling migrants into the sites. This kind of survey would have been an ambitious undertaking and more expensive than the one attempted. But it also would have added a lot more to current knowledge.

Conclusions

In the last dozen years social experiments have become an established part of the arsenal of government in its efforts to devise and evaluate public policies. They are perforce—in their design, execution, analysis, and ultimate interpretation—mixtures of political and scientific influences. Because it takes so long for those functions to occur, the concern and interest that prevailed at the beginning of an experiment will have changed somewhat by the time it is completed. The political forces that define the feasible range of policy alternatives changed in the 1970s, altering the questions that seem most urgent. Similarly, the state of knowledge or conventional wisdom in the scientific community appears to change—partly because of genuine progress in understanding social and economic processes and partly because there are tides of fashion or fascination in the behavioral sciences.

When the Experimental Housing Allowance Program was designed, social experimentation was relatively new and enjoyed a great deal of attention. It is far from clear whether this was because of its potential for increasing knowledge in the conventional scientific sense or as a substitute for full-scale policy innovation. It was appealing as a low-cost, prestigious sort of demonstration that still retained the primary objectives of showing feasibility and developing sufficient credibility to enlist political support. There was also optimism that substantial new redistributive policies were politically feasible. Even though Nixon's welfare reform flopped, it came near enough to success that policy planners could plausibly consider costly options providing benefits for millions of low-income families.

In this context, then, the idea of a housing allowance emerged. It opened up the possibility of using an approach to getting families into satisfactory housing quite different from previous ones, which relied much more heavily on constructing housing for the poor. The idea of using existing market mechanisms had substantial appeal then, as it still does, as a way of making the many allocational choices involved in deciding who is going to live where and under what conditions. But it also offered a means of providing immediate assistance to those who were unsatisfactorily housed.

The experimental program was thus conceived, by both congressional and HUD proponents, as a means of showing that housing allowances "work" and of providing the informational foundation for rapid national implementation based on refined estimates of impact, cost, and so forth. The precise definition of "work" was and is, of course, ambiguous. Those who generally favored larger and more equitable benefits for the low-income population in almost any guise could be enthusiastic if purchasing power was effectively bolstered, quite apart from any effect on housing expenditures or the quality of housing. For persons who regard housing quality as a pivotal influence on human development and social welfare, "working" would surely involve a disproportionate effect on housing of the transfer relative to cash benefits made on any other basis. For those whose livelihood depends on the level of construction activity, a program that tends to reallocate existing housing resources to low-income households without at the same time stimulating the construction of new units would have to be placed in the category of things that "don't work."

Given these origins, the features of the Experimental Housing Allowance Program as designed, and our experience to date, it must be asked, how well has the program worked and what does that answer imply about social experimentation? I shall consider its value under three headings, as a demonstration or pilot operation, as a basis for projecting short-term impacts and costs, and as a source of evidence about more long-run effects related to basic knowledge about housing markets.

As a demonstration that a housing allowance of the income gap variety can be set up and operated in a wide variety of settings, the program is a resounding success. No calamitous effects on local markets or other unpleasant side effects were uncovered. A lot of valuable experience, some recorded and some embodied in managers and administrators, now exists that would enable a national housing allowance program to be rapidly and efficiently put into place. Among the dozen research sites and the thousands of beneficiaries, a great deal of testimony on the merits of the program, most of it favorable, could be elicited.

If these results of a costly undertaking appear to have relatively little value, it is because the political climate has changed and is now less favorable toward large redistributional undertakings. Regarded as a part of the outcome expected and desired from the experimental program, and thereby influential in its broad design, the best composite of the whole experience is a strong tool for contributing to knowledge. If momentum for a housing allowance had developed during the mid-1970s, such "products" would have been of enormous value to HUD.

But the objectives of the program were clearly more ambitious than merely being a demonstration or pilot project. Policy analysis has become more sophisticated in the last dozen years, and policy makers need and expect detailed projections of the costs and effects of proposed programs.

How well has the program met the needs for such projections? Here it is fair to take the problem as one of predicting the impacts and costs on a given population of households, a given inventory of housing units, and a given distribution by housing tenure. Based on the evidence and analysis from the program, it seems to me that relatively firm estimates of eligibility, participation, and housing expenditures could be made. Such estimates could be adjusted to allow for changes in the level of maximum benefits or the tax rate, and some attempt could be made to provide adjustment for housing standards of varying stringency as well. Administrative costs and staffing estimates could also be projected with greater authority than is typically available for new programs.

It is when one considers relaxing the critical assumptions about household formation and tenure decisions that severe limitations must be recognized. The analytic and experimental design of the demand experiment is particularly inadequate for addressing such issues. The supply experiment may have a less inherently restrictive design, but the desire to examine these issues is not evident in its data-collecting or analytical approaches. Since there has been no significant effect on the housing markets in the supply experiment sites, analytic effort has been shifted to the fundamental structure of housing supply mechanisms and to the dynamics of eligibility and participation. It can be hoped only that further research can overcome the gaps in data needed for a thorough analysis.

An experimental design capable of exploring or estimating the full range of housing adjustment processes is certainly difficult to devise. The problem is that the background of theory and evidence on the dynamics and economics of household formation and of life-cycle consumption patterns, including housing, is relatively weak. The design of any experiment is bound by prior understanding as well as by issues that are important to the sponsoring agency. But the importance of the indirect effects of household fission or fusion and of tenure change simply was not recognized at the outset, and even the weak theory that exists was not used.

What general conclusions about social experimentation can be drawn from the Experimental Housing Allowance Program experience? It seems to me that at least two lessons, not entirely new, are well exemplified here. One is that because experiments take a long time (if they are carefully designed and executed) the objective ought to be to learn about issues that are likely to be of *continuing* importance. A narrow focus on a particular form of policy runs the risk of being outside the target of concern by the time experimental evidence is available and has been thoroughly and critically analyzed. The second is that drawing on the experience of other experiments, particularly on their structural design, can be overdone. Each analytic problem should be carefully considered and the design of experiments and coverage of the data-collection efforts tailored to suit the purpose. But despite these lessons, the program has produced some uniquely valuable data sets as well as an impressive array of analytic reports. In the longer run, provided that further analysis of these data files (in a form for public use) can be organized and supported, the most valuable contribution may come from more general and gradual improvement in the understanding of the microeconomic processes involved in housing markets rather than from the eventual legislative destiny of one or another form of housing allowance. In the meantime, we are all well primed for a debate on the immediate merits of a housing gap pro-

gram and have a much improved basis for seeking the knowledge required
for more comprehensive and long-run assessments.

Was the enterprise worth the cost? The total of more than $160 million
is very large. Half that amount represents benefits to low-income households and the attendant administrative costs; the other half is the bill for
data and research. The total cost of the Experimental Housing Allowance
Program is approximately twenty times the cost of the New Jersey income
maintenance experiment[14] and six times the amount of research funding
available annually from the National Science Foundation for all the social
sciences. If the program were evaluated purely on the basis of its contribution to general understanding of economic and social processes relating to the production, allocation, and consumption of housing services,
I conjecture that more could have been learned for less money by using a
different strategy. If, however, one considers how much research and development might be justified as a fraction of total public spending on
housing or as a fraction of the total costs of a new permanent policy, the
numbers do not look as large. Also, the program-specific findings and
the institutional learning that come from a large demonstration effort become the primary outputs of such research and development activity.
Viewed in this way, the total cost would be easily justified if there were a
movement to legislate and, if successful, to institute a housing allowance
program. I will not conjecture whether the evidence would help proponents any more than opponents. However, I feel certain that the debate
could be based on much better evidence than was available in 1970. More
as a matter of faith than of reckoning, I believe the added evidence would
prevent enough errors, large and small, to outweigh the cost.

As the nature of program evaluation has evolved, there has been a
tendency to embed more social experimentation, in the sense in which I
have used it, in large, multipurpose policy evaluations. The latest example is the Employment Opportunity Pilot Project initiated by the Department of Labor.[15] The design of this evaluation introduces guaranteed employment, following a period of job search, as a saturation treatment in
fourteen sites selected to represent a variety of labor market and demographic conditions. One additional site is to be a "scattered sample" with

14. David Kershaw and Jerilyn Fair, *The New Jersey Income-Maintenance
Experiment,* vol. 1: *Operations, Surveys, and Administration* (Academic Press,
1976), p. 18.
15. The following specifications for the Employment Opportunity Pilot Project
refer to the project's design as of fall 1979.

a control group. Intersite variations in the program are also being demonstrated, and a matched set of fourteen sites has been selected to provide
a basis for comparison with the saturation sites. One of the saturation
sites may also introduce variation in the wage paid for public employment. This project, like the Experimental Housing Allowance Program,
combines some closely designed experimental features with a large demonstration aimed at proving and improving the feasibility of a job entitlement policy. The Department of Labor needs to show that some basic
policy can be made to work and to find ways to make it work better
through "learning by doing." This project will probably cost three or
four times as much as the Experimental Housing Allowance Program.
(The net cost will almost certainly be smaller than that total because of
substitution from other activities under the Comprehensive Employment
and Training Act.) The larger size makes it possible to introduce variation
both within and among the saturation sites, to have control sites, and to
have a scattered sample site for more intensive study of variations. It
allows a wide range of evaluative activity, only part of which is experimental in the narrow sense. Case studies and simple cost accounting or
related management studies also play an important role.

It appears to me that the mixture of evaluative activities, including
various degrees of experimentation, embedded in a pilot project or field
trial of a new policy is a pattern, clearly established by the housing program, that is likely to continue. The Employment Opportunity Pilot Project is the latest example and, with a larger budget and more sites, it has
greater opportunities to refine its designs. It will remain important to
consider carefully the range of general and specific issues that can be
explored in each such opportunity and to choose the exploratory technique best suited to the level of current knowledge on each issue.

Comments on this paper follow the Aaron paper.

HENRY J. AARON

Policy Implications:
A Progress Report

It would be delightful to report that the housing allowance experiments provided unambiguous guidance about the best form of housing assistance. In the words of a bygone political figure, that statement would be easy, but it would be wrong.

The first part of this paper sets forth certain "facts" about housing that I shall assume without elaboration or proof and that underlie the rest of the paper, and then reviews the objectives of federal housing policies and the programs undertaken to advance them. The second part compares housing allowances with unconstrained cash assistance and concludes that either program will promote certain housing objectives but not others, and that running both programs independently is administratively inefficient. The third part compares housing allowances with construction-related subsidies. It concludes that subsidy programs tied to new construction try to cope with a wider range of objectives than housing allowances do, that their success in achieving those objectives is largely unknown, and that they cost too much. For political rather than analytic reasons, this part concludes that housing assistance programs that provide subsidies both to encourage demand for existing housing and to promote new construction should be retained. The paper ends with an examination of the value of social experimentation and concludes that social experiments are worth their cost if used sparingly, and that the housing allowance experiments, in particular, have repaid or will repay their cost.

I wish to thank C. Lance Barnett and his colleagues at the Rand Corporation, John Bayne, Marc Bendick, Jr., and his colleagues at the Urban Institute, Elizabeth Bernsten, Katharine L. Bradbury, Anthony Downs, Jerry J. Fitts, Stephen D. Kennedy and his colleagues at Abt Associates, Larry L. Orr, and James P. Zais for comments on a draft of this paper and for assistance on the final version.

Housing Policy and the Experiments

For more than four decades, successive Congresses and administrations have pursued similar housing goals with diverse policies. The housing allowance experiments were designed to find out whether some of these goals could be achieved more effectively by housing allowances than by other policies. It is important to keep in mind, however, that housing allowances are not relevant to many housing policy objectives, and that their effects depend on the structure of housing markets and underlying housing conditions.

Background Assumptions

The attractiveness of housing subsidies in general and housing allowances in particular depends on one's views of the nature of urban problems and of the adequacy of the housing stock in the United States. The remainder of this paper rests on several perceptions. First, the housing stock of the United States in general is abundant and of high quality; it is larger on a per capita basis and of better quality than that of any other country. Its size and excellence are due in part to American wealth, but they are also attributable to policies that encourage Americans to consume far more housing and to become homeowners far more often than they would in free housing and credit markets. These incentives include personal income tax rules that encourage investment in owner-occupied housing, depreciation rules on rental housing that are more favorable than those for nonresidential investment, and the corporation income tax, which encourages more capital to flow into the relatively lightly taxed housing sector.[1] These incentives are offset only partly (if at all) by property taxes, the burden of which may fall more heavily on capital invested in residences than on capital put to other productive uses. Also,

1. Henry J. Aaron, *Shelter and Subsidies: Who Benefits from Federal Housing Policies?* (Brookings Institution, 1972), pp. 53–73; David Laidler, "Income Tax Incentives for Owner-Occupied Housing," in Arnold C. Harberger and Martin J. Bailey, eds., *The Taxation of Income from Capital* (Brookings Institution, 1969), pp. 50–76; Harvey S. Rosen, "Housing Decisions and the U.S. Income Tax: An Econometric Analysis," *Journal of Public Economics,* vol. 11 (February 1979), pp. 1–23; Arnold C. Harberger, "The Incidence of the Corporation Income Tax," *Journal of Political Economy,* vol. 70 (June 1962), pp. 215–40; Joseph E. Stiglitz, "Taxation, Corporate Financial Policy and the Cost of Capital," *Journal of Public Economics,* vol. 2 (February 1973), pp. 1–34.

American financial markets are organized to direct a larger fraction of credit into housing than would occur through unfettered credit institutions.

Second, despite the general excellence of the American housing stock, seriously inadequate housing still exists. The probability of living in such inadequate housing varies inversely with income and rent, but the correlation is loose. Many low-income families live in housing that is physically adequate by conventional standards. In fact, with a few exceptions (such as the old-law tenements in New York City), the housing inhabited by the poor was built to standards adequate by today's criteria, and any inadequacies result from poor maintenance by owners or occupants. The correlation between rent and housing quality is especially loose. Housing may be inadequate because of physical shortcomings of the units, overcrowding, or deficiencies in neighborhoods (including in the concept of neighborhoods the quality of other units in a building). The proportion of the housing stock that was considered inadequate because of physical shortcomings of the units or overcrowding has declined dramatically in the last several decades. The proportion of occupied housing units that lack some or all plumbing, that are dilapidated, or that are severely overcrowded (more than 1.5 persons per room) has become negligible. Moreover, only a small part of the decline in these indexes of inadequate housing can be attributed to housing subsidy programs under even the most generous evaluation of their effectiveness; the declines have been due instead to the rise in per capita incomes and to the policies cited above that favor investment in housing. The fact that all new housing is built standard does not imply that it stays that way; large numbers of housing units, particularly those inhabited by low-income families, develop serious flaws.[2] Such deterioration is attributable to poor maintenance, not to poor construction.

Third, most problems faced by older cities are the inevitable consequences of trends that cannot be reversed in the short run. These problems reflect the general decline in density related to the greater availability of faster and less expensive transportation associated with the automobile and the movement of employment from the Northeast to the South and West caused by changes in the composition of productive activity and in the comparative advantages of different regions. The problems are height-

2. See David W. Budding, "Draft Report on Housing Deprivation Among Enrollees in the Housing Allowance Demand Experiment" (Cambridge, Mass.: Abt Associates, November 1978).

ened by the durability of the urban capital stock and by the interlocking character of housing, transportation, commercial, and social investments. These problems are compounded by and interact with social pathologies and discrimination. Against these formidable trends and problems, housing programs are at best a palliative that can ameliorate certain serious and painful consequences of the adjustment process. But housing policies cannot reverse, halt, or even significantly slow the adjustment process. Housing policies can, however, serve other important functions unrelated to the problems of older industrial cities, and those functions will be discussed later in this paper.

Goals of Federal Housing Policies

Housing allowances in varying degrees are relevant to at least eight traditional goals of American housing policy.[3] The first is a reduction in the amount of physically inadequate housing. Although most occupied housing now is uncrowded and equipped with adequate plumbing, heating, and cooking facilities,[4] millions of Americans live in housing most would regard as distasteful. A study done under the supply experiment finds that a large fraction of the housing inhabited by poor people has serious flaws, but that nearly all are traceable to poor maintenance, not to substandard construction.[5] Physically inadequate housing usually is dirty, poorly maintained, or located in the "wrong" neighborhood. But such methods of mass data collection as the census and the HUD annual housing survey seem unable to agree sufficiently on the inadequacy of individual units to permit measurement of other than gross physical characteristics.[6]

Housing allowances help recipients live in standard housing to the extent that either recipients move from deficient to standard units or recipients (or landlords) upgrade the units in which recipients live. The allowances reduce the stock of deficient housing only to the extent that landlords and tenants upgrade previously deficient units to acceptable

3. See Martin D. Levine, *Federal Housing Policy: Current Programs and Recurring Issues,* Congressional Budget Office, Background Paper (Government Printing Office, June 1978), p. 3.

4. See Ira S. Lowry, *A Topical Guide to HASE Research,* Rand/N-1215-HUD (Santa Monica: Rand Corp., June 1979), p. 15.

5. Ibid., p. 15.

6. Joseph J. Valenza, *Program Housing Standards in the Experimental Housing Allowance Program: Analyzing Differences in the Demand and Supply Experiments,* 216-30 (Washington, D.C.: Urban Institute, July 1977).

standards or that tenants move to standard units from deficient units that are then removed from the housing stock. If all income-eligible households participated in housing allowances, none would live in deficient housing. Even if participation were universal, however, income-ineligible households might reside in deficient housing. But participation is far from universal, so housing allowances probably eliminate only a fraction of deficient housing.

The second major goal of federal housing policy is to reduce crowding. The demand and the supply experiments stipulated that no unit could be regarded as standard if there were more than two people per acceptable bedroom.

Housing standards for occupancy, like all other elements of the minimum standards used in the experiments, are threshold standards. Units fail if they are below the threshold, but they receive no extra credit if they exceed it substantially. Thus a household that wants "too small" an apartment in a "good" neighborhood cannot indulge its preferences and qualify for aid. Failure to meet any one standard, however minor, cannot be offset by other qualities, no matter how highly valued by the tenant. The logic of the standards is inevitably arbitrary. There is no reliable evidence that variations from current standards governing the number of persons per room or bedroom or sleeping room has any particular effect on health, education, or other social outcomes. High population densities per apartment may increase wear and tear on the apartment or inflict external costs on neighbors, but both drawbacks could be reflected in rents.

Housing allowances may reduce overcrowding, leave it unaffected, or increase it in the aggregate if allowances do not affect the supply of housing.[7] No evidence is available on which outcome is most likely.

A third goal of federal housing policy is to reduce the financial burden of housing. In fact, the fraction of income that people spend on housing has been rising, and the poor spend proportionally more of their income on housing than do the middle- and upper-income classes. Between 1950 and 1976 the proportion of renter households spending 25 percent or more of their income on rent rose from 31 to 47 percent; more than three-

7. To illustrate the statement in the text, assume that there are three units with one, two, and three bedrooms and three households with two, four, and six persons. The households can arrange themselves in six ways in the three units, one of which leaves no household overcrowded, one of which leaves two households overcrowded, and four of which leave one household overcrowded. Depending on the initial situation and which households are eligible for allowances, the number of overcrowded units may rise, fall, or stay the same.

fifths of renter households with incomes below $10,000 spent at least 25 percent of their income on housing in 1976, compared with 1 percent of those with incomes of $20,000 or more.[8] Moreover, the variation around these averages is enormous.

There is nothing wrong with trying to reduce the financial burden of housing, but with one exception this goal has nothing to do with housing. The exception occurs when policies improve manufacturing efficiency, improve the efficiency of credit markets, or otherwise cut the quantity of real resources required to supply a given quantity of housing services. In general, housing allowances or any kind of housing subsidy or cash assistance reduces the financial burden of housing only to the extent that it does not result in increased housing expenditures. In other words, subsidies reduce the financial burden of housing in direct proportion to the degree by which they increase saving and the consumption of goods other than housing. Thus attempting to attain goal 3 directly conflicts with attaining goals 1 and 2, unless a decline in housing prices results.[9]

For many years federal policy has been based on the judgment that households should not have to spend more than 25 percent of their income on housing and that a rise in the proportion of households that spend more, such as has occurred in recent years, is evidence that the financial burden of housing has increased undesirably. The 25 percent norm may serve a useful purpose in some contexts. For example, lenders may find that a simple rule of thumb that mortgage borrowers should not have to spend more than a certain fraction of their income—such as 25 percent—on debt service is an efficient device for screening potential borrowers because the cost of more precise decision rules may exceed any gains.

8. Levine, *Federal Housing Policy*, pp. 10–11. The higher percentage of renter households that spent 25 percent or more of their incomes on rent may have resulted in part from the lower fraction of all households renting in 1976 than in 1950. When many relatively affluent renters shift to homeownership, the proportion of renting households that spend over 25 percent on rent may rise.

9. There seems to be some confusion in the reports on the experiments over how the effect of housing allowances on goal 3 should be measured. In some cases, the allowance is subtracted from rent and excluded from income in calculating a rent–income ratio. In others, the allowance is simply added to income in calculating the rent–income ratio. Neither approach measures the effect on the alleged lack of adequate income for purposes other than housing caused by high housing costs. The correct measure for progress on this problem is not a ratio at all, but simply the change in the difference between total income (including housing allowance benefits) and actual housing expenditures.

But there are two uses for which the 25 percent rule is inappropriate. The first is its most traditional use, as a normative guide to whether individual households or groups of households are overburdened by housing expenditures. It is ridiculous to regard a household that has been earning $10,000 and spending $2,500 on housing as newly distressed when it receives a raise of $1,000 and elects to spend it all on housing; yet the 25 percent rule implies precisely that. Unless it can be shown that markets are systematically and seriously distorted, it is also ridiculous to draw any conclusions from trends in the proportion of households that spend more than any particular fraction of their income on housing. Households can be expected to spend their incomes to maximize their welfare subject to prices for housing and other goods. Trends in the fraction of income spent on housing would show how the pursuit of economic well-being proceeded as incomes rose and relative commodity prices changed, but changes in the financial burden of housing are not, in themselves, good or bad.

The idea that 25 percent of income should be used for housing also crops up in actual housing programs and in the housing allowance experiments. In housing programs, it is the fraction of income most often used for reducing benefits as income rises, and in housing allowances it is the central value of b, the benefit reduction rate. Clearly, some benefit reduction rate must be used if eligibility for subsidies is not to be extended to everyone, and a central value of 0.25 in the experiments is as good as any other value for generating data. But I know of no justification for the 25 percent tax rate in policy. Ideally, to maximize the achievement of the objectives of a housing program, the rate at which benefits are reduced as income rises should be set jointly with the amount of assistance given to households with no income and with the housing requirements. A given budget can be distributed in various ways, and the degree to which program objectives are met can vary widely depending on how these three key parameters are set. To achieve the optimum, one would have to specify the objectives of a housing policy and their relative weights and have information on how families at various income levels would respond to offers of cash contingent on the satisfaction of housing requirements. I should be surprised if a 25 percent benefit reduction rate turned out to yield the best results.

A fourth goal emerged during the 1960s—to promote economic and racial integration, or at least to break down legal and market barriers to integration. In earlier years, housing programs had reinforced racially segregated living patterns. To the extent that racial segregation is enforced or reflects the preferences of affected households, housing allowances in principle are powerless to affect it. But to the extent that racial segregation is a proxy for economic segregation—the inability of the poor (disproportionally nonwhite) to afford housing near the middle class (disproportionally white)—housing allowances in principle can aid integration.

The housing allowance reports conclude that the experiments negligibly affected racial and economic integration.[10] I believe that even small effects on moving patterns may affect racial segregation more significantly than the authors suggest. Among black households who moved, the percentage of neighbors who were black declined as a result of the move by 3.7 percent in Pittsburgh and 4.3 percent in Phoenix; among black controls who moved, the percentages increased by 7.7 percent and 4.1 percent, respectively.[11] But even small differences in moving patterns can have great importance in the long run, as the imaginative simulations of Thomas Schelling dramatize.[12]

A wide range of programs has promoted a fifth goal, the encouragement of homeownership. These programs include mortgage insurance and guarantees, tax policy, and the creation of institutions to increase and stabilize the flow of mortgage credit. Housing allowances may retard homeownership if allowances are available only to renters.[13] When hous-

10. Reilly Atkinson, William Hamilton, and Dowell Myers, "Draft Report on Economic and Racial/Ethnic Concentration in the Housing Allowance Demand Experiment" (Abt, January 1979); Jean MacMillan, "Draft Report on Mobility in the Housing Allowance Demand Experiment" (Abt, June 1978); Rand Corporation, *Fourth Annual Report of the Housing Assistance Supply Experiment,* R-2302-HUD (Rand Corp., May 1978), pp. 128–33.

11. Atkinson and others, "Draft Report," p. 47. The authors point out the possibility that this difference may represent regression to the mean, as black recipients of the allowance who moved lived in more segregated neighborhoods than did black controls who moved. A later table shows the same pattern in predominantly black or boundary neighborhoods. The small number of blacks in white neighborhoods prevents any meaningful statistical comparisons.

12. Thomas C. Schelling, "Dynamic Models of Segregation," *Journal of Mathematical Sociology,* vol. 1 (July 1971), pp. 143–86; "Models of Segregation," *American Economic Review,* vol. 59 (May 1969; *Papers and Proceedings, 1968*), pp. 488–93; "On the Ecology of Micromotives," *The Public Interest,* no. 25 (Fall 1971); "The Process of Residential Segregation: Neighborhood Tipping," in Anthony H. Pascal, ed., *Racial Discrimination in Economic Life* (Lexington Books, 1972), pp. 157–84.

13. The effect is unclear, however. In addition to the quasi-substitution effect that underlies the statement in the text, housing allowances generate an income effect, increasing the resources from which families can amass a down payment. If illiquidity is a sufficiently important barrier to homeownership, the quasi-income effect might predominate.

ing allowances are available to both renters and homeowners, housing allowances should promote homeownership because they add to income, and the income elasticity of demand for homeownership is positive. Also, the effect of housing allowances on housing consumption is likely to be greater if both homeowners and renters are eligible to receive them, because renters can then use the allowances not only to rent better apartments but also to buy housing.[14]

Federal policy has sought not only to affect housing directly, but also to promote neighborhood revitalization and preservation and community development. The precise meaning of this sixth goal is unclear and has changed over the years. But an evolving roster of programs—urban renewal, model cities, the community development block grant, urban development action grants—has been intended to change and improve the environment in which housing exists. By a looser definition, all housing programs—and indeed all programs that have a major impact on cities and towns, especially food stamps and welfare—may be regarded as instruments for advancing this objective.[15] In this sense, housing allowances are also such an instrument, but the experiments indicate that the kind of allowances tested would have minor direct effects on neighborhood revitalization and community development. Another kind of allowance—one limited to particular areas or to groups living in such areas—could be used in rapidly appreciating areas to stem the departure of low-income people, thereby promoting or preserving economic integration.

A seventh goal of federal policy is to increase the supply of housing tailored to the needs of particular groups such as the aged and the needy. This goal resulted from the belief that private industry would not provide the kinds of housing best suited to these groups. Housing allowances limited to such groups could further this objective if they enabled these

14. Data from the income maintenance experiments suggest that the income elasticity of demand for housing is greater when both renters and homeowners are included than when only renters are included. See James C. Ohls and Cynthia Thomas, "The Effects of the Seattle and Denver Income Maintenance Experiments on Housing Consumption, Ownership and Mobility," Draft Report (Denver: Mathematica Policy Research, January 1979), pp. 26–27.

15. Joseph Friedman and Daniel Weinberg point out that food stamps are equivalent to a percent of rent housing allowance payable in food vouchers with a value in 1976 of nearly $1 billion. This is because food stamp bonuses at that time depended on net income and housing expenses in excess of 30 percent of income were subtracted from income to reach net income. In 1977 Congress changed the rules for computing net income, reducing the importance of "excess" housing cost. See "Draft Report on the Demand for Rental Housing: Evidence from a Percent of Rent Housing Allowance" (Abt, September 1978), pp. 33–38, A-41–47.

groups to bid successfully for available units or if they encouraged the construction of special units. But results from the experiments cast doubt on the effectiveness of a general housing allowance in promoting these objectives, especially if currently overcrowded families of moderate size began to compete with large families for the meager quantity of large units or if nonelderly families living in substandard housing began to compete for standard units now occupied by the elderly.

As the eighth goal, federal policy has sought at various times to increase and stabilize residential construction. Regulations affecting investments of savings and loan associations and the creation of the Federal National Mortgage Association, the Federal Home Loan Bank Board, the Federal Home Loan Mortgage Corporation, and the Government National Mortgage Association were intended in part to increase the flow of credit to housing; some were designed to reduce the instability introduced by other elements. There was little reason before, and there is no reason at all now that results from the experiments are coming in, to expect housing allowances to have much effect on either objective.

The experiments sought information on how housing allowances would affect each of these objectives of public policy. Most of the research questions were related to specific effects and addressed positive questions. Who participates in housing allowance programs, and how do variations in program characteristics affect rates of participation? Do housing allowances increase mobility, and if so, where do people move? How much do housing expenditures increase under a housing allowance, and how are such increases divided between improved housing and higher prices? Would housing allowances cause general inflation in housing markets? In what ways do housing allowances affect the supply of housing— through maintenance, rehabilitation, or new construction? What administrative problems does a housing allowance program encounter?[16]

The answers to these questions are essential components of any normative statement about whether or not housing allowances are better suited than other housing policies to advance housing goals.

---

16. For detailed statements of the research questions, see Garth Buchanan and John D. Heinberg, *Housing Allowance Household Experiment Design: Part I— Summary and Overview*, 205-4 (Urban Institute, May 1972); John D. Heinberg and others, *Integrated Analysis of the Experimental Housing Allowance Program*, 210-3 (Urban Institute, November 1973); Abt Associates, *Summary Evaluation Design: The Demand Experiment* (Abt, June 1973), pp. 5–9; Rand Corporation, *Fourth Annual Report*, pp. 2–4; and U.S. Department of Housing and Urban Development, *Experimental Housing Allowance Program: A 1979 Report of Findings* (GPO, 1979), pp. 3–6.

Housing Allowances as a Subsidy to Demand

Housing allowances are payments to households of cash with certain strings attached. The housing gap allowance is calculated according to a formula that is structurally indistinguishable from formulas tested in the income maintenance experiments. The negative income tax formulas examined in the income maintenance experiments stipulated that households were to be paid a certain sum if they had no outside income (the guarantee) and that the payment was to be reduced by a certain fraction of income (the "benefit reduction" rate). The housing gap allowance assures each household some multiple of the estimated cost of standard housing, C^*, if the household has no income and reduces that guarantee by some fraction, b, of income. Thus the structure of housing allowances differs from that of negative income taxes only to the extent that conditions are imposed on housing allowances but not on negative income taxes. The conditions cause recipients to spend the housing allowance benefits differently from the way they would spend unrestricted cash assistance.

The cost of a housing allowance or any other housing program, T, may be divided into two main parts—the allowance payment, P, and the administrative cost, A, of providing that payment, including the salaries and expenses of the administering agency and the costs of inspections; that is, $T = P + A$. The allowance payment can be divided into two parts—the amount of the allowance payment that the household spends on housing, H, and the amount that the household has available to spend for other goods and services (including saving), Y; that is, $P = H + Y$. The extra expenditures on housing, H, may be well or poorly spent. If housing is collectively produced, the process may be more or less costly than an equivalent privately constructed unit; this cost differential is D. Because a housing program makes households spend more on additional housing than they would without restriction, the value of the housing to the recipient, V, is usually less than its market value, $H - D$; that is, $V(H - D) < (H - D)$. Society presumably derives some return from the induced housing outlay, S. Housing expenditures are worth undertaking when the private and social value of the induced housing outlay, plus the value to recipients of the increase in their capacity to buy other goods, is at least as great as the cost of the program including administrative costs; that is, $V(H - D) + S(H - D) + Y \geq T$.

When Is a Housing Program Not a Housing Program?

Because housing allowance formulas so closely resemble those of un-constrained income support, it is interesting to measure the degree to which housing allowances (and other housing programs) are income maintenance and the degree to which they are really housing programs. For this purpose a scale is essential. One point on the scale is generated by unrestricted income support, exemplified by the negative income tax formulas tested in the income maintenance experiments and by the un-constrained housing allowance variants tested in Pittsburgh and Phoenix. These programs increase housing expenditures by some fraction of the payments made to households. The remainder of the payment is used to purchase other goods and services. The fraction of the payment spent on housing under such an unrestricted program, $H/(Y + H)$, measures one point on the scale. Data from the Seattle and Denver income maintenance experiments indicate that 4.5 to 10.6 cents out of every assistance dollar go for housing.[17] Data from the housing allowance demand experiment indicate that recipients of unconstrained payments spent 6 percent on housing in Pittsburgh and 19 percent in Phoenix.[18] Thus the "zero point," corresponding to the effect of one dollar spent without any effort to increase expenditures on any commodity, shows a ratio of increased housing expenditure to subsidy cost of 0.05 to 0.19.

All other points on the scale are arbitrary, but I shall define a "pure housing program" as one in which all program costs, other than those for administration, result in increased housing expenditures. In other words, $Y = 0$ and $H/(T - A) = 1$.

A few comments about these two points are in order. First, not all pro-grams will lie between these points. Programs that encourage the con-sumption of goods other than housing may reduce housing consumption or increase it less than unrestricted cash assistance does; in other words, $H/(Y + H) < (0.05$ to $0.19)$. Conversely, it is easy to conceive of sub-

17. Using their combined measure of rent and homeownership, Ohls and Thomas report that 10.6 cents of every dollar of allowance payments go into housing but argue that these estimates are nearly double the true value because of inadequate controls for initial conditions. If attention is focused on renters, only an estimated 4.5 cents out of each income maintenance dollar go to housing. Based on data in "Effects of the Seattle and Denver Income Maintenance Experiments," pp. 19, 25, 28.

18. Joseph Friedman and Daniel Weinberg, "Draft Report on Housing Con-sumption Under a Constrained Income Transfer: Evidence from a Housing Gap Housing Allowance" (Abt, April 1979), p. 146.

sidy formulas that increase housing expenditures by more than program costs net of administrative expenses; in other words, $H/(T - A) > 1$.[19]

Second, a pure housing program is not necessarily efficient. Administrative costs, though not included in these definitions, should not be ignored. Distortions in consumption patterns $(V < H)$ or production inefficiencies $(D > O)$ may result in increases in utility to recipients and to society that are worth far less than program cost. The converse is also possible; subsidy programs may break down inefficiencies or provide recipients with benefits that society values highly even if they are produced inefficiently.

Are Housing Allowances a Housing Program?

Data from the housing allowance experiments make clear that housing allowances fall somewhere on the scale between unrestricted income support and pure housing programs but are far nearer the former than the latter. The demand experiment indicates that in Pittsburgh and Phoenix 9 and 27 percent, respectively, of housing allowance payments received by households subject to minimum standards went for increased housing expenditures.[20] In Pittsburgh, 3 percent more of the minimum standards housing allowance than of an unconstrained payment went for housing; in Phoenix, the corresponding figure was 8 percent. Thus, based on evidence from the housing allowance experiment, housing allowances are 3 to 8 percent housing program and 92 to 97 percent income maintenance.[21]

It is worth pointing out that one of the major programs of in-kind assistance, food stamps, is also nearly entirely income support and is a food program to only a negligible extent. Evaluations of the food stamp program before 1977 reached the conclusion that only a small proportion of food stamp payments went for food purchases above those that would have been made if benefits had been paid in cash. Program changes enacted in 1977 reduced this fraction still more.

19. If subsidies were offered on the condition that they be spent entirely on increased housing consumption, utility of recipients would increase. Clearly, it would be possible to require some increase in housing consumption and still leave recipients better off than they would be without any subsidy.

20. Friedman and Weinberg, "Draft Report on Housing Consumption," p. 139.

21. The housing allowances are *not* income maintenance to the extent that the increase in housing expenditures under the allowance exceeds the increase under unconstrained assistance.

The Importance of Housing Standards

Why did the experimental housing allowances increase housing expenditures so little? One explanation may be that the housing standards were so lenient that they could be met with a small investment in remodeling or repair, and some of these outlays may have been diverted from normal maintenance. Evidence from both the demand and supply experiments, especially the latter, seemed at first glance to support this explanation. The median cost of upgrading rented and owned units that initially failed the standard and were later repaired in both supply experiment sites was only $8 to $11, and the average cost was between $35 and $81 (these estimates exclude the value of the labor of tenants and owners).[22]

The hypothesis that housing expenditures rose so little because standards were so lenient tells part of the story, but a second hypothesis must be considered—that housing expenditures increased so little because a disproportionate number of households living in units that would have been costly to upgrade failed to obtain allowances. The proportion of failed units that were upgraded declined markedly in both sites with the number of faults discovered. The drop-off was striking in the demand experiment sites; 22 percent of households living in units that failed only one element of the housing standards (and that passed the occupancy standard) upgraded their units, but only 3 percent of households living in units that failed four or more elements upgraded their units.[23] The drop-off was less marked in the supply experiment sites; in Green Bay, Wisconsin, and South Bend, Indiana, 67 and 73 percent, respectively, of households whose units failed one element of the standards upgraded their units, while 31 and 32 percent, respectively, upgraded if their units failed four or more elements of the standards.[24]

The difference between the behavior at the demand experiment sites and that at the supply experiment sites may be due in part to discrepancies in the housing standards.[25] At the supply experiment sites, the fraction of persons who moved increased with the number of deficiencies, so that

22. See James L. McDowell, *Housing Allowances and Housing Improvement: Early Findings,* Rand/N-1198-HUD (Rand Corp., September 1979), p. 28; David B. Carlson and John D. Heinberg, *How Housing Allowances Work: Integrated Findings from the Experimental Housing Allowance Program,* 249-3 (Urban Institute, February 1978), pp. 25–27; and HUD, *1979 Report of Findings,* p. 60.

23. Unpublished tabulation contained in letter from Stephen D. Kennedy, July 31, 1979.

24. HUD, *1979 Report of Findings,* p. 48.

25. See Valenza, *Program Housing Standards.*

participation declined slightly as the number of deficiencies increased. In the demand experiment sites, there was no such increase in the tendency to move, so that overall participation declined sharply as the number of flaws increased. The difference between the demand experiment and the supply experiment sites is probably attributable to the ways in which the participants were selected: supply experiment site participants were self-selected, but in the demand experiment sites a random sample of the income-eligible population was invited to enroll.[26] Furthermore, the planned duration of the supply experiment was longer (ten years) than was that of the demand experiment (three years). As a result, making the effort to achieve compliance was more worthwhile in the supply than in the demand experiment. The decline in participation as the number of defects increased occurred even though households living in units with more deficiencies than average were entitled to larger than average allowance payments because of their relatively low incomes as a group.

Both explanations raise a question about how different housing standards would have affected participation and total expenditures. Unplanned variations between the demand and supply experiments and the contrast between these sites and the unconstrained plan offer some scope for judging the impact of housing standards on participation, moving, and upgrading. Furthermore, additional variations in standards occurred in the sites where the administrative agency experiments were carried out. However, data from these sites are confounded with the many other unique features of each site, making it difficult to identify the special circumstances that explain variations of behavior. The differences in behavior under the unconstrained plan, the standards enforced at the supply experiment sites, and the standards enforced at the demand experiment site are sufficiently gross to support the conclusion that stiffer standards reduce participation. In fact, the effect that stricter standards would have had on participation and on housing expenditures can be estimated, and the contractors have done so.[27] It appears that the probability that a

26. Kermit Gordon illustrated the pitfalls of drawing conclusions from a self-selected sample by recounting his effort to illustrate the decline in the birthrate by asking members of an economics class at Williams College to tell him the number of children in their families. To his surprise the number was about one child greater than the national average. In explaining the paradox, one student observed dryly that "the offspring of childless couples are underrepresented in this class."

27. These conclusions about the effects of variations in standards cannot be conclusive, however. Stephen D. Kennedy and Jean MacMillan, "Draft Report on Participation Under Alternative Housing Allowance Programs: Evidence from the Housing Allowance Demand Experiment" (Abt, October 1979).

household not initially in compliance will eventually meet the housing requirements is negatively related to the gap between the actual rent and the estimated cost of standard housing and positively related to the level of the payment schedule. According to these estimates, raising the housing standards would sharply reduce participation. Higher payment levels would increase participation, but it is estimated that to increase the participation among households that would not normally have met the housing standards from 25 percent to 50 percent would require payment levels that would add 50 to 100 percent to total transfer costs. The decline in participation as the number of disqualifying flaws increases can be explained in whole or in part by the fact that those who care about housing live in units with the fewest flaws and respond most flexibly to inducements to upgrade their housing. To the extent that this explanation is correct, tightening the standards might reduce participation somewhat, but it would also increase the proportion of allowance payments spent on housing. The absence of planned variation in the housing standards in the experiments makes it hazardous to predict the degree to which particular variations in standards would affect participation, expenditures, and housing quality.

In general, I believe that the design of the experiments was deficient in exploring the effects of different housing standards. Neither the percent of rent formula nor the minimum rent requirement is a feasible housing policy because each creates an incentive for collusion between tenants and landlords; even worse, the incentive is obvious.[28] Two variants of minimum standards were used, but since participants were sampled in the demand experiment sites but volunteered in the supply experiment sites, the comparability of behavioral response is limited. It is regrettable that the considerable effort and expense lavished on testing variations in income maintenance parameters C and b were not devoted to examining the effects of variations in the severity, breadth, and composition of the housing standards—the only feature of a housing allowance that distinguishes it from unconstrained cash assistance.[29]

28. Under the percent of rent formula, the landlord and tenant can agree to a "paper" increase in the rent. That raises the allowance payment, which the landlord and tenant can then divide. Under the minimum rent standard, the tenant who is paying too little rent to qualify has the incentive to get his rent raised, on paper or in fact, so that he can get the allowance payment. Again, the landlord and tenant can share the spoils.

29. Truth-in-criticism requires me to acknowledge my own participation in planning the four components of the experimental housing allowance program and of

Housing Allowances versus Unrestricted Cash Assistance

I believe that a program of housing allowances makes little sense if it is not integrated with existing programs of cash assistance. A separate program would duplicate administrative costs because the overlap of the populations served by housing allowances and by cash assistance would be substantial.

Administrative Costs

A freestanding housing allowance program would incur administrative costs estimated at roughly 23 percent of total program costs.[30] Average administrative costs under existing welfare programs run about 10 percent of program expenditures. A housing allowance program would thus cost roughly 10 to 13 percent more in administrative expenses than the average public assistance program in order to increase housing expenditures by 3 to 8 percent of program cost. Administrative costs associated with the housing allowance experiments were smaller per case, though larger as a percentage of total program costs, than administrative costs per case under AFDC (aid to families with dependent children). The explanation for this minor paradox is that payments per case under the housing allowance experiment were much smaller—$64 to $81 a month—than average AFDC payments—$256 a month.[31]

But the explanation of why it did not cost more per case to administer housing allowances than cash assistance must be inherent in administrative methods. For example, the supply experiment used semiannual in-

---

the demand experiment in particular. The points just made in the text were not made during those planning sessions until near the end of the planning process when implementation was getting under way, and even then they were made without sufficient force.

30. The 23 percent estimate appears in Carlson and Heinberg, *How Housing Allowances Work,* p. 47.

31. For average payments under the housing allowance experiment, see Friedman and Weinberg, "Draft Report on Housing Consumption," p. 109. The cited figures refer to Pittsburgh and Phoenix, respectively. The average monthly payment under the supply experiment during 1978 was $77 a month. Rand Corporation, *Fifth Annual Report of the Housing Assistance Supply Experiment,* R-2434-HUD (Rand, June 1979), p. 15. For average payments under AFDC, see *Social Security Bulletin* (June 1979), p. 55.

come recertification, which is less frequent than the average in most welfare systems.[32]

The interpretation of these differences in administrative expenses is far from straightforward. On the one hand, the administratve costs under the housing allowance experiments represent the initial experience with a new program, and learning by doing might reduce costs. On the other hand, the costs of administering welfare are lower in the two states in which the supply experiment is being conducted than in the nation as a whole, largely because the national statistics on the cost of administering welfare are heavily influenced by California and New York, both of which spend far more than the national average.[33]

In fact, the comparison between the administrative costs of a separate program of housing allowances and those of an increase in cash assistance costing the same amount is less favorable to housing allowances than these numbers suggest. First, the marginal administrative cost of increasing public assistance would be lower than the average cost if the average payment per household were increased. One of the reasons administrative costs of housing allowances are larger in relation to program costs than are administrative costs of public assistance is that average subsidy payments per household are so much smaller under housing allowances than under public assistance. Thus the difference between the administrative costs of a new, separate housing allowance program and the costs of corresponding additions to public assistance expenditures may be larger than the cited average administrative costs suggest. This statement presumes that any expansion in cash assistance would not require large increases in administrative costs per case. Any large expansion of cash assistance to two-parent families would probably come only if linked to work requirements and public job creation. President Carter's Program for Better Jobs and Income and his later and more modest welfare reform plan both stressed that the provision of economic support through private jobs, if possible, and public jobs, if necessary, is the preferred way to help needy two-parent families. Indeed, expenditures to create public jobs accounted for most of the estimated cost of both plans. The estimated administrative costs of the Carter administration's later welfare reform plan amounted to 10 percent of estimated outlays. As a fraction of total outlays, these estimates are far below those of housing allowances.

32. Rand Corporation, *Fourth Annual Report,* p. 57.

33. New York spent $582 per AFDC case on administration, and California spent $441; the national average was $295 a case. Rand Corporation, *Fourth Annual Report,* p. 150.

Second, administrative costs use up real resources, dollar for dollar, but the expenditure of one more dollar on housing under a housing allowance than would be spent under unrestricted cash assistance comes at the expense of one less dollar spent on goods other than housing. The household suffers a perceived loss from the distortion of its expenditure priorities. The gain to society from the increase in housing expenditures under housing allowances relative to expenditures on housing under unconstrained cash assistance equals the valuation society places on one more dollar of housing expenditure by the recipient household, less the value society places on one more dollar of expenditure on consumption of other goods by the recipient household, less the perceived loss to the recipient household from having its consumption distorted.

Are the Benefits Worth the Added Administrative Costs?

Unless the social value of increased housing expenditures by the recipient household is very high—two to five times the value of other consumption by the recipient household—a freestanding housing allowance of the kind tested in the experiments is a bad buy. To illustrate, if one assumes average administrative costs of 23 percent for the separate housing program and 10 percent for cash assistance, a housing allowance like that tested in the experiments uses $13 more in administrative costs for each $100 transferred than public assistance does, reduces household consumption of goods other than housing by $3 to $8, and imposes a welfare loss on the household (relative to the same expenditure on unconstrained assistance) of some fraction of the $3-to-$8 shift in consumption. When the welfare loss, which is probably small relative to the other magnitudes, is ignored, a $3 increase in housing consumption must have a social value of at least $16, and an $8 increase in housing consumption must have a social value of $21, for such a shift to be worthwhile.[34] It would be nice to know whether housing standards other than those tested would have led to similarly high ratios.

I do not presume to know the value to society of the shifts in expenditures toward housing accomplished by the housing allowances (or for that matter, by other housing programs). The social value may far exceed the

34. These assertions rest on the assumption that the social value, S, of the extra housing consumption induced by the housing allowance relative to cash assistance must equal the sum of the extra real resource costs used in administration and the reduction in consumption of goods other than housing induced by the housing allowance relative to cash assistance.

market value for some housing improvements. My guess is that society would willingly incur high costs to save children from being bitten by rats or to spare them the temptation of nibbling peeling lead-based paint. But my guess also is that society would not place a value much above that of the market, and hence not above that of the occupants, on improved railings and stairways or on bigger or more easily opened windows, the two most frequently encountered inadequacies in the supply and demand experiments, respectively. It seems extremely unlikely, however, that society would choose to incur large administrative costs to redistribute inadequate units from those who participate in the program to those who do not, which is the outcome in roughly half of the cases in the demand experiment and roughly one-third of the cases in the supply experiment. I conclude that, if society were deciding whether to spend a given sum on housing allowances or on unrestricted cash assistance, it should choose unrestricted cash assistance.

While the foregoing evaluation of housing allowances is instructive, it should not be considered conclusive for at least two reasons. First, even if one considers the tendency of each congressional committee to ignore what other committees are doing, the chance that a full housing allowance program, which would cost $7.4 billion (in 1976 dollars) according to the Urban Institute,[35] would be enacted without some degree of integration with existing cash assistance seems small. (One might even hope that the secretary of housing and urban development would support such integration.) The degree of integration is almost infinitely variable. Congress might redesign matching formulas under the federal-state program of aid to families with dependent children so that housing allowances served primarily to replace part of existing cash assistance, though the administrative structures of AFDC and housing allowances remained distinct. Perhaps more plausibly, Congress might require that cash assistance and housing allowances be administered jointly and stipulate that public assistance formulas for computing need take account of housing allowance benefits. Under the latter approach, housing allowances would be devices for injecting some added intrastate variability into state payment standards and could be used to promote code enforcement or other housing standards. Administrative costs would still include the expenses of inspection, but these seem to be roughly one-fifth of total direct administrative costs.[36] Increases in housing expenditures and effects on the

35. Carlson and Heinberg, *How Housing Allowances Work,* p. 47.
36. HUD, *A 1979 Report of Findings,* p. 66.

supply of housing similar to those encountered in the experiment could be achieved at much lower administrative cost.

Second, the extra administrative costs of a housing allowance program may be viewed as the necessary price for welding a coalition consisting of builders, labor, housing and community officials, and representatives of recipients that would be capable of enacting a large increase in assistance to the poor. For that reason, housing assistance may be enactable when the expansion of cash assistance is not. Nor would a housing program have to wend its way through that graveyard of welfare reform, the Senate Finance Committee. Thus, it could be argued, housing allowances should not be compared with welfare reform, which has no chance of passing, but with other public expenditures or tax cuts that increase neither the housing expenditures nor the other consumption of recipients. In this framework, all benefits to recipients should be evaluated in appraising housing allowances.

I shall return to this argument below, because the question of political coalitions and legislative feasibility is central to any consideration of the policy implications of the experiment.[37] At this point I shall simply assert, without supporting argument, that the political prospects for welfare reform seem to me to be no worse than those for a full housing allowance program costing roughly the same amount.

Housing Allowances versus Construction-linked Subsidies

Traditionally, American housing subsidies have been linked to the construction of new units. Builders or contractors have undertaken to construct new units or rehabilitate existing units, with the assurance that the federal government would provide subsidies—in addition to the rents the low-income occupants could afford—sufficient to assure the builder or developer a fair rate of return. This rather crude description characterizes low-rent public housing, section 236 rental assistance, section 235 homeownership assistance, and section 8 new construction and substantial rehabilitation. Construction has ended under section 236, is continuing slowly under section 235, and is increasing slowly under section 8. Only under section 8 existing housing and section 23 leased public housing are subsidies tied to units in the existing stock that need not have been

---

37. In technical terms, such political considerations define the counterfactual.

newly constructed or substantially rehabilitated under the program. History suggests, therefore, that it may be reasonable to view housing allowances as an alternative to construction-linked housing subsidies rather than to unconstrained cash assistance.

Construction-linked housing subsidies have a dual character. Like housing allowances, they increase housing expenditures and provide some income support. However, construction-linked subsidies also directly result in new construction, which adds standard units to the housing stock and, as in the case of substantial rehabilitation, may also remove a substandard unit from the stock.

To compare housing allowances with construction-linked subsidies would require, for each program, data on total program cost and the distribution of that cost between administrative overhead of the governmental agency or housing authority and payment for the increase in housing. Of this payment, one would need to know how much goes for housing, H, and how much for other goods and services, the income maintenance component, Y. One would also want to know how much of H was absorbed by the cost differential, D, between public and private production.

The only information on the division between H and Y of which I am aware has been compiled in connection with the housing allowance demand experiment. Mayo estimates that 68 percent and 64 percent of the total benefit to low-rent public housing tenants in Pittsburgh and Phoenix, respectively, accrues to them through change in income rather than through improved housing. Section 236 is not income maintenance at all in Pittsburgh, and it is 42 percent income maintenance in Phoenix. For section 23 (which closely resembles housing allowances), the corresponding figures are 69 percent and 65 percent, respectively.[38] If these measures generally characterize the operation of these programs in other sites, it appears that low-rent public housing newly built or leased provides more benefits in the form of increased incomes than in the form of increased housing.

---

38. Stephen Mayo and others, "Draft Report on Housing Allowances and Other Rental Housing Assistance Programs—A Comparison Based on the Housing Allowance Demand Experiment," pt. 1: "Participation, Housing Consumption, Location, and Satisfaction" (Abt, November 1979), p. 94. Mayo measures benefit as the change in the value of housing expenditures as indicated by a hedonic housing index, rather than the change in housing expenditure, H, used in this paper. His measure corresponds to V as described above plus any deadweight loss from distortion of consumption.

The High Cost of New Construction

Housing may cost more when provided under one program than under another. Furthermore, expenditures may differ from benefits under all of them. Mayo and others present additional evidence relevant to this question that suggests that the cost of providing a unit through new construction, whether public housing or section 236, is far greater than the cost of providing an equivalent unit through housing allowances.[39] The extra cost results in part from federally mandated standards other than those in housing codes, from the requirement that workers be paid "prevailing wages," as defined under the Davis-Bacon Act, that exceed wages at which workers can actually be hired, and from long delays by officials in processing applications. Mayo and others report that housing with a market value of $1,000 in 1975 required program costs of $1,150 and $1,090 under housing allowances in Pittsburgh and Phoenix, respectively; $2,200 and $1,790 under newly built low-rent public housing; and $2,010 and $1,470 under newly built section 236 housing.[40]

The same issue came up several years ago during the Department of Housing and Urban Development's review of federal housing subsidies.[41]

With the foregoing information, H or the relationship between H and Y cannot be specified, because both hinge on an estimate of the kind of housing that subsidy recipients would have obtained and what they would have spent for it had they been ineligible for the subsidy. So the degree to which construction-related subsidies are housing programs and income maintenance programs cannot be measured. The compilation of such estimates should be feasible from the data on which the estimates of Mayo and others are based. Their data do, however, suggest that construction-related subsidies are needlessly expensive as a device for improving the housing of subsidy recipients. It is possible to put income-eligible people in standard housing at far lower cost through section 23 leased public

39. Stephen Mayo and others, "Draft Report on Housing Allowances and Other Rental Housing Assistance Programs—A Comparison Based on the Housing Allowance Demand Experiment," pt. 2: "Costs and Efficiency" (Abt, August 1979), p. S-3.

40. Ibid., p. S-5.

41. See Department of Housing and Urban Development, "Suspended Subsidy Programs," in *Housing in the Seventies* (GPO, 1973). For a critical review of the HUD report that questions the precision of the results but does not present alternative estimates, see Henry B. Schechter, *Critique of "Housing in the Seventies,"* Senate Committee on Banking, Housing, and Urban Affairs (GPO, 1974), pp. 38–59.

housing, housing allowances, or (though not covered in their work) section 8 existing housing than through programs tied to new construction. They present no information—nor, to my knowledge, has anyone else— on whether a larger fraction of the occupants of subsidized new construction or of subsidized existing housing previously resided in substandard units. Thus it is impossible to tell which type of program has been more effective in upgrading housing of the occupants.

Because it costs more to provide a standard unit through construction-related subsidies than through existing housing subsidies such as housing allowances, some people conclude that construction-related subsidies are cost-ineffective and that housing allowances (or other demand subsidies) are superior to construction-related subsidies. While the conclusion may be correct, it does not follow from this argument.

Allowances versus Construction-related Subsidies

The only way to evaluate the relative attractiveness of housing allowances and construction-related subsidies is to compare the degree to which each advances the objectives listed at the outset of this paper. Table 1 lists my conclusions about the effectiveness of construction-related subsidies and of housing allowances in achieving each of the eight goals. Most of the evaluations of construction-related programs are guesses because the available data and analyses are inadequate to support an informed opinion and are grossly inferior to the data and analyses now available on housing allowances.

REDUCING INADEQUATE HOUSING. The effect of construction-related subsidies on the general supply of physically inadequate housing is unknown. Such programs create standard units. Some fears have been expressed that these standard units deteriorate rapidly because the programs concentrate families with high rates of antisocial behavior. While data from the demand experiment suggest that concentration of subsidy recipients is greater under public housing and section 236 than under housing allowances, no information is available about whether such concentration actually increases antisocial behavior or results in more deterioration than would occur if such families were dispersed.[42]

The critical issue of construction-related subsidies is their impact on

42. See "Location," in Mayo and others, "Draft Report on Housing Allowances," pt. 1.

Table 1. The Effect of Housing Policies on Goals[a]

Goal	Housing allowances	Construction-related subsidies
1. Reduce the amount of physically inadequate housing	+	?
2. Reduce overcrowding	+ (?)	+ (?)
3. Reduce financial burden of housing	+ +	+
4. Promote racial and economic integration	0, +	− (in the past) ? (today)
5. Promote homeownership	+ (if both renters and homeowners are covered) − (if only renters are covered)	+ (sections 235 and 502) − (other construction-related subsidies)
6. Revitalize neighborhoods	0	?
7. Increase supply of housing for particular groups	0, +	0, +
8. Stabilize housing construction	0	?

a. + + Indicates a strong positive effect.
   + Indicates a small positive effect.
   0 Indicates no perceptible effect.
   − Indicates a negative effect.
   ? Indicates that there probably is an effect, but its direction is unclear or is variable over time or from place to place.

the unsubsidized housing stock. In the best case, tenants would move into subsidized units from substandard existing units, which are then removed from the housing stock. In the worst case, tenants would move into subsidized units from standard units, which then deteriorate rapidly because of reduced cash flow to owners, leading perhaps to contagious blight and abandonment. To the best of my knowledge, no one knows which effect is predominant; hence there is a question mark in table 1 for goal 1 under "construction-related subsidies." Data from the experiments make it clear that housing allowances deserve a small plus—housing expenditures rise somewhat, adding to the cash flow of landlords, and modest physical improvements are made.

OVERCROWDING. A similar argument applies to overcrowding, although in this case the positive effect of construction subsidies seems much more likely. By creating a new unit, subsidized construction directly contributes to reduced densities, an effect that can be reversed only if the worst case described above takes place. In general, housing allowances reduce overcrowding. Recipients occupy more housing, and unless the supply is increased, nonrecipients will occupy less housing, raising their density. Nevertheless, few nonrecipients seem likely to be forced into overcrowded conditions.

SUPPLY AND PRICE. Both housing allowances and construction-related subsidies increase the capacity of recipients to buy nonhousing goods and reduce the financial burden of housing. To the extent that they add to the stock of housing in the long run, construction programs also tend to reduce housing prices in general, thus affecting the burden of housing on households other than those participating.

Unfortunately, no solid estimates of the overall effect of construction programs on the housing supply exist. There is some evidence that subsidized construction results in offsetting reduction in nonsubsidized construction by diverting credit that would otherwise go to unsubsidized starts; more recent research suggests that subsidized starts may be completely offset if financed through conventional mortgage markets (as is customary under sections 235, 236, and 8) but will not be offset at all if financed by direct government borrowing (as is customary under low-rent public housing and the Farmers' Home Administration programs).[43] Furthermore, the same uncertainties that make it difficult to determine whether construction subsidies will increase or decrease the amount of substandard housing make it difficult to determine their overall effect on the housing stock.

INTEGRATION. The goal of promoting economic or racial integration is new to housing programs. For many years preservation of traditional (meaning segregated) housing patterns was a stated objective of the Federal Housing Administration, a policy that was deliberately pursued with low-rent public housing as well. This policy has now been officially reversed, but the degree to which subsidized housing programs promote racial or economic integration has not, to the best of my knowledge, been measured. The continuing racial segregation in public housing raises concern about the effects of and the intent behind the current program. No doubt the story differs markedly from place to place, as well as from time to time. If one accepts the contractors' interpretation of the experiments, housing allowances have a negligible impact on racial integration; as noted earlier, I read the results as indicating some positive effect on racial integration. The income maintenance experiments in Seattle and Denver

43. See Michael P. Murray, "Subsidized and Unsubsidized Housing Starts 1961–1977" (Duke University, Center for the Study of Policy Analysis, June 1980). See also Craig Swan, "Housing Subsidies and Housing Starts," *American Real Estate and Urban Economics Association Journal*, vol. 1 (Fall 1973), pp. 119–40.

found clear evidence that recipients of unrestricted cash assistance dispersed themselves in the metropolitan areas of Seattle and Denver more than nonrecipients did, but this dispersion had no effect on racial integration.

HOMEOWNERSHIP. If housing allowances are available to homeowners as well as to renters, they appear to have a clear advantage in promoting homeownership over all housing programs except sections 235 and 502. If housing allowances were limited to renters only, they would appear to discourage homeownership just as existing housing programs other than sections 235 and 502 do.

NEIGHBORHOODS. Evidence from the experiments gives no reason to expect that a general system of housing allowances will have any particular effect on neighborhood revitalization or on the supply of housing for particular groups. A housing allowance limited to certain demographic or geographic groups could enable those groups to compete more effectively for housing or to remain in communities that they would otherwise be unable to afford. Construction-related housing subsidies clearly can increase the supply of housing for particular groups, such as the elderly; housing allowances too may be paid only to such groups, which increases their capacity to compete for available housing but probably does not add to the supply. For the reasons presented earlier, one cannot be sure whether construction-related subsidies will promote or retard neighborhood revitalization. The term "neighborhood revitalization" has several meanings, none of which is clearly defined. It could mean building up previously bulldozed land, "gentrification" of formerly lower-class neighborhoods, or restoration of community spirit in poor neighborhoods. Furthermore, which neighborhoods one is talking about must be specified. The impact of existing housing programs is too diverse and complex and the goal is too undefined to permit a general judgment on whether or not construction-related programs promote neighborhood revitalization and community development.

Reaching a Judgment: Analysis and Politics

This survey of the effects of housing allowances and of construction-related subsidies leaves me with two distinct impressions. First, the lack of solid information on housing programs, some of which have been in existence for decades, is appalling. The housing allowance experiments have produced information far superior to that available on existing programs. The lack of information of remotely comparable quality on construction-related subsidies testifies not only to the numbing complexity of many of the research questions but also to the inadequacy of data collection and research efforts in the past.

Second, housing allowances are at least as effective as existing construction-related subsidies in promoting six of the eight objectives listed above. The major possible exception is the capacity of such programs as section 202 and low-rent public housing to augment the supply of housing for target groups, and even here the advantage of construction-related programs is clear only if the target groups, such as the handicapped, require special structural features that the market will not supply. Housing allowances are a clear winner in reducing the financial burden of housing for the very reason that this goal is not really a housing goal at all, but an income maintenance goal, and housing allowances tested in experiments are aimed more at income maintenance than existing housing subsidies are.

What conclusions can be reached? The answer depends on whether one responds as an analyst or as a policy maker.

As an analyst, I would list the following findings.

First, a general program of housing allowances is inferior to unconstrained cash assistance.

Second, a general program of housing allowances is not inferior, on available evidence, to existing construction-related subsidies in advancing the traditional goals of housing policies and is much cheaper per household served. Given the fact that construction-related subsidies are far more costly per household served than housing allowances (or the closely analogous section 8 existing housing program), housing allowances are preferable to construction-related programs except where specific shortages of certain kinds of housing exist that the market is unlikely to satisfy—such as housing for large families or for the handicapped.

Third, selected housing problems—inadequate supplies of housing for particular groups, the decay of particular neighborhoods—are unlikely to be met by any general housing program and will require special programs.

As an analyst, I would conclude that the federal government should not institute a general program of housing allowances or rapidly expand existing construction-related subsidies. Instead, I would urge that, at the margin, resources should be directed to reforming the system of unconstrained cash assistance (in other words, welfare reform) and to continuing programs of modest scale to meet the housing needs of particular groups. I would also emphasize the desirability of project-grant authority to assist in restoring or preventing decay in particular neighborhoods with new construction or demand subsidies, as the particular needs of diverse communities dictate. It has been suggested, for example, that by combining grants or loans for rehabilitation with allowance payments, neighborhood revitalization could be promoted without forcing low-income residents to move.

As a policy maker, I would judge the foregoing findings and conclusion as incomplete and oversimplified for two reasons. First, for many years the American political system has supported something best described as "commodity egalitarianism." By that term I mean the tendency of Congress to provide earmarked income-tested benefits that enable recipients to buy larger amounts of certain commodities than they would voluntarily purchase with the levels of unrestricted income-tested cash assistance Congress is prepared to offer. Congress has consistently provided subsidies for the purchase of more and better food, housing, and medical care than people would purchase with the income support Congress has provided through any program. This policy mirrors the results of public opinion polls in which respondents declared themselves willing to increase spending to assure adequate food, housing, and health care but opposed to further increases, or even maintenance of existing levels, in welfare.

Second, subsidizing commodities permits political alliances to develop between advocates of assistance to the poor and producers of the commodities. The alliance between farm state representatives seeking income support for farm incomes and urban representatives seeking food stamps for the poor that supposedly makes possible periodic enactment of agricultural legislation is the clearest example of such political symbiosis. The alliance in support of construction-related subsidies of builders, housing officials, construction unions, and representatives of the poor and of minorities is another example. This alliance is symbolized by the diverse backgrounds of those who attended this conference.

For those who feel that the government has done enough or too much to equalize the distribution of consumption, this political feature of housing subsidies is a drawback. For those who feel that the government should take further steps to equalize consumption, this political feature of housing allowances is a distinct advantage.

As a policy analyst interested in giving more help to low-income households, I would support a link between construction-related subsidies and demand subsidies similar to housing allowances. In short, I would support a program with the same elements as the section 8 program—a combination of construction-related subsidies and demand subsidies in one program. I would try to keep the part of the program devoted to allowances as large as possible, certainly larger than the part devoted to construction and certainly relatively larger than section 8 existing housing as compared with section 8 new construction or substantial rehabilitation. Local housing authorities are an important repository of expertise and political influence, and this justifies their continued role in planning, executing, and managing subsidized construction. But there seems to be no clear reason why low-rent public housing and section 8 should remain administratively distinct.

The struggle may be expected to continue between those who want more emphasis on new construction and those who want more emphasis on the existing stock. And it should be welcomed. If either side wins, either efficiency or political viability will suffer.

Are Social Experiments Worth the Cost?

One of the important policy implications of the housing allowance experiments and of the other social experiments is that social experimentation, at least where it has been conducted so far, has been a very good buy for the U.S. taxpayer. Also, from the experience to date, Congress should view well-designed proposals for additional experiments favorably.

The preceding statement can be sustained even if the information gathered from the experiments is considered worthless. The housing allowance experiments will cost $160 million: $80 million in payments to families, which would have been spent under the section 23 program if the experiments had not been undertaken, and $80 million for data collection and research. The four income maintenance experiments in Seattle and Denver cost approximately $110 million: $31 million in payments to individuals and $79 million for data collection and research. The health insurance experiment, funded by the Department of Health and Human Services (formerly HEW) and administered by the Rand Corporation, which is at a much earlier stage than the housing or income maintenance experiments, is expected to cost $71 million: $15 million for medical services and $56 million for data collection and research.

The housing and income maintenance experiments have paid for themselves through serendipitous findings that had nothing to do with the
research objectives originally used to justify them.

A direct outgrowth of the requirements of the income maintenance
experiments for continuous information on income and earnings was the
system of monthly retrospective reporting. Further experimentation with
this administrative procedure in regular welfare offices in Boulder and
Denver, Colorado, indicates that its application reduces case loads and
cuts program costs by roughly 4 percent. Monthly reporting also reduces
the frequency of underpaying benefits. Further tests are beginning in several other states to determine if the same procedures yield similar, larger,
or smaller savings in other sites. If savings of 4 percent could be achieved
nationwide, the savings would approach $300 million a year. And these
savings would not include other benefits from monthly reporting such as
accurate addresses that permit a reduction in the number of medicaid
cards incorrectly sent to ineligible persons.

The housing allowance experiments have also produced information
that has reduced, or can reduce, administrative costs or incorrect payments sufficiently to pay for the experiments. At present, the elderly are
recertified for eligibility biennially. On the basis of experience from the
housing experiments, it is estimated that annual recertification could save
$12 million a year. Most of the savings come from taking into account
annual increases in social security payments one year sooner than under
present practices. From data developed in the experiments, it is estimated
that the payment of a credit to recipients of section 8 assistance equal to a
fraction of the amount that actual rents are below estimated "fair market
rents"—the highest rent that can be paid by tenants eligible for section 8
assistance—would save more than $50 million a year. HUD officials as-
sert that data from the administrative agency experiment induced them to
set the fees paid to local housing authorities for administering section 8
existing housing at 8.5 percent of fair market rents rather than the 10
percent or more that they would have paid on the basis of data from
other sources. The 8.5 percent fee reduces payments by HUD for administrative costs $25 million a year from what would have been paid
with a 10 percent fee. Again because of results from the administrative
agency experiment, HUD has introduced stricter methods than heretofore
used in the section 8 program for the certification of tenant income. These
methods are expected to reduce program costs $15 million a year. The
health insurance study is not yet far enough along to have generated find-

ings, but experience to date suggests that incidental benefits should be expected from it too.

In considering these numbers, it is important to keep in mind that many of the savings represent savings in transfers while real resources are used for data collection and research in the experiments. The social value of not spending a dollar on people who are ineligible but may be needy by many standards is in the eye of the observer. But the social value of being sure that those who are eligible for payments receive at least as much as their entitlements is probably high. Monthly reporting for aid to families with dependent children and annual reporting for housing assistance to the elderly will promote both objectives. It is also important to keep in mind that these administrative improvements might have been made sooner or later at lower cost even if the experiments had not been undertaken. This point can be raised in connection with any kind of research and is unanswerable, but it is seldom used to oppose other kinds of research.

Several aspects of these incidental benefits from the experiments deserve comment. First, the benefits are very large relative to the total cost of the experiments. The savings from monthly income reporting, if implemented nationally, would exceed the total cost of the income maintenance experiments in less than five months. The savings from the administrative changes attributable to the housing allowance experiments would pay for those experiments in about two years. Second, the changes have nothing to do with the original purpose of either experiment and are straightforward and simple. The changes arose because research on the actual operations of both the welfare system and housing programs was scandalously scarce before the experiments were undertaken. In the process of developing data for subsequent analysis, the managers of both experiments were forced to examine the details of program administration in a way that analysts seldom or never do. I am persuaded that social experimentation in other areas would yield similar benefits. Third, all of these benefits are windfalls added to the provision of unprecedentedly high quality data on which to plan for the reform of programs that already cost billions. I believe that these data have repaid, and will continue to repay, the cost of the experiments by improving the information on which public policy is based; but for those who demand tangible evidence, these incidental benefits establish, a fortiori, that Congress did a good day's work when it provided funds for the housing allowance and income maintenance experiments.

Comments by Frank de Leeuw on the Aaron Paper[44]

Suppose this were not a housing conference but a health conference considering the results of an experimental health program. Suppose that three hypothetical facts about health and the experimental program were generally agreed on. First, the health of the adult population, including illness-prone groups, had improved steadily and significantly over the years without this program. Second, the experimental program was one in which most eligible people in good health participated, but which people in chronically poor health were much less inclined to join. And third, the people who did join the program spent little of the benefits on improving their health and most of them on other goods and services. My first reaction would be that this was not a successful health program. It might have other virtues; for example, it might distribute income to people who most feel should have more income. But as a program to improve the nation's health, it certainly would look unappealing.

Substituting the word "housing" for the word "health" gives a first approximation to a description of the housing allowance experiments. Maybe that first approximation is not very accurate. Maybe it is even seriously misleading. But I do think it would be the impression of a fair-minded observer after looking at the results of the experiments for the first time. I would like to take this first approximation as a working hypothesis about the housing allowance experiments and use it to examine Henry Aaron's paper.

This first-approximation view is *not* the conclusion of Aaron's paper. The paper, which merits careful study, makes many closely reasoned points and reaches a set of analytical conclusions rather than one single conclusion. The first-approximation view does, however, provide a useful perspective for bringing together and evaluating much, though not all, of the material in the paper.

I will therefore proceed to consider first what the paper says about the facts underlying the first-approximation view—facts about housing improvement, participation rates, and earmarking. After that, I will consider the possibility that even if the facts underlying the first-approximation view are largely correct, the paper contains counterarguments to the conclusion that the results of the experiment are disappointing. After

44. I have benefited from discussions with Marc Bendick, Jr., Larry J. Ozanne, and Ann B. Schnare. The views expressed, however, are my own.

reviewing facts and counterarguments, I will draw my personal conclusions about the first-approximation view.

Facts about Housing and Housing Allowances

The first-approximation view rests on three propositions: first, that there has been steady improvement in the housing conditions of major segments of the population; second, that those in the poorest housing were much less likely to participate in the Experimental Housing Allowance Program than those in housing that met the standards; and third, that participants devoted only a small fraction of the additional income they received to housing.

I think that there is little, if any, disagreement about these facts. The steady decline, up through the latest annual housing survey, in numbers of units with inadequate plumbing, severe crowding, and other indicators of poor housing is well known. Aaron's paper, after referring to the decline, goes on to say, "Moreover, only a small part of the decline in these indexes of inadequate housing can be attributed to housing subsidy programs under even the most generous evaluation of their effectiveness; the declines have been due instead to the rise in per capita incomes and to the policies cited above [that is, tax incentives] that favor investment in housing."

The paper does not conclude from this improvement—as indeed no one should—that there is no inadequate housing left; it points out that there are, in absolute numbers, still many people living in unsatisfactory housing. However, the improvement that has taken place suggests to me that market forces can do a good deal about poor housing conditions.

Concerning the second fact, there is no question that the rate of participation in the experiment was low—far lower, I believe, than any of the planners expected. In both the demand and supply experiments, observed participation rates (as a fraction of eligible households) were below 50 percent, although one study concluded that in the supply experiment the steady-state participation rate was about 50 percent.[45]

Furthermore, a failure to meet minimum housing standards was one of the major causes of failure to participate. Aaron's paper notes that "the proportion of failed units that were upgraded declined markedly . . . with the number of faults discovered. The drop-off was striking in the demand

45. C. Peter Rydell, John E. Mulford, and Lawrence Kozimor, *Dynamics of Participation in a Housing Allowance Program* (Rand Corp., June 1978), p. v.

experiment sites; 22 percent of households living in units that failed only one element of the housing standards . . . upgraded their units, but only 3 percent of households living in units that failed four or more elements upgraded their units." The drop-off was less marked in the supply experiment sites; but even the supply experiment supports the proposition that a minimum-standards type of housing allowance makes participation much more likely for households in satisfactory housing than for those in unsatisfactory housing.

Finally, there seems also to be general agreement on the fact that only a small proportion of allowance payments was used to increase housing outlays. The proportions were 9 and 27 percent in the two demand sites (when compared with control groups receiving no subsidy). Proportions not far below these were spent on housing even by households receiving unconstrained income maintenance. The paper concludes that in the demand sites housing allowances were "3 to 8 percent housing program and 92 to 97 percent income maintenance."

Overall, then, I find no quarrel with the facts that private market forces have greatly improved housing conditions over the decades; that the experimental program appealed much more to people already living in satisfactory or nearly satisfactory housing than to those living in poor housing; and that among the households that participated, only a small fraction of the payments actually increased housing outlays.

I believe that the findings on participation and earmarking surprised those who planned the experiment and were not predicted by models of metropolitan housing markets. I know that was true in the case of the Urban Institute model, which greatly overestimated participation rates and the degree of earmarking in South Bend and Green Bay. Some have suggested that this was a mistake peculiar to the Urban Institute model, implying that others knew better all along. I do not think that was the case. I believe that those who built models and those who did not made exactly the same mistake and that the experiments have been valuable in educating both groups.

I hope that the policy implications of these findings are also beginning to be appreciated. A general housing allowance program, for example, used to be defended on the ground that it would give benefits equitably to all low-income households rather than to a few who managed to get to the top of the waiting list for a subsidized project; this kind of program used to be attacked on the ground that it would increase the price of housing. The low participation rates in the experiments suggest that the equity advantage of a housing allowance was seriously exaggerated. Low participation and low earmarking suggest that the inflationary fear was also exaggerated, even if housing supply turns out not to be highly elastic over a period of a few years.

Counterarguments

Since there is general agreement on the facts, I will now turn to arguments about why these facts should *not* lead to the conclusion that housing allowance programs are unsatisfactory. There are five such arguments in the paper.

Three of the five counterarguments relate to the numerous goals of housing policy distinguished and analyzed in the paper. When I first was interested in housing policy, there were only two goals—a decent home and a suitable living environment for all Americans. Since then, the number of goals has expanded from two to eight, a fourfold increase. Perhaps coincidentally, during the same period the fraction of undesirable dwellings in the housing stock, according to some measures, has declined to about one-quarter of its initial level. The number of goals seems to be inversely related to the size of the problem. Perhaps someday, if the fraction of undesirable dwellings (somehow measured) has declined by another 50 percent, I will come to a conference and be instructed that there are now sixteen major goals of housing policy.

THE GOAL OF "REDUCING THE FINANCIAL BURDEN OF HOUSING." In any case, one of the eight goals of housing policy is to "reduce the financial burden of housing." If this is a goal, then a subsidy that has no effect on housing expenditures but is spent on other goods is nevertheless meeting a housing goal.

The paper is quite clear on the paradoxical nature of counting this as one of the goals of housing policy. It points out that in many circumstances, "subsidies reduce the financial burden of housing in direct proportion to the degree by which they increase saving and the consumption of goods other than housing." The solution to this problem often "directly conflicts" with the solution to problems of unsatisfactory or overcrowded housing conditions. Thus the paper, while listing this goal, recognizes that it is a weak basis for defending housing allowances. It is really a way of saying that the principal interest should be in general income maintenance rather than housing alone—an argument to which I will return later.

THE GOAL OF ECONOMIC AND RACIAL INTEGRATION. Economic and racial integration has, in recent years, been another goal of housing policy. The first-approximation view of housing allowances might be inappropriate if housing allowances succeeded in furthering this goal.

The findings are that the experiments had only a small direct effect on integration. However, Aaron suggests that "even small effects on moving patterns may affect racial segregation more significantly than the authors suggest." In support of this proposition, the paper cites Thomas Schelling's articles on segregation. But the paper does not give this counterargument much weight in support of the housing allowance approach.

I believe this counterargument should be given even less weight than the paper gives it. In a Schelling world, it seems to me, the most likely way that a small, direct effect on integration could lead to large, indirect effects would be if a small increase in integration resulted in "neighborhood tipping" and thereby eventually decreased rather than increased the amount of racial integration in an entire area. In actuality, however, I accept the conclusion that the experiments had little effect on racial segregation.

THE GOAL OF ENCOURAGING HOMEOWNERSHIP. Promoting homeownership is another of the eight goals of housing policy. Clearly, a housing allowance directed only at renters does not promote homeownership, but it seems likely, as the paper points out, that a housing allowance available to homeowners as well as to renters does promote homeownership.

I doubt that allowance payments would permit many renters to switch to owner occupancy, but allowance payments might enable some homeowners—mainly elderly households—to stay in their houses rather than sell them and become renters. Although the numbers involved are probably small, I agree with the paper that this is one counterargument to the first-approximation view of the housing allowance experiment.

A POLITICAL COALITION FOR HOUSING ALLOWANCES. Much more frequently heard than points about integration or homeownership is the argument that even if allowances are largely general income maintenance rather than specifically targeted for housing, they may receive the support of powerful interest groups—landlords and local officials as well as the direct recipients—who would not support a program of general cash assistance. Those interested in general cash assistance but not specifically in housing might therefore support a housing allowance program as a second-best way of furthering an income support goal.

Aaron notes this argument but does not support it. He certainly concurs that housing allowances are a second-best form of income maintenance. He bases that conclusion mainly on the administrative costs of allowances. I believe that low participation rates and the likelihood that nonparticipants live in the poorest housing support the same conclusion.

Aaron does cite the argument that it may be worth proceeding in this second-best way nevertheless, because the extra administrative costs of a housing allowance program may be "the necessary price for welding a coalition consisting of builders, labor, housing and community officials, and representatives of recipients that would be capable of enacting a large increase in assistance to the poor." I am not sure why builders and construction unions should be expected to support an allowance program with as low an earmarking effect as the experimental programs. Evidently Aaron is not sure either, for his final judgment is that "the political prospects for welfare reform seem to me to be no worse than those for a full housing allowance program costing roughly the same amount," which I interpret as a rejection of the "coalition" argument for allowances.

The Aaron paper does give weight to a "coalition" argument in favor of a construction-related subsidy as opposed to either housing allowances or general income maintenance. It seems to me that this is a correct assessment of political realities. Certainly it should be a correct assessment once everyone understands how small a proportion of housing allowance money goes into housing.

THE INEFFICIENCY OF CONSTRUCTION-LINKED SUBSIDIES. The final counterargument to the first-approximation view of housing allowances is the argument that however good or bad housing allowances may be, construction-related subsidies are worse. Aaron's paper gives a good deal of weight to this argument. It cites findings that "the cost of providing a unit through new construction, whether public housing or section 236, is far greater than the cost of providing an equivalent unit through housing allowances. The extra cost results in part from federally mandated standards other than those in housing codes, from the requirement that workers be paid 'prevailing wages,' as defined under the Davis-Bacon Act, that exceed wages at which workers can actually be hired, and from long delays by officials in processing applications."

The extra cost might be worth incurring if construction-related subsidies met the goals of housing policy more effectively than allowances— for example, if construction-related subsidies added more (per million dollars spent) to the supply of decent housing than allowances do. But

Aaron argues that there is no clear choice between housing allowances on the one hand and construction-related subsidies on the other with respect to the eight goals. Construction-related subsidies may be preferable for achieving some goals, but housing allowances are probably preferable for achieving others. In making this comparison, Aaron stresses the likelihood that an increase in subsidized housing starts under construction-related subsidy programs will be offset at least in part by a decrease in unsubsidized starts.

Thus Aaron concludes that housing allowances have a cost advantage over construction subsidies. I think he is right regarding the two types of program in the aggregate. However, I would like to see research directed at looking behind these aggregates. I think it has been amply demonstrated that while public housing in the aggregate has severe cost, morale, and deterioration problems, there are a great many individual public housing projects that are successful and appreciated. Predicting what combination of circumstances leads to a successful project would be extremely useful. Similarly, with respect to housing allowances, it would be extremely useful to be able to predict where and for what kind of families housing allowances may result in major and welcomed improvements in housing conditions. I think that existing records of the housing allowance experiments could be searched for answers to these questions. We might find that for some households in some locations, housing allowances are a much more effective way of improving housing conditions than they seem to be in the aggregate.

Conclusion

My own verdict, after reviewing the facts and the counterarguments, is that the first-approximation view has been battered a bit but that it nevertheless emerges as a basically accurate view. Housing allowances may have minor effects on racial integration, homeownership, and other goals. But many households in the poorest housing did not participate in the allowance experiments, and those who did devoted most of the money to nonhousing goods. These results were not anticipated on nearly the scale that they occurred, and I think that they are disappointing results.

I believe that there are two reasons why Aaron did not reach this skeptical view of housing allowances. The first is the argument, just summarized, that construction-related subsidies are even less efficient than housing allowances. This argument favors housing allowances—at least as long as we look at programs in the aggregate—but I believe that it is a weak argument, since neither a dollar devoted to housing allowances nor a dollar devoted to construction subsidies is as efficient as a dollar devoted to housing in the private market. For construction subsidies, the main reason is excessive costs of production; for allowances, the main reason is that very little of the subsidy is effectively earmarked for housing.

Private market forces, aided by tax incentives, have resulted in considerable progress in improving housing. It seems to me that results for both the allowance experiments and construction subsidies suggest that public programs to speed up or improve on the workings of the private housing market have not, so far, shown much promise.

The second reason for not being disappointed at the results of the experiment is that for those whose real interest is in the general welfare of low-income households, housing allowances do not look as bad as for those who focus only on housing conditions. The fact that most of the money does not go to housing is no longer a disadvantage. I think that many of us—including myself—are in fact interested in income generally rather than, or at least in addition to, housing specifically.

However, I feel very uncomfortable about pronouncing the housing allowance results satisfactory or successful when the main reason for that assessment has nothing to do with improved housing conditions but rather with spending on other goods and services. I would feel the same way about pronouncing a health program a success if its main effect were to permit certain people to buy more food and housing. Statements of that sort, it seems to me, contribute to public confusion, while our job as analysts ought to be to help to clear up confusion. Aaron is aware of this point; he makes that clear in skeptical remarks about including reduction of the financial burden of housing as a goal of housing policy. But in the end, he seems to accept that goal as legitimate.

In closing, let me state once more that I have been looking at Aaron's paper from a special point of view. There are many points in the paper that I have not touched on at all and that well repay careful study.

Comments by Alice Rivlin on the Watts and Aaron Papers

Since the papers by Henry Aaron and Harold Watts seemed to me excellent overviews of the general advantages and flaws of the Experimental Housing Allowance Program, I thought it might be useful for me to compare and contrast their views on the questions the experiments were supposed to answer and how well they were designed to do so.

Policy makers considering a new type of assistance to individuals have two sets of questions on which empirical information can usefully be brought to bear. First, should we do it at all? And second, now that we have decided to do it, how should the program be designed? The first set of questions involves comparing one set of policies, such as housing allowances or negative income taxes, with alternative policies designed to do roughly the same thing. The alternatives to housing allowances are unconstrained cash assistance programs, construction-related subsidies for low-income housing, and various other options, including doing nothing at all.

It is typical of this situation that the alternatives have somewhat different goals than the policy one starts out to examine, and that the alternative policies reflect different philosophies of what the role of government ought to be; therefore, they appeal to different political coalitions. Hence, empirical evaluation alone cannot yield definitive choices; it can only help a little. As Watts so well puts it: "What can be hoped for is a progressive narrowing of the grounds for dispute, as forecasts of the costs and consequences of alternative policies become ever more precise, until the remaining grounds for argument lie in the realm of values and priorities attached to known outcomes."

The second set of questions—how do we set up the program?—can be divided into two parts. One part is determining the appropriate provisions—benefit levels, tax rates, housing standards, and so forth—of the program that has been decided on. The other part is determining how the program can be made workable and how it will best function in the community.

We thus have really three questions. Should we do it at all? What should it be like? And how do we make sure it is workable? Clearly, these are not independent questions. To answer the first question, one has to know something about the program's characteristics and its expected effectiveness. But to some extent these are separate issues, and I suspect they used to be even more separate back when people worried about whether the federal government should have *any* programs to deal with housing, poverty, or retirement.

In recent years the design decisions have been brought to the attention of the decision makers. Presidents and congressmen are now concerned with concepts such as marginal tax rates and benefit reduction rates. Indeed, the discussion of these technical design questions has almost superseded the more basic questions of whether we want a program at all and what for.

Aaron's paper focuses on the following set of questions: how much did the Experimental Housing Allowance Program tell us about the effectiveness of housing allowances, and how do housing allowances compare with alternatives such as unconstrained cash assistance programs and construction subsidies? As Aaron says, "The housing allowance experiments were designed to find out whether some of these [federal housing policy] goals could be achieved more effectively by housing allowances than by other policies."

Aaron finds evidence in the experiments to confirm both common sense and pre-experiment analysis, including his own predictions before the experimental results were available. One of his conclusions is that housing allowances do not significantly increase expenditures on housing. They increase such spending slightly more than unconstrained income maintenance programs, but not much more.

Aaron points out, and I agree, that it would have been interesting to vary the housing standard more than it was explicitly varied in the experiments.

Aaron concludes that conducting a separate housing allowance program along with the administrative costs entailed by such a program is an inefficient way to increase housing expenditures. He concludes furthermore that unless society places a higher value on increasing housing expenditures than on just increasing incomes, an unconstrained cash assistance program is probably a better buy.

That is not a very surprising result. I suspect that most congressmen would have been prepared to believe that even before the experiments. Even so, as Aaron points out, they might still have preferred housing allowances to unconstrained cash assistance for the same reasons that they prefer food stamps: the earmarked money goes through a different set of committees and appeals to a different political coalition and to a broader set of supporters.

The second basic point that Aaron makes is that housing allowances are a cheaper way of providing housing per unit than new construction subsidies are. Again this result is not surprising; it confirms what was thought before.

In sum, Aaron considers the experiments useful for comparing housing allowances with unconstrained cash assistance programs and construction subsidies. He finds in them confirmation of prior views that housing allowances do relatively little to improve housing quality but compare favorably on most scores to construction subsidies. He does not examine the question of whether other experimental or nonexperimental designs for acquiring information would have been more effective in contrasting housing allowances with unconstrained cash assistance and construction subsidies. Aaron concludes that the experiments were a good buy, but largely because of serendipitous findings such as the effectiveness of monthly retrospective reporting. These findings relate to my third type of question about making the program workable: one might not have needed such an elaborately designed experiment to find out about the accounting period.

But there remains the second set of questions—namely, once it is decided to embark on a housing allowance program, how should it be designed? Watts evaluates the contribution of the experiments primarily, but not exclusively, by how they help us to design a housing allowance. The spectrum that Watts lays out, ranging from pure experiments through orderly demonstration to a purposeful grope, seems to me very useful. It is clear that randomization is very important for evaluating the effect of varying provisions within a program like housing allowances. But it is also clear, as Watts points out, that some assumptions must be made about which uncontrolled variables are important and which are not.

I would submit that in a country of such great geographic and ethnic diversity as the United States, location-specific variables should have had more attention in the experiments. These variables are very important to our location-specific decision makers. Conducting the demand experiment in two sites allowed experimenters to ask if location makes a difference. The answer was yes, probably, but maybe not very much. Two sites do not permit one to say much more than that, however. Watts raises the question of whether more sites would have been useful and concludes that a few more would not have helped much.

Watts believes that the experiments yielded useful information on the effect of varying the incentive to get people to improve their housing. He rejects the notion raised by Aaron that varying the standards would have been useful, because he does not see a good way of doing that. He suggests—very provocatively, I think—that a better design for evaluating ways of getting people to improve their housing might have focused more on household formation and dissolution, the moments when the incentive offered might be expected to matter, and on the transitions between owners and renters.

Watts has not solved the problem of how to design an experiment focused on household formation and dissolution. A portable housing allowance that went with the person rather than with the household unit is possible but awkward, especially in an experiment treating only part of the universe. People with allowances would be differentially attractive at household formation and dissolution moments.

Watts is right when he says that the so-called supply experiment was really a demonstration or two demonstrations. The unit was the market, there were only two markets, and, unfortunately, the market effects were not very interesting.

The demand effects were not big enough to generate a supply effect. Therefore the supply demonstrations were most useful in obtaining information on demand factors and in answering, rather expensively, the workability questions. The big question, at least in hindsight, is, could the smallness of the demand effect have been predicted, and, if so, would one have undertaken the saturation (supply) experiments at all? Would it have been preferable to have conducted a more elaborate set of demand experiments that included both owners and renters, more sites, more years of treatment, and more variation in the standards, and in some way concentrated on the formation and dissolution of households? In hindsight, that might have yielded more information per dollar than we gained from the existing combination of the demand and the supply experiments.

This kind of design would also have yielded some workability information and, presumably, some useful administrative clues. More geographic diversity would have made the results more plausible to our geographically oriented politicians, even if it did not yield more rigorous knowledge about location effects.

My own conclusions about the lessons in these papers are these, stated as strongly as possible to provoke discussion.

First, much was learned from the experiments, but most conclusions confirmed common sense or (what should have been) prior hypothesis.

Second, I question whether the experiments were useful to policy makers choosing among major policies, because they were not designed to compare major alternatives, and because the goals of major policies are only partially overlapping; these decisions involve philosophical questions and tactics of political coalition-building.

Third, the experiments were useful in providing information for setting specific provisions of a program, but it would have been useful, in hindsight, to have designed the experiments to allow more focus on moments of change and transition, if only by oversampling certain age groups. One might have used the resources devoted to the supply experiment in a more elaborate and lengthy series of demand experiments.

Finally, the experiments were useful as demonstrations of the workability of housing allowances. It is ironic that such elaborate experiments should end in shining up the tarnished image of the demonstration.

MAHLON R. STRASZHEIM

Participation

This paper describes participation results in the Experimental Housing Allowance Program, which tested several housing allowance programs that offered participating households the opportunity to
increase their housing consumption or reduce their housing cost burden.
A household is considered here to be a participant if it received subsidy
payments; the participation rate is defined as the ratio of participating
households to all eligible households. Participation rates in a housing
allowance program are influenced by program rules and administration;
the magnitude of benefits; and by households' awareness of opportunities, attitudes toward public assistance programs, and ability to comply
with program regulations (for example, to obtain housing meeting minimum quality standards). Participation rates in the Experimental Housing
Allowance Program provide important information for projecting participation rates, participant profiles, and costs of a universal housing allowance program. The program results are also useful in assessing vertical
and horizontal equity consequences of a universal housing allowance.

The housing conditions and cost burdens of households without a
housing allowance program will be an important consideration in choosing between a housing allowance program that imposes minimum housing
quality standards and an unrestricted income transfer program. If the
problem facing low-income households is excessive rent burdens rather
than poor-quality housing, an income transfer program might be preferred to a housing allowance. The Experimental Housing Allowance
Program provides additional information on housing cost burdens,
crowding, and housing quality. The data reviewed in this paper reveal
that the great majority of low-income households are paying a large frac-

The author acknowledges the help and comments of Anthony Downs, Katharine L. Bradbury, Jerry J. Fitts, C. Lance Barnett, Stephen D. Kennedy, and Marc
Bendick, Jr.

tion of their incomes for housing, and that many live in housing that is crowded or has deficiencies in quality.

One of the principal factors that might distinguish a housing allowance program from an income maintenance program is a housing quality standard. Program data reveal that housing quality standards have a major effect on participation rates. Approximately 80 percent of eligible households in the demand experiment participated in programs that did not restrict housing choices. Participation rates were about half as high in programs that imposed housing quality minimums.[1] Households whose preprogram housing does not meet quality standards are often deterred from participation by the high costs of moving or the difficulties of securing improvements from their landlords. Search and moving costs are important considerations for many households. These barriers do not exist in many income transfer programs. The closest analogy is the former requirement to purchase food stamps at less than their market value in the food stamp program; under this program, the household's initial outlay can be converted almost immediately to benefits through food purchases. In the housing allowance programs, however, moving costs are large and are probably offset only after several months of rent subsidy.

Housing quality standards also affect the distribution of benefits by age and income level. When quality minimums are imposed, allowances are paid to many households that already occupy housing above the quality minimums, whereas many households in units that do not meet the quality minimums cannot participate. Eliminating or lowering the quality standards would increase participation rates and reduce the average income of participants.

The demand experiment relied on individual briefings of households, so households probably understood their options as well as they ever would in an operational program. These results can be used to assess how alternative program rules affect participation and other household behavior. The supply experiment is best viewed as a reflection of participation in a universal, open-enrollment program relying on mass outreach efforts. The results of these experiments are reviewed later in this paper.

The last section of this paper uses the Experimental Housing Allowance Program participation data to address certain issues in the design of a universal housing allowance program. The role of housing standards

1. U.S. Department of Housing and Urban Development, *Experimental Housing Allowance Program: A 1979 Report of Findings* (Government Printing Office, 1979), p. 22.

as they affect horizontal and vertical equity is discussed. Another issue is whether a universal housing allowance should be an open-enrollment (entitlement) program, that is, available to all interested households meeting stated eligibility limits; or whether a housing allowance should be limited to some subset of applicants that can be supported by available funds. Existing federal housing programs are an exception to most of the major income security programs, which use the open-enrollment principle. The choice between these two approaches involves a consideration of available budgets, income eligibility rules, and horizontal equity. If participation rates are high, program costs of a universal, open-enrollment approach may be such that income eligibility limits must be set at very low levels. Alternatively, higher income eligibility limits imply that many more persons may be interested in participation than can be supported by budgeted funds, and a rationing problem results. In this circumstance, participants receive large benefits while equally needy and eligible nonparticipants are not helped. Possible solutions to these problems of horizontal equity, given a limited total budget, involve changes in quality standards, income eligibility limits, and the tenants' share of income devoted to housing.

Housing Conditions of Potential Participants

Housing conditions of low-income households are an important determinant of participation rates and the extent of housing benefits and rent relief realized by program participants. Participation rates should be directly related to housing cost burdens of eligible households and inversely related to their present housing consumption as influenced by their income. The magnitude of housing improvements associated with participation is also important in the political debate over the choice between an unrestricted income transfer and a housing assistance program that imposes housing quality minimums. It has not been determined whether requiring that income transfers be spent on increased housing quality rather than on other commodities increases economic welfare for inhabitants or others.[2] This issue aside, if only a small proportion of eligible households have housing quality deficiencies or are overcrowded,

2. Weicher's survey indicates that there is little hard evidence on this question. John C. Weicher, "Urban Housing Policy," in Peter Mieszkowski and Mahlon Straszheim, eds., *Current Issues in Urban Economics* (Johns Hopkins University Press, 1979), pp. 490–92.

imposing housing quality standards will have little practical effect, and an unrestricted income transfer program would seem as attractive. Either program will reduce the burden of excessive housing costs for low-income households. Conversely, if the minimum standard requirement is well above the housing quality that low-income households are able to consume without such a requirement, then a housing allowance program might be more attractive.

Measuring housing quality or housing cost burdens and drawing welfare inferences is difficult because the willingness of households to pay for housing will vary with income and tastes. With respect to the latter, people who devote a large fraction of income to housing may be no more disadvantaged than those who spend a large fraction of their income on any other commodity. It is typically assumed that welfare and income are related. Since the income elasticity for aggregate housing expenditures is positive but less than unity, housing cost burdens decline with increases in income. It is not evident that any more information is conveyed about a household's welfare by knowing its housing cost burden in addition to its income.

Conventional measures of housing quality include whether the unit is in sound condition, has complete plumbing, and is not overcrowded. Using these measures, several recent papers based on the 1970 census and the 1976 annual housing survey have argued that physical deficiencies in housing units have diminished to nearly marginal levels. Weicher shows that, if the traditional measures of "lacking complete plumbing" or "overcrowding" (more than 1.5 persons per room) are used, only a few percent of all units did not qualify as satisfactory in 1976, though the incidence of quality deficiencies was somewhat higher among lower-income households.[3] Using the 1970 census, Birch estimated that 26 percent of households with incomes of less than $5,000 were in physically inadequate or crowded housing.[4] Levine developed a quality index using fifteen measures of housing quality in the annual housing survey and found that in 1976, 13 percent of all renter households eligible for federal housing assistance were in what he deemed physically inadequate housing and 7 percent lived in crowded conditions.[5]

    3. Ibid., pp. 470–71.
    4. David Birch and others, *America's Housing Needs: 1970 to 1980* (Massachusetts Institute of Technology–Harvard University, Joint Center for Urban Studies, 1973).
    5. Martin D. Levine, *Federal Housing Policy: Current Problems and Recurring Issues,* Congressional Budget Office, Background Paper (GPO, 1978), pp. 5–9. Levine classified a unit as physically inadequate if any of the following six condi-

Table 1. Trends in Housing Conditions, 1940–76
Percent

Housing condition	1940	1950	1960	1970	1976
Units					
Lacking some or all plumbing	44.6	34.0	15.2	5.1	2.6
Dilapidated	18.1	9.1	5.8	3.7	n.a.
Lacking some or all plumbing or dilapidated	48.6	35.4	17.0	7.4	n.a.
In need of rehabilitation	n.a.	n.a.	n.a.	n.a.	7.8
Households					
More than 1.5 persons per room	9.0	6.2	3.6	2.0	1.0
More than 1.0 person per room	20.3	15.7	11.5	8.0	4.6
Renter households paying more than 25 percent of income on housing	n.a.	30.8	35.2	39.6	46.6

Source: Martin D. Levine, *Federal Housing Policy: Current Programs and Recurring Issues*, Congressional Budget Office, Background Paper (GPO, 1978), pp. 6, 9, 10.
n.a. Not available.

While the quality of housing occupied by the poor has improved considerably over the past two decades, housing costs have risen more than incomes. Levine reports that 46.6 percent of all renter households paid 25 percent or more of their income for rent in 1976, based on the annual housing survey, whereas only 30.8 percent paid one-fourth or more of their income for housing in 1950 (see table 1).[6] Recent increases in utility costs, interest rates, and land prices are such that housing rent–income ratios have probably increased further since 1976.

The Experimental Housing Allowance Program provides additional and more up-to-date information on housing quality, the adequacy of space available, and housing cost burdens. These data show high housing-cost burdens for the poor and serious housing quality deficiencies. The program data are based on detailed physical inspections of each property. The quality inspections examined seventy-eight quality characteristics, including the soundness of the structure, the plumbing, the heating and

---

tions existed: absence of complete plumbing; absence of complete kitchen facilities; absence of a public sewer connection, a septic tank, or a cesspool; three or more breakdowns of six or more hours each in a sewer, septic tank, or cesspool during the past ninety days; three or more breakdowns of six or more hours each in the heating system (unit without water) during the past ninety days; or three or more breakdowns of the flush toilet for six or more hours each during the past ninety days. Units were also deemed inadequate if two or more additional but less serious quality deficiencies existed.

6. Ibid., p. 10. Some of this change may be attributable to the rise in the proportion of households that own their own homes and the resulting decline in the average income of tenants relative to homeowners.

utilities, the kitchen and bath facilities, and safety features such as fire exits, ventilation, and stairways. The inspectors also made an overall evaluation of the unit.

Under the conventional measures of housing quality, the sample results of the Experimental Housing Allowance Program are similar to the results of Birch and Levine for low-income renters using nationwide data. Twenty-two percent of poverty-level renters in Phoenix and Pittsburgh occupied units that either were dilapidated or lacked complete plumbing. However, program inspections revealed a large number of units with other deficiencies. Quality inspections resulted in 43 percent of the housing units of enrolled households being classified as "clearly inadequate" and 26 percent as "ambiguous."[7] The best way to interpret this classification of units is to examine the specific housing deficiencies reported in table 2. Of the units classified as "clearly inadequate," most units failed more than one specific test, the median being 4.4 quality indicators failed.

Similar data from the section 8 evaluation study revealed the same result—that households occupied properties with many structural defects prior to participation and that substantial improvements in housing quality were associated with participation.[8] The program results indicate that the quality information in the annual housing survey is not complete and that many poor households occupy housing with many quality deficiencies. The presence of these deficiencies raises questions about the quality standards that taxpayers will want to provide. This issue is at the heart of the debate over the adequacy of fair market rents in the section 8 program and the discussions on quality standards in public housing and other publicly assisted housing programs.

The Experimental Housing Allowance Program data reveal that the poor have very high housing cost burdens. The median rent–income ratio was 0.31 for all eligible households in the demand experiment. Of all eligible households, 68.4 percent had rent–income ratios in excess of 0.25, and 28.5 percent had ratios in excess of 0.40.[9] Similar results were evi-

7. David W. Budding, "Draft Report on Housing Deprivation Among Enrollees in the Housing Allowance Demand Experiment" (Cambridge, Mass.: Abt Associates, November 1978), pp. 32, 26.

8. Urban Systems Research and Engineering, Inc., *Research and Evaluation Regarding the Section 8 Housing Assistance Program in Sector A—Section 8 Research Summary Report* (HUD, 1978); and U.S. Department of Housing and Urban Development, *Lower Income Housing Assistance Program (Section 8): Nationwide Evaluation of the Existing Housing Program* (GPO, 1978), pp. 69–76.

9. Budding, "Draft Report," pp. 54–55.

Table 2. Housing Deficiencies Found in Sample[a]

Type of deficiency	*Percentage of clearly inadequate units with deficiency*
Poor physical condition	51
Structure	25
Surface	46
Lacking basic housing services	51
Plumbing	36
Heat	8
Kitchen	8
Electrical service	20
Health or safety hazards	35
Inadequate fire exits	11
Unvented space heater	16
Rats	12
Other indicators	84
Window condition	62
Window opening	55
No window or vent	14
Ceiling height	16
Overall rating	
0 (good)	4
1 (minor repairs)	26
2 (major repairs)	61
3 (unsound or unfit)	10
Number of items failed	
1	10
2–5	46
6–10	30
11 or more	14
Addendum:	
Median number of indicators failed	4.4

Source: David W. Budding, "Draft Report on Housing Deprivation Among Enrollees in the Housing Allowance Demand Experiment" (Cambridge, Mass.: Abt Associates, November 1978), p. 22.

a. The sample of 1,456 consisted of all enrolled households in clearly inadequate units (except those with enrollment incomes over the eligibility limits).

dent in the section 8 evaluation studies. Section 8 participants had, on the average, very low incomes ($3,535 nationwide in 1976); households had a mean rent–income ratio of 0.39 before entering section 8.[10] Both the section 8 and the Experimental Housing Allowance programs make a sizable transfer of real income to participants.

10. HUD, *Lower Income Housing Assistance Program,* Technical Supplement, pp. 33, 209.

Information from the program indicates a higher incidence of crowding or inadequate space among potential participants than earlier studies
did. According to one of the conventional measures of crowding (more
than one person per room), 15 percent of the enrolled households in the
demand experiment were severely overcrowded.[11] HUD regulations have
recently adopted "persons per bedroom" as a more appropriate measure
of crowding. Generally, a standard of 2.0 persons per bedroom gives a
higher incidence of crowding than a standard of 1.0 person per room.
The incidence of crowding among the program enrollees was highest for
larger families and poorest households. Twenty-three percent of all enrolled renters had more than two persons per bedroom. Crowded conditions were found in 31 percent of households with incomes below the
poverty line and in 68 percent of all low-income renters' households containing at least five members.[12]

The seriousness of crowding as conventionally measured may be further understated when the number of extended families among the poor
is considered. Budding suggests that extended families containing more
than the so-called nuclear family may require more space than conventional standards, which consider only persons per room, persons per bedroom, or adults per bedroom. Among the poor, there is a high incidence
of extended families, a living arrangement that provides much-needed
financial assistance and emotional support for elderly persons and separated households. The high incidence of separation and divorce among
poor and minority households and the small percentage of these households that receive court-ordered support payments create an especially
acute housing problem for many low-income households. Of women ever
married, 12.2 percent of white women and 34.9 percent of black women
over sixteen years of age in 1977 were divorced or separated. One in four
divorced women and one in ten separated women received alimony or
child support payments.[13]

Increasing space for low-income households would be one of the most
costly objectives of an allowance program. The rents for units with more
space or more bedrooms are considerably higher. My analysis of the 1976
annual housing survey data, estimating hedonic price equations for rental
units in twenty-one standard metropolitan statistical areas, indicated that

11. Budding, "Draft Report," p. 42.
12. Ibid., p. 47.
13. U.S. Department of Labor, Bureau of Labor Statistics, *Divorced and Separated Women in the Labor Force—An Update,* Special Labor Force Report 220
(GPO, 1978).

the added rent for a second bedroom is approximately $27 a month, approximately the same amount again for a third bedroom, and $22 more for a fourth, or about 12 percent of the mean rent of units recently occupied. Estimates vary by city size and location within the city. The added rent that must be paid for a second bathroom is also substantial.[14] If additional bedrooms and bathrooms are to be provided, program costs will be substantially increased unless households choose units with other quality deficiencies.

Program Characteristics and Participation: The Demand Experiment

The demand experiment is best viewed as a test of the responses of all income-eligible socioeconomic groups to alternative program features.[15] All such socioeconomic groups received the same outreach efforts. The biggest differences are between programs that require households to consume a minimum level of housing services and programs that do not. A principal finding from the Experimental Housing Allowance Program is that housing quality standards had a major effect on participation rates; for a variety of reasons discussed below, many households did not acquire housing that met the minimum standards.

The decision to participate by households that were offered enrollment could be viewed in two stages—first, the decision to enroll, and second, the decision to acquire housing meeting quality standards and hence qualifying for subsidy. These stages occur simultaneously in the unconstrained program. Enrollment requires that the household provide information periodically. Presumably, households would not enroll if they anticipated that their existing housing would not pass inspection, that landlords would not make necessary repairs, or that they were unable to relocate. Enrollment rates were only slightly lower in the housing gap plans (74 percent in Pittsburgh and 83 percent in Phoenix) than in the

14. Mahlon R. Straszheim, "Setting Housing Entitlements in the Section 8 Housing Allowance Program," *Research in Urban Economics,* vol. 2 (forthcoming).

15. For a survey of the participation results from the demand experiment, see HUD, *A Summary Report of Current Findings from the Experimental Housing Allowance Program* (GPO, 1978); Stephen D. Kennedy and Jean MacMillan, "Draft Report on Participation Under Alternative Housing Allowance Programs: Evidence from the Housing Allowance Demand Experiment" (Abt, October 1979); and HUD, *A 1979 Report of Findings.*

Mahlon R. Straszheim

Table 3. Participation Rates in the Demand Experiment, by Program Type
Percent

Item	No restrictions		Minimum quality restrictions			
			Housing gap, subprograms			
	Percent of rent	Uncon- strained	Mini- mum stan- dards	Low mini- mum rent	High mini- mum rent	All housing gap sub- groups
Pittsburgh						
Enrollment rate	82	78	75	74	73	74
Rate at which enrolled households met standards	100	100	40	81	58	56
Participation rate	82	78	30	60	42	41
Phoenix						
Enrollment rate	87	90	84	82	81	83
Rate at which enrolled households met standards	100	100	54	74	54	59
Participation rate	87	90	45	61	44	49

Source: Stephen D. Kennedy and Jean MacMillan, "Draft Report on Participation Under Alternative Housing Allowance Programs: Evidence from the Housing Allowance Demand Experiment" (Abt, October 1979), pp. 24, 25.

unconstrained plans, suggesting that most households expected to be able to meet the quality standards (see table 3). Reasons for declining enrollment are shown in table 4. These include objections to excessive paperwork, to government assistance, to such experimentation, or to revealing information about themselves. Reasons for refusal are not correlated with socioeconomic characteristics. Objections to reporting requirements would be less severe in an operational program since less elaborate procedures would be used than in an experimental program such as the Experimental Housing Allowance Program, which collected large amounts of data. The other objections—loss of privacy, the recurring means test, or the welfare stigma—are often voiced by persons eligible for other income assistance programs, and these objections would probably exist in a universal housing allowance program as well.

Among socioeconomic groups, enrollment rates were slightly higher for households whose members were younger, that had moved more often in the past three years, or that had received welfare or food stamps (see table 5). With the exception of slightly lower enrollment rates for the lowest income class, income appeared uncorrelated with enrollment rates.

Table 4. Reasons for Declining Enrollment
Percent

Reason for not enrolling[a]	Pittsburgh		Phoenix	
	Gave reason	Gave reason as only reason for not enrolling	Gave reason	Gave reason as only reason for not enrolling
Requirements, bother, paperwork	50	12	49	5
Objected to participating in a transfer program	41	12	47	12
Benefits from other programs would be reduced	8	1	5	1
Thought they were ineligible	14	1	24	4
Payment too small	18	1	26	1
Did not want to move	14	2	14	1
Personal reasons	18	4	18	1
Did not understand the offer	12	1	11	2
Mean number of reasons given	1.8		1.9	

Source: Kennedy and MacMillan, "Draft Report," p. 77.
a. A household could give more than one reason.

The size of the income transfer affected enrollment rates. Enrollment rates were about 67 percent for households that were told they could expect a subsidy of only $10, about 87 percent for households that would receive $31 to $50 transfers, and only marginally higher for those receiving larger expected transfers.[16] The percent of rent plan was a price subsidy, whereas the others were income subsidy plans. Two factors could explain why there was no difference in acceptance rates between these plans: either households did not understand the subtleties of the program when they enrolled or housing price elasticities were low relative to income elasticities so that income effects dominated the results of both types of programs.

The most striking findings about participation involve the role of quality standards. Since the demand experiment included only two types of housing standards—the unconstrained plan with no standards and the housing gap plan with a single standard—it is not possible to determine precisely the effects of alternative types of standards. The results demonstrate that the standard imposed in the housing gap plan significantly reduced participation. Of the households that accepted enrollment in the

16. Kennedy and Macmillan, "Draft Report," p. 27.

Table 5. Enrollment and Participation Rates in the Demand Experiment, by Household Characteristic

Percent

	Pittsburgh		Phoenix	
Household characteristic	Enrollment rate in housing gap experiment	Rate at which enrolled households met standards	Enrollment rate in housing gap experiment	Rate at which enrolled households met standards
Age of household head				
Under 30	81	60	86	68
30–61	75	58	82	53
62 or over	61	49	79	54
Household size				
1 person	63	47	80	59
2 persons	73	65	81	67
3–4 persons	74	59	86	63
5–6 persons	79	51	79	51
7 or more	75	37	86	32
Mobility in past 3 years				
No moves	67	49	76	42
1 move	75	58	83	63
2 moves	81	67	82	55
3 or more	88	62	88	69
Race of head				
Nonminority	71	59	85	66
Black	79	45	78	39
Spanish-American	n.a.	n.a.	78	47
Sex of household head				
Male	70	52	82	56
Female	76	59	84	64
Income (dollars)				
1,000–1,999	66	45	81	40
2,000–3,999	77	55	85	56
4,000–5,999	75	63	86	65
6,000–7,999	73	54	82	65
8,000–9,999	66	n.a.	82	56
10,000 and over	62	n.a.	74	43
Welfare recipient				
Yes	80	55	85	45
No	68	58	82	64
Food stamp recipient				
Yes	81	53	87	54
No	67	60	81	61

Source: Kennedy and MacMillan, "Draft Report," pp. 31, 45.
n.a. Not available.

Table 6. Participation Rates of Households in the Demand Experiment, by Preprogram Housing Consumption[a]

Program	Minimum standards	Low minimum rent	High minimum rent	All housing gap households
Pittsburgh				
Proportion of enrolled households that met requirements at enrollment	0.15	0.64	0.35	0.33
Participation rates of households that did not meet requirements at enrollment	0.30	0.48	0.35	0.34
Participation rate, all enrolled households	0.40	0.81	0.58	0.56
Proportion of all participants that met requirements at enrollment	0.36	0.79	0.60	0.60
Phoenix				
Proportion of enrolled households that met requirements at enrollment	0.19	0.53	0.27	0.29
Participation rates of households that did not meet requirements at enrollment	0.44	0.46	0.37	0.42
Participation rate, all enrolled households	0.54	0.74	0.54	0.59
Proportion of all participants that met requirements at enrollment	0.34	0.71	0.50	0.50

Source: Kennedy and MacMillan, "Draft Report," p. 35.
a. The sample consisted of housing gap households eligible at enrollment.

housing gap plans, only about half subsequently lived in housing that made them eligible to receive subsidy payments. Sixty-seven percent of enrolled households in Pittsburgh and 71 percent of enrolled households in Phoenix lived in units that did not meet minimum quality standards at the time of enrollment, although the necessary repairs were often minor. Of those who did not initially meet minimum standards, 34 percent in Pittsburgh and 42 percent in Phoenix eventually received payments (see table 6). The standards may also have discouraged some eligible households from enrolling in the housing gap plans. These results reveal that the imposition of housing quality minimums is a major deterrent to participation. Even when generous income transfers are involved, many households are unable to relocate or improve their housing sufficiently to receive subsidies. The majority receiving subsidy payments lived in housing that met quality minimums at the time of enrollment.

Where income transfers of 20 percent of income are available and large housing improvements are possible, the imposition of housing quality minimums may not appear to be a significant barrier to participation. On the assumption that the administratively determined rent payment was sufficient to acquire housing that met the quality standard, and that relocations were costless, housing standards would have little role. Sellers should offer the appropriate quality level at the higher rent, or the household could move to another unit.

In the Experimental Housing Allowance Program, considerable attention was devoted to establishing payment levels that reflected local market prices.[17] Inaccuracy in setting payment levels does not explain participation results. In a nationwide program, fewer resources will be devoted to setting payment levels, and there will be considerable variation across local markets in opportunities for households. If payments are set below market rents, lower-quality units will be offered to potential participants than program administrators expect. (In the section 8 program, fair market rents are more generous in some markets.) This variation in benefits will influence participation rates.

One possible explanation for refusing participation involves assumptions about preference functions. To abstract from income considerations, if a household preferred to consume housing well below the housing quality levels required under the program, both before and after the income transfer, participation in the housing gap programs would not be desirable since little gain in household welfare would result from meeting the quality minimum imposed. Such a household would probably be devoting a smaller fraction of income to housing before participation than other households. Households that devote a larger fraction of income to housing also might decline to participate if they placed a low value on the increase in housing quality needed to meet the quality standards. The Experimental Housing Allowance Program results indicate that many households did not consider their present housing deficient and would not devote even small sums to repair certain quality deficiencies.

The majority of eligible households in the program devote appreciably more than 25 percent of income to housing before participation and live in housing well below the quality standards. For this group, a different explanation must be found for nonparticipation. The answer may lie in relocation and transaction costs. Relocation costs affect mobility and also influence the outcome of tenant-landlord bargaining. For many households, ties to their existing houses and neighborhoods and a desire

17. Abt Associates, *The Experimental Housing Allowance Program, the Housing Allowance Demand Experiment—First Annual Report* (Abt, March 1974); Abt Associates, "The Experimental Housing Allowance Program, the Housing Allowance Demand Experiment—Working Paper on Early Findings" (Abt, January 1975), app. 2; and HUD, *A 1979 Report of Findings*, pp. 85–89.

to avoid relocation costs will encourage bargaining with landlords to make the necessary repairs. A landlord's bargaining position will be enhanced by the knowledge that the tenant has a significant real income transfer at stake if the landlord participates. Some of the real income gains intended for households may therefore be shifted to landlords in the form of above-market rents for a given quality level or unreported quality defects.

The elaborate quality inspections conducted in the program are not easily replicated in a nationwide program. The inspections meant that tenants in the program usually obtained the quality of housing specified in the requirements for participation.[18] However, many households may not have participated because their landlords would not make the necessary improvements and the households were also unable to move.

Households that cannot obtain necessary repairs from their landlords must compare the costs of moving with the income transfers associated with participation. For households with close ties to their present neighborhoods, relocation costs may outweigh the income transfer associated with participation. That a significant fraction of households did not search for new housing indicates that search costs are also significant.[19]

The likelihood of a household moving without an allowance plan should be a useful predictor of participation in the program. Households more likely to move without an allowance program either perceive relocation costs to be less or are undergoing more frequent changes in income, work place, location, or family composition.[20] For higher-income households, the real income transfer resulting from participation is smaller; hence relocation costs may outweigh program benefits. On the other hand, poorer households may be least able to afford the move.

The Experimental Housing Allowance Program results clearly demonstrate the role of relocation costs. Participation rates are positively related to the frequency of prior moves and inversely to age. Kennedy and MacMillan's statistical analysis of the role of relocation costs is persuasive. The effects of the size of payment offered, the household's normal probability of moving (that is, that it would move without an allow-

18. David W. Budding, *Inspection: Implementing Housing Quality Requirements in the Administrative Agency Experiment* (Abt, 1977); and Joseph J. Valenza, *Program Housing Standards in the Experimental Housing Allowance Program: Analyzing Differences in the Demand and Supply Experiments,* 216-30 (Urban Institute, 1977), p. vii.

19. HUD, *A Summary Report,* p. 17.

20. See the paper by Peter H. Rossi in this volume.

Table 7. Logit Estimation of the Probability of Participation for Housing Gap Households Not Meeting Requirements at Enrollment

| | Minimum standards requirement | | | Minimum rent requirement | | | | | |
| | Sites combined | | | Pittsburgh | | | Phoenix | | |
Independent variable	Coefficient	t-statistic	Partial derivative[a]	Coefficient	t-statistic	Partial derivative[a]	Coefficient	t-statistic	Partial derivative[a]
Constant	-1.724	-5.48**	n.a.	0.626	1.04	n.a.	-1.480	-2.45	n.a.
Quality deficiency (units of $10)	-0.113	-5.17**	-0.026	-0.639	-5.31**	-0.149	-0.134	-3.31	-0.031
Probability of moving (units of 0.10)	0.067	1.84†	0.016	0.163	2.37*	0.038	0.038	4.19**	0.031
Payment level (units of $10)	0.222	6.27**	0.052	-0.042	-0.49	-0.010	0.118	2.02*	0.028
Residual payment (units of $10)	0.048	1.13	0.011	-0.022	-0.24	-0.005	0.067	1.37	0.010
Addendum:									
Likelihood ratio (significance)				97.523**					
Sample size				710					
Mean of dependent variable				0.370					
Coefficient of determination				0.104					

Source: Kennedy and MacMillan, "Draft Report," p. 118.
n.a. Not available.
† Significant at the 0.10 level (two-tailed).
* Significant at the 0.05 level (two-tailed).
** Significant at the 0.01 level (two-tailed).
a. Derivatives computed at sample mean.

ance program), and the difference between the household's current housing quality and that required to meet minimum quality standards on participation were estimated using a logit model.[21] This model provides a statistical test of the separate effects of each factor.

$$(1) \qquad \ln \left(\frac{\pi_E}{1 - \pi_E} \right) = \alpha_0 + \alpha_1(QD) + \alpha_2 P_M + \alpha_3 S_1 + \alpha_4 S_2$$

where

π_E = the probability that a household not meeting standards at enrollment participated

QD = quality deficiency (expenditure required to meet quality standards, less housing expenditures at time of enrollment)

P_M = the estimated normal probability of moving during the experiment

S_1 = the payment level at enrollment (computed as the payment the household would have received as a household of size four with the sample mean income)

S_2 = the residual payment (the difference between the actual payment offered at enrollment and S_1).

The results are shown in table 7. Expected moving rates were positively related to participation. The difference in probability of participating between a person with an estimated probability of moving of zero versus an estimated probability of moving of one was approximately 16 percent.[22] Only modest effects on participation rates were associated with increasing payment levels. Contrary to the hypothesis suggested earlier, Kennedy and MacMillan report that households whose housing quality was furthest from the minimum standards required in the housing gap plans were least likely to participate.[23] The addition of demographic variables did not improve the equation. Demographic factors are captured in the variable representing the normal probability of moving.

An additional measure of program impact is to relate housing consumption under the Experimental Housing Allowance Program to what would be expected without an allowance. Households' incomes and abilities to acquire sound housing fluctuate through time. Of households that did not meet standards at the time of enrollment, some would subsequently ac-

21. Kennedy and MacMillan, "Draft Report," pp. 115–16.
22. Ibid., p. 119.
23. Ibid., p. 117.

quire housing that met minimum standards without any program. These households may still sustain high housing-cost burdens. Using the control group, Kennedy and MacMillan estimated that 40 to 50 percent of households that did not meet standards at enrollment would have subsequently met them without an allowance plan. Many would have improved their housing by moving. Combining these households with those that met standards at the time of enrollment, between 67 and 90 percent of all participants were households that would have met standards without an allowance. The proportion of households participating in the program that would not have normally met housing standards was only 25 percent.[24]

This procedure may give a somewhat misleading picture of program results, since it does not account for households that are currently meeting minimum standards but that will subsequently find themselves with lower incomes and more serious housing problems in the absence of a program. This category includes households in which one or more working members will become unemployed, ill, or unable to work, or in which a divorce or separation will occur. These households may enjoy considerable benefits in the future under an allowance program.

The demand experiment demonstrates dramatically one of the dilemmas confronting a housing allowance program. If the program adopts minimum standards, it will exclude many poor households. A majority of participants will be households that already live in, or would be expected to live in, adequate housing without an allowance program. The imposition of quality standards increases the average income of participants and reduces the proportion of minority and elderly households. On the other hand, in a program without quality standards, many participating households may remain in inferior quality units. The latter circumstance makes a housing allowance program closely resemble an unrestricted income transfer program. This is discussed further in the final section of this paper.

Comparison of participation rates in the Experimental Housing Allowance Program with rates in other income transfer programs suggests that the housing quality minimums are higher than the barriers discouraging households from participating in other programs. Nationwide participation rates of the eligible population have been estimated to be 87 percent for aid to families with dependent children (AFDC) in 1975, 60 percent for supplemental security income/aid to the aged, blind, and disabled in

24. Ibid., pp. 128–29.

1976, and 55 percent for the food stamp program in 1975.[25] The first
two programs require that the households apply and meet eligibility requirements, whereas the food stamp program until recently required that
the household make cash outlays to purchase food stamps. Relocation
costs play a role similar to the necessity to make outlays in the food stamp
program. Only if all restrictions on housing consumption are removed
will participation rates approach the high levels in the AFDC program.

Participation Profiles in Open Enrollment: The Supply Experiment

The supply experiment (which ends in 1984) tests the effects of a universal, open-enrollment housing allowance operating over an extended
period of time. Instead of individual outreach and interviewing, mass
publicity was used. Because the cities in the supply experiment were small
and a large amount of data was collected, considerable attention was
focused on the program. The public's awareness was probably greater
than would be realized in a nationwide universal housing allowance program. Ellickson and Kanouse report that more than three-quarters of the
households in the supply experiment sites had heard of the program.[26]
Households in the two supply experiment sites received more assistance
and friendlier treatment than would be typical in other welfare programs
or likely in a universal housing allowance program.[27]

The discussion here focuses principally on the descriptive statistics on
participation. The contractors have provided statistics on household participants, prices, housing quality, and supply but have conducted little
behavioral modeling of household decision making. For example, no
modeling has been attempted of households' decisions to participate or
relocate in the supply experiment.

Just as in the demand experiment, eligibility standards are based on
age, income, assets, and family size. Eligible one-person households include elderly (sixty-two years old or over), handicapped, or disabled persons, or persons displaced by public action. Households of two or more

25. Marc Bendick, Jr., "Failure to Enroll in Public Assistance Programs," *Social Work*, vol. 2 (July 1980), p. 269.
26. Phyllis L. Ellickson and David E. Kanouse, *Public Perceptions of Housing Allowances: The First Two Years*, Rand/WN-9817-HUD (Santa Monica: Rand Corp., 1978), p. 67.
27. Bendick, "Failure to Enroll in Public Assistance Programs."

Table 8. Characteristics of Participants in the Supply Experiment, 1978
Percent unless otherwise specified

| | Brown County, Wisconsin | | St. Joseph County, Indiana | |
Household characteristic	Eligible population	Participants	Eligible population	Participants
Tenure				
Own	53	31	70	54
Rent	47	69	30	46
Age of household head				
Under 62	58	63	46	54
62 or over	42	37	54	46
Race of household head				
White	97	97	83	75
Other	3	3	17	25
Size of household				
1	23	43	30	45
2	27	26	34	26
3–4	25	24	22	21
5–6	16	6	9	6
7 or more	9	2	5	1
Annual gross income, 1978 (dollars)				
Owners	n.a.	5,490	n.a.	4,604
Renters	n.a.	4,646	n.a.	3,467

Sources: Eligible population from Lawrence W. Kozimor, *Eligibility and Enrollment in the Housing Allowance Program: Brown and St. Joseph Counties through Year Two*, Rand WN-9816-HUD (Rand Corp., 1978), pp. 17, 19, 96, 100, 106, 133, 143. Participants from Rand Corporation, *Fifth Annual Report of the Housing Assistance Supply Experiment* (Rand, June 1979), pp. 21, 23.
n.a. Not available.

Table 9. Enrollment Rates by Adjusted Gross Income

Income (dollars)	Brown County (percent)	St. Joseph County (percent)
Under 1,000	...	35.8
1,000–1,999	35.5	46.1
2,000–2,999	52.2	33.4
3,000–3,999	79.4	53.2
4,000–4,999	39.7	24.3
5,000–5,999	32.2	19.9
6,000–6,999	18.1	a
7,000–7,999	20.6	a
8,000 or more	6.7	a
All incomes	42.4	33.9

Source: Kozimor, *Eligibility and Enrollment*, pp. 103, 140.
a. Not reported because sample size was less than 10.

related persons of any age are eligible if adjusted income falls below administratively established levels. The income limit is established at four times the standard cost of adequate housing for a household of a given size. Adjustments in income are made for assets, work-related expenses, dependents, and unusual medical expenses. This differs from the approach in section 8, which establishes income limits on a county basis at 80 percent of median county income for a family of four, with adjustments up or down for families of different sizes. Kozimor estimates that about 20 percent of all households were deemed eligible by income under these rules.[28] The highest eligibility rates were for single-head families with children and elderly single-person households.

The profile of participating households reflects persons enrolled in the past, the probability of their securing housing that met quality standards and hence made them eligible to receive a subsidy, and the changes in their incomes over time. Many younger households enroll and receive assistance for a time, but ultimately become ineligible because their income increases. The elderly constitute a smaller fraction of applicants but are less likely to leave the program because of income increases; consequently, they constitute a larger percentage of participants than the nonelderly at any given time relative to their representation in the pool of applicants.

The characteristics of participating households in 1978 appear in table 8. The elderly, owner-occupants, and large households (more than four persons) are underrepresented in the participant profile relative to their share of the eligible population. Income tends to be inversely related to enrollment rates, but not monotonically (see table 9). The mean income of participant households in 1978 (shown in table 8) was less than half the median household income in the two sites ($11,500 in Brown County in 1973, $10,900 in St. Joseph County in 1974); more recent household income data for the sites are not available.

It is difficult to isolate the role of the quality standards in the supply experiment since only a single standard was used and there was no control group. The enrollment will probably exclude most people who anticipated being unable to meet the quality standards because they or their landlords would not repair the unit and they were unable to move. Since many with deficient housing would not enroll, it is to be expected that

28. Lawrence W. Kozimor, *Eligibility and Enrollment in the Housing Allowance Program: Brown and St. Joseph Counties through Year Two,* Rand/WN-9816-HUD (Rand Corp., 1978), p. 13.

most who enrolled would be able to acquire housing that met the standards. About half of all enrollees' dwellings initially met standards in the supply experiment (52 percent in Brown County, 44 percent in St. Joseph County),[29] with quality failures more frequent among large households, nonelderly households, and white households. Most of the defects were small; the most frequent were stairways lacking handrails, inadequate bathrooms, and unsafe utilities.[30] About two-thirds of all units that initially failed inspection were successfully repaired by either the landlord or the tenant, generally at an average cost of less than $60.[31] There is a self-selection bias because only those who reasonably expected to meet the standards would choose to enroll. Hence the fact that most enrollees met the quality standards in the supply experiment does not contradict the demand experiment's finding that imposing a quality standard has a significant impact on participation.

Other factors must be considered in comparing the results of the demand and supply experiments. A slightly less stringent minimum housing standard was used in the supply experiment.[32] Landlords were probably more willing to upgrade units in the supply experiment. To refuse repairs and force a tenant to leave would mean finding a tenant who would accept a substandard unit. In the supply experiment sites, landlords may have realized that all low-income households would be in exactly the same bargaining position, needing a suitable unit to receive the subsidy. Some noneligible households might still prefer low-quality units. However, the program effectively placed a minimum quality on many units. Conversely, in the demand experiment a small percentage of households participated. Tenants were in a poor bargaining position since the landlord could expect to find another tenant who would not require a minimum quality standard.

An approximation can be made of steady-state participation rates, defined as the equilibrium number of households receiving subsidies divided by all eligible households, by examining the data for several years. Simple models of enrollment and termination rates as they affect overall partici-

29. Rand Corporation, *Fifth Annual Report of the Housing Assistance Supply Experiment* (Rand, June 1979), p. 25.

30. Bruce W. Lamar and Ira S. Lowry, *Client Responses to Housing Requirements: The First Two Years,* Rand/WN-9814-HUD (Rand Corp., February 1979), pp. 12–27, and app. A, pp. 69–76.

31. HUD, *A 1979 Report of Findings,* p. 60.

32. See Valenza, *Program Housing Standards;* and HUD, *A 1979 Report of Findings.*

pation have been constructed.[33] Households terminate—that is, no longer receive subsidies—because their incomes (adjusted for assets) become too high, they die or migrate to other areas, or they leave the program due to a change in household composition, opposition to the concept of receiving aid, entry into another program, and so forth. Increases in income account for three-fourths of nonelderly terminations, but only one-half of elderly terminations. Fifty-one percent of eligible nonelderly households enroll in a given year, but only 20 percent of eligible elderly households enroll. Forty-five percent of nonelderly participants terminate in a year, whereas 21 percent of elderly participants do so. Steady-state participation rates of about 50 percent of all eligible households have been estimated (53 percent for the nonelderly and 49 percent for the elderly), levels that should be fairly closely approximated after five years.[34] These estimates should be regarded as preliminary, given the limited time series data available.

Policy Considerations

Information on participation in the Experimental Housing Allowance Program is useful in designing a universal housing allowance program and projecting its costs. Cost estimates will be important in the political debate about an allowance program. Experience in other major income transfer programs is reviewed briefly below, with special emphasis on the increase in costs, which has reduced the political support for these programs.

Transfer payments increased almost fivefold from 1965 to 1975, rising from 3.9 percent of the gross national product in 1965 to 9.1 percent in early 1975.[35] A summary of growth rates in major transfer programs is shown in table 10. After 1975 the growth in income assistance transfer payments slowed substantially but still exceeded the rate of inflation. Existing transfer programs have been affected by inflation, legislative changes in benefits or in the number of eligible households, fluctuations in the economy, changes in geographic coverage or outreach, and changes

33. John E. Mulford, Grace E. Carter, and Phyllis D. Ellickson, *Eligibility and Participation Research Plan for the Housing Assistance Supply Experiment,* Rand/WN-10328-HUD (Rand Corp., October 1978).

34. C. Peter Rydell, John E. Mulford, and Lawrence Kozimor, *Dynamics of Participation in a Housing Allowance Program,* Rand/WN-10200-HUD (Rand Corp., June 1978), pp. 14, 21–23.

35. Martin Holmer, "Why Have Transfer Payments Grown So Rapidly?" (Department of Health, Education, and Welfare, October 1976), p. 1.

Table 10. Growth in Income Transfer Programs, 1965–79

Percent

	Change in expenditures, 1965–75 (1)	Change in federal outlays, 1975–79 (2)
Social security (old-age, survivors, and disability insurance)	247	64
Supplemental security income	167	34
Medicare	1,420	94
Medicaid	827	92
Unemployment insurance	678	−18
Aid to families with dependent children	456	−11
Food stamps	733	54

Sources: Column 1, Martin Holmer, "Why Have Transfer Payments Grown So Rapidly?" (Department of Health, Education, and Welfare, October 1976), p. 2. Column 2, *The Budget of the United States Government, Fiscal Year 1981*, pp. 263, 267, 277. Holmer's figures include federal, state, and local expenditures.

in participation rates. Holmer contends that policy liberalizations have been the principal source of growth.

Growth in AFDC transfers was concentrated in the period 1967 to 1972, when the case load more than doubled, with little growth since. Most of this increase is traceable to increases in participation rates of eligible households as a result of changes in administrative practices, court rulings, and an apparent decrease in the stigma attached to receiving welfare.[36] Increases in the number of households headed by females (from 5.5 percent in 1960 to 7.7 percent in 1975) accounted for about 18 percent of the growth. Between 1972 and 1975 the effects on the program of growth in households headed by females were almost offset by stricter administrative standards on eligibility.[37]

The experience with food stamps has been quite different. Food stamps are available to all persons, with a single nationwide benefit standard in effect. The value of transfers was increased sharply after 1971, when benefits were indexed to the price of food, and by liberalized national eligibility criteria in 1970 and in the amendments to the Food Stamp Act. Geographic coverage of the program expanded in the 1970s, and the

36. Frances Fox Piven and Richard A. Cloward, *Regulating the Poor: The Functions of Public Welfare* (Pantheon, 1971), pp. 330–37; Sheldon Danziger, Robert Haveman, and Robert Plotnick, "Income Transfer Programs in the United States: An Analysis of Their Structure and Impacts," prepared for the Joint Economic Committee, 96 Cong. 1 sess. (May 1979).

37. Holmer, "Why Have Transfer Payments Grown So Rapidly?" pp. 14–19.

1973 amendments to the Food Stamp Act required that the program operate in all jurisdictions. Holmer estimates that the indexing of benefits to food prices rather than to the consumer price index increased payments by about 25 percent. The major source of the increase in beneficiaries and payments prior to 1975 is traceable to policy liberalizations and expanded geographic coverage.[38]

Growth in social security disability payments can be traced about equally to larger numbers of recipients and higher average benefits per recipient. Since the definition of disability has not changed in the Social Security Act, the increase in recipients reflects a more liberal administrative interpretation of eligibility and higher participation rates by eligible persons (in the absence of growth in the number of disabled persons). Medicaid growth can also be divided about equally between an increase in recipients and an increase in benefits per recipient. About two-thirds of benefit increases are traceable to higher medical prices and one-third to higher real benefits. Virtually all of the increase in numbers of recipients is traceable to increases in the number of AFDC recipients, who automatically qualify for medicaid.

This overall expansion in transfer programs was not anticipated at the time of their legislative approval. It would appear possible to eliminate most of the budgetary uncertainties that led to unanticipated budget increases in other transfer programs if a universal housing allowance program were to be adopted. Estimates of income-eligible households by family size can be accurately made. Variations in participation rates by family size and income level could have considerable effects on total program costs. A program that serves the lowest-income households or the largest households—households that often devote more than 40 percent of income to housing yet acquire poor-quality units—will cost far more per household than a program that assists higher-income households or elderly households. Since the allowance decreases as household income increases, the elasticity of program costs per household with respect to income exceeds unity, and lowering the average income of participants will less than proportionally reduce total program costs. However, participation rates in the supply experiment have stabilized over a relatively short period of time. It should be possible to make reasonably accurate projections of participation by income and family size and hence estimate program costs accurately.

38. Ibid., pp. 22–24.

Other sources of uncertainty in predicting participation are housing quality standards and housing prices. The interpretation of quality standards will depend on local administrative decisions. It is not easy to devise appropriate incentives for local administrators with responsibility for quality certification. Prices of housing units that meet a given quality standard will vary across local markets, and periods in which housing price increases exceed the overall rate of inflation are possible. However, given the amount of data available from the Experimental Housing Allowance Program and section 8, reasonably accurate budget projections for a universal housing allowance would be possible. (See, for example, John Kain's paper in this volume.)

A major policy decision in the design of a universal allowance program that affects both vertical and horizontal equity and the costs of the program involves the choice between a program with open enrollment and one in which participation is limited by available budgets. Unless budgets are large, an open-enrollment program requires that income eligibility limits be low. Alternatively, if numbers participating are to be limited by budgets, either applicants must be rationed or benefits per household must be reduced. This problem has arisen in section 8 and all federal low-income housing assistance programs to date, where far more households are income-eligible than can be assisted. If all eligible persons are equally well informed of opportunities, randomly choosing participants from applicants might be regarded as fair and equitable. In practice, these conditions are difficult to achieve. As a result, participants receive large benefits while equally needy nonparticipants are not aided.

Anthony Downs has suggested that funds might be rationed by limiting eligibility to persons residing in certain areas, perhaps targeting aid to especially needy areas or neighborhoods where other local and federal programs are being concentrated to foster neighborhood revitalization. Targeting aid to particular geographic areas has a long history and was the principle used in the urban renewal program. This approach has serious weaknesses. If the objective is to aid households, tying the assistance to particular housing units or neighborhoods may create unwarranted income transfers to owners of particular units and at the same time restrict households' choices to certain areas. Assisting households without limits on what they consume and where they reside is the only means of promoting free market choices by recipients and potential geographic mobility, both of which are necessary for an efficient outcome. Tying aid to certain residential areas creates potential windfalls for property owners in one area but not in another; the politics of making these geographic designations and the associated invitations for corruption were serious problems in the urban renewal program.

There are several solutions to the implied horizontal inequity other than increasing program size: average benefits could be lowered by reducing the target housing quality or by increasing the tenant's contribution. Reducing the subsidy cost per household would make it possible to assist more households for the same budget. Either of these changes lowers the income level at which benefits are zero and thereby reduces the average income of eligible households. This would permit a higher percentage of eligible households to be served than if benefits were higher.

Among these methods of coping with limited total funding, lowering benefits by increasing the tenant's contribution seems the most desirable. It is difficult to justify on social welfare grounds the need to define tenant benefits on the basis of a tenant contribution of only 25 percent of income (as opposed to 30 or 35 percent) if a program can aid only a tiny fraction of the renter households with rent payments in excess of 35 or 40 percent of income. It should also be noted that housing payments as a share of income have risen considerably in the unassisted housing market in recent years.

The role of quality standards in an allowance program presents complex policy issues. The evidence above clearly demonstrates the constraints imposed by quality minimums on many households, particularly the poorest and older households. Questions can also be raised about the effectiveness of quality standards in a nationwide program. While households were able to secure quality improvements in the housing allowance experiments, they received more assistance than they would have in an operational program. Tenants may have little leverage with landlords in many cases. Many poor households are neither skilled in shopping nor astute in tenant-landlord negotiation.

The burden of quality enforcement may rest on local administrators. In many cases, the tenant and the landlord both stand to gain if a deficient unit passes inspection. Barriers to moving allow the landlord to share in some of the gains of the income transfer. Nor is it simple to design administrative procedures to ensure that local officials enforce standards. If administrative fees are paid for households receiving benefits, the incentives for local administering agencies to interpret standards loosely is obvious. Administrative regulations will not be as easily enforced in a nationwide program operating in all geographic markets as in the experimental program, in which much more administrative surveillance took place.

Whether Congress would ever endorse a housing allowance program that omitted requirements for the type of housing consumed is doubtful, since such a program would essentially be an income transfer program. One possible justification for an allowance program without quality minimums is the need to establish benefit payments for each applicant. Since housing needs vary by household composition and size, and because housing prices vary considerably across local communities, a simple formula based on income and household size might be judged too imprecise, providing some households with too large a benefit and others with too little. It is debatable whether this justifies establishing an elaborate administrative procedure to assess housing needs of each applicant in each geographic market, or whether what these needs are could be judged in a better way than by using only income, family size, and other variables in a simple formula.

A housing allowance program that did not impose a minimum quality standard might also assist households in shopping and negotiating with landlords. As discovered in evaluation studies of the section 8 program, many low-income households have little or no knowledge of leases, tenants' rights, enforcement of codes or leases, or methods of shopping for another unit. The benefits of an informed public able to shop effectively for housing are obvious, even in the absence of a housing allowance program; an informed public can be an important assurance that the government's commitment of resources does not become a transfer to landlords. An active role by the federal government in assisting low-income households in house hunting, lease negotiations, and tenant-landlord disputes could be controversial.

It is true that no amount of legal or administrative enforcement activity will ensure that the private market will provide tenants with housing of good quality at below-market prices. If tenants cannot pay rents that reflect market prices for sound housing, or if payments of that amount are not made on their behalf, quality standards and enforcement will not be helpful. It might also be argued that housing standards are unnecessary if tenants can pay for adequate housing. A housing allowance program without standards would ensure that households had the resources to secure adequate housing and would help them in their search.

Comments by Ann B. Schnare[39]

Over the past few years, several of my friends and colleagues have been involved in the housing allowance experiment. On occasion, I have participated more directly in the process, either by critiquing a technical paper or by reviewing reports to make statements on some aspect of the Experimental Housing Allowance Program experience. In the process of my admittedly superficial involvement with the program, I have discovered a strange phenomenon that I shall call the "EHAP trap."

An enormous number of reports and much empirical data were produced during the experiment's nine-year history. Trying to assimilate the facts and theories presented in these reports—and trying to remember, if not to reconcile, the different patterns that occur in the twelve sites—is a monumental task. The "EHAP trap," which I personally find difficult to avoid, is when one becomes so immersed in minor details that one loses a sense of perspective. Every attempt to make a generalization seems to be almost immediately met with a new piece of data that questions, if it does not disprove, the original hypothesis.

With this in mind, I think that Mahlon Straszheim's paper deserves special commendation, because it is obvious that he spent much time and effort to present the more salient aspects of program participation. My only criticisms are on emphasis or focus. The paper covers a variety of topics that are related to the issue of participation. While such breadth is welcome, I think that the various sections of the paper could have been tied together more effectively to present a more cohesive, positive statement about the Experimental Housing Allowance Program participation experience. Although I am aware that the "EHAP trap" works against such generalizations, I think additional efforts in this direction would be worthwhile.

From my own perspective, there are four basic questions pertaining to program enrollment or participation. Most have been covered in Straszheim's paper. However, I think it would be useful to summarize the major findings of the program as they relate to each question and to emphasize some issues that Straszheim ignores. Let me raise and address these basic questions one by one.

39. The author thanks Frank de Leeuw for his helpful comments. Any errors and omissions, of course, are mine.

The first question is, "Are households willing to participate in the program?" The supply experiment provides the best information on this, since it involved an open-enrollment program. After four years of operation, about 45 percent of the eligible population was enrolled, and about 35 percent received program benefits.[40] These relatively low enrollment and participation rates came as a surprise to many observers. To put them in some perspective, the latest estimates of participation rates are about 70 percent in the food stamp program and about 90 percent in AFDC.[41]

Experimental Housing Allowance Program data also suggest that enrollment rates will vary over different subgroups of the eligible population. Female-headed households with children, households on welfare, and minorities tended to be the most likely to enroll. Enrollment rates were considerably lower among homeowners, the working poor, and elderly households. These differences in enrollment rates apparently reflect a variety of factors, including lack of program awareness and perception of a welfare stigma. While there is some evidence that changes in outreach procedures can bring enrollment rates to a level more reflective of the general population, there appears to be a bias in the types of households the program attracts.

The second question is, "Are there any significant barriers to participation?" The program findings in this regard are not encouraging. The proportion of enrolled households that were able to participate ranged from a low of 33 percent in Jacksonville, Florida, to a high of 86 percent in Tulsa, Oklahoma, and Bismarck, North Dakota.[42] While eight of the twelve experimental sites had "success rates" of 70 percent or more, the lower rates in the other areas—as well as differences in the experiences of certain types of households—give some reason for concern.

The most important factor affecting the enrollees' success in receiving program benefits was the quality of the initial housing. Households whose units failed the initial inspection could move to a better unit, convince their landlords to make the necessary repairs, or repair their units themselves. In the supply experiment, upgrading was fairly common, perhaps because of the relatively minor expenses involved, the large scale of the program, or the longer time span of the experiment. However, in the

40. HUD, *Experimental Housing Allowance Program: Conclusions, the 1980 Report* (GPO, 1980), p. 6.

41. Bendick, "Failure to Enroll in Public Assistance Programs," p. 269.

42. David B. Carlson and John D. Heinberg, *How Housing Allowances Work: Integrated Findings from the Experimental Housing Allowance Program*, 249-3 (Urban Institute, February 1978), p. 14.

remainder of the program sites, a majority of households met program requirements by moving.

From a policy perspective it is important that the opportunity to participate in the Experimental Housing Allowance Program had only a minor impact on a household's decision to move. As a result, the successful participants in the program tended to be households with relatively good initial housing or with relatively high mobility rates. Not too surprisingly, large families and minorities had a lower probability of success, since such households were more likely to live in units that failed to qualify for the program.[43]

One may naturally ask why the prospect of an allowance had so little effect on a household's decision to move. In most cases, the size of the transfer payment was large enough to cover the rent increase incurred when the household moved to standard housing. Nevertheless, about one-third of the households in ineligible units did not look for new housing. When interviewed, most indicated that they liked their current units and neighborhoods and that it was too much trouble to move.

The remaining households in ineligible units did attempt to locate suitable housing. However, there is some evidence that certain households encountered barriers when attempting to move. For example, blacks who searched in Pittsburgh were less likely to move than similar households elsewhere.[44] Twenty-one percent of all black households moving in Pittsburgh reported that they encountered racial-ethnic discrimination during their housing search.[45] These factors combined to make the success rates of minority households at least ten percentage points lower than those of white households.

Participation among elderly households also proved problematic. On the one hand, the general success rate among elderly enrollees was relatively high in the majority of program sites. For example, in both the administrative agency experiment and the supply experiment, the proportion of elderly enrollees that achieved recipient status was about ten percentage points higher than for younger households. On the other hand, most of the elderly households that enrolled in the program began with units that met program standards. There is some evidence that potential

43. Abt Associates, *Third Annual Report of the Administrative Agency Experiment* (Abt, August 1976), p. 27.

44. Jean MacMillan, "Draft Report on Mobility in the Housing Allowance Demand Experiment" (Abt, June 1978), p. 96.

45. Avis Vidal, "Draft Report on the Search Behavior of Black Households in Pittsburgh in the Housing Allowance Demand Experiment" (Abt, July 1978), p. A-42.

elderly applicants were discouraged from enrolling because their housing would not pass program standards. In addition, elderly enrollees in housing that did not meet program standards had lower participation rates than other households. This pattern is not surprising, given the fact that older households have a relatively lower propensity to move.

These differing patterns of success raise a third important question that was not addressed in Straszheim's paper: "What administrative procedure could be adopted to increase the enrollee's chance of securing an acceptable unit?" The administrative agency experiment offered a variety of supportive services to facilitate the household's search for housing. Apparently, one of the most frequently requested services was a list of available units. While the evidence related to the effectiveness of these supportive services is somewhat tenuous, an initial report by Abt Associates concluded that supportive services were effective tools in tighter housing markets, especially for minority households. It may thus be possible to lessen some of the problems that I noted earlier, but significant moves in this direction would jeopardize the administrative simplicity of the program.

The last question I raise is, "How effective is a housing allowance approach, given the participation patterns that were observed across the different program sites?" As Straszheim and Aaron state in their papers, there has been a dramatic decline in the number of inadequate dwelling units in this country over the last couple of decades, at least when measured against some fairly simple quality indicators. Given this decline—and the limited resources available for housing subsidies—it seems reasonable that the nation's housing policy should be targeted to households in the lowest-quality dwellings, if not to the dwellings themselves.

The disappointing evidence from the program experience is that this logical target group will be the *least* likely to participate. Thus if the objective of the program is to improve the housing conditions of low-income households, the program will be relatively inefficient. As Straszheim highlights in his paper, increasing the minimum housing requirements exacerbates the problem by excluding the neediest or the least mobile households. Reducing the minimum standards would encourage participation but at the expense of the housing-related focus of the program.

However, it is also important to note that the general effectiveness of the housing allowance approach will probably vary with the characteristics of housing markets and with the type of household served. It thus seems safe to assume that the program would be successful in areas with high mobility rates, a young population, and a good housing stock. However, it also appears that participation rates would be low in cities and neighborhoods where households are attached to a particular place, where the housing stock is unusually poor, where vacancy rates are low, or where segregation is fairly intense. While such findings do not negate the usefulness of the housing allowance approach, the findings imply that more targeted demand or supply approaches would be needed to reach households in the lowest-quality dwellings or to serve locales with the most serious housing needs.

PETER H. ROSSI

Residential Mobility

It is no mystery why the issue of residential mobility is important in the Experimental Housing Allowance Program. To be effective, housing allowances should stimulate recipients to occupy better housing. One way to accomplish this goal would be to induce households to move to better housing, thereby possibly increasing overall amounts of moving. Because they have less control over their housing, renters may be induced to move, whereas owners may have more options to upgrade the quality of their housing. For housing allowances to affect housing quality relatively quickly, additional residential shifting among recipient households would have to be stimulated. On the aggregate level, for housing allowances to diminish housing segregation by income or ethnicity, the spatial patterning of such induced shifts should also be affected by allowances. Hence, higher levels of residential mobility are an important potential intermediate outcome of housing allowances. Stimulating additional mobility may be important in improving housing, especially for renters. Affecting the locational distribution of persons who move is essential if the allowances are to reduce economic and ethnic residential segregation.

Two important issues in the evaluation of housing allowances as social policy are (1) the extent to which residential shifts are stimulated by housing allowance eligibility and (2) the extent to which shifts that do occur move households into areas in which they can contribute to increasing the mix along socioeconomic and ethnic lines. Of course, the incidence of shifting or mixing would have to be greater than could be "ordinarily expected," an estimation problem that is met squarely by the randomized design of the demand experiment and met less adequately in the design of the supply experiment.

Measuring residential mobility seems to be a remarkably simple task. For all practical purposes, most people in the United States have an ad-

147

dress to which they return frequently enough to receive mail and messages, where they often sleep, eat, and so on. A shift in address defines a move, usually involving associated shifts in the consumption of housing and in activities that are conditioned by residential location. These activities include employment, participation in kinship and friendship networks, consumption of private and public services and other goods, expressions of political and ethnic solidarity, ethnic and racial antagonisms, and so on. Because residence is believed to be correlated with so many other aspects of life, residential mobility is a prime concern in a number of social science fields. These correlates of residential location are also reasons for policy makers' interest in residential mobility, aside from their direct interest in the differentials of housing consumption.

Residential mobility is regarded with some ambivalence. On the one hand, policy makers are concerned that persons can and do move from inappropriate housing to housing that is more compatible with their needs. Housing policy is biased toward homeownership; thus a move from rental housing to owned housing is regarded positively. Residential shifts that would in the aggregate increase residential mixing by race, ethnicity, and socioeconomic level are also regarded positively, and explicit legislation attempts to remove barriers to such shifts. On the other hand, transiency of individuals and high turnover of neighborhoods are viewed negatively. Stable neighborhoods and residents who are loyal to their neighborhoods are considered desirable. This ambivalence is evident in the policy interests of the Experimental Housing Allowance Program: housing allowances should help poor families to upgrade their inadequate housing and leave depressed neighborhoods, but at the same time housing allowances should not radically reduce the neighborhoods of higher-income families. The program does not change this ambivalence because housing allowances appear to do little of either.

Residential shifts, although easy to detect, have several characteristics that complicate attempts to understand why people move. First, persons rarely move as individuals; household units are involved. Second, location decisions often are not simply housing decisions but are based on other factors or exogenous events. Dwellings may be destroyed, tenants evicted,[1] deaths or illnesses experienced, households formed or dissolved,

1. Jean MacMillan, "Draft Report on Mobility in the Housing Allowance Demand Experiment" (Cambridge, Mass.: Abt Associates, June 1978), estimates that 8 to 9 percent of moves in Pittsburgh and Phoenix over the first two years of the demand experiment were "forced" by either eviction or destruction of the dwell-

and so on. All these events imply moving. Long-distance migration is rarely motivated by housing considerations per se. Forced or derivative moves represent a large proportion of all residential shifts. Thus it is not possible to reduce mobility to zero.

When derivative and forced moves are viewed as a component of the total amount of residential shifting, their aggregate amount is high. Close to one-third of residential shifts involve migration across county lines. As much as another third may be the result of household formation and dissolution or forced by the destruction of dwelling units or evictions. In short, as many as two-thirds of all residential shifts appear to be caused by nonhousing considerations. This estimate is stated imprecisely because it is an inference drawn from a variety of sources.[2]

Finally, some residential shifts do involve housing considerations. For already formed households in the middle years before mortality takes its toll, perhaps the majority of shifts undertaken are discretionary and involve housing considerations.[3] An important conceptual and measurement issue involves what characteristics of the housing bundle count in such discretionary moves. A residence implies a set of housing and housing-associated services, including the physical structure—its size, design, adequacy of heating, plumbing, and so forth—its costs, surrounding structures and their inhabitants, the locational characteristics of the dwelling, the symbolic meanings of dwelling and neighborhood, and so on. The complexity of the housing bundle makes it difficult to understand residential mobility and to discern the aspects of housing to which inhabitants are sensitive. In this regard, the demand and supply experiments have contributed significantly through the computation of "hedonic indexes" that measure the sensitivity of rent to dwelling unit characteristics. Assuming that market forces capture and express in rent differences the

---

ing unit. Other estimates yield much higher proportions of moves that are either forced or derived from other decisions. See introduction to new edition of Peter H. Rossi, *Why Families Move* (Sage Publications, 1980).

2. A critical issue is the extent to which housing considerations may be involved in what appear to be nondiscretionary moves. Thus a long-distance migration may be partially motivated by the desire for better housing opportunities, and a divorce decision may be reinforced by deep dissatisfaction with the housing or community involved in the marriage. In short, the boundary between discretionary and nondiscretionary moves is not easy to draw.

3. Of course, the eligibility requirements imposed by the experiments minimize some of the nondiscretionary moves, particularly those associated with household formation and dissolution.

characteristics of housing that renters seek to obtain, these indexes help us understand housing bundle complexity.[4]

A useful working theory of discretionary residential mobility has been stated by Quigley and Weinberg[5] as follows: a household tends toward equilibrium in its housing choice, an equilibrium that is represented by that choice, in comparison to which an alternative choice would produce no additional benefits that exceed the costs of moving. This general statement verges on the tautological since a restatement of the proposition is that households move when it is clearly advantageous for them to do so, as they see it. The main advantage of the statement, however, is that it focuses attention on three important aspects of mobility. First, it emphasizes a view of residential stability as a distribution of equilibrium points at which the households involved are doing the best they can. Hence most households should be satisfied with their housing. Second, there are moving costs, presumably not only out-of-pocket costs but others as well. Third, the statement directs one to look for events that move households from their equilibrium points as sources for residential mobility. This last point translates in the present context into the question of whether the experimental treatments involved in the Experimental Housing Allowance Program constitute sufficient stimuli to move households from their equilibrium points.

Although there is some disagreement on this score, most microlevel

4. The hedonic indexes appear to be post hoc analyses using available data on rental units in the data files. They may be too carefully fitted to the specific localities and hence not fully generalizable to other markets and to other parts of the housing market. For example, they may capture what rents (and, by implication, housing tastes) are sensitive to in the low-rent markets of Phoenix and Pittsburgh and may not be as useful in other places and in other markets. Indeed, the researchers comment that because of the behavior of the hedonic index for Phoenix, specification errors probably exist in the index for that city, meaning that the list of variables describing low-cost rental housing in Phoenix is probably incomplete. A recent Urban Institute study confirms that there is considerable variation in hedonic indexes across standard metropolitan statistical areas. James R. Follain and Stephen Malpezzi, *Dissecting Housing Value and Rent: Estimates of Hedonic Indexes for 39 Large SMSA's* (Washington, D.C.: Urban Institute, February 1980).

5. John M. Quigley and Daniel H. Weinberg, "Intra-Urban Residential Mobility: A Review and Synthesis," *International Regional Science Review*, vol. 2 (Fall 1977), pp. 41–66. This general model is used in an interesting operational form in Daniel H. Weinberg, Joseph Friedman, and Stephen K. Mayo, "A Disequilibrium Model of Housing Search and Residential Mobility," in U.S. Department of Housing and Urban Development, *Occasional Papers in Housing and Community Affairs* (Government Printing Office, forthcoming).

models of mobility distinguish between a household's decision to move and its decision to select a new dwelling.[6] When dissatisfaction with housing passes a certain threshold, the household makes plans to move, and disequilibrium manifests itself. A plan or intention to move becomes an actual search for a new dwelling, resulting in a choice of a new dwelling among the alternatives evaluated in the search. The major advantage of distinguishing these stages in the household mobility process is that attention is drawn to the distinctive roles played by different influences at separate stages. Thus the characteristics of the housing bundle in interaction with household characteristics are important in determining levels of satisfaction. Search behavior, in contrast, may be more influenced by friendship patterns, media exposure, or familiarity with residential neighborhoods in the city in question. Whether or not dissatisfaction is converted into plans for moving may depend heavily on calculation of moving costs. This mobility process model helps to specify how a policy works or where a prospective policy might intervene. For example, discrimination in the housing market probably constricts search behavior or raises the cost of searching.

Some version of the mobility process model described above is used in the analyses of the demand and supply experiments. Housing allowances might work through changing threshold conditions or enlarging search patterns. This model will be discussed under experimental findings in a later section of this paper.

Past Research

Empirical studies of residential mobility extend back for several decades. It is worthwhile to review these studies to provide a background for assessing findings from the housing allowance experiments.

Perhaps the most puzzling aspect of residential mobility is its relative stability over time. In 1948 the Bureau of the Census began publishing annual mobility data from current population surveys based on March survey questions, asking whether or not the members of the household were still living in the same dwelling unit as they had on April 1 of the

6. An early formulation of this scheme can be found in the first edition of Rossi, *Why Families Move* (Free Press, 1955), and is more fully developed in Alden Speare, Jr., Sidney Goldstein, and William H. Frey, *Residential Mobility, Migration, and Metropolitan Change* (Ballinger, 1975).

previous year. These "annual ever-moved" measures[7] are summarized in table 1.

For the three decades for which data are available, the annual ever-moved rates show a remarkable stability. At the highest point in the series, 1950–51, 21 percent of the population was found to have moved at least once. At the lowest point in the series, 1975–76, the proportion that had ever moved was 17 percent. There appears to be a gradual decline to this low point from about 1965–66. It is not yet clear whether this decline is a trend that can be distinguished from "normal" fluctuation.

Table 1 divides the total ever-moved rates into two components—proportions who moved across county boundaries and proportions who moved within county boundaries—or proxies, respectively, for migration and for residential mobility. Long-distance migration seems the more stable of the two rates, fluctuating between 5.6 and 7.1 percent. Intracounty moves show more apparent annual fluctuations, ranging from a high of 13.9 percent in 1950–51 to a low of 10.8 percent in 1975–76. Indeed, it appears that the decline in the total ever-moved rate after 1965–66 largely reflects the decline in residential mobility (intracounty moves).

If there is a decline in mobility rates since 1965–66, as the data in table 1 seem to suggest, it is neither large nor precipitous. For about thirty years, the total annual ever-moved rate has been about 20 percent and the intracounty ever-moved rate has been about 13 percent. This persistence in magnitude is all the more remarkable considering that the post–World War II period started out with a severe housing shortage and went through two small military engagements, two relatively severe recessions, a large increase in the proportion of the population owning their own homes, decisive changes in fertility, changes in age at first marriage, and at least two booms of prosperity. *Whatever drives migration and mobility in the aggregate must be dominated by processes that are relatively insensitive to major events and trends in the economy, vital processes, and the housing market.*[8]

7. These rates are the proportions of persons one year old or older who lived at a different address on April 1 of the previous year. Note that each person is counted separately, not as households, and that multiple moves within a year are ignored. Note also that larger households contribute proportionately more than smaller households. A five-person family is counted five times, whereas a single-person household is counted only once.

8. It may well be the case that the small absolute change from year to year should be regarded as significant change. The annual mobility rates may be sensitive to some set of market forces, responding in a systematic manner but on a scale that only appears to be small.

Table 1. The Percentage of People That Had Ever Moved, 1947–76, by Type of Move[a]

Period (April 1 through March 31)	Total ever moved	Ever moved intercounty	Ever moved intracounty
1947–48	19.9	6.4	13.6
1948–49	18.8	5.8	13.0
1949–50	18.7	5.6	13.1
1950–51	21.0	7.1	13.9
1951–52	19.8	6.6	13.2
1952–53	20.1	6.6	13.5
1953–54	18.6	6.4	12.2
1954–55	19.9	6.6	13.3
1955–56	20.5	6.8	13.7
1956–57	19.4	6.2	13.1
1957–58	19.8	6.7	13.1
1958–59	19.2	6.1	13.1
1959–60	19.4	6.4	12.9
1960–61	20.0	6.3	13.7
1961–62	19.1	6.1	13.0
1962–63	19.4	6.8	12.6
1963–64	19.6	6.6	13.0
1964–65	20.1	6.8	13.4
1965–66	19.3	6.6	12.7
1966–67	18.3	6.7	11.6
1967–68	18.8	7.0	11.8
1968–69	18.3	6.6	11.7
1969–70	18.4	6.7	11.7
1970–71	17.9	6.5	11.4
1971–75[b]	...	...	...
1975–76	17.1	6.4	10.8
Mean	19.3	6.5	12.8

Sources: U.S. Bureau of the Census, *Current Population Reports*, series P-20, no. 235, "Mobility of the Population of the United States, March 1970 to March 1971" (GPO, 1972), p. 8, and series P-20, no. 305, "Geographical Mobility, March 1975 to March 1976" (GPO, 1977), p. 6. Figures are rounded.
a. The sample was drawn from the U.S. civilian noninstitutionalized population, one year old or over.
b. Data for April 1971 through March 1975 not available on annual basis.

When computed over longer periods, the ever-moved proportion increases. Over a five-year period (1970–75) the ever-moved proportion is 41.3 percent, with 17.1 percent having moved between counties and the remaining 24.2 percent having moved within counties. Since these cumulative ever-moved proportions do not count multiple moves within a period, the total amount of moving is underestimated.

Strong and persistent regional differences also have been recorded in the ever-moved rates, with cities in the fast-growing western and south-western states persistently showing higher ever-moved rates than the relatively declining northeastern and mid-Atlantic states.[9] These regional differences also survive when tenure, age, and other compositional differences among regions are held constant. One such regional difference is reflected faithfully in the demand experiment by the higher level of mobility in Phoenix than in Pittsburgh.

The distances involved in residential mobility shifts are not very large. In a study of several metropolitan areas, Zimmer estimated that 62 percent of moves originating in central cities were less than three miles; longer distance moves involved shifts within areas that had less dense settlement patterns and shorter moves within the more densely built-up residential sections of standard metropolitan statistical areas.[10] Lansing and Mueller found that despite the many moves households typically experience over a lifetime, 45 percent of household heads were still living in localities within fifty miles of where they were born.[11]

The probability of moving is not uniform across households. The empirical literature shows that the stability of those who own their homes is greater than of those who rent. Several researchers have asserted that tenure is the single most important predictor of residential mobility.[12] In addition, studies indicate that owning a home is regarded almost uniformly as preferable to renting.

It is not clear why homeownership, ceteris paribus, should induce more stability than renting. American norms apparently favor owning over renting, but there is no evidence that the norms prescribe residential stability for homeowners and not for renters. The costs of moving are probably greater for homeowners, but if this were the major factor, residential

9. For example, regional rates for 1975–76 were as follows:

Region	Proportion that did not move	Proportion that moved, same county	Proportion that moved, different county
Northeast	87.7	7.8	4.0
North Central	84.4	9.8	5.6
South	80.0	11.7	7.7
West	76.5	14.4	8.1

Bureau of the Census, "Geographical Mobility," pp. 9–10. Note that the residential mobility (intracounty) rates in the West are almost twice (1.85 times) those of the Northeast, a proportionality that has remained fairly constant over the period since the early 1950s, when census reports first tabulated moving rates by region.

10. Basil G. Zimmer, "Residential Mobility and Housing," *Land Economics*, vol. 49 (August 1973), p. 346.

11. John B. Lansing and Eva L. Mueller, *The Geographic Mobility of Labor* (University of Michigan, Institute for Social Research, 1967).

12. See, for example, William Michelson, *Environmental Choice, Human Behavior and Residential Satisfaction* (New York: Oxford University Press, 1977).

mobility would be far more sensitive to the costs of moving than empirical evidence suggests.[13] It also may be the case that the ceteris paribus conditions have not been fully met, particularly those relating to the characteristics of the housing involved. Rental and owner-occupied units vary considerably in size, location, interior design, and so forth, in ways that may not have been fully controlled for in previous research.

Self-selection processes may also be at work. MacMillan suggests that because of the greater moving costs and the investment in time involved in selling a house, households may not purchase a house until they are ready to stay in one place for a while. Hence homeowners may simply consist of more stable households.

A second extremely powerful predictor of residential mobility is a set of household characteristics that have been summarized as "life cycle stages." While the literature has not settled on any standard set of stages, all agree that the components of such a definition include household composition, especially the presence or absence of children; who heads the household; and the ages of members of the household. Households headed by older persons are more stable than those headed by younger persons, and households that are in the earliest periods of child rearing are less stable than households with older children.[14]

Perhaps the most unequivocal finding is that the older the head of the household, the more stable the household. Why this should be the case is not clear, especially since this finding holds up under all sorts of ceteris paribus conditions. Older households are least responsive to the incentives offered by Experimental Housing Allowance Program payments.

Past mobility behavior is also a good predictor of current mobility. Families that have moved in the recent past are likely to move again. Whether this means, as some have claimed, that one learns how to move

13. Some of the demand experiment analyses show that moving costs are considerably greater in Pittsburgh than in Phoenix and that the costs of moving are greater for blacks than for whites, a factor that depresses the residential mobility of blacks below what one would expect from their levels of dissatisfaction with housing occupied. Francis J. Cronin, *Racial Differences in the Search for Housing*, 1510-4 (Urban Institute, May 1980). Additional evidence on the role of moving costs is shown in Weinberg and others, "A Disequilibrium Model of Housing Search and Residential Mobility," which is discussed in greater detail later on in this paper.

14. Most of the findings are somewhat confounded by the fact that "life cycle stage" is measured after the move rather than before. Hence the fact that families with small children are most likely to have moved may mean only that such families are most likely to have experienced an increase in family size that led to their move and not that families with small children are more mobile. Similarly, the finding that recently married persons are more likely to have moved may mean only that getting married produced a move.

and how to search for better housing by experience with moving or whether some inherent propensity to move exists is not clear. What this finding does mean, however, is that some families contribute more than their proportionate share to the ever-moved rates.[15]

Research on residential mobility has not produced clear findings on the effects of household income on moving. It is difficult to understand the role of income because income is so entangled with apparently stronger correlates of moving; for example, higher-income families are much more likely to be homeowners. Drastic shifts in household income are associated with shifts in family composition, and family income changes with life cycle stage. The estimates of income elasticity of housing expenditures as calculated from cross-sectional studies do not appear to be particularly stable from one study to another, nor do they appear to be uniform over various income classes.

An even more inconsistent set of findings concerns the effects of locational characteristics of housing on residential mobility. For example, while there is some evidence that the aggregate number of white families tends to decline in areas where the number of blacks increases, it is not clear whether these effects are created by greater-than-expected moving out of such areas or less-than-expected white moves into such areas. Indeed, given the amount of mobility to be expected on the basis of demographic shifts in any population, it is easy for an area to be emptied of a large proportion of its inhabitants over a relatively short period of time simply by lack of replacements for the inhabitants who are moving because of household formation and dissolution reasons.

Another locational characteristic to which a great deal of attention has been paid is the relationship between residential and employment locations. Indeed, some of the early models of mobility attempted to use minimizing distance to employment as a prime factor in intrametropolitan population redistribution.[16] A more recent formulation considers a mu-

15. Of course, this tendency is dampened by the factors outlined earlier. For example, young families that are chronic movers move less when they age, but more than others in their age bracket. In addition, some researchers have speculated (Rossi, *Why Families Move*) that such findings reflect tentative moves involving the exploration of neighborhoods as residential locations with return moves to the original location when the attempt to change failed to yield greater housing and neighborhood satisfaction.

16. William Alonso, *Location and Land Use: Toward a General Theory of Land Rent* (Harvard University Press, 1964); and Richard F. Muth, *Cities and Housing: The Spatial Pattern of Urban Residential Land Use* (University of Chicago Press, 1969).

tually interacting influence in which either moving residences or moving employment location reduces the journey-to-work burden.[17] All told, locational characteristics of residences have either a weak or a contradictory set of influences on residential mobility.[18]

The main purpose of reviewing existing knowledge on residential mobility was to provide a background for evaluating the housing allowance experiment findings on residential mobility. Perhaps the main lesson to be drawn from this review is that the major processes that drive residential mobility are not touched very deeply by the experimental treatments. In the aggregate over time, the amounts of moving appear to be stable, changing slowly rather than in response to identifiable short-term trends in the economy at large or the housing market. Since tenure and family life cycle appear to be the major correlates of residential mobility, it seems unlikely that the housing allowance payments are going to have much effect on moving; at best they will accelerate or retard changes that might otherwise have occurred rather than drastically altering the levels of residential mobility for the households to whom housing allowances were offered.

It should also be noted that the mobility experiences of the Experimental Housing Allowance Program participants are going to be strongly conditioned by the ways in which eligibility requirements shape the distribution of enrolled families. In the demand experiment, mobility will be high because only renters are eligible, a tendency counteracted by the income requirements that will make many older persons eligible for enrollment.

Mobility and Housing Allowances

One of the goals of the housing allowance program was to induce families to live in better housing and to lower their degree of economic and racial-ethnic residential segregation. Better housing meant either upgrading the housing families occupied or moving to better accommodations.

17. Daniel H. Weinberg, "Intra-urban Household Mobility" (Ph.D. dissertation, Yale University).
18. It is also possible that the proper specification of effects requires so much disaggregation that the usual research design employed in mobility studies (relatively sparse area probability samples) cannot sustain the appropriate analyses. It should also be noted that neither the demand nor the supply experiment paid any attention to journey-to-work considerations in analyses available up to this point.

Reduction in economic and racial-ethnic segregation implied moving from areas of high concentrations of poor families or of whites, blacks, or Chicanos to areas of lower concentration. In either case, residential mobility was to be an important means to these ends. The question then arises, to what extent did the housing allowance plans induce moving over and above what would have ordinarily occurred?

The inducements to moving offered by the housing allowances are complicated. Indeed, for some of the families the incentives are apparently negative: more may be gained by staying in one place than by moving.

Under the minimum standards housing allowance plan, families are offered the difference between the established rent for reasonable accommodations for families of the same size and a fraction of their income, provided that they occupy housing that passes a test of minimum adequacy. Under this plan the incentive for moving varies according to (1) whether existing accommodations at enrollment pass or fail the test, (2) whether the family is occupying housing that is a bargain relative to similar housing on the market, and (3) moving costs. Clearly, families that are eligible for payments immediately upon enrollment (that is, whose housing meets standards) may have little to gain and perhaps much to lose by moving, especially because of moving costs and probably higher housing costs.[19] Families whose enrollment housing fails the standards test have the option of moving to a dwelling that would pass the standards test, repairing the dwelling unit to be in conformity, or remaining and forgoing payments. In short, the plan that was used exclusively in the supply experiments and was one of the major plans in the demand experiment provides a set of mixed incentives for moving.

Similar considerations apply to the minimum rent plans in the demand experiment, in which families receive allowances if they pay more than a given percentage of standard housing costs estimated in that city for families of that size. Apparently, this plan rewards families that occupy poor housing bargains.

Finally, the percent of rent plans, which amount to rent rebates, and the unconstrained housing gap plan provide no particular incentive for moving other than rent and income subsidy effects.

The considerations given above apply mainly to the direction of the

19. In all sites, housing costs rise more slowly if one remains stable than if one moves. The estimated rent discount for stability is estimated at as much as 10 percent over five years.

incentives offered by housing allowances and do not consider the question of size. Thus it is clear that for families in the supply experiment whose housing does not meet standards there is some incentive for moving. But the size of that incentive is unclear and presumably varies depending on the particular circumstances faced by the families in question, including such things as tenure, current housing costs, moving costs, involvement in local social networks, and satisfaction with housing.

It should also be noted that once a household has moved to comply with minimum standards, it faces a different incentive structure. There may then be more to be gained from stability than from additional mobility. The positive effects of a housing allowance on mobility ought to be progressively weaker as more and more substandard households come into compliance and hence into the opposite incentive condition. Of course, with periodic inspections and some deterioration of housing over time, some households would always be going out of compliance, providing new recruits for the pool of households whose incentives for moving are positive.

Not only are the plans complicated at the outset, but the distribution of the incentives fluctuates over time, depending on rates of coming into and going out of compliance; these rates are in turn related to the rates of deterioration of the housing stock and the response of households to the incentives offered for moving.

Whether housing allowances provide any incentive for the dispersion of poor families is even less clear a priori. No special location tie-ins are provided in any of the plans in either the supply or the demand experiment. Presumably dispersion would result from the housing allowance policy only if the housing changes induced by the plans implied movement out of areas of concentration at a rate greater than would be expected. If families offered housing allowances have strong motivations to move out of neighborhoods with heavy concentrations of poor people or with heavy racial or ethnic concentrations, then housing allowances may enable them to realize those aspirations, assuming also that the allowances are sufficient for that purpose.

The effects of housing allowances on housing segregation for these reasons cannot be expected to be large and can be expected to occur only if a considerable amount of moving is induced[20] and if moving implies

20. There are also technical problems, especially in the demand experiment, that tend to obscure relocation effects. These problems arise out of the sampling design and are discussed more fully later on.

neighborhood relocation. This double contingency can be expected to keep the desegregation effects small.[21]

The results of the demand experiment are particularly important for assessing the mobility-inducing effects of housing allowances. Ceteris paribus conditions can be estimated fairly well through the use of the controls in Pittsburgh and Phoenix. The supply experiment, in contrast, is not useful in these respects since no controls are available. Ceteris paribus conditions can only be estimated in the supply experiment through heroic assumptions.

The experiments are useful for two purposes in the present discussion. First, the analyses describe mobility processes in the poor and near-poor segments of urban populations in four cities, providing more information on this important segment of the American population than is available in the literature. Second, the experiments evaluate the impact of the housing allowances in their several forms on mobility and population dispersion. Although both experiments are relevant to the first purpose, only the demand experiment provides useful estimates of the housing allowance impact. Hence my discussion will be based on both experiments in the next section and only on the demand experiment in the section following that.

Residential Mobility of the Urban Poor

Although urban poor families have been included in most previously published research on residential mobility, the detailed attention given to this group in the analyses provided by the two experiments has been lacking. MacMillan's report on moving behavior of families during their first two years in the demand experiment provides an excellent prospective analysis.[22] McCarthy's reports, based on prebaseline mobility in Green Bay, Wisconsin, and South Bend, Indiana, as well as Menchik's analysis of allowance recipients in the two sites based on moving during the experimental period, provide data from the supply experiment.[23]

21. A housing allowance program conducted under the model cities program in Kansas City and Wilmington tied receipt of allowances to moving, but found no deconcentration effects in the pattern of resulting moves. See John D. Heinberg, Peggy W. Spohn, and Grace M. Taher, *Housing Allowances in Kansas City and Wilmington: An Appraisal* (Urban Institute, 1975), pp. 36–37.

22. MacMillan, "Draft Report."

23. Kevin F. McCarthy, *Housing Choices and Residential Mobility in Site I at Baseline*, Rand/N-1091-HUD (Rand Corp., October 1979), and *Housing Choices*

Despite the differences in approaches taken, the heterogeneity among the four sites studied, and differences in the ways in which crucial variables were measured, all four studies tend to converge on the same set of generalizations. Even more impressive is the fact that there are no essential differences in the sources of residential mobility in this segment of the urban population compared with more general samples analyzed in existing literature.

MacMillan's analysis is of particular interest because she attempted to employ a version of the microlevel process model of mobility behavior outlined earlier in which a household moves from satisfaction to planning to move, searching for new housing, and finally moving. This analysis is particularly appropriate since it is possible to take advantage of the longitudinal nature of the demand experiment, in which satisfaction and plans are measured at the beginning of the experiment, with search behavior and moving observed over the first two years. MacMillan's analysis shows that the microlevel model is only a rough description of what occurs. First, while fewer than half of the demand experiment households (41 percent in Pittsburgh and 34 percent in Phoenix) were dissatisfied with their housing or their neighborhood at the outset of the experiment, somewhat larger proportions (57 percent in Pittsburgh and 61 percent in Phoenix) were willing to move if they were given an additional $50 a month to spend on rent.[24] About the same proportions engaged in searching at some time during the two years of the experiment (58 percent in Pittsburgh and 70 percent in Phoenix), but smaller proportions eventually moved during that period (37 percent in Pittsburgh and 59 percent in Phoenix).[25] Even more significant, factors predictive of dissatisfaction were also related to plans, search behavior, and moving even after the earlier stages had been held constant. Thus older households were less likely to move even if they had indicated at baseline that they were willing to do so and had engaged in a search during the two years. Dissatisfaction and "propensity to move" acted less like stages in a process than like factors that continue to play roles all through the process, if there was an orderly process.

The inability of MacMillan's analysis to sustain the microlevel process

---

and Residential Mobility in Site II at Baseline, Rand/N-1119-HUD (Rand Corp., October 1979); and Mark David Menchik, *Residential Mobility of Housing Allowance Recipients,* Rand/N-1144-HUD (Rand Corp., October 1979).

24. MacMillan, "Draft Report," pp. 30, 35.

25. Ibid., p. 72.

model should not be taken as proof that the model is faulty. In part, Mac-Millan's test is not a good one since dissatisfaction and moving propensity are measured by single questions at a particular time, whereas the model may be more appropriately specified as a process in which housing satisfaction and propensity to move may change over time and be influenced by inadvertent search behavior, such as noticing a vacancy sign in a desirable apartment house. As in other areas, decision-making models appear to be more complicated empirically than formal a priori models, no matter how convincingly rational they are.

The absence of clear-cut stages leading from dissatisfaction through search behavior to moving has been noted in other studies in which better measures of satisfaction and more elaborate accounts of search behavior were obtained.[26] These findings suggest that the decision-making process concerning moving has not been properly modeled as a set of stages. It appears that simultaneity characterizes at least some of the moving processes, in which satisfaction, search behavior, and moving decisions interact. Also, threshold levels of the decision apparently vary, with older households, for instance, reacting to higher levels of dissatisfaction than younger counterparts. Perhaps some households are always engaging in search behavior and move when a housing bargain is located; in these cases, the discovery triggers dissatisfaction with the old housing unit.

In any event, it is clear that a definitive study of household mobility decision making has yet to appear. The policy relevance of this topic lies in the importance of understanding the characteristics of dwelling units that trigger dissatisfaction and the even stronger possibility of policy that would intervene to facilitate search patterns. A more detailed discussion of the search behavior aspects of the experiments is contained in the comments by Wilhelmina Leigh at the end of this paper.

The analyses based on the supply experiment stress once again the influence of tenure on residential mobility. McCarthy's analysis of pre-experimental moving behavior (based on retrospective accounts of pre-baseline moves) and Menchik's imaginative analysis of expected length of residence both indicate that homeownership is the strongest indicator of stability, even among poor people.[27] For example, once enrolled in the experiment, the expected length of stay was 2.7 years for renters and 18.0 years for homeowners.[28]

26. Rossi, *Why Families Move;* Speare and others, *Residential Mobility;* and Michelson, *Environmental Choice.*

27. Information on this issue is available only from the supply experiment because the demand experiment dealt only with renters.

28. Menchik, *Residential Mobility,* p. 32.

Especially interesting in Menchik's analysis is the use of hazard functions to model length of stay. Hazard function curves are fitted to length of stay data computed over the periods of time families were enrolled in the housing supply experiment; then the curve is used to extrapolate for each household type an expected length of stay that can be projected beyond the period of enrollment. Unfortunately, the expected lengths of stay for homeowners are based on few observations of moves in that category, but the technique appears to be especially appropriate to mobility data.

The approaches taken in measuring life cycle stages differed in the analyses presented of the supply and demand experiments. MacMillan's analyses avoided any attempt to measure stages, using instead age of household head and number of children as well as a dummy variable representing families with single-parent household heads. In contrast, McCarthy's analyses used detailed, categorical classifications based on age of household head, ages of children, and household composition, and Menchik's analyses used a truncated version of McCarthy's life cycle classification. However, despite these differences, findings tend to converge. MacMillan's analyses consistently indicated that age had a strong effect on mobility; the probability of moving declined strongly as the age of household head increased, with each decade of age lowering the probability of moving by 5 percent over two years. Single-parent families, regardless of age, were more likely to move than were intact families (7 percent greater probability of moving over two years).[29] In McCarthy's and Menchik's analyses, households in the later stages of the life cycle were less likely to move than those in the earlier stages, with single-parent households being especially likely to move (or have a shorter duration of stay). MacMillan's findings indicated that number of children played a minor role in moving, a possibly discordant note were it not for the fact that life cycle stages and age are strongly related.[30]

A third set of findings concerns the effect of previous mobility on current mobility. MacMillan found that families that have moved in the recent past are more likely to move again. Similarly, preenrollment length of stay is a significant determinant of postenrollment length of stay. These findings also are consistent with those in previous studies on residential mobility.

29. The probability was computed using logit analysis and evaluated at the mean of the independent variable. MacMillan, "Draft Report," p. 96.
30. Clearly, few households whose heads are over forty-five years old are likely to have children under school age.

Because appropriate data were available in the demand experiment, MacMillan was able to show that subsequent mobility was affected by certain characteristics of the dwelling unit occupied, particularly satisfaction with the dwelling in general and satisfaction with the amount of space in the dwelling. The more dissatisfied a family is in these respects, the more likely it is to move. Comparable data were not available in the supply experiment.

Finally, there were important site differences. Strong differences were noted in the general level of mobility between Phoenix and Pittsburgh: 59 percent of families in Phoenix and 37 percent in Pittsburgh moved during the first two years of the experiment.[31] This difference between the two sites mirrors but also exaggerates the differences between the two regions involved. It is difficult to make much sense of this difference in mobility rates. Various analysts have provided the following explanations: the vacancy rate among rental units is much higher in Phoenix than in Pittsburgh; the costs of moving tend to be higher in Pittsburgh; there are differences in the population composition between the two sites; and there are elusive (and perhaps fictional) "cultural differences."[32]

An ingenious attempt to model the experimental effects is as important as the findings summarized above.[33] The model's conceptual scheme sees mobility as an attempt by households to maximize their housing utilities subject to a budget constraint and their utilities derivable from other goods. Under this model, a household will move if the benefits from moving bring it closer to its desired housing consumption and if the benefits exceed the costs of moving and the increase in costs of the new dwelling.

Estimating the costs and benefits to be derived from moving, Weinberg and his colleagues found that the benefits of moving for low-income households are far smaller than expected. The contours of housing demand among low-income households are such that large changes in

31. Mobility rates are for households that were enrolled and active two years after enrollment and that were not above income-eligibility limits or living in ineligible housing units.

32. Especially intriguing was the finding that the costs of moving were considerably higher in Pittsburgh (Weinberg and others, "Disequilibrium Model," p. 15) and that estimated moving costs were important factors in moving. Expected out-of-pocket moving costs amounted to $61 in Pittsburgh and $16 in Phoenix, with standard deviations small enough to indicate that there was scarcely any overlap in the distributions of the two cities. While it is not clear what causes the differences between sites in these respects, these findings suggest that subsidization of moving costs for poor households may be a relatively powerful stimulant to mobility.

33. Weinberg and others, "Disequilibrium Model."

housing prices and household income result in small changes in household demand for housing. In other words, income and price elasticities for housing for low-income households are small.[34] Because households that do not move to their optimum housing are at least partially compensated for this deficiency by the other goods that they can purchase with the cost savings, the benefit from moving is further decreased. Thus Weinberg and his colleagues estimated that a household spending $150 for rent per month and offered a price rebate of 40 percent (or $60 per month subsidy) can expect a net benefit upon moving of only about $3 per month.

The costs of moving are also a consideration. Weinburg and his colleagues found that many households were paying below-market prices[35] for the housing they occupied, a condition enjoyed because of discounts landlords offered for longer tenure and also because some landlords, out of ignorance, did not charge market rents. In both Phoenix and Pittsburgh, households that moved experienced a larger increase in their rents than those that did not move, while the increase in housing quality enjoyed by movers was not as great proportionately as was the increase in rent. The "good deals" enjoyed by some households are probably lost on moving, more so in Pittsburgh, with its tight housing market, than in Phoenix.

One line of interpretation that flows from these findings goes as follows: within the range of housing quality available to low-income families, few families appear interested in improving quality if offered price discounts or additional income. Other goods and services seem to yield higher utilities.

The nonfindings reported are as significant as the positive findings given above. Perhaps the biggest disappointment from the policy viewpoint was the insensitivity of mobility to the housing characteristics measured in the housing standards test. True enough, families tended to move out of housing that lacked major facilities, but there is apparently a wide range of tolerance for housing defects that are seemingly important to the American Public Health Association[36] but not to these families. Although housing with defects noted in the standards test tended to rent for less, it is apparent either that the rent differences must have com-

34. Estimated price elasticities in Pittsburgh and Phoenix, respectively, were −0.17 and −0.21, and income elasticities were 0.29 and 0.34.

35. Market prices were estimated using hedonic indexes.

36. Standards applied were devised by the American Public Health Association as part of a suggested model housing code for states and communities.

pensated for the inconveniences and lack of amenities involved or that such defects were well below the thresholds triggering dissatisfaction.

While each of the American Public Health Association standards appears to be a reasonable measure of desirable housing features, it is clear that most of the features included in the standard are not essential to a dwelling's status as healthy or habitable. To "fail" a dwelling because of some of the lesser features (for example, too small a window area relative to the floor area in a room) may have been to impose standards that seem unnecessary to the resident. This observation leads to the suggestion that the subsidy offered should have considered quality—that is, a higher subsidy for better housing—or that the acceptability thresholds should have been limited to major defects that most persons would agree make a dwelling uninhabitable.

It is puzzling that dwelling unit characteristics other than those represented in the housing standards applied and the perception of overcrowding are missing in the analyses. After all, mobility concerns housing and its location in space. Perhaps such things as the number of rooms, floor location, presence of elevators in high-rise apartments, distance to schools, work or shopping places, and so on, are not considered relevant to moving by poor people. But perhaps they are. In either event we have learned little about their roles from the experiments.

Housing Allowance Effects on Residential Mobility and Dispersion

The only firm evidence on housing allowance effects on residential mobility comes from the demand experiment. Because of the absence of randomization and hence control observations in the supply experiment, any estimates constructed from data derived from there are necessarily flawed to some unknown degree.[37] Hence this summary draws exclusively on the analyses provided by the Abt Associates researchers and is concerned entirely with the demand experiment results.

37. Nor did the analysts make any serious attempt to estimate the effects of allowances. Although an attempt is made in one of the annual reports issued by Rand (*Fourth Annual Report of the Housing Assistance Supply Experiment*, R-2302-HUD [Rand Corp., May 1978], pp. 122–23) to compare moving rates among housing allowance recipients with moving rates for all households in the two sites, the analysts reported that this comparison cannot be taken seriously because the recipient and enrolled populations differed in important ways (life cycle, income, household composition, and tenure) from the general population of households in both sites.

Table 2. The Effect of the Demand Experiment on Mobility, by Treatment Group[a]

City and type of household	Number of households		Partial derivative of experimental variable[b]
	Experimental	Control	
Pittsburgh			
Total	767	270	0.052 (1.56)
Percent of rent	341	270	0.053 (1.62*)
Housing gap	374	270	0.045 (1.44)
Unconstrained	52	270	0.111 (1.65*)
Phoenix			
Total	567	228	0.096 (3.07**)
Percent of rent	237	228	0.106 (2.95**)
Housing gap	297	228	0.101 (2.77**)
Unconstrained	33	228	0.122 (1.31)

Source: Jean MacMillan, "Draft Report on Mobility in the Housing Allowance Demand Experiment" (Cambridge, Mass.: Abt Associates, June 1978), p. 57.
* Significant at the 0.10 level (two-tailed).
** Significant at the 0.01 level (two-tailed).
a. Partial derivatives from logit estimations of the probability of moving. The sample comprises experimental and control households active at two years after enrollment, excluding those with enrollment incomes over the eligibility limit, those living in their own houses or in subsidized housing, and those that moved between the baseline interview and enrollment.
b. The numbers in parentheses are *t*-statistics.

As suggested in the beginning of this section, the effects of housing allowances were complicated, varying within the constrained plans by whether or not the housing occupied met minimum standards of either housing quality or rent, as appropriate. Overall, experimental households were significantly more likely to move in Phoenix but not in Pittsburgh when compared with the appropriate controls in each site. The experimental effect in Phoenix was calculated to be a 0.096 increase in the probability of moving over a two-year period, while the corresponding increase (not significant) in Pittsburgh was 0.052 (see table 2).

It is difficult to determine whether the experimental effects in Pittsburgh and Phoenix are large or small. From a statistical point of view, the effects are too small to be distinguished from no effect in Pittsburgh and are not much beyond the 0.05 threshold in Phoenix. Compared with

Table 3. The Effect of Compliance with Requirements at Enrollment on the Mobility of Housing Gap Households[a]

City and type of household	Number of households		Partial derivative of experimental variable[b]
	Experimental	Control	
Pittsburgh			
Total	374	270	0.045 (1.44)
Meeting requirements at enrollment	131	87	−0.036 (−0.62)
Not meeting requirements at enrollment	241	182	0.091 (1.94*)
Phoenix			
Total	297	228	0.101 (2.77†)
Meeting requirements at enrollment	80	61	0.128 (1.37)
Not meeting requirements at enrollment	216	167	0.107 (2.51**)

Source: Jean MacMillan, "Draft Report," p. 60. Information is missing on whether some households met requirements.
* Significant at the 0.10 level (two-tailed).
** Significant at the 0.05 level (two-tailed).
† Significant at the 0.01 level (two-tailed).
a. Partial derivatives from logit estimations of the probability of moving.
b. The numbers in parentheses are t-statistics. For Pittsburgh, the t-statistic for the difference in the experimental effect for households that met and did not meet requirements is 1.66*; for Phoenix, it is 0.20.

the overall mobility rates in the control groups in those two cities (35 and 53 percent moving over the two-year period in Pittsburgh and Phoenix, respectively), the experimental effects appear larger (an 18 percent relative increase in Phoenix and a 15 percent relative increase in Pittsburgh).[38] These differences are considerably greater than the annual variations in the mobility rates for the United States, as shown in table 1.

The overall effects of the experiment, as shown above, are not as interesting as the differential effects according to the specific plans used in the demand experiment. Since sample sizes at this point tended to become small, especially for some of the plans, the estimates of effects often bordered on statistical insignificance. The percent of rent treatment turned out to have significant effects both in Pittsburgh (0.053) and in Phoenix (0.106), indicating some degree of sensitivity to housing prices. As shown in table 3, the housing gap plans that imposed constraints of either minimum standards or minimum rent produced significant increments of

38. MacMillan, "Draft Report," p. A-39.

moving in both sites among households not meeting requirements at enrollment. This plan also apparently reinforced residential stability among those whose initial housing met requirements, an effect that was especially strong in Pittsburgh. Finally, families on the unconstrained plans (whose payments may be regarded as ordinary income transfers) were more likely to move than were the controls, a difference that is significant in Pittsburgh (see table 2). This last finding reflects an income effect on moving.[39]

It should be mentioned that the results shown in table 3 may be incorrect estimates of the effects of payments on mobility. The classification of households into those that met or did not meet housing requirements, as shown in the table, is as of the time of enrollment. As mentioned earlier, a household's classification changes over the course of the experiment depending on housing deterioration and recertification and on the household's moves. Thus a household that did not meet requirements at enrollment and moved after six months to a dwelling that met requirements was in the condition that favored moving for only six months and in the condition that did not favor moving for the remaining eighteen months of the experiment. A measure that would be more sensitive to the incentives offered by the plans would reckon the probability of moving per unit of time exposed to a given set of experimentally imposed incentives. Since moves occur both into and out of experimental conditions that offer incentives for moving, it is difficult to assess a priori whether the movements occurring in the two years of the demand experiment balanced each other out or whether a reanalysis along the lines suggested would show that mobility was over- or underestimated in the calculations of table 3.

Several observations can be made about the findings in table 2. First, the effects tend to be similar in sign in Pittsburgh and in Phoenix. Second, the effects tend to be higher in Phoenix than in Pittsburgh, possibly reflecting the greater ease in making residential shifts in a city where the vacancy rate is higher. Third, there appears to be little difference among the plans,

39. The similarity in findings between the demand experiment and the mobility-inducing effects of general income maintenance as found in the Denver income maintenance experiment suggests that despite efforts to tie housing allowances to housing quality, about the same level of mobility can be achieved by general income maintenance payments. James C. Ohls and Cynthia Thomas, "The Effects of the Seattle and Denver Income Maintenance Experiments on Housing Consumption, Ownership, and Mobility," Draft Report (Denver: Mathematica Policy Research, January 1979), pp. 44–45.

with the major exception of the stabilizing effect of the housing gap plan occurring under the conditions that enrollment housing met the housing standards. Finally, the results indicate that it is possible to stimulate a small increment in residential mobility by providing either additional income or rent subsidy. The obverse is that it is also possible to promote residential stability by tying income payments to housing standards, provided, of course, that housing occupied meets those standards. In short, housing allowance plans are viable policies, if increased residential mobility or stability is desired. Whether these plans are efficient policies is clearly problematic.

After mobility, the other major issue in the Experimental Housing Allowance Program experiments is the extent to which housing allowances tend to promote economic and racial and ethnic deconcentration. Presumably such plans would accomplish this by making it possible for poor families to afford more expensive housing in less concentrated neighborhoods. The analyses made of the demand experiment data and reported by Atkinson, Hamilton, and Myers[40] can be summarized briefly, as follows: when experimental households are compared with controls in either Pittsburgh or Phoenix, there appears to be no tendency for experimental households to move more frequently into areas of lesser concentration of poor persons or their own racial-ethnic groups. Hopes or fears that white flight to the suburbs would be encouraged or that blacks and Chicanos would break out of their ghettos appear to be groundless, at least from the demand experiment results. Nor do housing allowances appear to be a way to achieve residential integration along class or ethnic lines.[41]

While this summary of findings about residential location decribes the analyses performed, it should be noted that the demand experiment is not the best means for testing the integrative possibilities of housing allowances. First, the clustered sampling plan used in locating a sample of eligible households systematically excluded from consideration poor families in locations occupied largely by relatively affluent families. While

40. Reilly Atkinson, William Hamilton, and Dowell Myers, "Draft Report on Economic and Racial/Ethnic Concentration in the Housing Allowance Demand Experiment" (Abt, January 1979).

41. Nor does this finding appear to depend on the low level of additional mobility fostered by the housing allowances. As indicated earlier, a demonstration of housing allowances in which moving was a condition for payments, thereby stimulating more mobility, did not result in greater deconcentration. See Heinberg and others, *Housing Allowances in Kansas City and Wilmington*, pp. 36–37.

census tracts are mostly homogeneous, they are not entirely so, and some poor families live within most of the tracts that are affluent according to central tendencies. Indeed, it is families that have managed on their own to break out of the ghettos of race-ethnicity or poverty whose behavior in response to housing allowance plans may be most interesting; such allowances possibly permit them to retain their residential locations. Second, the numbers involved in the two experiments are simply too small to make firm estimates of locational tendencies. Possible destinations are large in number and sample members tend to be diluted in analyses. Finally, the use of 1970 census tract data to characterize moves taking place in the mid-1970s makes errors in measurement likely, especially in expanding Phoenix. Such errors work both ways: origin neighborhoods and destination neighborhoods may both be incorrectly classified. For example, some moves classified as moves from concentrated to integrated neighborhoods may not be correctly classified, because the destination neighborhood changed drastically between the 1970 census and the move.

The design and measurement defects pointed out above affect experimental and control families equally. The measurement errors, of course, tend to confuse the comparisons between the two groups and hence lessen the power of the experiment to detect real experimental effects. Perhaps the best that can be said at this point is that the locational effects of housing allowances, if any, are not strong enough to overcome design and measurement error.

Policy Implications

Social policy interest in residential mobility is not in the moves themselves but in the resulting redistribution of housing quality and in the redistribution of population. Mobility that improves the quality of the housing occupied by poor people and that effects a deconcentration of the poor and racial-ethnic minorities is clearly of primary policy interest. While it is clear from the review of the experimental findings that housing allowances can induce more moves than would have occurred without a program, it is not clear that the resulting shifts appreciably increased the quality of housing occupied by poor people. Certainly families recruited into the housing gap plans whose enrollment housing did not qualify them for payments were induced to move, presumably into acceptable housing that was better in some sense than the housing initially occupied.

We have to look into other analyses of the Experimental Housing Allowance Program data for information that would definitively determine whether the induced mobility under the housing gap or other plans produced enough change upward in housing quality to justify housing allowances as compared to more general income transfers.[42]

As for the locational redistributional effects of the housing allowance plans, the data are not free enough from design and measurement defects to provide definitive answers. Certainly the redistributional effects, if any, are likely to be slight. Hence, as an instrument of social policy promoting economic and racial-ethnic integration, the housing allowance program appears to be weak.[43]

In short, if housing allowances are to succeed in getting the poor out of inadequate housing and ghettos, the proper method is not to induce large amounts of additional residential mobility.

Comments by Wilhelmina A. Leigh[44]

A reading of relevant reports from the Experimental Housing Allowance Program leaves me substantially in agreement with Peter H. Rossi's conclusions. The definition of mobility and his review of the research findings on mobility were useful and comprehensive. His use of current population survey data to describe national mobility trends also provides a helpful framework for discussion. Reference to an ambivalence in federal policy and its manifestation in the Experimental Housing Allowance Program is certainly germane to an evaluation of this experiment.

Rossi relied heavily on the findings from the housing allowance demand experiment to take advantage of differentials reported between the behavior of experimental and control group households. He noted that the eligibility requirements of the demand experiment had shaped the

42. See the papers in this volume by Hanushek and Quigley and by Aaron.

43. Of course, the critical issue may be, "compared to what?" Housing allowances may be the best means of producing this redistributional end because nothing else works any better.

44. The work that provided the basis for these comments was supported by funding under a grant from the Department of Housing and Urban Development. The substance and findings of that work are dedicated to the public. The author is solely responsible for the accuracy of the statements and interpretations contained in this article, and such interpretations do not necessarily reflect the views of the government.

distribution of enrolled families and thereby strongly conditioned the mobility patterns observed. Also, only 63 percent of all eligible households applied for the program. The more mobile black households tended to leave the demand experiment before the end of its first two years. These facts suggest that a self-selection process may have gone on within the demand experiment, due in part to the knowledge that this was only a short-term, experimental program. Whatever its cause, the result for race and income groupings is very small subsamples on which to base subsequent mobility analyses. I think it is important that such a constraint be acknowledged before further discussion of search and mobility trends observed in the program.

Although the subject to be covered in Rossi's paper was mobility and search behavior implications of the Experimental Housing Allowance Program, search behavior was neglected. Also, the trade-off between upgrading in place and moving made by potential recipients was not fully addressed. These topics will be covered below, based on findings from the demand experiment, the supply experiment, and the administrative agency experiment. The first section discusses search behavior, as characterized both before and by the Experimental Housing Allowance Program. The next section expands on other points of interest regarding search and mobility behavior; the trade-off between upgrading in place and moving is covered there. The final section states conclusions from this commentary.

Search Behavior Implications

The theoretical and empirical findings from the general research on household search behavior will be presented first. Because the literature has developed primarily around home buyers' search behavior, the results of the supply experiment, which enrolled both owners and renters, are especially comparable to previous findings. These and other program findings on search behavior will be presented and compared with the results obtained from the broader literature evaluation. Whether or not household characteristics condition the search behavior will be examined, with special attention given to racial differences and the role that discrimination, either real or perceived, plays in creating these differences.

Donald Hempel defines three dimensions of the home purchaser's search process: length of time, number and type of information sources, and the degree of the searcher's active participation.[45] The basic sources of information during the search are (1) friends, relatives, and business associates; (2) real estate agencies; (3) mass media; (4) signs on or directing searchers to a particular location; (5) banks and lending institutions; and (6) builders and contractors. Hempel found that families with annual incomes of less than $10,000 rely more on friends and relatives, newspapers, and personal inspection to locate houses than do families in the $10,000 to $15,000 income bracket. The following socioeconomic characteristics were noted by other researchers to increase the intensity of the search or the active participation of the searcher in the process.[46]

- Consumer is in the middle-income (as opposed to the high- or low-income) class.
- Consumer has a college education.
- Consumer is under thirty-five years of age.
- Consumer's education would place him or her in the white-collar occupational class.

In his 1955 mobility study based on data from Philadelphia neighborhoods, Rossi noted differentials in the type of information sources used by lower and upper socioeconomic status renters in their search. Lower-status renters found places mainly through personal contact and direct search, whereas upper-status renters used newspapers and real estate agents more effectively.[47]

In a 1971 study of 137 black and 156 white families matched by income who were searching for housing in Knoxville, Tennessee, Neufeld and Kenney made several useful findings about racial differentials in the search process.[48] Categories of information to assist in the search were newspaper ads, driving around, friends and relatives, real estate agents,

45. Donald J. Hempel, *Search Behavior and Information Utilization in the Home Buying Process* (Center for Real Estate and Urban Economic Studies, University of Connecticut, 1969), as cited in George Sternlieb and W. Patrick Beaton, "The Housing Hunt: An Analysis of Buyer Behavior and Market Structure in Light of Recent Research," in U.S. Department of Housing and Urban Development, *Housing in the Seventies: Working Papers,* vol. 1 (GPO, 1976), pp. 362, 369.

46. James F. Engel, David T. Kollat, and Roger D. Blackwell, *Consumer Behavior* (Holt, Rinehart and Winston, 1968), as cited in Sternlieb and Beaton, "Housing Hunt," p. 362.

47. Rossi, *Why Families Move,* p. 162.

48. J. L. Neufeld and K. B. Kenney, *The Lack of Relation Between Race and Housing Costs: A Case Study of Knoxville, Tennessee* (Civil Defense Project, Oak Ridge National Laboratory, 1971), as cited in Sternlieb and Beaton, "Housing Hunt," exhibit 12, pp. 369–70.

rental agents (renters only), and current landlords (renters only). They found that the largest percentage of black searchers in any category (34 percent) found information from friends and relatives of most use in finding their present homes; the largest percentage in the distribution of information sources for white households, 30 percent, found driving around to see what was available of most use. In addition, 11 percent of black families and 28 percent of white families said newspaper ads were of most use in finding their present homes; this category reflected the largest difference by race. Although both blacks and whites relied very little on real estate and rental agents, the percentages of blacks doing so (16 percent and 4 percent, respectively) were greater than the percentages of whites relying on agents (11 percent and 0.7 percent, respectively).

The supply experiment baseline studies in Brown County, Wisconsin, and St. Joseph County, Indiana, indicate that housing search behavior is strongly conditioned by income and the probability of encountering discrimination (either because of race or because of children). Low-income renters are reluctant to search the market thoroughly because prospective landlords often respond negatively to their age, marital status, race, family composition, or source of income.[49] This result is generally consistent with the finding noted above that income level affects the intensity of the search, with those at either the lower or upper extremes making less of a search effort. Another finding from the supply experiment is that housing bargains are usually acquired through personal contact rather than through diligent search.

Under the administrative agency experiment (for renters) in Jacksonville, Florida, difficulties were encountered in enrolling the desired number of participants because black households were reluctant to search in other than predominantly black neighborhoods; this reluctance stemmed from fear of discriminatory practices in other parts of the city. Their reluctance limited their enrollment because the housing stock in the predominantly black neighborhoods was of poorer quality than in the rest of the city. Searching in only the black neighborhoods of Jacksonville also suggests the reliance of blacks on personal contacts, as noted in the Neufeld and Kenney study of Knoxville. Many of these contacts are probably black and are knowledgeable only of the same areas in the segregated housing market.

49. Ira S. Lowry, *A Topical Guide to HASE Research,* Rand/N-1215-HUD (Rand Corp., June 1979), pp. 32–33.

The findings on search behavior from the demand experiment cited here are based on Vidal's analysis of Pittsburgh data.[50] Newspapers, real estate agents, vacancy signs, and friends and relatives are the information sources used to facilitate search in the demand experiment. The caveat about dangerously small sample sizes certainly applies to all the results by race from Pittsburgh.

It was found that blacks in Pittsburgh concentrated their housing search in predominantly black neighborhoods and in neighborhoods with clusters of black residents. This was true regardless of the information source used by black households. Since only one of the four socioeconomic characteristics cited above that positively affect the intensity of search (that the consumer is under thirty-five years of age) is possessed by sizable numbers of black households, it is consistent both with previous research findings and with the legacy of racial discrimination that blacks would limit the scope and intensity of their search. The neighborhoods chosen by black households that moved reflect the restricted set of neighborhoods in which they searched.

The information sources used by blacks and whites were not equally effective. Although friends and relatives were the information source used most frequently by both black and white households searching for housing in the demand experiment, black searchers were significantly less likely to move into a dwelling located in this manner than were white searchers. This result conflicts with the finding of Neufeld and Kenney that the information source category of most use to blacks in locating their present homes was "friends and other personal contacts."

Presumably because personal contacts were less effective for blacks than for whites, blacks in the Pittsburgh demand experiment were more dependent than whites on real estate agents and vacancy signs. This is again slightly inconsistent with a Neufeld and Kenney finding that blacks relied more heavily on real estate agents than whites did but that this reliance was not because personal contacts were ineffective. This demand experiment finding also conflicts with the results from Rossi's Philadelphia study, in which upper-status renters were found to have relied more heavily on real estate agents than did lower-status renters. The exclusion from Rossi's study of areas with heavy black or foreign-born white populations may temper this finding and render its conflict with the demand experiment result less serious.

50. Avis Vidal, "Draft Report on the Search Behavior of Black Households in Pittsburgh in the Housing Allowance Demand Experiment" (Abt, July 1978).

Later in the Rossi study, the use of certain information sources is related to the types of areas in which one is searching.[51] For instance, if black households in Pittsburgh are searching in locations similar to the low-status areas of Philadelphia, their greater reliance on vacancy signs is appropriate. Houses for rent or sale in such areas rarely are advertised in newspapers and even less frequently in the multiple listing service. These houses can best be acquired by a search process that relies upon signs seen from the street.

What conclusions can be drawn about the search behavior implications of the Experimental Housing Allowance Program? First, the program analyses reflect the search behavior of both owners and renters, whereas much of the earlier research with which it is compared reflects findings only of home purchasers. Second, the most striking program finding is that blacks make use of the formal market search information sources more than whites, even though they limit this search to predominantly black and cluster black neighborhoods. The final conclusion is that, given the small likelihood of making personal contacts work more effectively to widen the range of search of blacks and to secure housing that would enable them to enroll in a housing allowance program in greater numbers, efforts should be directed toward making the formal market mechanisms (real estate agents, vacancy signs, and newspaper ads) work even more effectively for blacks. Such a mission is more difficult to satisfactorily achieve now than it might have been five or ten years ago, because discriminatory practices within the formal housing market have become more sophisticated and subtle and therefore more difficult to counteract.

Other Issues

Three issues are discussed in this section. The first is the influence of household and market characteristics on mobility. The second issue is factors underlying the choice between upgrading in place and moving to gain recipient status in the program. The final area is that of neighborhood changes due to the program. Rossi has addressed all but the second issue; thus, this commentary is largely an elaboration of his analysis.

HOUSEHOLD CHARACTERISTICS AND MOBILITY. As Rossi noted, a major program result—that life cycle factors, general dissatisfaction with the dwelling, and dissatisfaction with the amount of space in the dwelling

51. Rossi, *Why Families Move*, p. 172.

are the primary determinants of mobility—is consistent with the findings of other research. Rossi also notes the ambiguity of previous research findings on the impact of income on mobility patterns. In an effort to shed further light in this gray area, research other than that cited by Rossi is discussed, and these findings are contrasted to those from both the supply and demand experiments.

Elizabeth Roistacher, in an analysis based on the Panel Study of Income Dynamics, found that the strongest predictors of mobility are age (a life cycle factor) and initial ownership status.[52] She also noted that those households experiencing the most extreme changes in income or family size (either increases or decreases) were more likely to move than those with only moderate changes.

In a study of homesteading neighborhoods, Ann B. Schnare found that high-income owners and low-income renters had the greatest tendencies to move.[53] A finding from the supply experiment in Brown County corroborates Schnare's finding. McCarthy, in his baseline analysis, shows that higher-income households (that is, those earning $15,000 or more) are more likely to have mortgages than are lower-income households at all stages of the life cycle.[54] This can be interpreted to reflect the greater willingness of those owners with higher incomes to move in order to equilibrate their housing and their needs. It could also simply reflect the greater ease with which the wealthier acquire mortgages or perhaps the duration of mortgages in general.

Further evidence from the supply experiment in both Brown and St. Joseph counties concurs with earlier research findings on the importance to mobility of life cycle factors and carves out another role for income in the housing equilibration process. From baseline surveys in both counties, it is noted that the pattern of space adjustment (a primary reason for moving) over the household life cycle is unaffected by income. Life cycle stage is found to be more important to explain differences in the

52. Elizabeth Roistacher, "Residential Mobility," in James N. Morgan, ed., *Five Thousand American Families—Patterns of Economic Progress,* vol. 2: *Special Studies of the First Five Years of the Panel Study of Income Dynamics* (University of Michigan, Institute for Social Research, 1974), p. 50.

53. Ann B. Schnare, *Household Mobility in Urban Homesteading Neighborhoods: Implications for Displacement* (Washington, D.C.: Urban Systems Research and Engineering, 1979), p. 30.

54. McCarthy, *Housing Choices and Residential Mobility in Site I at Baseline,* p. 47.

types and sizes of dwellings occupied, while income is more important to explain how much is spent for housing.

MARKET CHARACTERISTICS AND MOBILITY. Several housing market characteristics can be expected to affect household mobility. The ones to be covered here are discrimination in all forms, the type of housing stock available, the market vacancy rate, and house prices.

As noted in the section on search behavior, discrimination against households on any grounds proscribes search and ultimately limits household mobility. Discrimination on the basis of race, presence of children, sex of household head, and sources of income were noted above. Another type of discrimination that can limit the mobility of any household is difficulty in getting mortgage financing.

The type of housing stock in a given neighborhood can be especially crucial to mobility patterns. If only single-family houses that are not suitable for subdivision and too saleable to be rented exist in a given neighborhood, the mobility of renters in an adjacent neighborhood, for whom this would be a logical area of search, could be limited. This of course depends on the distance from their neighborhoods that households are willing to search.

The following scenario from the supply experiment in St. Joseph County illustrates how vacancy rates and house prices could interact to affect mobility rates. St. Joseph County has a high vacancy rate and low house sale prices. Partly because of this, 40 percent of the young singles in St. Joseph County (but only 6.5 percent of the young singles in Brown County, the other supply experiment site) own homes.[55] This could lead to an expectation of lessened mobility among St. Joseph County residents relative to Brown County residents because a large proportion of young singles, usually a very mobile population subgroup, have become owners, usually a rather nonmobile status. On the other hand, this could lead to the expectation of increased mobility if the young singles status and behavior dominates that of the homeownership status.

In concluding this discussion of housing market characteristics and their influence on mobility, the finding by Rossi that national trends in migration and mobility are insensitive to major events and trends in the economy and the housing market must be mentioned. Disaggregation to a smaller geographic level than current population survey data allow would

55. McCarthy, *Housing Choices . . . Site II*, p. 20.

probably reveal a sensitivity of mobility to housing market conditions. The differential mobility rates for households in the demand experiment in Pittsburgh and Phoenix could be indicative of this.

MOVING VERSUS UPGRADING IN PLACE. The prevalence of moving versus upgrading in place can be examined by using evidence from the supply experiment, the administrative agency experiment, and the demand experiment. In the supply experiment, about two-thirds of the households whose dwellings initially did not meet the standards requirements upgraded in place, one-tenth moved, and one-fifth terminated without qualifying for payments.[56] Data on client requests for evaluation of other units suggest that occupants of unacceptable dwellings decided on their next actions (to repair, move, or terminate) without much exploration of alternatives.

After the first year of the administrative agency experiment, moves were more prevalent than upgrading. Forty-five percent of the recipients in eight administrative agency experiment sites moved within three months of acceptance into the program.[57] In the demand experiment, among minimum standards households not meeting the standards at enrollment, upgrading was chosen over moving in Phoenix and Pittsburgh by 30 percent and 45 percent, respectively, of the households that met the requirements some time after enrollment.[58]

Several conclusions can be drawn about the prevalence of upgrading in place versus moving. In the supply experiment, upgrading appears to dominate moving, and the enrollment of owners (that is, those with lower mobility rates) in this part of the experiment no doubt affects this outcome. In the administrative agency experiment and the demand experiment, both of which are for renters only, moving appears to be the dominant form of adjustment.[59]

How does the initial unit condition appear to affect the choice between moving and upgrading? The supply experiment found that the worst dwellings are the least likely to be repaired. The proportion of enrollees

56. Bruce W. Lamar and Ira S. Lowry, *Client Responses to Housing Requirements: The First Two Years,* Rand/WN-9814-HUD (Rand Corp., 1979), p. v.

57. U.S. Department of Housing and Urban Development, *Housing Allowances: The 1976 Report to Congress* (GPO, 1976), p. 31.

58. Sally R. Merrill and Catherine A. Joseph, "Draft Report on Housing Improvements and Upgrading in the Housing Allowance Demand Experiment" (Abt, February 1979), p. S-3.

59. The finding for the administrative agency experiment is based on only a year's worth of data.

who move rather than repair rises sharply with the number of postevaluation defects noted. The number of housing defects was found to be related to both tenure and age of head; it is this relationship that may partly explain the pattern of response. For instance, homeowners generally have fewer defects in their units and are less likely to move and more likely to upgrade than renters. On the other hand, the elderly also generally have fewer defects in their homes and are less likely to move and more likely to upgrade than are the nonelderly.

Similar findings emerged from the demand experiment. Upgrading was generally concentrated in better-quality units and usually involved small changes to units with no above-normal rent increases. As one would expect, upgrading rather than moving was found to be the route to participation chosen by those households for which it was a relatively inexpensive means of meeting program requirements. A logit regression analysis reveals the following statistically significant (at 0.10 level or better) determinants of the probability of upgrading: satisfaction with neighborhood and unit, number of persons per room, quality of each room, distance from meeting minimum standards (that is, number of physical components failed), and number of moves made in the preceding three years.[60] Three of these five significant explanators relate to unit condition. One could thereby conclude that initial unit condition does affect the choice between moving and upgrading in place.

Do movers improve the quality of housing consumed overall or do they improve only those dimensions required by the Experimental Housing Allowance Program? There is little evidence to address these questions. Since both landlords and tenants in the demand experiment normally make repair and maintenance expenditures without the program incentives and since additional maintenance and repair expenditures are not made when program enrollment is sought, it is assumed that there is a refocusing of the normal maintenance and repair expenditures away from other things to satisfy the program housing requirements. A report on the housing gap form of housing allowance notes that the existence of housing requirements caused the affected households to focus housing changes directly on meeting these requirements and thereby resulted in, as one would expect, a much larger proportion of housing gap households meeting housing standards than did households receiving the unconstrained income transfer under the demand experiment.

60. Merrill and Joseph, "Draft Report," p. 39.

NEIGHBORHOOD CHANGES DUE TO THE PROGRAM. As Rossi stated, the effects on neighborhoods of household mobility responses to the Experimental Housing Allowance Program have been very limited. The fourth annual report on the supply experiment noted that although three out of four moves cross neighborhood boundaries, the net effect on neighborhoods is small. Only a few neighborhoods at each site gained or lost ten or more households because of moves by participants. Only the worst neighborhoods in each site lost program participants, and these participants moved, on balance, to better neighborhoods.

Because the program does so little to alter the residential patterns in neighborhoods, it is worth determining the prevailing patterns that it can be deemed to complement de facto. Again in St. Joseph County, it was determined that local movers were forsaking older central parts of South Bend and Mishawaka, Indiana, to settle in outlying areas. By not altering this trend, the program probably contributes to a continuation of the trend, whereby central neighborhoods are losers and outlying neighborhoods are gainers of households in a given metropolitan area.

If the life cycle theory for neighborhoods (that is, neighborhoods themselves go through stages of stability, change, and deterioration) is invoked in light of the above findings, it might stimulate one to try to ascertain what mix of neighborhoods, in terms of life cycles, had been selected for the program. If an equal number of stable and deteriorating neighborhoods had been fortuitously selected, the geographical balance of movers between areas could have this selection as a partial explanation.

As for mobility effects on neighborhood homogeneity or on segregation by race and income, when the experimental and control households from the demand experiment in Pittsburgh and Phoenix are compared, there is no statistically significant trend for experimental households to move more frequently than control households into areas of lesser concentration of either poor households or of racial or ethnic groups. Vidal noted explicitly that the demand experiment did little to alter patterns of residential segregation by race in Pittsburgh. In another study based on the demand experiment, Atkinson and others warned that small sample sizes made it difficult to confidently evaluate differences between control group and experimental movers by race and income.[61]

Results from the supply experiment in St. Joseph County indicate that at most the program may have slightly speeded up black dispersion and

61. Atkinson and others, "Draft Report on Economic and Racial/Ethnic Concentration."

white retreat within central South Bend. The additional finding for St. Joseph County that over 40 percent of the white and minority owners prefer to live in neighborhoods with others like themselves[62] suggests that lessening the extreme homogeneity by race and income at that site would be difficult.

Conclusions

The Experimental Housing Allowance Program has taught us about the nature of housing market search and mobility, even though it has done little to alter the patterns normally observed. We now know essentially what the program does *not* do. By inference, we can determine what it does accomplish and use this knowledge to restructure its incentive system to meet policy goals.

To reiterate a point made by Rossi, this program is one of several currently funded HUD programs that suffer from an ambivalence in federal policy with regard to two objectives—stabilization of neighborhoods and deconcentration of poor and minority group populations. As currently designed and operated, the program does little to achieve either objective. However, if it were redesigned and if a different incentive system were incorporated into its enrollment criteria, either of the above objectives could be supported explicitly. An example of such an incentive scheme is the use of bonuses, above the regular program payments, to steer searchers to or from designated neighborhoods.

It is important that the federal government assess the information on residential search and mobility provided by the Experimental Housing Allowance Program from the perspective of its primary future policy objectives. It is even more important that any subsequent housing allowance program be clearly structured with a tilt toward achieving these goals and objectives.

62. McCarthy, *Housing Choices . . . Site II*, p. ix.

ERIC A. HANUSHEK

JOHN M. QUIGLEY

Consumption Aspects

This volume documents the public expenditure of more than $163 million to analyze the behavioral impact and housing market implications of specific economic incentives that were intended to improve housing quality for low-income households. Analysis of the rich experimental data generated by responses to varying housing subsidies can potentially increase our understanding of complicated consumption decisions and reduce uncertainty about the impact of a range of social policies. This paper reviews and evaluates the currently available research from the Experimental Housing Allowance Program, with particular emphasis on analyses of housing consumption and quality improvement induced by housing allowances.

The notion of a housing allowance policy represents the confluence of two distinct social programs. Since the 1930s the quality and availability of adequate housing has been the subject of active federal concern. Through public housing programs and a variety of construction subsidies, the government has sought to ensure "safe and decent" housing for the poor.[1] At the same time, a variety of income transfer entitlement programs that are only tangentially related to housing concerns have emerged. A housing allowance program brings the two types of programs together.

A major criticism of current housing programs is the inequity caused by the limited availability of subsidized units, so that equally needy households actually receive different subsidies. Further, the limited supply of

This paper has benefited from comments and suggestions by C. Lance Barnett, Katharine L. Bradbury, Marc Bendick, Jr., Francis J. Cronin, Anthony Downs, Jerry J. Fitts, Joseph Friedman, Stephen D. Kennedy, Ira S. Lowry, and Daniel Weinberg.

1. See the paper by Henry J. Aaron in this volume for a discussion of different goals of housing programs.

subsidized units, along with the incentives built into the various program structures, has meant that the most needy—usually defined in income terms—are frequently not the first served. This has led to the charge that the programs are inefficient because they do not accurately target subsidies according to need.[2]

Existing income-entitlement programs, which also focus on the welfare of the poor, have been subject to a different criticism. The incentive structure built in through eligibility rules can cause substantial work disincentives. These disincentives are magnified by complicated interactions among different income and in-kind support programs where combined eligibility rules often imply very high marginal tax rates on earnings.

These criticisms have led to reform movements both in the housing and the welfare areas. The inequities of past housing programs suggest targeting subsidies to needy families, that is, providing entitlement subsidies to housing demanders based on need criteria. The work disincentives of welfare plans have led to suggestions of a negative income tax, designed to eliminate notches in payment schedules and in general to reduce marginal tax rates on work income. The housing allowance plan, as applied in the experiments, has integrated reforms suggested for both areas; it takes the basic structure of a negative income tax plan and modifies it into a "housing" program. Subsidy levels are scaled to reflect either (1) household income and the cost of decent housing in different regions of the country or (2) housing expenditures. More important, however, household eligibility for a subsidy is related to actual housing choices through a complex set of entitlement rules or housing restrictions.

The immediate reaction of most economists, schooled in notions of consumer sovereignty, is, "Why not just give money?" The answer to this question seems twofold. First, a program tied to housing conditions, which has ample historical precedent, might be politically more feasible than a pure cash transfer. Donor sovereignty is not inconsistent with paternalism. Second, there may be important external factors in housing consumption that warrant overriding recipients' choices. These externalities may include neighborhood effects on the nonpoor, such as reduced

2. These programs have also been labeled inefficient in a different sense: to the extent that they directly subsidize new construction, such programs tend to cost more per quality-equivalent unit than subsidies that use existing units. See Stephen Mayo and others, "Draft Report on Housing Allowances and Other Rental Housing Assistance Programs—A Comparison Based on the Housing Allowance Demand Experiment," pt. 2: "Costs and Efficiency" (Cambridge, Mass.: Abt Associates, August 1979).

neighborhood housing values or even visual and aesthetic effects. Even though the housing allowance experiments are not designed to answer fundamental normative questions, the research should support evaluation in the contexts of these different purposes.

A crucial issue in evaluation involves the kinds of housing restrictions imposed under a housing allowance plan. If the restrictions are very loose (or nonexistent), the program is simply a negative income tax program with special features: a "housing gap" transfer recognizes regional cost of living differences as reflected in local housing prices; and a "percent of rent" transfer recognizes individual differences in tastes for housing. In the situation where housing restrictions are initially binding for a proportion of the population, households that already meet the restrictions— those who previously expressed a taste for "standard housing"—again receive a simple income transfer. For households that do not initially meet the standards but subsequently adjust to meet them, the program looks like a combination of a pure transfer program and an in-kind benefits program; the pure income transfer equals the gross transfer payment less the cost of upgrading to meet the standards.

There are four crucial issues in considering the housing restrictions. (1) Do the restrictions adequately reflect the goals of the housing program? (2) How binding are the restrictions in terms of the proportion of eligible households that initially fail the standards? (3) How much upgrading of housing is induced by the program? (4) How does recipient behavior compare under transfer programs with different restrictions?

As particular requirements become more binding, and as less upgrading by eligible households is induced, a housing allowance program incorporating restrictive standards looks more like a general welfare or income transfer program, with eligibility based on household tastes for a given type of housing. The inequities of past housing programs, determined by supply constraints on available units, are replaced by inequalities determined by housing tastes. The key difference, of course, is that housing tastes are not immutable; they can be overridden by sufficiently strong incentives. The effectiveness of any specific form of housing allowance, gauged either as a welfare program or as a housing program, relates directly to housing restrictions and behavioral responses.

The massive effort at data collection and analysis sponsored by the Department of Housing and Urban Development (HUD) provides the raw material for comparing alternative forms of housing allowance programs. The behavior of recipient households, made in response to various program incentives, can be compared with the behavior of control households, and such comparisons can be made across quite different local markets.

The scope of this chapter is, however, somewhat narrower than "What happened?" The primary focus is what we have learned about households' consumption choices for housing, measured in either expenditure or quality terms, and how these choices might be modified by different forms of housing allowances. In this, we compare and contrast the behavioral results generated by the experimental programs of the housing allowance supply and demand experiments.[3] The discussion considers the specific analyses conducted by the researchers at Abt Associates, the Urban Institute, and the Rand Corporation, along with the strengths and limitations of the overall experimental design. Finally, to a lesser extent, we also consider research on housing decisions under unconstrained subsidies as analyzed by Mathematica Policy Research for the Seattle and Denver income maintenance experiments.

Although the sheer volume of research reports, conference papers, and working papers is intimidating, it is also highly unbalanced, and this affects the form and content of our discussion. At one extreme, the reports available on the demand experiment are unusually detailed and meticulous examples of applied research. Virtually every inference teased from the data is subjected to some form of sensitivity analysis and evaluated for potential bias; each investigation is faithfully reported in one of the many appendixes to the reports. From these (but within the limits imposed by the experimental design, inherent data problems, and the existing economic models and statistical methods employed by the researchers), some statements can be made with reasonable confidence. At the other extreme, little analytical (as opposed to descriptive) information is yet available from the supply experiment, although it has been in operation for more than seven years. Presumably this difference in currently available analysis reflects variations in timing and data collection between the supply and demand experiments.[4] Nevertheless, regardless of the

3. The administrative agency experiment did not focus on participant behavior and therefore is not relevant to this discussion.
4. The supply experiment has more of the character of a demonstration than of an experiment. Since the experiment saturated the housing markets, there is no control group to provide comparisons of what would be expected without subsidies. Further, since there was no variation in the subsidy plan, there is no way of identifying the impact of the subsidy per se. While such an experiment may be useful for analysis of administrative activities, any analyses of participation or consumption are conditional on the specific subsidy plan, and there is no clear way of inferring how this plan modifies behavior.

reasons for this disparity, our discussion must focus less than we would have hoped on the supply experiment, which has consumed two-thirds of all research expenditures.

The plan of the paper is as follows. Building on the textbook case of the competitive market, we investigate the effect of pure income and price subsidies on household behavior. While the analysis gets more complicated and problematic when departures from the textbook case are recognized, it nevertheless provides a standard of comparison. The next sections review the estimated behavioral responses to allowance programs that impose restrictions on the physical character of the housing consumed by recipients or their minimum rental payments. We then evaluate this evidence for the design of social policy.

The Key Market Relationships

Parameters of the Demand for Housing Services

Although a key element of housing allowance programs is the effect of specific housing requirements, a logical starting point is the examination of pure transfer programs that contain no such restrictions. If social scientists could provide policy makers with reliable estimates of the parameters of supply and demand schedules for housing, the consequences on aggregate housing consumption of a program that either provided cash transfers to low-income households or provided price reductions for housing could be readily forecast. Consider the following stylized example.[5] With known parameters reflecting the income elasticity of housing demand α, the price elasticity of demand β, and the supply elasticity γ, the following four equations on the left describe equilibrium in the market for low-income housing without public intervention.

5. This example is simplified in several ways, chiefly for expositional ease. It relies on the convenient log-linear representations of supplier and demander behavior, on the definition of housing as a single valued scalar function, and on the assumption of a single unsegmented market. In addition, this example ignores the spatial variation in housing prices in response to transport costs, so emphasized by urban economists. See John Yinger's comments on this paper. Transport considerations per se are ignored on empirical grounds, based on the careful analyses of the housing price structure in Pittsburgh and Phoenix by Sally R. Merrill, "Draft Report on Hedonic Indices as a Measure of Housing Quality" (Abt, December 1977). The more general issue is also discussed in the section on "Housing Requirements and Tied Subsidies" below.

Market conditions	Unrestricted subsidies
(1a) $H_i^d = A(Y_i)^\alpha (P_i^d)^\beta$	(1b) $H_i^d = A[Y_i(1 + \phi_i)]^\alpha (P_i^d)^\beta$
(2a) $H^s = B(P^s)^\gamma$	(2b) $H^s = B(P^s)^\gamma$
(3a) $H^s = \sum_i H_i^d$	(3b) $H^s = \sum_i H_i^d$
(4a) $P_i^d = P_j^d = P^s$	(4b) $P_i^d = (1 - \theta_i)P^s$

The quantity of housing demanded by household i (H_i^d) depends on its income (Y_i) and the price of housing it faces (P_i^d), as well as the elasticity parameters, α and β, and an arbitrary constant A (equation 1a). The quantity of housing supplied in the market (H^s) depends on the supply price (P^s) as well as the elasticity parameter γ and an arbitrary constant B (equation 2a). Market equilibrium in an unregulated market implies that supply equals market demand—that is, the quantity supplied equals the sum of household demands (equation 3a), and that prices are equal for all suppliers and demanders (equation 4a).

Now consider the effect of housing gap allowances that increase the income of household i by $100\phi_i$ percent, or percent of rent allowances that reduce the housing prices they face by $100\theta_i$ percent. The four equations on the right describe the equilibrium of the housing market subject to these policies. Under these conditions, the effect of policy intervention can be forecast in a straightforward manner.[6] The effects on the housing consumption of any household, or group of households, depend on the price, income, and supply elasticities, on the specific housing gap or percent of rent offer made to household i, *and* on the distribution of such subsidies throughout the local market.

Obviously, the effect of a price or income subsidy on housing consumption will be greater (1) if households are more responsive to price or income variations in choosing their levels of housing services, (2) if the

---

6. In general, the proportional increase in housing consumption by household i induced by these forms of a housing allowance is

$$(5) \qquad \frac{\Delta H_i^d}{H_i^d} = (1 + \phi_i)^\alpha (1 - \theta_i)^\beta \left[\frac{\sum_i (Y_i)^\alpha (1 + \phi_i)^\alpha (1 - \theta_i)^\beta}{\sum_i Y_i^\alpha} \right]^{\beta/(\gamma-\beta)} - 1.$$

Housing gap subsidies, as described below, differ from this stylized example in that the subsidy rate is a function of household income. Introducing this feature would change the aggregate market calculations for universal subsidies but would leave the qualitative results unchanged.

rate of price or income subsidy is larger, and (3) if the housing supply is more sensitive to increased demand over a suitable time horizon.

Suppose, for example, the price elasticity of housing demand were minus one ($\beta = -1$) and the income elasticity were plus one ($\alpha = 1$). Under these conditions, if a small fraction of the households in the market received a 10 percent rent subsidy and a 10 percent income subsidy ($\phi_i = 0.1; \theta_i = 0.1$), this policy would lead to a 22 percent increase in housing consumption by recipient households, regardless of the supply elasticity of housing.[7]

The effects of a universal housing allowance will clearly depend on the supply elasticity. For example, in the long run, if supply is completely elastic ($\gamma = \infty$), a particular program such as a 10 percent price subsidy ($\phi_i = \phi_j = 0; \theta_i = \theta_j = 0.1$) will increase housing consumption by 10 percent for each household.[8]

There are two different ways of evaluating the effects of subsidy policies on the behavior of recipient households. First, the results can be analyzed in terms of their "effectiveness" in stimulating housing consumption by low-income households—for example, by examining the fraction of the subsidy used by recipients to consume more housing services. Second, the results can be analyzed in terms of their effect on the high "rent burdens" faced by poor people—for example, by examining changes in the fraction of income devoted to housing expenditures.

Note the contradictory implications of these two ways of evaluating program impact. If the housing consumption of low-income households is highly responsive to price or income subsidies, such subsidies would be relatively effective in terms of housing outcomes but would have little impact on the rent burdens of low-income households. Conversely, if housing consumption is insensitive to price or income subsidies, then housing gap or percent of rent allowances would be relatively ineffective

---

7. If the fraction of households receiving subsidies is small, the term in square brackets in equation 5 is almost one and the change in housing consumption is

$$(6) \qquad \frac{\Delta H_i^d}{H_i^d} \simeq (1 + \phi_i)^\alpha (1 - \theta_i)^\beta - 1.$$

8. If the subsidy program is universal ($\phi_i = \bar{\phi}; \theta_i = \bar{\theta}$), the bracketed term in equation 5 can be simplified and the change in housing consumption is exactly

$$(7) \qquad \frac{\Delta H_i^d}{H_i^d} = (1 + \bar{\phi})^{\alpha/(1-\beta/\gamma)} (1 - \bar{\theta})^{\beta/(1-\beta/\gamma)} - 1.$$

If supply is perfectly elastic, this expression reduces to equation 6.

Table 1. Effectiveness in Stimulating Housing Consumption and Impact on Relative Rent Burdens of Percent of Rent Subsidies at Various Price Elasticities

Price elasticity (β)	Relative increase in housing expenditures by subsidy rate (θ)[a]			Relative reduction in rent burden by subsidy rate (θ)[b]		
	20%	40%	60%	20%	40%	60%
0.00	0.00	0.00	0.00	0.20	0.40	0.60
−0.20	0.22	0.24	0.28	0.16	0.34	0.52
−0.40	0.43	0.46	0.51	0.13	0.26	0.42
−0.80	0.81	0.84	0.87	0.04	0.10	0.17
−1.00	1.00	1.00	1.00	0.00	0.00	0.00

a. Fraction of public subsidy used to improve housing conditions, *e*. From equations 1b through 4b, $e = (1/\theta)[1 - (1 - \theta)^{-\beta}]$.

b. Proportionate reduction in the ratio of rental payments to income, *r*. From equations 1b through 4b. $r = 1 - (1 - \theta)^{\beta+1}$.

in stimulating consumption but would significantly reduce the rent burdens of low-income households.

Table 1 illustrates the complementary relationship between the consumption effects of various price subsidies and their impacts on relative rent burdens at different price elasticities.[9] If the price elasticity were −0.2, then a 20 percent price subsidy would reduce the rent burdens of low-income households by 16 percent, but only 22 percent of the subsidy money received by a household would be spent on increased housing consumption. If the price elasticity were −0.8, however, the same subsidy would reduce rent burdens by only 4 percent, but 81 percent of the subsidy money would be devoted to additional housing consumption. Similarly, a given income subsidy would have greater effects on housing consumption and smaller effects on rent burdens with a larger income elasticity.

If the housing market parameters were clearly determined, then the desirability of a particular program—that is, an income or price subsidy rate—would depend on policy makers' views about the importance to the larger society of these different outcomes. Subsidies may result in an *increase* in the housing consumption of poverty households, reflecting the housing goals of subsidy policies; they may also result in a *decrease* in the large fraction of the incomes of poor people that must be devoted to shelter, reflecting the welfare goals of subsidy policies. Any transfer must lead to an improvement in one of these dimensions. However, without

9. The calculations in table 1 assume that the subsidized households are a small fraction of all households in the market. (Alternatively, the calculations are identical for a universal price subsidy program if the long-run supply elasticity is infinite.)

basic information on the parameters governing market behavior, a subsidy policy that recognizes these or other goals cannot be evaluated at all.

Despite extensive empirical research on housing market behavior,
there was considerable uncertainty at the time the allowance experiments
were undertaken about the basic parameters (α, β, and γ) reflecting supplier and demander behavior in the housing market. In part this uncertainty reflected standard problems in econometric work—problems of
generalizing from particular samples, selectivity bias in samples of observations stratified by ownership or rental status, and problems related
to the typically aggregate nature of observations on behavioral units, especially housing suppliers.

In large part, however, the uncertainty reflected several peculiarities of
the housing market. First, the high costs of moving suggest that the
relevant concept of income for housing demanders is some long-run or
permanent income. Second, direct observations of housing prices are
never available. Market transactions generate observations on monthly
rents or housing values, expressed in units of price times quantity ($P^s H_i^d$),
not simply market prices (P^s). Third, the housing services that command
monthly payments include a large number of components not provided
by the private actions of individual suppliers, for example, neighborhood
characteristics and public services. This makes it difficult to interpret information on landlords' investment or maintenance strategies that alter
parts of the housing bundle.

The Bundle Choice Problem

Lurking behind these three complications is a major conceptual problem of central importance in housing allowance programs that tie subsidies
to consumption of specific standards. Housing is a complex collection of
attributes. The decision to rent a given dwelling unit involves evaluating
its spaciousness, quality, layout, and location. For many purposes, it is
reasonable and useful to aggregate these components into a single valued
index of "housing services," measured by consumption expenditures.[10]
However, as discussed below, when policy interests and program restrictions concentrate on specific components of the bundle, simply knowing
the effects of a program on total consumption is no longer sufficient.

10. When there is a competitive housing market and each attribute valued by the
household has the same supply elasticity, it is possible to aggregate across these
attributes and to use housing expenditures as an index of total housing services.

Experimental Data and Statistical Inference

We can divide the experimental questions and findings into investigations of (1) households whose market choices were not distorted by particular standards or earmarking requirements and (2) households that were offered some form of tied subsidy.

The first group of households includes (a) experimental subjects in Seattle and Denver income maintenance experiments, (b) unrestricted housing gap households (demand experiment), (c) percent of rent households (demand experiment), (d) control households (demand experiment), (e) occupants of sampled dwelling units (supply experiment), and (f) baseline (preexperimental) households (demand and supply experiments).

The second group of households includes (g) households subject to minimum rent or minimum standards constraints (demand experiment), and (h) all recipient households (supply and administrative agency experiments).

These rich bodies of data will undoubtedly support a wide range of housing research for many years. Data from the first group of households, unrestricted in their housing choices, facilitate housing market and microeconomic research in many new areas. The reactions of households to exogenous subsidy offers (a, b, and c above) provide direct information about the basic demand parameters (α and β) of low-income households. The experimental manipulation of housing prices (c) permits a direct analysis of price elasticities of demand. The longitudinal nature of the data supports analyses of the dynamic behavior of households in response to subsidies (a through c) and variations in sociodemographic characteristics (d and e). Moreover, because of the detailed housing information, it is possible to go beyond simple analyses of expenditures and to consider the quantity and quality of housing attributes consumed in response to direct subsidies (a, b, c) and to natural variations in household circumstances (d, e, f).

The second group of households (g, h), whose subsidy amounts are constrained by varying restrictions on choice, permits further insight into housing demand. For these households, there are direct observations on consumption choices, modified by a combination of specific restrictions and experimental incentives. Here again researchers have the benefit of unusually rich and detailed longitudinal data about household characteristics and housing consumption.

What new insights into housing demand have been obtained from these experimental data? Are the findings relevant to the choice of housing policies? Before we address these questions in detail, it is worth emphasizing several inherent problems of inductive inference from the experimental observations.

First, and most important, the income and price subsidy treatments were of limited duration and the experimental subjects knew this. Price and income subsidies were offered for three years by the housing demand experiments; income subsidies were offered for periods up to five years by the income maintenance experiments and up to ten years by the housing supply experiments. For a majority of households, certainly for most renters, substantial improvement in housing conditions implies a residential move and nontrivial transaction costs. Thus the limited duration of the experiment may inhibit households from making adjustments and incurring these relocation costs. This is an even greater problem for households receiving tied subsidies, since the restrictions often distort normal consumption patterns and thus lower the effective benefits of any given subsidy.

Second, even if households behaved during the experiment as if their subsidies would last indefinitely, there may be moderate lags in adjustment even to permanently changed circumstances—lags induced by household inertia, by ties to familiar surroundings, and by the cost of searching for alternative housing. For analytical purposes, the information from the demand experiment is a two-year historical record, and some fraction of the long-run response to subsidy treatments may simply not be observed in this period. For the income maintenance and housing supply experiments, where the duration of treatment is longer, this problem is presumably less severe. However, these longer experiments do not include price subsidy treatments at all, and the supply experiment data do not allow direct analysis of the effects of income subsidies or of subsidies tied to housing consumption.

Third, enrollment and attrition of experimental households may not be random. Nonrandom enrollment and attrition probably occur even in a universal, operational program, since households with stronger tastes for housing, other things being equal, are more likely to remain in the program. However, there is no assurance that attrition during the experiment mirrors the attrition that would be expected in an actual ongoing program. This nonrandom sample selection will certainly influence the estimation of housing demand relationships. Problems arising from the nonrandom selection of participants are also likely to be most severe in the samples subjected to earmarking or physical standards restrictions. These problems are exacerbated by subsidy eligibility rules based on income and, in the demand experiment, by restriction to rental households.

Fourth, resource limitations on the experiments implied that they could be introduced in only a few local housing markets. To the extent that characteristics of the housing markets interact with the consumption decisions of households, generalizing from these results to universal programs is problematic. Differences in the operation of the supply and demand experiments, coupled with differences in the local markets, further complicate any analysis of potential biases arising from the limited duration of the experiments and selective attrition. Conceptually, differences in the period of subsidy between the supply and demand and income maintenance experiments could provide insights into time horizon biases, but only if other differences among these experiments could be readily incorporated into the analysis. As discussed below, this is hardly the case.

Evidence on Behavioral Demand Parameters

Direct Evidence on the Price and Income Elasticity of Demand

The most direct information about the demand parameters comes from analyzing the reactions of unconstrained experimental households to various forms of subsidies. A total of 385 renter households in Pittsburgh and 280 households in Phoenix received percentage rebates on rent (θ's of various levels) of between 20 and 60 percent.[11] In addition, 59 low-income households in Pittsburgh and 37 households in Phoenix received unrestricted cash payments (ϕ's of various levels) representing the difference between the estimated cost of standard housing and 25 percent of their incomes. (The subsidy levels [ϕ's] offered were thus not independent of household income.) The behavior of these households can be compared with a control group of 289 households in Pittsburgh and 252 households in Phoenix, households from which identical data

---

11. While the subsidies were actually given for up to three years, the last year involved moving households into other programs. Therefore, for analytical purposes, only the first two years are relevant.

Table 2. Percentage Changes in Rent after Two Years for Households Receiving Price and Income Subsidies

Percent

Subsidy		Pittsburgh		Phoenix	
		Households in original sample active after two years	Average change in rent	Households in original sample active after two years	Average change in rent
θ	ϕ				
0[a]	0	74	18	54	18
20	0	71	17	55	24
30	0	78	25	60	24
40	0	78	27	56	24
50	0	90	27	70	24
60	0	82	39	66	45
39[b]	0	80	26	...	...
43[c]	0	...	...	61	26
0	30[d]	84	22	57	35

Sources: Joseph Friedman and Daniel Weinberg, "Draft Report on the Demand for Rental Housing: Evidence from a Percent of Rent Housing Allowance" (Cambridge, Mass.: Abt Associates, September 1978), pp. 8, 9, A-19, A-94; Joseph Friedman and Daniel Weinberg, "Draft Report on Housing Consumption Under a Constrained Income Transfer: Evidence from a Housing Gap Housing Allowance" (Abt, April 1979), p. A-14.

a. Control group households receiving neither price nor income subsidies.
b. Average for percent of rent households in Pittsburgh.
c. Average for percent of rent households in Phoenix.
d. Average for unconstrained housing gap households in both Pittsburgh and Phoenix.

were gathered over the same period but which received no direct subsidies.

Table 2 summarizes the changes in housing consumption, as measured by rental expenditures after two years of subsidy. In both sites the housing expenditures of control households increased by 18 percent; on average, the rental payments of those receiving pure price reductions increased by 26 percent, or an additional 8 percentage points. Assuming that households were randomly assigned to treatment groups and that attrition from the various treatment groups was random,[12] a rough estimate of the price elasticity of demand, β, is -0.2. This is calculated by simply comparing the net increase in housing consumption to the average price discount.

For the smaller samples of households receiving unrestricted income

12. As table 2 shows, the attrition rates for the control groups, 26 percent and 46 percent in Pittsburgh and Phoenix, respectively, are somewhat higher than for those receiving rent subsidies, 20 percent and 39 percent, respectively. Moreover, the experimental attrition rate at both sites apparently varied inversely with the rate of subsidy.

subsidies, the average subsidy ϕ was 30 percent of income at both sites. In Pittsburgh, the group receiving this subsidy increased their housing consumption by 22 percent, or by 4 percentage points more than the control group receiving no subsidy. In Phoenix, the income subsidy group increased their housing consumption by 35 percent, or by 17 percentage points more than the control group. These crude comparisons yield income elasticity estimates, α, of 0.13 for Pittsburgh and 0.57 for Phoenix. When these small samples are combined, a 30 percent increase in unrestricted income for these ninety-six households is associated with an increase in housing expenditures of 9 percentage points more than the control group, or an income elasticity of about 0.3.

Estimates of the change in housing consumption induced after two years of experimental payments have also been obtained by standard multivariate analysis by pooling observations on the control households and on those receiving percentage rebates.[13] From equations 1b and 4b, with $\phi=0$, the demand for housing in logarithmic form is

$$(8) \qquad \log (H_i^d P^s) = \log R_i = \log A + \alpha \log Y_i + \beta \log (1 - \theta_i),$$

where the left-hand side is the monthly rental payment R_i of the ith household and A is an arbitrary constant. If the unit price of housing is constant, estimates of α and β may be obtained by ordinary least squares regression of log rent upon log income and the log of 1 minus the fractional rent subsidy, which varies from zero to 0.6.[14]

As noted, the appropriate conceptual definition of income is a permanent, normal, or long-run concept. Friedman and Weinberg use the three-year average income of each household, probably a far better definition than that relied on in single cross sections. Direct estimates of equation 8 along with estimates from a linear specification, instead of the logarithmic one, are presented by Friedman and Weinberg; these are based on the pooled samples of control households and households receiving percent of rent subsidies. Table 3 summarizes their results. The

13. For technical reasons, the small samples of households receiving income transfers cannot be included in this analysis since the amount of the transfer was determined by household income.

14. More specifically, as long as income and the subsidy rate are independent of the unobserved price of housing and no other factors influence demands, ordinary least squares is appropriate for the estimation of equation 8. In practice, since other characteristics of households systematically affect demands, these characteristics should be included as regressors. When not included, as frequently is the case, the parameter estimates will be less efficient if other factors are uncorrelated with incomes and subsidies and will be biased when correlated.

estimated price elasticities, −0.16 to −0.18 in Pittsburgh and −0.21 to −0.23 in Phoenix, are almost identical for the two specifications and are similar across the two sites.[15]

The income elasticity estimates derived from regression estimates of equation 8 do not arise from experimental payments of income but rather from the natural experiment arising because "otherwise identical" households of varying incomes are observed to have made different choices. As expected, estimates of the responsiveness of housing consumption to income are slightly larger when average income is used, although the differences are remarkably small. Depending on the specification, the elasticity of demand from long-run income is estimated to be 0.29 to 0.33 in Pittsburgh and 0.38 to 0.44 in Phoenix.

An additional analysis of income sensitivity was performed by combining the control group and those receiving unrestricted income transfers (of π dollars a month over the period). Regressions of the form

$$(9) \qquad \log R_i = \log A_1 + \alpha \log (Y_i + \pi_i),$$

that is, regressions of log rent upon a constant and the log of average income including any transfer payments, were estimated. Dummy intercept and slope variables, representing individuals receiving unrestricted transfer, proved insignificant, leading to the conclusion that "the responses of unconstrained households are adequately characterized in terms of additions to income that are treated like any other income."[16]

Ohls and Thomas replicated this analysis for the sample of 824 households receiving unrestricted transfers in the Seattle and Denver income maintenance experiments. Linear regressions related housing expenditures to average income over a three-year period and separately to average transfer income, holding constant the race and composition of households. Table 3 also summarizes the results of the Ohls and Thomas investigations. Results are reported separately for owners and renters and for the subsample of mover households. The results imply income elasticities of demand of 0.22 to 0.33 for renters and 0.18 to 0.32 for owner-occupants.

The familiar economic case depicted in equations 1 through 4 and the empirical analyses summarized in tables 2 and 3 are rooted in the notion

15. Indeed, the point estimates of the price elasticity are apparently indistinguishable on statistical grounds. Joseph Friedman and Daniel Weinberg, "Draft Report on the Demand for Rental Housing: Evidence from a Percent of Rent Housing Allowance" (Abt, September 1978), pp. A-106–09.

16. Ibid., p. 79.

Table 3. Estimates of Price and Income Elasticities of Demand from Experimental Data[a]

Parameter and functional form	Static model				Dynamic model, movers only	
	All households		Movers only			
	Pittsburgh	Phoenix	Pittsburgh	Phoenix	Pittsburgh	Phoenix
Price elasticity estimate						
Control and percent of rent						
Logarithmic form	−0.178	−0.234	−0.211	−0.219	−0.237	−0.310
Linear form						
At sample mean	−0.164	−0.213	−0.222	−0.198	n.a.	n.a.
Average estimate	−0.172	−0.211	−0.227	−0.216	n.a.	n.a.
Income elasticity estimate						
Control and percent of rent						
Logarithmic form						
Annual income	0.291	0.371	n.a.	n.a.	n.a.	n.a.
Three-year average	0.333	0.435	0.363	0.364	0.368	0.387
Linear form						
At sample mean (three-year average)	0.291	0.377	0.375	0.330	n.a.	n.a.
Average estimate (three-year average)	0.323	0.404	0.403	0.380	n.a.	n.a.

Control and housing gap: logarithmic form

				Seattle and Denver		
Control and housing gap: logarithmic form	n.a.	n.a.	0.292	0.340	n.a.	n.a.

Income transfer households: linear form, at sample mean (three-year average)

				Seattle and Denver	
Nongrant income					
Renters	0.219	⋮		0.314	
Owners	0.320	⋮		0.406	
Combined	0.477	⋮		n.a.	
Experimental grant income					
Renters	0.329	⋮		0.418	
Owners	0.179	⋮		0.246	
Combined	0.420	⋮		n.a.	

Sources: Friedman and Weinberg, "Draft Report on the Demand for Rental Housing," pp. 64, 73, 80, 126, A-106; James C. Ohls and Cynthia Thomas, "The Effects of the Seattle and Denver Income Maintenance Experiments on Housing Consumption, Ownership, and Mobility," Draft Report (Denver: Mathematica Policy Research, January 1979), pp. 19, 28, 31.
n.a. Not available.
a. Pittsburgh and Phoenix were in the demand experiment; Seattle and Denver in the Seattle and Denver income maintenance experiments.

of equilibrium—equilibrium in the market sense, but also equilibrium in the sense that each household chooses the optimal quantity of housing, given the market or subsidized price of this commodity. The tabular or statistical comparison of household choices two years after enrollment presumes that households have, in fact, chosen the quantity of housing services desired, given the subsidized prices they face or the income transfers they receive.

However, choosing a substantially different quantity of housing services is associated almost invariably with a residential move, at least for renters. Moving, in turn, incurs real costs—not only the transaction costs of moving household possessions and so forth, but also the costs of searching for accommodations, of disrupting familiar neighborhoods, and so forth. It is entirely possible that the responses of households observed after two years are not their true equilibrium levels of consumption. The researchers for the demand experiment and Seattle and Denver income maintenance experiments have investigated this possibility in a number of ways. The first method is to estimate the parameters of the demand curve, equation 8, for the subset of households that actually moved during the two-year period after enrollment. Presumably households that are observed to have incurred the substantial costs of relocation will choose their long-run equilibrium quantities of housing services. As other households move, Friedman and Weinberg argue, they "may respond more like the households that moved during the experimental period."[17] The authors present an extensive analysis of the sample of control and experimental households that moved during the two-year period after enrollment. The principal results from the demand experiment, indicated in table 3, suggest that in Pittsburgh income and price elasticities are slightly larger for movers than for all households. Results suggest similar price elasticities for all households in Phoenix, and slightly smaller income elasticity estimates.[18]

For the samples of income maintenance households that had moved, the results in table 3 suggest somewhat larger income elasticities, on the order of 0.31 to 0.42 for renters and 0.25 to 0.41 for owners. In addition, information on households receiving payments for five years suggests a slightly larger income elasticity. This finding is discussed further below.

Additional evidence provided by Friedman and Weinberg focuses on

17. Ibid., p. 71.
18. The authors also present estimates at the two sites for minority households and for households of different size and composition. These estimates indicate some differences across groups, but they are generally small or insignificant.

an explicit model of dynamic adjustment rather than an equilibrium model. The authors postulate a version of a partial adjustment process where desired housing consumption at time t depends on prices and income as in equation 8, but where actual adjustment in housing consumption in any interval is only some fraction, η, of the difference between desired consumption and consumption in the previous period.

These postulates yield a logarithmic relationship of the form

(10) $\log R_{it} = \log A_2 + \alpha\eta \log Y_{it} + \beta\eta \log (1 - \theta_i) + (1 - \eta) \log R_{i,t-1}.$[19]

From observations on control and experimental households in each site, equation 10 is estimated using appropriate instruments for lagged rent $R_{i, t-1}$. Table 3 also presents these estimates, which are somewhat larger than those derived from a purely static model.

Three points are worth making in considering this evidence. First, the sample is confined to households that moved during the two years after enrollment. Second, the dynamic analysis considers only the end points of the two-year time interval. Since identical data were gathered at four points in time, it would have been possible to incorporate more information in the estimation of these dynamic relationships. Third, there is some evidence that slightly different specifications of the short-run dynamic process lead to still larger estimates of the price elasticity.[20]

As these data are ransacked over the next few years, there will undoubtedly be a great deal of attention to refinements of the short-run

19. The model expressed in equation 10 is derived from the relationship between desired housing consumption at time t, $\tilde{H}_{it}^d$

(11) $\tilde{H}_{it}^d = A(Y_{it})^\alpha (P_{it}^d)^\beta,$

the assumed adjustment relation

(12) $\dfrac{P_t^s H_{it}^d}{P_{t-1}^s H_{i,t-1}} = \left[\dfrac{P_t^s \tilde{H}_{it}^d}{P_{t-1}^s H_{t,t-1}^d} \right]^\eta,$

and the assumption

(13) $P_t^s = P_{t-1}^s.$

20. For example, our early work, initially sponsored by Abt Associates, relied on a slightly different specification of the adjustment process and yielded price elasticity estimates of -0.36 to -0.64 in Pittsburgh and -0.41 to -0.45 in Phoenix. Eric A. Hanushek and John M. Quigley, "The Dynamics of the Housing Market: A Stock Adjustment Model of Housing Consumption," *Journal of Urban Economics*, vol. 6 (January 1979), pp. 90–111; Eric A. Hanushek and John M. Quigley, "What Is the Price Elasticity of Housing Demand?" *Review of Economics and Statistics*, vol. 62 (August 1980), pp. 449–54. The principal differences were that our work relied upon a linear, as opposed to the log-linear, adjustment model in equation 11, that our analysis used data for each year of the program rather than merely the endpoints, and that our analysis used instrumental estimates for equilibrium demand based on exogenous factors. See also note 21.

dynamics of household adjustment to price subsidies. Indeed, with such a short time series, it may be difficult or impossible to choose among alternative representations of the adjustment path. If one suspects that households adjust their housing consumption only slowly in response to economic incentives, and that transaction costs lead to moderate lags in response, then the problem of extrapolation from a two-year period is formidable.[21]

Let this not obscure the basic message of the impressive and careful analysis of price sensitivity reported in great detail and subjected to a variety of sensitivity tests. A decade ago, many economists assumed, on the basis of practically no evidence, that the price elasticity of housing demand was about −1.0 or even more elastic. Experimental observation suggests a much lower price sensitivity, at least for low-income households. In the longer run, consumer response to price variation may be somewhat more elastic, but on the basis of this research an elasticity of −1.0 appears much too large numerically. Indeed, unless one believes that the experiment is fatally flawed by its three-year time limit, it is impossible to conclude that a 10 percent reduction in housing prices would increase the housing consumption of low-income households by more than 5 or 6 percent.

The experimental evidence on households receiving unrestricted income transfers indicates that these payments are treated as ordinary income over a three-year period, but that households are only moderately sensitive to income in their housing consumption. It would appear from these analyses that an upper limit on the income elasticity of demand is about 0.5.

Indirect Evidence on Price and Income Elasticities

The price of housing is never simply observed in the market. The advantage of the demand experiment percent of rent study, and the evi-

---

21. Friedman and Weinberg, "Draft Report on the Demand for Rental Housing," pp. 120–26, point out in detail that if there are individual specific variations in demand (or serially correlated stochastic errors in the demand function), it is extremely difficult to project the time path of price responsiveness from such a short time series. These considerations also suggest that the technique of direct substitution (as compared to the instrumental estimation used by Friedman and Weinberg) is likely to provide estimates suggesting more elastic price responsiveness. See also Stephen K. Mayo, *Housing Allowance Demand Experiment: Housing Expenditures and Quality,* pt. 2: *Housing Expenditures Under a Percent of Rent Housing Allowance* (Abt, 1977).

dence derived from it, is that experimental variations in relative prices are sufficient to estimate price responsiveness. The baseline and longitudinal information on control households alone provides little additional evidence, at least not if one presumes that the market for low-income housing is reasonably competitive, so that differences in observed rents (that is, prices times quantities) reflect different quantities of housing services enjoyed.

The relationship between income and housing expenditures can, however, be directly estimated without relying upon the experimental manipulation of subsidies. Thus the analysis of households unaffected by the experiments can provide additional evidence on the income responsiveness of housing consumption by poor households.

Both the demand and supply experiment research designs generated a detailed sample of baseline observations—that is, a rich cross-sectional sample of households and their housing consumption before experimental treatment. In addition, in the supply experiment, a longitudinal sample of dwelling units and their occupants was collected in Brown County, Wisconsin, and in St. Joseph County, Indiana. In contrast to the demand experiments, the longitudinal samples of the supply experiment include a large fraction of owner-occupied units. The analysis of these samples provides additional evidence on housing responses to changed economic circumstances.

Mulford estimated several variants of equation 8, assuming that at each site households face the same price for housing services; regression analysis relates the log of rent (or for owners, the log of a transformation of housing value) to the log of income, holding minority status and household composition constant.[22] Three analyses are presented. One uses the cross-sectional information on income and housing consumption available from the baseline surveys in Brown and St. Joseph counties. The other two use the two-year longitudinal survey of dwelling units—that is, they are based on samples of households who resided in the same units for at least two years. Elasticity estimates are presented based on annual income and three-year average income.

The results of these investigations appear in table 4.[23] For the baseline

---

22. John E. Mulford, *Income Elasticity of Housing Demand*, R-2449-HUD (Santa Monica: Rand Corp., July 1979).

23. These analyses measure housing consumption at baseline and either annual income at baseline or average income over a three-year period. Presumably average income includes supply experiment transfer payments. Thus there are three prob-

Table 4. Indirect Estimates of the Income Elasticity of Demand from Control and Baseline Data

Parameter and stratification	Sample			
	Pittsburgh	Phoenix	Brown County	St. Joseph County
Annual income; baseline analyses				
Renters				
All households	0.291	0.371	0.119	0.018
Minority	0.210	0.270	n.a.	n.a.
Nonminority	0.170	0.310	n.a.	n.a.
Recent movers	n.a.	n.a.	n.a.	n.a.
Minority	0.270	0.320	n.a.	n.a.
Nonminority	0.190	0.290	n.a.	n.a.
Owners: all households	. . .[a]	. . .[a]	0.383	0.283
Three-year average income				
Renters				
All households	0.333	0.435	. . .[b]	. . .[b]
Nonmovers	n.a.	n.a.	0.219	0.152
Recent movers	0.363	0.364	. . .[b]	. . .[b]
Owners: nonmovers	. . .[a]	. . .[a]	0.513	0.395

Sources: Francis J. Cronin, *The Housing Demand of Low-Income Households*, 249-35 (Washington, D.C.: Urban Institute, August 1979), pp. 40, 43; Friedman and Weinberg, "Draft Report on the Demand for Rental Housing," pp. 64, 73; John Mulford, *Income Elasticity of Housing Demand*, R-2449-HUD (Santa Monica: Rand Corp., July 1979), p. 21.

n.a. Not available.

a. Samples of Pittsburgh and Phoenix households include renters only.

b. Three-year samples of Brown and St. Joseph counties households include nonmovers only.

sample, the relationship between annual income and housing expenditures suggests low elasticities for renters, 0.11 to 0.12, and somewhat larger elasticities for owners, 0.28 to 0.38. When three-year average income is used, the estimated income elasticity is 0.15 to 0.22 for renters and 0.40 to 0.51 for owners. However, restricting the samples to nonmoving households surely leads to an underestimate of the sensitivity of housing consumption to income variations, especially for renter households.

An elaborate cross-sectional analysis of the baseline data on rental households from the demand experiment was also conducted by Cronin.[24] Cronin defines income as the annual household income at baseline and

---

lems with the permanent income analysis: (1) the sample is restricted to nonmoving households; (2) receipt of the subsidy is contingent on meeting housing requirements (see the later discussion); and (3) it is not possible to estimate the effects of the subsidy per se, since the subsidy rate is the same for all households.

24. Francis J. Cronin, *The Housing Demand of Low-Income Households*, 249-35 (Washington, D.C.: Urban Institute, August 1979), pp. 40, 43.

produces separate estimates of income elasticities for minority and non-minority households for four stratifications of duration of occupancy.

Table 4 presents the income elasticities estimated for all households and for the subsample of recent movers.[25] The results noted in table 4 are actually obtained from a complex procedure that uses the technique of hedonic regressions to impute a housing price to each observation in the sample.[26] Because this procedure is open to serious question, as discussed later, we are somewhat skeptical of the results.

These two indirect analyses are difficult to interpret; the supply experiment analysis is conducted on a somewhat unusual sample, and the demand experiment analysis is conducted subject to a number of heroic assumptions about the specification of hedonic indexes. Nevertheless, the analyses do support the principal inferences drawn from the direct experimental evidence—that the responsiveness of housing consumption to changes in household income is rather low.

25. Actually Cronin's investigation is not focused on the linear logarithmic relationship (Cobb-Douglas), equation 8, but on the more general Stone-Geary relationship between housing consumption, income, and relative prices. Estimates are presented for four different specifications of the Stone-Geary relationship.

26. The regression of monthly rent upon the correct specification of the physical components of the housing, locational, and neighborhood attributes enjoyed (for example, amount of space and quality of neighborhood), together with such non-housing attributes as length of tenure and relationship to the landlord, yields a set of implicit prices for the qualitative and quantitative attributes of housing, together with estimates of the discounts available for longer-term occupancy or relationship to the landlord.

If this hedonic relationship is known a priori, and if the functional form is correct, then the qualitative and quantitative attributes of housing consumed by any household can be multiplied by these marketwide implicit prices to yield an estimate of the market rent for the attributes consumed by that household. For any household, the ratio of its actual rental payment to this estimate of the impersonal market rent yields a relative price for the dwelling unit chosen by that household. Cronin's analysis uses this methodology to compute a relative price for each household in the baseline survey conducted at the demand sites of Pittsburgh and Phoenix. He then uses these relative prices to estimate equations similar to the form of equation 8. The price elasticity estimates are on the order of −0.6 when this technique of cross-sectional analysis is used.

These results should be viewed with skepticism; they are based on the ratio of the hedonic residual to the predicted value of rent. Indeed, they exploit the theoretical notion that if the hedonic regression is specified properly, then the residual error for any single dwelling unit is a measure of the deviation of the observed rental price of that unit from the market relationship, that is, its premium or discount. In fact, the residual for any observation in a sample includes stochastic components, measurement error, and the influences of left-out variables. See also the "Expenditures, Consumption, and Measures of Adequacy" section of this paper.

*Implications of Unconstrained Price and Income Subsidies
for Housing Consumption Patterns*

The extensive investigation of the parameters of the demand curve for
housing supports the conclusion that the housing expenditures of low-
income households are insensitive to price and income subsidies. The
price elasticity appears to be bounded by -0.5 or -0.6 and is perhaps
even closer to zero; the income elasticity estimates are never above 0.5,
which may be an upper limit. Clearly the main effect of a housing allowance that provided either of these subsidies would be a reduction in the
rent burdens of poor households; only a small fraction of the subsidy
would be spent on housing.

Table 5 compares the direct effects of unconstrained price and income
subsidies on the experimental households in Pittsburgh and Phoenix after
two years. In Pittsburgh, the average payment to households receiving
price reductions was $50 a month. These payments substantially reduced
the rent burdens of households, from 32 percent of income to 21 percent,
or by about one-third. Only about 14 percent of the payments were used
to purchase housing. As expected, for households receiving pure income
transfers of the same average amount ($55), a much smaller fraction was
spent on housing, and relative rent burdens were reduced even more
dramatically.

In Phoenix, the average payments of $59 a month reduced rent burdens
by 25 percent; less than one-fourth of the payments were used to purchase
additional housing. Households receiving pure income transfers received
substantially higher average payments ($108), which reduced their rela-
tive rent burdens from one-third of income to one-eighth; only about 12
percent of the transfer payment was used to purchase housing.

Expenditures, Consumption, and Measures of Adequacy

The analysis of the determinants of aggregate housing expenditure is
important for program design. However, the chief concerns of housing
policies relate to the physical conditions and the adequacy of space in each
unit and to externalities such as the quality of neighborhoods. Moreover,
other things equal (including housing quality, space, and neighborhoods),
it would clearly be desirable if low-income households could spend less,
not more, for housing. Although analyzing aggregate expenditures is often

Table 5. Experimental Evidence on Effectiveness and Relative Reduction in Rent Burden after Two Years

| Payment | | | | Rent burden | | |
Average monthly payment (dollars)	Percent used for increased housing expenses	Percent rebate θ	Percent rebate ϕ	Median At baseline	Median After two years	Relative change (percent)
			Pittsburgh households			
0	0.0	0[a]	0	0.29	0.26	−10.3
24	−4.0	20	0	0.29	0.22	−24.1
37	13.0	30	0	0.33	0.25	−24.2
54	14.2	40	0	0.31	0.20	−35.5
62	12.3	50	0	0.33	0.17	−48.5
79	16.4	60	0	0.40	0.18	−55.0
50	14.0	39[b]	0	0.32	0.21	−34.4
55	5.4	0	30[c]	0.35	0.20	−42.9
			Phoenix households			
0	0.0	0[a]	0	0.32	0.30	−6.3
29	23.0	20	0	0.37	0.31	−16.2
44	21.4	30	0	0.31	0.26	−16.1
61	18.4	40	0	0.31	0.22	−29.0
82	11.5	50	0	0.33	0.20	−39.4
92	23.6	60	0	0.39	0.19	−51.3
59	24.0	43[d]	0	0.32	0.24	−25.0
108	12.0	0	30[c]	0.33	0.13	−60.6

Source: Friedman and Weinberg, "Draft Report on the Demand for Rental Housing," pp. 11, A-95, A-103.

a. Control group households receiving neither price nor income subsidies.
b. Average for percent of rent households in Pittsburgh.
c. Average for unconstrained households.
d. Average for percent of rent households in Phoenix.

useful, these analyses have obvious limitations in the context of housing allowance programs.

First, even though the market for low-income housing appears to be competitive, there is probably some variation in the observed prices of identical dwelling units in the market. Part of this variation indicates that some units are a "bargain" and some units are "overpriced" relative to the housing services they provide. For both suppliers and demanders, information may be imperfect. If the distribution of households across units providing the same services at higher and lower rents were random, reflecting luck or perspicacity on the part of demanders, this would have little effect on point estimates of consumer responses to subsidies. However, when housing subsidies depend on housing decisions, as with both pure price subsidies and the more restrictive subsidies tied to minimum rents, recipients have weaker incentives to shop carefully for housing than do other consumers. In these instances, since part of the rent will be borne by someone else, the private returns to a more thorough search for bargains are correspondingly reduced.[27]

In Pittsburgh, control households that moved reported more days of searching, more calls about housing, and more units inspected than households that received price subsidies. In Phoenix, however, a similar comparison reveals no systematic pattern.[28] Thus there is no clear evidence that households receiving pure price subsidies devoted fewer resources to searching or to shopping carefully for housing than did unsubsidized households. Nevertheless, there is some evidence of overpayment when restrictions on minimum rental expenditures are imposed.

Second, given the heterogeneous nature of the housing bundle, simple expenditure analyses mask much of the nature of consumption changes. Indeed, it is possible for households to change their housing consumption substantially without changing their expenditures at all—for example, by consuming more space in a lower-quality unit. This is important when the housing policy dictates concern about specific components of the housing market that differ from the market weights reflecting consumer preferences and market prices.

Finally, when specific housing requirements are levied on households as a condition for receiving subsidies, this is effectively a change in the relative price schedule for certain housing attributes. When all households no longer face the same prices, analyzing the level of expenditures alone is inappropriate. It is important to know how the bundle of attributes chosen by households varies in response to distortions in relative prices.

Two basic approaches to the analysis of housing components have been applied in past research (and have been carried out, to some extent, within the experimental analyses). Each method involves different ways of aggregating particular features of housing bundles. The first involves initially estimating a hedonic price equation, quantifying the implicit prices attached to particular attributes. These estimated prices are then used to

27. At the extreme there are incentives for collusion between landlord and tenant to overprice dwelling units for reporting purposes. There is no direct evidence that this happened during the experiments. However, such behavior might evolve if an ongoing, national program were instituted.
28. Friedman and Weinberg, "Draft Report on the Demand for Rental Housing," p. A-129.

aggregate housing attributes, either for the total bundle or specific subsets of the bundle, in subsequent analyses of consumption behavior.[29] The second method concentrates on specific features through the development of quality-weighted indexes of consumption; typically, exogenous notions of quality or adequacy are imposed, and dwellings are given dichotomous scores (such as acceptable or not acceptable) for either specific components or the total bundle. The latter is, for example, used to define the criteria for adequate housing required in the minimum standards allowance programs.

The discussion first considers the application of each approach to the unconstrained groups of households in the experiments. Then the constrained groups, whose subsidies are linked to specific housing requirements, are considered.

Hedonic Price Equations

The heterogeneous nature of the bundle of housing services received in exchange for rental payments has frustrated housing analysts for a decade. Despite a number of studies, empirical evidence on the underlying marginal rates of substitution, or market demands for the components of housing services, is notably weak.[30] Yet this is precisely the information required for a comprehensive evaluation of tied subsidy programs.

The demand experiment researchers have addressed the conceptual distinction between housing expenditures (in units of price times quantity) and housing consumption (in quantity units) through the technique of hedonic indexes. Merrill presents an extensive investigation of the hedonic regressions of monthly rent on a diverse collection of housing attributes—measures of location, physical, and quality conditions of dwelling units, parcels, and neighborhoods—as well as measures of duration of occupancy and landlord-tenant relations.[31] Friedman and Weinberg use the results of this analysis to compute a Laspayres index of the quantity of housing initially consumed by each household and the quantity consumed two years later. A detailed comparison of these indexes

29. See, for example, John F. Kain and John M. Quigley, *Housing Markets and Racial Discrimination: A Microeconomic Analysis* (New York: National Bureau of Economic Research, 1975).

30. Reviewed in John M. Quigley, "What Have We Learned About Urban Housing Markets?" in Peter Mieszkowski and Mahlon Straszheim, eds., *Current Issues in Urban Economics* (Johns Hopkins University Press, 1979).

31. Merrill, "Draft Report."

reveals only small differences between control and percent of rent households in the average increase in housing quantity over the two-year period.

However, when equation 8 is reestimated for the sample of percent of
rent and control households, with this index as the dependent variable,
the analysis implies lower price and income elasticities of demand at both
sites for a number of stratifications—movers, nonmovers, and so forth.[32]

The interpretation of these results is problematic. If the hedonic regressions are properly specified in terms of the "right" set of variables and
the "right" functional form, if a single structure of underlying prices
characterizes each market, and if this structure of relative prices remains
constant for two years, then and only then is interpretation of statistical
demand estimates based on these indexes straightforward. In this case,
the parameter estimates may be interpreted as the price and income elasticities of the quantities demanded; parameter estimates based on housing
expenditures will be biased and inconsistent to the extent that there are
systematic shopping differences (that is, different obtained price distributions) across groups. Unfortunately, it is difficult to establish whether
these conditions are met, despite heroic attempts by the Abt Associates
researchers to exploit the data.[33] The limited information available is
nevertheless consistent with the conclusion that the small changes in housing expenditure induced by price subsidies represent still smaller changes
in physical housing conditions.

But the evidence is also consistent with an alternative interpretation:
the price and income elasticities of unmeasured housing quality dimensions are larger than for easily measured items, such as size; dwelling units
renting for more than the predicted hedonic index are simply of higher
quality than those with the same measured attributes but lower rents.

32. Friedman and Weinberg, "Draft Report on the Demand for Rental Housing," pp. A-132–35.
33. Indeed, the authors present an exhaustive, but inconclusive, analysis of the
potential bias in estimates resulting from the procedures. In particular, see the ingenious analysis in Stephen D. Kennedy and Sally R. Merrill, "The Use of Hedonic
Indices to Distinguish Real Changes in Housing Expenditures: Evidence from the
Housing Allowance Demand Experiment," paper presented at the Research Conference on Housing Choices of Low-Income Families, Washington, D.C., March 8–9,
1979. They attempt to decompose errors in hedonic price equations between control
and percent of rent households into search efficiency and an attribute misspecification component. They conclude that overpayment may be important, but, at least
for Pittsburgh, model misspecification may also be important and indistinguishable
from overpayment. This analysis, however, requires strong assumptions about the
structure of the regression errors, the nature of search behavior, and an assumption
that hedonic price relationships are unchanged over the two-year period.

Regressions relating housing expenditures to prices and incomes contain measurement error due to bargains and overpriced units. However, regressions relating hedonic indexes to prices and incomes also contain measurement error because of the omission of certain components of quality. It is virtually impossible to distinguish between these interpretations on the basis of this evidence.

It is therefore worth noting that with this hedonic technique the estimated income elasticities of demand are lower for both demand experiment households and Seattle and Denver income maintenance experiment households.[34] While theory suggests that the private returns to search are reduced by offering percent of rent subsidies, households receiving income subsidies still pay the full marginal cost of any inefficiency in their search behavior. Therefore, the overall results seem consistent with the hypothesis that the problem of "left-out quality" in the hedonic demand relations is more important than the problem of "inefficient search" in the expenditure relations.[35]

34. For households receiving unrestricted income transfers under the Seattle and Denver income maintenance experiment program, a comparable analysis was performed using a hedonic index as the dependent variable. See James C. Ohls and Cynthia Thomas, "The Effects of the Seattle and Denver Income Maintenance Experiments on Consumption, Ownership, and Mobility," Draft Report (Mathematica Policy Research, January 1979), p. 34. For samples of renter and owner households receiving income subsidies for three and five years, the estimated income elasticities of demand are also somewhat lower with this technique.

35. The marketwide sample of dwellings (preexperimental from Brown County) is also used by the supply experiment researchers to estimate hedonic price equations. C. Lance Barnett, *Using Hedonic Indexes to Measure Housing Quantity,* R-2450-HUD (Rand Corp., October 1979). While the estimated equations yield plausible price estimates, the most interesting part involves testing for submarket differences and consideration of demands for particular attributes. Tests for differences in relative prices for particular housing attributes by dwelling unit type (for example, single family, duplex, and so forth) indicate that the prices for duplexes seem to diverge from other types of dwellings. No other definitions of submarkets, such as by race or geographic location, are considered. The second analysis, following the design used by Kain and Quigley, *Housing Markets,* considers how the demands for five aggregations of attributes (space, interior quality, exterior quality, location, and residential services) differ by income class. This analysis indicates that most of the additional expenditures by higher-income groups go toward quality, both interior and exterior. Interpretation of these latter results is difficult for two reasons: first, no consideration is given to other household attributes (such as family size) that might affect demands for particular attributes (such as space); second, this analysis ignores complications introduced by joint pricing of attributes and the interrelatedness of bundle decisions. No application of this analytic strategy has yet been made to the experimental data.

Quality Indexes and Housing Standards

An alternative approach is the development of direct quality indexes—an attempt to translate the abstract notions of decent, safe, and sanitary housing, which motivate the housing allowances as a *housing* policy, into operational measures. Clearly, this is complicated—there is little consensus about what constitutes "adequate" housing and even less about how to measure explicitly the various elements of adequate housing. The experimenters were, nevertheless, required to develop and use such measures for housing requirements in eligibility determination. This subsection discusses the interrelationships among the alternative definitions and notes the choices of unconstrained demand households (controls, unconstrained housing gap, and percent of rent treatments) in terms of these measures. The next subsection describes the households whose subsidies were tied to particular housing requirements.

The primary set of standards involved fifteen elements of the physical condition of dwelling units and specific occupancy requirements. The explicit requirements differed somewhat between supply and demand experiment sites and were determined by individual operating agencies in the administrative agency experiment sites.[36]

The application of these standards requires detailed inspections of individual dwelling units. There would be obvious gains—lower costs and a less intrusive program operation—from housing standards that do not require individual dwelling unit evaluations.[37] Therefore, the demand ex-

36. See the discussion in this volume on the components of physical standards and Joseph J. Valenza, *Program Housing Standards in the Experimental Housing Allowance Program: Analyzing Differences in the Demand and Supply Experiments,* 216-30 (Urban Institute, July 1977), pp. 22–24, for contrasts between supply and demand experiment standards. For example, the occupancy standards were nominally the same for both experiments: no more than two household members per "adequate" bedroom. However, the definitions of an "adequate" bedroom differed, and the interpretation of "adequacy" differed across demand and supply site evaluators, so that even such apparently direct comparisons of standards are difficult across experiments and sites.

37. Unfortunately, reliable estimates of inspection costs from the administrative agency and demand experiments are unavailable. In the administrative agency experiment, standards, cost accounting, and methods of inspection differed by site and preclude estimation of costs. See the paper by David N. Kershaw and Roberton C. Williams, Jr., in this volume. Estimates of the marginal costs of housing inspections from the supply experiment are $58 and $81 per recipient per year in Brown and St. Joseph counties, respectively. See Rand Corporation, *Fourth Annual Report of the Housing Assistance Supply Experiment,* R-2302-HUD (Rand, May 1978), pp. 148–50.

periment also measured adequacy by minimum rent requirements for
some experimental groups.[38]

At the same time, it is clear that "adequate" housing is neither well-
defined at any point in time nor a static concept.[39] Therefore, for analytical
purposes, the demand experiment researchers used other definitions of
adequacy, in part to analyze the sensitivity of the program to the specific
measures used.[40] Using the same data available from housing inspections, Budding developed an alternative set of measures that might better
correspond to notions of physical deprivation in housing.[41] Housing units
were classified in the following categories:

(1) clearly inadequate—"clear evidence of one or more serious defi-
    ciencies";
(2) minimally adequate—"no serious deficiencies plus an evaluator
    overall rating consistent with such a classification"; or
(3) ambiguous—"unit falls in neither of above categories."

The researchers also defined a "low standard," a subset of "physical standards" (six of the fifteen physical "program standards" requiring minimal
kitchen, bath, and one other room, and adequate exterior walls and
roofing).

The relationship between housing requirements in the program and
these alternative measures is best illustrated by considering the control
group at the baseline. Table 6 shows the percentage of units considered
clearly inadequate and minimally adequate by whether or not the households concurrently passed or failed the three program housing requirements. Passing the program standards implies a higher probability of living in a unit classified as minimally adequate and a lower probability of
living in a house that is clearly inadequate. Yet there are substantial differences across measures, and only part of these differences can be attributed
to the occupancy standard. Further, as many as 39 percent of the units in
various samples fall in the ambiguous category, which implies even larger
potential discrepancies. Finally, even though the patterns of the quality

38. The specific standards are discussed below.

39. See, for example, the historical change in notions of standards described by
William C. Baer, "The Evolution of Housing Indicators and Housing Standards:
Some Lessons for the Future," *Public Policy*, vol. 24 (Summer 1976), pp. 361–93.

40. Note, however, that all tied subsidies required either the program minimum
standards or the minimum rent requirements. Therefore, all analyses related to reactions to housing requirements are restricted to the narrower definitions above.

41. David W. Budding, "Draft Report on Housing Deprivation Among Enrollees
in the Housing Allowance Demand Experiment" (Abt, November 1978).

Table 6. Distribution of Control Households by Measures of Housing Adequacy and Program Standards at Baseline

Percent

Program standards status	Pittsburgh			Phoenix		
	Minimally adequate	Am- biguous	Clearly inadequate	Minimally adequate	Am- biguous	Clearly inadequate
Minimum standards						
Passed	84	14	2	94	4	2
Failed	14	39	47	20	24	56
Low minimum rent						
Passed	41	36	23	59	26	15
Failed	9	30	61	14	15	71
High minimum rent						
Passed	54	33	13	71	21	8
Failed	17	34	49	22	20	58

Source: Friedman and Weinberg, "Draft Report on Housing Consumption," pp. 22, 60, 61.

indexes are similar across the two sites, it is also evident that they yield systematic differences in aggregate measures of adequacy. These comparisons underscore the need for understanding the housing "bundle choice" problem.

While table 6 displays the relationships among the alternative standards and measures of housing condition, table 7 indicates the natural choices of households and the adjustments elicited by unconstrained transfers. This table describes the proportion of control, percent of rent, and unconstrained housing gap households meeting program minimum standards, separate components of these program standards—that is, low, physical, and occupancy standards[42]—and the alternative summary measures devised by Budding. These data are presented at baseline and after two years of program operation.[43] The table indicates, for example, that in Pitts-

42. Meeting the "low standard" implies complete plumbing, heating, and kitchen facilities, as well as sound roof structure and exterior walls. The "physical standard" includes the low standard plus interior features like adequate lighting fixtures and ceiling height. The "occupancy standard" requires a minimum of one adequate bedroom for every two occupants. For more details, see Friedman and Weinberg, "Draft Report on the Demand for Rental Housing," p. A-30.

43. For none of these households is the receipt of any subsidies contingent on attributes of the dwellings they occupy. Therefore, the distributions of housing outcomes for controls at both times and subsidy groups at baseline indicate the preferences for the different levels of adequacy, conditional of course on incomes, prices, and the availability of different kinds of units. The two-year data for the subsidy groups show how unrestricted subsidies affect choices.

burgh at baseline only 21 percent of the control households and 13 percent of those receiving price subsidies lived in dwelling units that met program physical and occupancy housing requirements.

Conclusions about the extent of improvement from subsidies depend on the specific measure used. For the first three measures of adequacy, there is no evidence that households receiving price reductions chose to live in better or less-crowded dwelling units than the control group that receives no subsidy. There is some evidence that the change in the fraction of households meeting the combined housing requirements (that is, program and occupancy standards) was greater for unconstrained housing gap households than for control households. It also appears that households receiving transfers improved their housing under the last two criteria, relative to the control group. Yet none of the individual comparisons is very persuasive, since each notion of standards appears on the surface to be reasonable.

For Seattle and Denver income maintenance experiment households, demand experiment housing gap households receiving unrestricted transfers, and demand experiment percent of rent households, several other comparisons of the housing chosen are available. A probit analysis of the Seattle and Denver experiment data base reveals that the probability of living in a dwelling unit that meets certain normative physical standards is not affected by unrestricted income transfers.[44] However, experimental payments seem to have significantly increased the average propensity for homeownership. A 10 percent increase in transfer payments is associated with a 2 percent increase in probability of homeownership. Payments seem to have substantially increased the probability of home purchase among minority households. For example, it is estimated that $2,000 in annual transfers increases the probability of homeownership by 9 or 10 percentage points.[45] In addition, an analysis of upgrading behavior suggests that income subsidies are associated with housing improvements or upgrading among nonmovers, especially renters.[46]

In summary, it appears that unrestricted price and income subsidies to low-income households caused them to increase their housing expendi-

44. Ohls and Thomas, *Effects*, p. 23.
45. Ibid., p. 41. Note that tenure choice cannot be analyzed in the demand experiment research since the experiment was restricted to renters. In the supply experiment sites, where payments are open to both owners and renters, aggregate statistics suggest that change in tenure is not frequent.
46. Ibid., p. 72.

Table 7. Percentage of Households Residing in Alternative Measures of Adequate Housing for Demand Experiment Control Groups and Those Receiving Unrestricted Transfers at Baseline and after Two Years

Measure of adequacy and treatment group	Pittsburgh households passing standard			Phoenix households passing standard		
	At baseline	After two years	Percent change	At baseline	After two years	Percent change
Program minimum standards						
Low standard						
Control	81	80	−1	66	74	12
Percent of rent	81	84	4	72	75	4
Physical standard						
Control	33	29	−12	28	36	29
Percent of rent	37	34	−8	33	41	24
Occupancy standard						
Control	46	41	−11	38	53	39
Percent of rent	49	47	−4	43	55	28
Physical and occupancy standard[a]						
Control	21	28	33	19	36	89
Percent of rent	n.a.	n.a.	n.a.	n.a.	n.a.	n.a.
Unconstrained housing gap	13	23	77	23	46	100
Alternative adequacy measures						
Minimally adequate housing						
Control	29	25	−14	34	37	9
Percent of rent	31	28	−10	36	39	8
Unconstrained housing gap	18	31	72	26	44	69
Minimally adequate and ambiguous housing						
Control	62	65	5	54	59	9
Percent of rent	59	65	10	56	61	9
Unconstrained housing gap	52	66	27	44	69	57

Sources: Friedman and Weinberg, "Draft Report on Housing Consumption," pp. 17, 22; Friedman and Weinberg, "Draft Report on the Demand for Rental Housing," p. 95.
n.a. Not available.
a. Meeting both physical and occupancy standards is equivalent to meeting minimum standard requirements.

tures, their consumption of housing services, their probability of home-ownership, and their propensity to upgrade rental units. However, the expenditure and consumption increases are relatively small, which again implies that such policies have their largest impacts on rent burdens. There is little or no evidence that the housing bundles chosen with the help of unconstrained subsidies are more "adequate," when adequate is defined according to narrow program criteria.

What does it all mean? Conclusions about adequacy depend somewhat on the specific standards applied; plausible alternative definitions may yield different conclusions.

Housing Requirements and Tied Subsidies

The key distinction between a housing allowance program and a pure income transfer is the imposition of certain housing requirements. These requirements presumably relate to the specific housing goals that underlie a housing policy. The demand experiment housing gap program applied two different approaches to the question of housing requirements. First, some households were required to meet the specific standards on occupancy and quality discussed previously. Second, other households were required to meet certain minimum expenditure requirements (set at 70 and 90 percent of the estimated average market rent for "minimally adequate" housing of a given size) with no restrictions on the physical characteristics of the housing bundle chosen.

Two issues are important. The first is the array of housing consumption outcomes when rent requirements, and only rent requirements, are imposed; the second is how individual households react to explicit physical standards requirements. Some may choose not to participate because the requirements are too onerous. Others may opt to meet the requirements, but to do so in ways that are peculiar to the form of the requirements.[47] Some households might meet the physical standards precisely even though they live in dwellings that are inadequate by other reasonable standards. In the last case, the issue in part is whether program regulations and standards can be devised that precisely characterize a view of adequacy.

47. Under a minimum rent requirement, for example, some households may find it desirable to simply pay current landlords more (or split the difference between current rent and required rent); thus, they could meet the requirements with no change in actual housing services.

The analytical problems in unraveling the relationship between tied subsidies and the consumption of particular components of the housing bundle are not trivial. Different households place different values on various components of the housing bundle. The aggregate demand for and supply of dwellings with different attributes determines the price attached to the separate attributes (that is, the hedonic prices); given a change in income or relative prices and given the underlying individual demands for and supplies of attributes, households will make different choices. For example, large families may prefer space to overall quality; families with two workers may highly value location; and families with school-aged children may be most concerned with the quality of neighborhood schools. When individuals are required to purchase units with certain attributes in order to receive payments, the effective prices of those attributes are changed by the housing allowance program. In deciding whether or not to participate in the program, a household must compare the utility of housing and nonhousing consumption at the higher subsidized income with the level of well-being without the subsidy. Program requirements may restrict the choice of dwellings to a subset of the market where the prices and availability of other attributes may be different from the housing market as a whole. Further, the range of dwellings—both in terms of attributes and prices—that meet the requirements in specific dimensions may differ significantly across housing markets.

This suggests that participation in the program and the housing changes observed from the housing allowance will differ across household types and across housing markets, where historical supply conditions for attributes vary. In particular, characteristics of the aggregate housing market may influence the observed decisions of households, even in a demand experiment where a small segment of the housing market receives subsidies and where any effects on the aggregate housing market may be small.

A model that describes both aggregate housing choices and the disaggregation of these across housing attributes is clearly needed, but previous analyses provide little guidance. First, before the housing allowance experiment few data sources contained detailed information about attributes of the bundle; none of these sources had a longitudinal perspective. Second, the simultaneous choice of attributes involves parameters, reflecting differing valuations of attributes, that vary across different households and supply conditions that vary across markets. The analytics of dealing with such a problem are quite undeveloped.

The housing allowance experiment solved the first problem. Considerable resources were devoted to inspecting dwellings, measuring various attributes, geocoding locations, and merging information about neighborhood attributes. To date, little use has been made of these data; they have been used only to estimate hedonic price equations to yield average market prices for different attributes and to analyze program standards and participation decisions. Neither of these analyses directly addresses the bundle choice problem, and neither yields much information about the effect of instituting a national housing allowance program that incorporates standards or housing requirements—particularly if they differ at all from the experimental standards. (Note, however, that the supply experiment analysis on baseline data in Brown County by Barnett, *Using Hedonic Indexes*, may eventually address part of this problem.)

The information gathered on dwelling attributes remains largely unexploited.[48] This is particularly unfortunate, given the structure of the experiments. The tied subsidies provide information about the reactions of households to a single set of standards, standards that are unlikely to be the exact ones applied in any future program. Without detailed information about demands for specific attributes, it is extremely difficult to predict how the experimentally observed behavior might be modified in the face of housing requirement changes.

Table 8 shows the failure rates of standards applied in the supply and demand experiments. The most notable feature of the table is the high failure rates of dwellings initially occupied by experimental subjects.[49] A second feature is the difference in failure rates across sites and between

48. Jeanne E. Goedert, *Earmarking Housing Allowances: The Trade-off Between Housing Consumption and Program Participation*, 249-19 (Urban Institute, May 1979), pp. 5–21, attempted to analyze consumption decisions—the probability of meeting sixteen different components of the minimum standards housing requirements. She also examined the probabilities of meeting overall standards under each of the constrained plans. This does not provide much information about the general demand question and the joint nature of participation and consumption decisions. In particular, the consumption of each component is taken to be independent of other consumption choices, is restricted to the operational program standards, and ignores any marketwide constraints on choices.

49. Note that the data from the supply and demand experiments were gathered by very different sampling rules. In the demand experiment, a sample of households was randomly chosen from a population passing the income eligibility rule. In the supply experiment, the sample was limited to households that voluntarily enrolled in the program. One would expect enrolling households to live in dwellings that are more likely to pass the housing standards than those of the entire population meeting the income eligibility limits.

Table 8. Percentage of Enrollees in Constrained Housing Allowance Plans That Failed Minimum Standards Requirements at Enrollment

	Demand experiment[a]		Supply experiment[b]	
Type of defect	Phoenix	Pittsburgh	Brown County	St. Joseph County
Exterior property area	...	...	4.6	1.3
Building exterior	...	...	18.6	31.9
Roof structure	4.4	0.9	...	...
Exterior walls	8.5	0.4	...	...
Building interior	...	...	35.9	55.9
Room structure	10.9	1.4	...	...
Room surface	24.5	9.1	...	...
Floor surface	20.9	3.9	...	...
Core rooms	2.5	7.5	...	...
Ceiling height	9.8	9.4	...	...
Light fixtures	7.0	5.8	...	...
Light/ventilation	63.6	63.7	...	...
Adequate exits	1.1	8.9	...	...
Utility systems	...	...	11.2	15.6
Electricity	5.9	8.8	...	...
Heating equipment	18.8	3.2	...	...
Kitchen facilities	5.5	3.3	5.3	18.6
Bathroom/plumbing	18.2	17.7	14.3	28.3
Occupancy	58.1	52.4	9.6	20.5
Failed at least one component	78.4	82.0	49.8	61.2

Sources: Jeanne E. Goedert, *Earmarking Housing Allowances: The Trade-off Between Housing Consumption and Program Participation*, 249-19 (Washington, D.C.: Urban Institute, May 1979), p. 10; Rand Corporation, *Third Annual Report of the Housing Assistance Supply Experiment*, R-2151-HUD (Rand, February 1977), pp. 96, 98.

a. Phoenix and Pittsburgh households assigned to minimum standards or minimum rent treatment groups.

b. Dwellings occupied at enrollment by owners and renters at each site.

experiments. The difference between experiments reflects differences in standards, differences in sampling rules (see note 49), differences in emphasis between the evaluators at the two sites, and, probably, differences in the available housing stock. The major point of the comparison among sites is variation in the definition of what is "adequate." Further, apparently small variations in the definition of standards can have large impacts on eligibility.[50]

50. For example, the demand and supply experiment standards applied to an identical set of houses by evaluators for the supply and demand experiments yielded an estimated difference in failure of the occupancy requirement of 28 percent even though both experiments used the same nominal standard (no more than two per-

These differences have three implications. First, the definition of adequate in housing is important, and the definitions applied in the experiments may not correspond to those that would be chosen in an operational program. Second, even identical criteria may result in a different program across the country. Third, the differences across the experiments make participation and housing consumption results incomparable across experiments.

The key questions are whether requirements affect participation in an important way and whether participating households do anything more than just meet the explicit requirement. In other words, what is the relationship between meeting standards—which are necessarily a set of specific, measurable features of housing—and more general notions of improvements in housing conditions?

The relationship between participation and housing requirements is shown in tables 9 (demand experiment) and 10 (supply and administrative agency experiments). The determinants of participation are the subject of a separate analysis (see Straszheim's paper in this volume), but the low participation rates have implications for analysis of housing changes. The low participation resulted in very small samples of households receiving subsidies and dramatically reduced the ability to evaluate alternative program effects. Further, there is a real possibility that attrition and selection biases affected the results of consumption analyses. In Pittsburgh 56 percent of active households at the end of two years did not meet the minimum standards and thus did not receive subsidies; for Phoenix, 47 percent. In addition, a significant proportion of enrolled households were not active in the program at all and had completely dropped out at the end of two years (27 percent in Pittsburgh and 47 percent in Phoenix). Combining eligibility and standards data, we find that less than one-third of the initially enrolled households in each site were both active and met the

---

sons per adequate bedroom). Valenza, "Program Housing Standards," p. 20. Most of this difference is explicable by differences in the definition of an adequate bedroom, although there is even disagreement about just how many bedrooms are available. For Phoenix, there is a discrepancy of 12 percent in the count of the total number of bedrooms. In three of the four sites, the estimated number of adequate bedrooms differed by over 20 percent between the supply and demand experiment evaluators. This difference appears to arise from the light and ventilation standards of the demand experiment that were not present in the supply experiment, and the bedroom heating requirement present in the supply but not the demand experiment. Ibid., p. 23.

Table 9. Participation Status for Demand Experiment Households Offered Subsidies Tied to Housing Requirements

Treatment	Pittsburgh		Phoenix	
	Number	*Percent*	*Number*	*Percent*
Minimum standards				
Enrolled households at baseline[a]	281	100	329	100
Passing at baseline	51	18	61	19
Enrolled after two years[b]	204	73	174	53
Passing at baseline	43	22	33	20
Passing after two years	39	91	28	85
Failing at baseline	156	78	134	80
Passing after two years	50	32	65	49
Low mimimum rent				
Enrolled households at baseline[a]	166	100	175	100
Passing at baseline	103	62	94	54
Enrolled after two years[b]	128	77	98	56
Passing at baseline	78	62	47	48
Passing after two years	78	100	45	96
Failing at baseline	47	38	50	52
Passing after two years	28	60	30	60
High minimum rent				
Enrolled households at baseline[a]	179	100	191	100
Passing at baseline	56	31	50	26
Enrolled after two years[b]	117	65	109	57
Passing at baseline	35	30	21	20
Passing after two years	35	100	20	95
Failing at baseline	82	70	84	80
Passing after two years	26	32	33	39

Source: Friedman and Weinberg, "Draft Report on Housing Consumption," pp. 14, 15, 45–48.
a. Income-eligible households enrolled in subsidy plan.
b. Enrolled households two years after enrollment excluding those with incomes over eligibility limits, those owning homes, and those in subsidized housing.

standards by the end of two years. Thus, consumption decisions are related to participation, and attrition decisions and analyses confined to subsidy recipients are likely to be based on unrepresentative samples.[51]

51. The joint modeling of participation and consumption decisions is very difficult in this case. Most empirical demand analysis relies on an underlying consumer utility maximization argument where consumers face linear budget constraints. The implied budget constraint, with subsidy tied to consumption, is not only nonlinear but also discontinuous. This suggests that modeling of the joint decisions must incorporate assumptions about the form of underlying utility functions. While some work has been done with nonlinear budget constraints, it has considered only continuous constraints. See, for example, Gary Burtless and Jerry A. Hausman, "The Effect of Taxation on Labor Supply: Evaluating the Gary Negative Income Tax Experiment," *Journal of Political Economy,* vol. 86 (December 1978), pp. 1103–30.

Table 10. Participation Rates for Supply Experiment and Administrative Agency Experiment Households Offered Subsidies Tied to Housing Requirements
Percent

Site	Renters	Owners
Enrollment[a]		
Brown County, Wisconsin	53	33
St. Joseph County, Indiana	54	25
Enrollees who became recipients		
Bismarck, North Dakota	86	...
Brown County, Wisconsin	79	85
Durham, North Carolina	71	...
Jacksonville, Florida	32	...
Peoria, Illinois	65	...
St. Joseph County, Indiana	70	84
Salem, Oregon	85	...
San Bernardino, California	82	...
Springfield, Massachusetts	70	...
Tulsa, Oklahoma	86	...

Source: U.S. Department of Housing and Urban Development, *Experimental Housing Allowance Program: A 1979 Report of Findings* (Government Printing Office, 1979), pp. 19, 20.
a. Percentage of estimated number of households with incomes less than eligibility limits enrolled in program as of September 1977.

For the supply experiment (table 10), percentages are based on estimates of the eligible population after about three years of operation. These statistics again show that many of the eligible households did not enroll. However, for those enrolling, a higher percentage passed the housing requirements and became recipients than in the demand experiment.

Turning to the effects of tied subsidies, table 11 presents the most optimistic appraisal of the housing improvements elicited by the housing allowance program. This table displays the changes in the different measures of adequacy for households that initially did not meet the requirements for payments but subsequently did meet them. Only a minority of households that met the minimum expenditure limits also met the minimum physical standards of the program or moved to dwellings rated as "minimally adequate." A significant fraction of the minimum rent households remain in "clearly inadequate" housing, although there was a distinct movement into "ambiguous" housing. The relationship between meeting the program standards and the alternative measures is stronger, but it should be, since the alternative adequacy measures are based on many of the same notions as the program standards. The table also shows

Table 11. Quality of Housing Chosen by Those Demand Experiment Households Meeting Requirements at Two Years but Not at Enrollment

Housing requirement imposed	Pittsburgh: outcome after two years				Phoenix: outcome after two years			
	Met minimum standards	Adequacy rating			Met minimum standards	Adequacy rating		
		Minimally adequate	Clearly inadequate	Ambiguous		Minimally adequate	Clearly inadequate	Ambiguous
				Percent				
Minimum standards	100	49	10	41	100	72	5	23
Low minimum rent	14	17	31	52	30	32	29	39
High minimum rent	23	23	35	42	39	41	10	49
			Change since enrollment (percentage points)					
Minimum standards	100	39	−31	−8	100	36	−36	0
Low minimum rent	11	14	−35	21	16	3	−17	14
High minimum rent	8	0	−23	23	20	10	−42	32

Source: Friedman and Weinberg, "Draft Report on Housing Consumption," pp. 56, 57, A-95–97.

distinct differences between the two housing markets. The relationship between the various measures of standards is uniformly stronger in Phoenix than in Pittsburgh.

This table, however, overstates the importance of the program requirements in improving housing. First, the sample from which this table is drawn represents a minority of the experimental groups because of the low overall participation rates, and the comparison is of a self-selected sample. Second, this comparison attributes *all* movement to the program requirements when, in fact, at least some of these households would have been expected to improve their housing in the absence of a housing allowance program or in the absence of explicit housing requirements.

Table 12 provides some evidence on the net effects of program requirements. This table presents estimated probabilities of changing housing quality for each category of housing requirements when compared with the control group.[52] Except for the probability of meeting minimum standards by the minimum standards experimental group, the only consistent difference from control group behavior seems to be a reduction in the

52. These estimates are based on logit models estimated for households (both experimental and control) that did not initially meet standards. For some inexplicable reason, the estimated models do not include household income, even though they do include several other factors that might affect household demands.

Table 12. Effect of the Allowance Offer on Measures of Housing Adequacy
Percentage points

Household group	Pittsburgh; change in the probability of [a]			Phoenix; change in the probability of [a]		
	Meeting minimum standards[b]	Living in minimally adequate housing	Living in clearly inadequate housing	Meeting minimum standards[b]	Living in minimally adequate housing	Living in clearly inadequate housing
Minimum standards	20**	4	−2	28**	11*	−14**
Low minimum rent	4	−2	1	4	5	−12*
High minimum rent	−1	−4	6	4	6	−11*
Unconstrained	1	8	−3	8	10	−22**

Source: Friedman and Weinberg, "Draft Report on Housing Consumption," p. 227.
* t-statistic of logit coefficient significant at the 0.05 level.
** t-statistic of logit coefficient significant at the 0.01 level.
a. Measured at two years after enrollment relative to control households, at the means of the other independent variables included in the logit models.
b. For households that did not meet minimum standards at enrollment.

probability of living in clearly inadequate housing in Phoenix.[53] However, even there the improvements were smaller by the groups with housing requirements than by those receiving unrestricted cash transfer.[54] There is no discernible difference in probabilities of improvement between the two minimum rent groups.

Because of the possibilities of perverse incentives when expenditure requirements are applied, Friedman and Weinberg examined the question of overpayment for housing. Their analysis, based on the hedonic price equations, is not conclusive; it suggests that the high minimum rent households are induced to overpay for housing,[55] sometimes by as much as 20

53. The estimated net improvement of the minimum standards group in meeting the minimum standards is an artifact of the sample selection. To be in the sample, a minimum standard household had to be active at two years and not have met the standard at enrollment. One would expect differential attrition by households to affect this estimate.

54. Some caution is required in comparisons with the unconstrained households. This is a small treatment cell, and other analyses of this group suggest erratic behavior probably related to sampling problems.

55. There are several reasons for a more cautious interpretation. The analysis is based on average residuals from a hedonic price equation. There is always some difficulty in labeling residuals in this way, particularly when the residual variance is high. Among other things, this analysis presumes that the specification of the hedonic price equation is correct in terms of variables and functional form. See also Kennedy and Merrill, "Use of Hedonic Indices," fn. 1, p. 33. Further, the hedonic

percent. There is also some evidence that overpayment may be related to overall housing market conditions; minimum rent households apparently make larger overpayments in Pittsburgh than in Phoenix.

Because of the small cells in the experimental groups, it is difficult to find out exactly what kinds of housing changes occurred within the different treatment groups. Did the households consuming the worst housing increase consumption, or did the changes occur among households that were close to meeting the requirements before the experiment? For the small group that met the requirements by physically upgrading units, it appears that those who were close to the standards did something. If installing a sash cord in a window or installing a stairway handrail opens up the cash transfers (which probably would exceed the costs of improvement in the first month), one would expect renters to meet the requirements, even in a program of limited duration. For example, in the supply experiment 86 percent of the households that eventually qualified for subsidies, but did not meet requirements at enrollment, undertook some upgrading of their units. These repairs were highly concentrated in meeting handrail and stair requirements or window requirements, and the median expenditure was about $9.[56] While the demand experiment showed higher expenditures on upgrading, it also indicated that there was little difference in probabilities of upgrading (and in housing expenditures) between control and experimental households.[57] Outside of this small subset for which minimal changes are required, little evidence on the pattern of upgrading relative to initial conditions exists. (Note that tabulating mean expenditures conditional on making improvements conveys very little in-

---

prices are an amalgam of supplies of different kinds of units and demands for these units. These cannot be interpreted as structural supply coefficients except under very restrictive circumstances. If there are taste differences in the population, interpretation of hedonic residuals is difficult. While one might argue that randomization in treatment groups ensures that the average tastes of households in the different groups will be the same, this argument is difficult here because the sample sizes in the different cells are very small. The sample size problem is particularly acute for unconstrained households. (The erratic estimates for the unconstrained households in terms of overpayments indicate a need for caution in comparing results for constrained households with those for unconstrained.)

56. U.S. Department of Housing and Urban Development, *Experimental Housing Allowance Program: A 1979 Report of Findings* (Government Printing Office, 1979), pp. 58, 60. This is not to say that some expenditures are not substantial. In the supply experiment, 1.3 percent (in Brown County) and 2.3 percent (in St. Joseph County) of those making repairs spent more than $300 in 1976–77.

57. Sally R. Merrill and Catherine A. Joseph, "Draft Report on Housing Improvements and Upgrading in the Housing Allowance Demand Experiment" (Abt, February 1979).

formation about the expenditures that would generally be required to improve houses; it conveys information only about how close some houses were to the cutoff. Further, information about the hedonic price discount related to substandard housing may give misleading information about the actual costs of improving a dwelling when there are restricted supplies of housing bundles with different characteristics.)

In summary, the evidence from the demand experiment suggests that households that received tied subsidies tended to concentrate on meeting the explicit and narrowly defined requirements. While there is some measured improvement in alternative definitions of housing adequacy, meeting a given specific standard by no means implied the achievement of other standards of adequacy. Further, it is unclear how much of the improvement in housing conditions can be attributed to the program. When the housing improvements for the constrained housing group are compared with the changes observed for the control group and the unconstrained housing allowance group, the improvements appear rather small. Finally, some of the housing requirements may have perverse incentives. In particular, the minimum rent requirement (that is, the requirement to make a given expenditure on housing) may induce households to live in dwellings with low "housing-services-to-rent" ratios. The evidence suggests that, at least for the households with high minimum rent requirements, this indeed takes place.

The Effects of Variations in Program Parameters

Within the demand experiment, there are three important design parameters: the basic payment level (or the subsidy that would be received by a household with no income), the tax rate on income (the rate at which subsidies are reduced as income increases), and the housing requirements.[58] An estimate of the cost of obtaining modest existing standard housing (C^*), which varies by site and household size, is used in calculating the basic payment level.[59] For eligible households, the subsidies to be received are calculated by the formula:

(14)   Subsidy $= C - t \times$ income.

58. The supply experiment, with a common program definition, can provide no information on the effects of variations in program parameters.

59. As an indication of the magnitudes involved, C^* for a two-bedroom unit was $150 in Pittsburgh and $190 in Phoenix in March 1975. HUD, *1979 Report of Findings*, p. 100.

The basic payment level (C) offered to a particular household was $0.8C^*$, $1.0C^*$, or $1.2C^*$. The tax rate, t, applied to the incomes of experimental households was 0.15, 0.25, or 0.35, but most households were taxed at 25 percent. The housing requirements were either program (physical and occupancy) standards, described previously, or minimum rent payment requirements (which were either $0.7C^*$ or $0.9C^*$).[60] The effects of variations in program parameters are obviously of central importance in designing a national policy. Three effects are crucial. First, these parameters will affect the level and pattern of participation in the program (where participation means meeting the physical, occupancy, or rent eligibility requirements). Second, they will affect the housing consumption by those households meeting the stated requirements. Third, the program parameters will have a substantial effect on the total amount of government subsidies, or the program costs.

The clearest effect is on program costs. With the same number of participants (that is, if no households are induced to meet housing requirements with a change in subsidy parameters), increasing the basic subsidy from $1.0C^*$ to $1.2C^*$ increases total program costs by 20 percent; decreasing the tax rate from 25 percent to 15 percent increases total program costs by 40 percent. Going from the least generous option ($0.8C^*$ and 35 percent) to the most generous option ($1.2C^*$ and 15 percent) yields a change in program costs of at least 183 percent, if no new households are induced to participate. Such changes would be clearly noticeable in a national program. Presumably, the more generous options would increase the number of eligible households (by raising the income eligibility cutoff), so variations in program costs would be considerably larger.

If the program is viewed as a straight income transfer program, the amount of subsidy is a political issue, not an analytical one; there is no real way for us to say whether more generous programs are better or worse. However, in this light it is clear that when participation is low, inequities of the transfer program are more pronounced if larger subsidies are given to households simply on the basis of past expressed consumption preferences for housing. If the program is viewed as a housing program, larger subsidies are better because they may stimulate greater changes in

60. As discussed above, one treatment group received an unrestricted income subsidy (a payments schedule with a basic subsidy of $1.0C^*$, a tax rate of 25 percent, and no housing requirements), and other groups received a pure percent of rent subsidy (reimbursements of 20, 40, or 60 percent of monthly rent with no housing requirements). Table 2 of the paper by Allen, Glatt, and Fitts in this volume shows all seventeen treatments used in the demand experiment.

housing consumption by new participants and by those who would not have participated under a less generous plan.

What is the effect of variations in the program parameters on the housing consumption of participants? The answer is, "We don't know." Table 13 shows the number of households that met the different housing requirements at the end of two years. The table also shows the number of different experimental treatments (that is, variations in basic subsidy and tax rates) for each type of housing requirement. As the table indicates, numbers of participating households in the different treatment groups are *very* small. This makes detection of differential effects extremely difficult, particularly if one allows for differences among those initially meeting and not meeting requirements, or among housing requirement categories. For example, eighty-seven participating households in Pittsburgh received subsidies for living in dwelling units that met minimum physical standards. These households were distributed among five experimental treatments (that is, five different sets of payment parameters). Thirty-eight of those households already lived in dwelling units at baseline that satisfied the minimum standards, and thus these households received pure income transfers.

Apparently because of these small samples, analysis of program effects on housing consumption within the demand experiment is almost exclusively related to aggregate effects within different housing requirements groups, and all variations in basic subsidy levels and tax rates are ignored.

With such a small number of observations, the only hope of detecting consumption differences is by combining the information across treatment groups. This is done in two ways in the demand analysis. First, the dollar subsidy is calculated for each household, and the effect of this transfer on above-normal rent expenditures is estimated. Second, the parameter differences relative to the modal program ($1.0C^*$ and $t = 0.25$) and the calculated subsidy under the modal program are used to explain above-normal consumption expenditures.[61] The latter analysis finds no positive effects; estimated effects are almost always insignificantly different from

61. In both analyses, the dependent variable is expressed as differences between log rent and estimated normal rent. In the first analysis, dollar subsidy level is the independent variable; in the second, the deviation of the basic subsidy from C^* and the deviation of the tax rate from 0.25 are the independent variables. The semi-log form seems peculiar in both analyses. In the former, the elasticity of subsidy varies depending upon income level—in a form that is different from all of the other estimates of income elasticity analyzed in the demand experiment. In the latter, the effects of differences in basic subsidy and in tax rates are constrained to be independent of income levels and of each other. See Friedman and Weinberg, "Draft Report on the Demand for Rental Housing," pp. 108–16.

Table 13. Number of Experimental Households Meeting Requirements at Baseline and after Two Years and Number of Experimental Treatments, by Type of Housing Requirement

Households meeting requirement	Type of housing requirement							
	Unconstrained		Minimum standards		Low minimum rent		High minimum rent	
	Number of households	Number of treatments	Number of households	Number of treatments	Number of households	Number of treatments	Number of households	Number of treatments
Pittsburgh								
Total	59	1	87	5	104	3	59	3
At baseline	59	...	38	...	77	...	33	...
After two years[a]	0	...	49	...	27	...	26	...
Phoenix								
Total	37	1	91	5	69	3	46	3
At baseline	37	...	27	...	42	...	18	...
After two years[a]	0	...	64	...	27	...	28	...

Source: Friedman and Weinberg, "Draft Report on Housing Consumption," pp. 14, 15, 45–48, A-46.
a. Comprises only those households that did not meet requirement at baseline.

Table 14. Implied Elasticity of Housing Consumption with Respect to Subsidy Amount at Mean Treatment Income Subsidy for Minimum Standards Households

Minimum standards households	Pittsburgh	Phoenix
All households	0.17	1.39*
Households meeting standards at baseline	0.10	0.74**
Households not meeting standards at baseline	0.24	1.39*

Source: Calculations based on Friedman and Weinberg, "Draft Report on Housing Consumption," pp. 109, 112.

* Regression coefficient significant at 0.05 level.
** Regression coefficient significant at 0.10 level.

zero and often of the wrong sign. The former estimates, available only for the minimum standards treatment, do not clarify much. The coefficient on the payment size variable for Pittsburgh is uniformly less than its standard error, and remains so when the sample is divided into households meeting and not meeting standards at enrollment. For Phoenix, the coefficients are significant at the 0.10 level or better, but the difference from the Pittsburgh results is hard to interpret. Table 14 presents the elasticities of consumption with respect to subsidies, using the point estimates of the subsidy co-efficients and the mean income and subsidies from the samples. For the group meeting the requirements at enrollment and thus receiving a pure income transfer, these estimates should presumably correspond to income elasticities. In fact, they are *very* different from those presented in table 3.

The differences across sites, here and elsewhere, raise serious questions of interpretation. Do these differences reflect fundamental differences in the tastes and preferences of households across sites? Do they arise from the characterization of the housing markets or the analytical methods? Or do they arise merely because samples are small and estimates of behavior are imprecise? With two sites, we have little basis for choosing among these alternatives. But the answer is important when considering a national program.

The basic problem in understanding the impact of different subsidy schedules is lack of data, not a failure of analysis. No amount of analytical ingenuity is likely to provide an answer to the fundamentally important policy question—what do you get for different levels of subsidies?

Regional Variations

One issue pervades the analysis of responses to housing allowance payments. Across the four sites of the supply and demand experiments, estimates of the basic demand parameters are comparable, but the estimated reactions to housing allowance requirements differ markedly. Initial failure of standards differs; participation differs; and consumption adjustments, estimated rent overpayments, and the probability of meeting alternative measures of adequacy all differ. These differences lead to serious and fundamental problems in interpretation.

One view would simply be that households in different locations have distinctly different tastes. In such a case, we would find that a national program would have different impacts on housing conditions in different locations. So long as the goals of the program were national in scope and so long as supply was reasonably responsive, no particular concern would be elicited. Yet the consistency of the overall demand parameter estimates, such as income elasticities, casts some doubt on the taste difference interpretation.

Another interpretation is perhaps more serious from a policy view. It argues that households in different markets make choices subject to very different constraints in the short run. Consequently, household demand behavior cannot be evaluated in isolation from the local housing market, even in an experiment with negligible impact on the local market. The existing supply of different kinds of units in different locations has a strong impact on the difficulty of meeting requirements and on the subsequent behavior of households.

If the experimental cities reflected the range of housing market conditions observed in the nation, it might be possible to view the observed responses to alternative experimental treatments as bounds upon household and market behavior. But surely this is doubtful. Without explicitly identifying the characteristics of housing markets that are important, such conclusions are pure speculation.[62] For example, in the analysis of over-

62. Jeanne E. Goedert, *Generalizing from the Experimental Housing Allowance Program: An Assessment of Site Characteristics* (Urban Institute, 1978), does compare experimental site characteristics with the distribution of housing market characteristics for all urbanized areas in the United States. In a bivariate analysis of such characteristics as age of housing stock, vacancy rates, percent of black or Hispanic population, and percent of overcrowded units, the experimental sites seem to be evenly distributed across the national distribution. A comparison of mobility rates is an exception. This hardly supports an argument for "bounding" the range since (1) experimental effects can be analyzed only in the two demand sites (only those have control groups and program variation), and these sites do not fall at the extremes except in housing stock age; (2) the sites differed (in terms of place in the distribution) across attributes considered, and there is no way of assessing which attributes were most important or even how they might have affected the results; and (3) these comparisons neglect the substantial portion of the distribution that is not in an urbanized area.

payment, Friedman and Weinberg found that minorities may overpay
more than whites; this would suggest that measures of housing submarkets
more localized than cities or metropolitan areas are appropriate.[63] The
overall experimental design severely limits the analytical possibilities.[64]

While the demand experiment researchers frequently suggested that
overall market conditions, such as the tightness of the Pittsburgh housing market, may have affected the site differences, there was no explicit
analysis of these factors. This has implications both for the generalizability of experimental findings and for the way one thinks about explicit
requirements. Housing stocks in metropolitan areas have developed at
different time periods and in different ways, and the incidence of certain
housing deficiencies will be considerably lower in certain markets.

Conclusions

This paper has two purposes: (1) to summarize and integrate the
analyses resulting from a major commitment to experimental housing research, and (2) to relate the findings from the experiments to the information that would be desired if one seriously considered implementing a
housing allowance program on a national scale. In both cases, however,
the discussion has been limited to issues revolving around housing consumption choices and the microbehavior of households. This limitation is
important, given the participation rates observed, and this paper must be
taken within the context of the related issues raised throughout this
volume.

The most consistent and unequivocal findings relate to the reactions of
households to unrestricted transfer programs. The experiments provide
strong additional evidence that the income elasticity of housing demand
from current income is surely less than one. The income elasticities from
permanent, or long-run, income are somewhat larger than those from current income but are still far less than one. This finding, also supported by
a number of studies completed since the beginning of the experiments, has

63. Friedman and Weinberg, "Draft Report on Housing Consumption."
64. If, in fact, there are distinct submarket differences that could be identified,
perhaps on the basis of geography within areas, it might be possible to analyze how
differences in market conditions affect the analysis. In other words, more observations on market conditions would be available, and variations in different attributes
might be included directly in the modeling. One example of attempting such an
analysis can be found in Mahlon Straszheim, *An Econometric Analysis of the Urban
Housing Market* (National Bureau of Economic Research, 1975).

obvious implications for any housing allowance providing unrestricted cash transfers. Low income elasticities imply that the welfare effects (that is, reductions in rent burdens) will be relatively stronger than the housing effects (that is, increases in the housing component of expenditures) of income transfers.

Second, the demand experiment design allows direct investigation of the price sensitivity of housing demand, a key relationship that heretofore could be inferred only through indirect analysis. These estimates, around -0.2, are uniformly less than the conventional guesses that, in the absence of this evidence, centered on -1.0. Again, the uncertain estimates of the long-run price responsiveness of housing demand are larger than those in the short run, but the low absolute values suggest that a housing allowance providing price discounts to low-income households will also affect rent burdens more than housing consumption.

Third, the collection of longitudinal data within several housing markets provides a unique glimpse into the dynamics of household behavior, a subject that has implications for a variety of questions about housing market operations and consumer behavior. The experimental evidence derived from longitudinal or dynamic analyses will surely be the subject of considerable future research based on the public use files generated by the experiments. At present, it is less conclusive than the static evidence. The estimates of dynamic adjustment lags vary considerably, depending on the precise specification of the model. Inference problems are complicated by the known limited duration of the demand experiment and by the selection bias in a longitudinal sample of experimental households.

At the same time, it must be recognized that investigations of aggregate demand parameters and market dynamics did not require a massive housing allowance experiment. In fact, alternative sampling schemes undoubtedly would have provided even more information about key parameters for the same public expenditure.[65] The unique information on aggregate demand parameters is confined to estimates of the price elasticity of demand, where the experimental manipulation of individual housing prices provides data about reactions to inherently unobservable factors.

---

65. In particular, in an unrestricted income transfer program the key element is knowing the income elasticity of demand, since there is little reason to suspect that transfer income would be treated differently than other income and since the search and shopping incentives would be unaffected. Therefore, all the transfer payments made in the experiment could have been put into expanding the household samples. Also, the number of cities could have been increased so that some effects of site differences could be analyzed.

This additional evidence would hardly justify the experiments. Instead, the justification must rely on new information about reactions to housing requirements that might be imposed as a condition for receipt of public subsidies. On this score, the experimental evidence is very inconclusive.

Decision makers would have to consider two types of information before implementing a national housing allowance program: (1) the response of households to different kinds of program parameters and housing requirements, and (2) the costs of particular entitlement programs keyed to these differences.[66]

The first issue requires a forecast of the effects of program variation on participation, changes in consumption decisions (for housing and other goods), residential location and neighborhood impacts, dwelling unit upgrading, impacts on tenure choice, and the physical characteristics of occupied dwellings. In a national program these responses, and the costs of alternative programs, may be critically related to local housing market differences.[67]

There is some information from the experiments related to each of these issues, but it is hardly enough to give a policy maker much confidence about the most effective program design or about the likely implications of any specific policy. Because of a combination of experimental design problems, bad luck or at least bad guesses on household participation, limitations of current analytical models, and currently incomplete analyses, there are large gaps in our ability to evaluate or predict many important aspects of a national housing allowance program.

Problems in experimental design enter at several points. First, the minimum occupancy and physical standards applied for subsidy eligibility did not vary within the demand and supply experiments, although there were some variations across the two experiments.[68] The precise set of demand

---

66. A third type of information, the aggregate response of local markets to these demand subsidies, is critical to the phase-in and short-run response to such policies. This was the chief motivation for the supply experiments, which were designed to demonstrate fully operational programs at two sites.

67. Several of these issues, such as participation decisions, household mobility, or extrapolations to national programs, are the focal point of other papers in this volume.

68. The administrative agency experiment allowed more variation since individual sites could establish their own housing standards. However, we could not find even a description of the variations used, let alone an analysis of their impacts. The design of the supply and demand experiments appears to reflect the presumption of consistency of individual behavior across local markets, while the administrative agency experiment apparently takes almost the opposite view.

or supply experiment standards almost certainly would not be applied in a national program, but the evidence on effects of program standards pertains only to them.[69]

Second, the experimental design presumes that characteristics of the local housing markets will not enter into the analysis of individual household behavior, but the ex post evidence calls this assumption into question. In principle, the choice of particular sites was intended to consider such possibilities, but when site differences are important, there is no real way to incorporate them into the analysis.[70] In reality, the choice of sites was not intended to bound the range of local differences but rather to provide two observations of different kinds of sites for each experiment.

Third, whether because of experimental design failure or simply bad luck, the samples of participants in different treatment groups within the demand experiment were so small that any real evaluation of the implications of program parameter variation is effectively precluded. Therefore, while the original design permitted consideration of the effects of widely different programs (with variations in program costs of a couple of hundred percent), analyses of different treatment groups within the housing gap program cannot provide estimates with any reasonable reliability.

Two major analytical problems also affect our ability to generalize from the experimental results.

First, related to the design problems, there is no indication of how housing market conditions constrain individual demand behavior. While estimates of the income and price elasticities across demand experiment sites appear similar, suggesting consistency in tastes across sites, the responses to housing requirements differ significantly. Together with other apparent differences across submarkets, such as for minorities, these results imply interaction with local market conditions. It is hard to know how to incorporate these features in the analysis.

Second, even though extensive data were collected on the characteris-

69. As discussed below, the analysis of the unrestricted choices by households of different housing bundles is possible. However, this differs from an analysis of reactions to different standards requirements when they are *binding,* the important issue in program design.

70. The design chosen clearly reflects experimental cost considerations. However, with hindsight, redirection of money from the supply demonstrations to an expanded number of demand experiments probably would have been desirable. For analysis of tied subsidies, only the two demand sites appear relevant.

tics of dwellings, neighborhoods, work locations, and so forth, the bulk of the analysis is confined to aggregate housing expenditures. Under certain conditions, housing expenditures can be taken as a reasonable index of housing services. However, to evaluate the imposition of various housing requirements, it is necessary to know more about the determinants of choice of specific attributes, that is, to disaggregate the housing bundle. This is most obvious for the analysis of participation decisions when the housing requirements are binding, but it also enters at other places. For example, if a household changes dwellings to meet housing requirements, does the household improve its housing conditions only in the explicit areas covered by the requirements?[71] Does it lower its consumption in other dimensions, for example, by meeting physical requirements in worse neighborhoods? The choices and trade-offs among various components of the housing bundle are clearly complex, and they have not been adequately considered in past housing research. Yet they are crucial elements in evaluating housing allowances, particularly given the rigid set of housing requirements considered in the experimental design.

These uncertainties are disturbing when one considers going from experiments to an expensive, nationwide program. There are, nevertheless, some suggestive but inconclusive findings from the direct analyses of reactions to housing requirements in the demand experiment. First, specific housing requirements appear to elicit specific responses; households that adjust to become eligible for subsidies show some, although significantly less, improvement in other measures of housing. Second, compared with unconstrained households, the groups placed under housing restrictions demonstrate little additional improvement, on average, in housing quality. Third, minimum rent restrictions may induce households to overpay for dwellings. Finally, under all variations, larger changes occur in reducing rent burdens than in increasing housing consumption. In other words, eligible households prefer higher consumption levels of other goods, and the restrictions imposed by the housing allowance are not usually sufficient

71. The only analysis that addresses this issue is the work by Goedert, *Earmarking Housing Allowances,* which relates a number of qualitative measures of dwelling units, parcels, and neighborhoods to dummy variables for major treatment groups. These regressions are estimated separately for each measure of quality and include dummy variables only for minimum standards households and high minimum rent and low minimum rent households, not for the particular subsidies received by households. Again, with only a weak theory, small samples, and crude qualitative measures, the results are problematic.

to override the preferences of these households. When unconstrained, the experimental households show even more clearly that they do not perceive housing as their most important economic problem.

Comments by John Yinger

Hanushek and Quigley have provided an excellent overview of the consumption aspects of housing allowances. They conduct a detailed tour through the complex and imaginative research on the topic, pointing out many of the conceptual and methodological pitfalls along the way and drawing out the implications of the research for public policy. I expect that their paper will become required reading for analysts and policy makers interested in housing allowances.

Their paper focuses on two key policy questions: How does a housing allowance affect housing consumption? How do variations in the design of a housing allowance or in local housing market conditions alter these effects? In the context of a simple model of the housing market, Hanushek and Quigley demonstrate that the answer to the first question depends on the income and price elasticities of demand for housing. Low elasticities imply small changes in housing consumption. Because the elasticities estimated from the Experimental Housing Allowance Program data are consistently low (about -0.2 for price and 0.4 for income), Hanushek and Quigley conclude that a housing allowance will decrease rent burdens instead of raising housing consumption.

Decisions about the details of a national housing allowance program should be based on the answer to the second policy question. As Hanushek and Quigley explain, however, the program has provided an incomplete answer. In fact, the only firm conclusion that emerges from their review of the research on this question is the virtual tautology that households receiving tied subsidies appear to meet the explicit requirements of the subsidies. Their understated summary is, "Because of a combination of experimental design problems, bad luck or at least bad guesses on household participation, limitations of current analytical models, and currently incomplete analyses, there are large gaps in our ability to evaluate or predict many important aspects of a national housing allowance program."

Their review is wide-ranging, but in my judgment one topic deserves far more attention than they give it: the relationship between theories about the housing market and the empirical research about the Experimental Housing Allowance Program. The extensive theoretical literature on urban housing markets supplies some important clues for untangling the effects of the program. Furthermore, precise tests of theories about housing require extensive data, and the data generated by the program provide an unprecedented opportunity to carry out such tests. A review paper should therefore ask two interrelated questions: Does the research adequately consider housing theory? Do the program results support existing theories about the housing market?

Two topics in housing theory—the impacts of location and of search costs on the price of housing—are particularly important for evaluating estimates of the income and price elasticities of demand for housing. I will therefore devote the rest of my discussion to the relationship between these topics and the elasticity estimates from the program data.

Location and the Price of Housing

The Hanushek and Quigley review, like most of the analyses in the Experimental Housing Allowance Program literature, is based on a simple formulation of the demand for housing services. As expressed in their equation 1b, this demand is

$$(15) \qquad\qquad H = A Y^\alpha [P(1 - \theta)]^\beta,$$

where θ, expressed as a percentage of rent, describes the housing allowance. (To simplify my analysis, I will not consider housing gap formulas or income transfers, although my comments apply to them as well.) Since housing services, H, are not observed directly, both sides of this equation are multiplied by the price of housing services, P, to obtain rent, R, as the independent variable:

$$(16) \qquad\qquad PH = R = A Y^\alpha P^{\beta+1}(1 - \theta)^\beta.$$

Because P is also not observed directly, it is dropped from the analysis, and the final demand function, estimated in logarithmic form, is

$$(17) \qquad\qquad R = A Y^\alpha (1 - \theta)^\beta.$$

As Hanushek and Quigley point out, this procedure is appropriate if P is constant, so that it becomes a part of the constant term, or if P is uncorrelated with Y and $(1 - \theta)$, so that it does not bias the estimates of α and β. Unfortunately, however, Hanushek and Quigley do not ask whether these conditions are reasonable but simply proceed as if the assumption needed to prevent bias were true.

I am puzzled about why Hanushek and Quigley, and indeed virtually all the program researchers, are so casual about this assumption. A central theoretical result of urban economics, supported by numerous empirical studies, is that the price of housing services varies with location. To assert that P is constant is therefore to ignore much of urban economics. Hanushek and Quigley point out that accessibility does not appear to influence housing prices in Pittsburgh and Phoenix. However, accessibility is only one of the locational variables that affect the price of housing services. As shown by analyses of the program data and by other research, air pollution, traffic, school quality, and other neighborhood amenities also influence the price people are willing to pay for housing services.[72]

The assumption that P is independent of income and of the subsidy rate is not much better. A key result in urban economics is that poorer households tend to live closer to the city center, where P is higher. If the true absolute value of β is less than unity, then the price variable has a positive coefficient, $\beta + 1$, and the omission of the price variable biases the income elasticity toward zero.

If all eligible households participated in the program, the subsidy rate, which is assigned at random, would be uncorrelated with anything, including P, and the coefficient of the subsidy rate would be unbiased. Because many eligible households do not participate, however, exclusion of the term might lead to bias. Suppose, for example, that black households are more likely to participate than are white households. Because, according to many studies, blacks pay more than whites for equivalent housing, this higher participation rate introduces a positive correlation between the market price variable and the price–subsidy variable, so that the coeffi-

---

72. The theory and evidence about amenities and the price of housing are carefully reviewed by A. Mitchell Polinsky and Daniel L. Rubinfeld, "Property Values and the Benefits of Environmental Improvements: Theory and Measurement," in Lowdon Wingo and Alan Evans, eds., *Public Economics and the Quality of Life* (Johns Hopkins University Press for Resources for the Future, 1977), pp. 154–80. For the theory and evidence about accessibility and the price of housing, see John Yinger, "Estimating the Relationship Between Location and the Price of Housing," *Journal of Regional Science,* vol. 19 (August 1979), pp. 271–89, and the references cited therein. Hedonic regressions for the demand experiment data are presented in Merrill, "Draft Report." Hedonic regressions for the supply experiment data are in Barnett, *Using Hedonic Indexes.*

cient of the latter is biased toward zero when the former is left out of the regression.[73]

These examples do not prove, of course, that the Experimental Housing Allowance Program elasticity estimates are biased. Nor are they meant to detract from the extensive efforts by the program researchers, many of which are described by Hanushek and Quigley, to avoid biases from other sources. But these examples illustrate the gap between theory about the price of housing services and the program research. To my knowledge, none of the program elasticity estimates is insured against the potential bias from leaving out the price term, despite the fact that this insurance could be purchased simply by including price variables—that is, accessibility and neighborhood amenities—in the estimating equation.

Search Costs and the Price of Housing

Theories about search costs should also be considered in estimating elasticities of housing demand. Several recent papers have shown that in markets like the housing market, where search costs are large, sellers have some market power; models of monopolistic competition are therefore more appropriate than models of perfect competition.[74] For convincing evidence that search costs are important in housing, one need only look at the program data on household search: about half of the households receiving housing assistance did not even bother to search for new housing.[75]

Hanushek and Quigley recognize that a housing allowance may change the market price for housing, but they do not consider the possibility that individual landlords may raise rents when a housing allowance boosts their tenants' demand for housing. If landlords do have this sort of market power, P is correlated with $(1 - \theta)$ and the estimated demand functions

73. For some evidence on racial rent differentials, see Robert Schafer, "Racial Discrimination in the Boston Housing Market," *Journal of Urban Economics,* vol. 6 (April 1979), pp. 176–96.

74. For a general treatment of search costs, see Michael Rothschild, "Models of Market Organization with Imperfect Information: A Survey," *Journal of Political Economy,* vol. 81 (November–December 1973), pp. 1283–1308. For an application to the housing market, see Paul N. Courant, "Racial Prejudice in a Search Model of the Urban Housing Market," *Journal of Urban Economics,* vol. 5 (July 1978), pp. 329–45.

75. A thorough review of the search results from the program can be found in Wilhelmina A. Leigh's comments on the paper by Peter H. Rossi.

involve another type of bias. One of the results cited by Hanushek and Quigley implies that landlords do behave in this way: rents paid by households facing high minimum rent requirements were 20 percent higher than rents predicted by a hedonic regression.

A simple model shows exactly how this second source of bias works. The demand function for housing, equation 15, can be solved for the price a household is willing to pay:

$$(18) \qquad\qquad P = (H/A Y^\alpha)^{1/\beta}(1 - \theta)^{-1}.$$

Hence a housing allowance raises what a household will pay for a given H by $(1 - \theta)^{-1}$. Now suppose that landlords have some market power so that they can capture some of the increase in their tenants' demand for housing. To be specific, suppose that

$$(19) \qquad\qquad P = P_o[(1 - \theta)^{-1}]^m,$$

where m is a measure of a landlord's market power. If $m = 0.1$, for example, the observed percentage increase in rent for a 40 percent subsidy is $[(1 - 0.4)^{-0.1} - 1]$, or 5.2 percent. This increase is consistent with the results in table 2 of Hanushek and Quigley's paper; it is about half of the observed rent increase (above the increase for control households) in Pittsburgh and Phoenix.

Substituting this expression for P into the demand function, equation 16, we obtain

$$(20) \qquad\qquad HP = R = A Y^\alpha[P_o(1 - \theta)^{-m}]^{\beta+1}(1 - \theta)^\beta$$

or

$$(21) \qquad\qquad R = A Y^\alpha P_o^{\beta+1}(1 - \theta)^{\beta - m(\beta+1)}.$$

Hence b, the estimated coefficient of the price subsidy variable, is not equal to the price elasticity of demand for housing. Instead,

$$(22) \qquad\qquad b = \beta - m(\beta + 1)$$

or

$$(23) \qquad\qquad \beta = (b + m)/(1 - m).$$

With $m = 0.1$, the program estimate for b of -0.2 implies a β of -0.11.

Income transfers or housing gap formulas also raise demand. The analogous derivation for these programs reveals that a, the estimated coefficient of the allowance income term, is not the income elasticity. Instead,

$$(24) \qquad\qquad a = \alpha[1 - m(1 + \beta)/\beta]$$

or

$$(25) \qquad\qquad \alpha = \beta a/[\beta - m(1 + \beta)].$$

Thus, to the degree that individual landlords have market power, the method used by the program studies overestimates both the income and price elasticities of demand for housing.[76]

To extract the income and price elasticities from the coefficients of income and subsidy rate variables, therefore, one must identify β from the coefficient of a market price variable. Because the market price of housing services is not directly observed, it must be obtained by decomposing a hedonic regression for housing. To be specific, the price of housing is a function of locational variables, such as distance from the city center and neighborhood amenities, and housing services are a function of the physical characteristics of an apartment. If L is a vector of locational variables and X is a vector of physical characteristics of housing, then

$$(26) \qquad\qquad R = P(L)H(X)$$

is the appropriate hedonic regression for rental housing. The coefficients of this regression can be used to construct the price variable needed for the demand regression.

In discussing other uses of hedonic regressions, Hanushek and Quigley argue that the exact specification of a hedonic regression is unknown, so that using one introduces unknown biases into the analysis. In my opinion, this argument misses the point. Hedonic regressions are not exact, but they are the only tool we have for separating housing price and housing quantity. In estimating elasticities, one can either ignore price altogether and introduce biases such as those described above, or use the available information to try to avoid these biases. I do not believe that throwing out information can improve one's analysis, so I am a strong supporter of the latter strategy.

---

76. This result provides a possible explanation for the finding of Mills and Sullivan in this volume that the estimated marginal propensity to spend allowance income on housing exceeds the estimated marginal propensity to spend nonallowance income.

Summary

Hanushek and Quigley, and the Experimental Housing Allowance Program researchers in general, appear to have neglected important aspects of housing theory. This neglect is unfortunate for two reasons. First, one cannot rule out the possibility that the program elasticity estimates are seriously biased. Until the locational dimension of housing prices and landlord market power are adequately considered, one should be cautious in interpreting these elasticity estimates. Second, the program research so far has missed an opportunity to test hypotheses about the impact of location and of landlord market power on housing prices. I hope these two interrelated issues will provide some grist for the mill of future research.

EDWIN S. MILLS

ARTHUR SULLIVAN

Market Effects

The Experimental Housing Allowance Program is certainly the most elaborate and carefully designed social experiment ever performed. Coming at the end of the negative income tax experiments, the program has benefited from lessons learned in those experiments. But the program is more complex than the negative income tax experiments because housing is such a complex commodity. The Department of Housing and Urban Development (HUD) and its contractors carefully designed the Experimental Housing Allowance Program. The Rand Corporation and Abt Associates have executed and analyzed the supply and demand experiments with care and imagination.

Many questions can be asked of the data obtained, but this paper will deal with market effects of the program. The key issue regarding market effects is the effect of the housing allowance program on market prices or rents and quantities of housing consumed.[1] Housing allowances entail a rightward shift in housing demand equations and a resulting increase in prices and/or rents and quantities consumed. The magnitude of the increase depends on characteristics of supply and demand equations. Thus, analysis of market effects entails measuring price, rent, and quantity changes resulting from the program and estimating properties of supply and demand equations that explain the shifts. The problem is complex because measurement of housing quantities is complex and because complex relationships exist between long- and short-run adjustments on both the demand and supply sides.

Evaluation of housing allowances as a national housing program depends on market effects. If housing demand hardly increases as a result of

1. In this paper, "price" means asset price per unit of housing, "rent" means the actual or imputed charge per unit of housing per unit of time, and "expenditure" means price or rent times quantity of housing consumed.

allowance payments, then doubts are raised whether housing allowances are better than income transfers as a way to help the poor. If housing allowances increase housing demand mainly because recipients are required to live in housing that meets minimum standards, then questions are raised about the justification for the standards. If housing allowances increase demand substantially but large price and rent increases result because supply is inelastic, questions are raised about the desirability of a national program. The desirability of transfer programs does not depend on exact magnitudes of supply elasticities, but the poor are not helped by transfers that must be spent on inelastically supplied commodities. Finally, if housing allowances result in substantial price and rent increases for housing consumed by persons whose incomes are somewhat above levels that qualify them for allowances, then welfare losses to nonrecipients offset the benefits to recipients.

The Experimental Housing Allowance Program consists of several related experiments, described in the paper by Allen, Fitts, and Glatt in this volume. Only the demand and supply experiments are relevant to our paper. The supply experiment conducted by the Rand Corporation was designed to elicit housing market supply responses to housing allowances. The demand experiment conducted by Abt Associates provided allowances to samples of eligible residents in several metropolitan areas. Providing allowances to carefully chosen samples of residents is adequate to elicit demand responses; indeed, restricting recipients to a sample minimizes the danger of confounding income and price or rent effects on demand. But to elicit supply responses, an entire housing market must be included in an experiment. A freestanding metropolitan area, such as Green Bay (Brown County), Wisconsin, or South Bend (St. Joseph County), Indiana, is the most natural definition of such a market. Costs of the experiments are kept low and problems of estimation are simplified by studying small metropolitan areas such as Green Bay and South Bend. Also, these sites were selected because of their variations in racial composition and original state of the housing market.

Theoretical Analysis

The Experimental Housing Allowance Program provides temporary income increases to recipients, although these increases may last a decade. Unless housing is an inferior good, which it is not, allowances induce recipients to increase their housing demand even if housing standards are not imposed. There are three ways that increased housing demand can result in increased housing consumption.

First, the quantity of housing can increase from the existing stock, without changes in residence. Residences can be rehabilitated, repaired, redecorated, or expanded, all of which mean increases in housing consumption. Beyond a doubt, such filtering up is an important way to increase housing consumption for poor people, although no one knows how important it is since it largely escapes official measurement. Each means of increasing housing consumption from a fixed stock requires valuable inputs: labor, materials, and sometimes construction equipment. Thus, actions to increase the quantity of housing from an existing dwelling certainly raise housing expenditure, and the effect on expenditure probably depends only slightly on tenure or on whether or not the landlord or tenant improves a rental dwelling. Theoretically, such filtering-up activities should increase housing prices, rents, and expenditures throughout the local housing market unless supplies are perfectly elastic. All housing requires maintenance and repairs, or else the quantity of housing services the dwelling provides will deteriorate rapidly. Thus, increased demand for maintenance and repair inputs must raise the prices of such activities to all dwellings in the local market unless supplies are perfectly elastic. To the extent that the same inputs are used in the construction of new dwellings, allowance-induced increases in maintenance, repair, and expansion also raise building costs of new dwellings.

However, there are rapidly diminishing returns to expanding housing consumption from the existing stock, as recent studies have shown.[2] Thus, if allowances lead to substantial increases in housing demand, many recipients should be expected to move. It is likewise inferred that allowances may result in modest housing expenditure increases by nonmover recipients but that market effects from increases in housing consumption by nonmovers are probably small.

The second way that housing allowances can increase housing consumption is by moves by some, but not all, of the residents of a dwelling. Household composition changes frequently and for many reasons in con-

2. See Gregory K. Ingram and Yitzhak Oron, "The Production of Housing Services from Existing Dwelling Units," in Gregory K. Ingram, ed., *Residential Location and Urban Housing Markets,* Studies in Income and Wealth, vol. 43 (Ballinger for National Bureau of Economic Research, 1977); and Larry Ozanne and Raymond J. Struyk, *Housing from the Existing Stock: Comparative, Economic Analyses of Owner-Occupants and Landlords* (Washington, D.C.: Urban Institute, May 1976).

temporary U.S. society. Events such as births, deaths, marriages, divorces, and children or roomers moving in or out change household composition. Whatever event halves the number of members of a household doubles housing consumption per capita for remaining residents. Some changes in household composition may be allowance induced, but most presumably are not. Nevertheless, a reduction in household membership may provide increased housing consumption for remaining members that otherwise would be provided by other means.

The third way housing allowances can increase housing consumption is by a move of an entire household. Moving is a discrete activity, undertaken infrequently and usually in response to an accumulation of changes in income, age, family composition, work place, and so forth. Housing allowances increase incomes, and the increase, by itself or when added to other causes of dissatisfaction, may induce the family to move.

Moves—whether by all or by part of a family—that are prompted by housing allowances should be expected to occur with varying lags. A few people probably receive large allowances or have several causes of dissatisfaction, and they may move quickly after housing allowances begin. But most people probably receive modest allowances and may not be sufficiently dissatisfied to want to move. Some may move later as they become more dissatisfied. In addition, some families need more time to find satisfactory alternative housing.

Demand effects of housing allowances are complicated by the minimum housing standards that are conditions of eligibility. Some people eligible for allowances by the criteria of income and family size already live in housing that meets the standards. For such people, increases in housing consumption either with or without a move reveal their demand equations. A family whose housing initially fails to meet the standards has three options: (1) the family can decide not to participate, (2) the family or its landlord can improve the dwelling to meet the standards, or (3) the family can move to a dwelling that already meets the standards. Of course, observed increases in housing consumption by those whose housing initially fails to meet the standards do not reveal whether the increased consumption is induced by the increased income the allowance provides or by the need to meet the standards. If the allowance were provided without imposition of standards, recipients might have increased housing consumption as observed. But common sense can help. If the housing fails initially to meet the standards only because of a missing stairway railing, and installation of the railing is the only change in housing consumption that ensues from the allowance, then the presumption is that the change is induced by the standards, not by the money. If the dwelling needs only a $15 railing to meet the standards and the family nevertheless moves, the presumption is that the increased housing consumption is induced by the money, not by the standards. But in many cases, the cause of the move may not be easy to find.[3]

The presumption should be that those households with substandard dwellings will be more likely to increase housing consumption to meet the standards the less costly the necessary increase in consumption is and the greater the allowance for which they will be eligible if they meet the standards.

Standards are a conundrum for housing allowances. Their theoretical justification is the neighborhood effect, the notion that neighbors benefit from a high-quality dwelling. The neighborhood effect is an external economy in housing markets, yet standards imposed by the Experimental Housing Allowance Program are mostly interior standards. The poorest people live in the worst housing and are eligible for the largest housing allowances, so it is uncertain whether standards are a deterrent to participation by families with lowest incomes.[4]

At the level of a local housing market, some distinctions need to be made on the supply side. There are three ways that the market supply of housing can be increased. First, the quantity of housing supplied from the existing stock can be increased by rehabilitation, maintenance, and expansion, as mentioned above. Second, the occupancy rate can be increased, which reduces the vacancy rate. Third, the housing stock can be increased by constructing new dwellings. The presumption should be that a housing demand increase induced by housing allowances will result in supply increases from all three sources.

In the United States, poor people live in newly constructed housing only if it is heavily subsidized by the government. An increase in housing demand by the poor has its greatest initial impact in housing near the lower end of the housing quality spectrum. To the extent that the result is moves by the poor into housing somewhat further up the quality spectrum, rents and prices of housing at that quality level increase. Some people living in housing of that quality would be induced to move up another quality notch. The effect would ripple up to the quality level at which new

3. See the paper by Peter H. Rossi in this volume for a discussion of mobility.
4. See the paper by Mahlon R. Straszheim in this volume for a discussion of the effect of housing standards on participation.

construction takes place, and the demand for newly built housing would increase. Recent papers by Sweeney and Ohls have clarified theoretical aspects of this process,[5] but empirical aspects, such as the length of lags and the magnitude of price ripples, are still unexplored. Housing construction is almost certainly a constant-returns-to-scale industry: doubling construction input doubles the rate of new housing production. But land costs increase with the size of the metropolitan area, so one important input price changes systematically as an urban area grows.

Changes in occupancy rates received little attention in housing economics literature until Rydell, inspired by results of the Experimental Housing Allowance Program, wrote a perceptive paper.[6] Rydell's model is somewhat complex, but the basic ideas can be stated in familiar terms. Dwelling rent is the payment for a flow of housing services for a given time period, say a year. The dwelling's asset value is the present value of future rents less operating expenses (maintenance and repair costs, taxes, and so forth). If rent is interpreted as imputed rent, the theory applies to owner-occupied housing. A landlord can affect a dwelling's occupancy rate, that is, the percentage of time the dwelling is occupied. If the rent level is below the market rent for similar dwellings, the occupancy rate is probably above the average for the market; if the rent level is above the market average, the occupancy rate is probably below the market average. The result is that rents and occupancy rates cluster around market averages.

Rydell defines the occupied supply curve as the schedule of rents at which housing is offered at various occupancy rates; fix the housing stock and ask how much rents would rise or fall as housing demand and the market occupancy rate increase. Until the occupancy rate is close to 1.0, the presumption should be that the occupied supply curve is extremely elastic. In a competitive housing market, rents approximate marginal cost; marginal cost is positive, but probably nearly flat, until the occupancy rate approaches 1.0.

There is presumably a positive equilibrium vacancy rate in each housing market. Equilibrium should be defined as the vacancy rate that maintains rents and the housing stock. If the vacancy rate is very close to zero,

5. James L. Sweeney, "A Commodity Hierarchy Model of the Rental Housing Market," *Journal of Urban Economics,* vol. 1 (July 1974), pp. 288–323; James C. Ohls, "Public Policy Toward Low Income Housing and Filtering in Housing Markets," ibid., vol. 2 (April 1975), pp. 144–71.

6. C. Peter Rydell, *Shortrun Response of Housing Markets to Demand Shifts,* R-2453-HUD (Santa Monica: Rand Corp., September 1979).

rents should rise, and dwelling values certainly rise, inducing an increase in supply of the housing type in question either by construction or by filtering, at least in the long run. The equilibrium vacancy rate is analogous to frictional unemployment in labor markets. Rydell does not discuss the possibility of a positive equilibrium vacancy rate, and his small data set provides no evidence on the matter.

The occupied supply curve removes what might be an apparent paradox in housing markets. If the occupancy rate is less than 1.0 and demand increases, rents rise very little if the occupied supply curve is highly elastic. But if rents exceed marginal operating costs, which they must in the vicinity of long-run equilibrium, then the asset value of the dwelling increases with present and prospective occupancy rates even at fixed rents. Thus, it is possible that increased housing demand may have a large effect on asset values but a small effect on rents if there is slack in housing markets. As occupancy rates approach 1.0, rents and asset values must rise in response to demand increases.

Little needs to be said about supply-side aspects of the first source of increased housing supply mentioned above, increasing the quantity of housing supplied from the existing stock. It has already been mentioned that maintenance, repair, and expansion activities with the existing stock use much the same inputs as construction of new housing does. Thus increases in housing supply by construction or by improvement of the existing stock are competitive activities, at least in the short run. For example, if housing allowances resulted in an increased demand to improve the existing stock, the result could be a slowdown in construction activity. Resources to improve the existing stock might be diverted from construction activity. The result would be a direct effect of housing allowances in slowing construction activity. In practical terms, it seems unlikely that the effect would be large.

Program Results

By the end of 1978, considerable evidence on housing market effects of the Experimental Housing Allowance Program was available. The supply experiment had operated at least four years, and the demand experiment three years. Market effects of the program result from interaction between market demand and supply equations. The demand experiment dealt with small samples of consumers in each metropolitan area. It was designed to permit estimation of family demand equations and, by appropriate aggregation, market demand equations. But it was carefully designed to avoid market effects on housing prices and consumption. Only the supply experiment, which blanketed two metropolitan areas, could have market effects. Thus, direct evidence about market effects of the program must come from the supply experiment. Insofar as explanations of market effects rely on characteristics of demand equations, findings from the demand experiment can be used to test explanatory hypotheses.

Findings about market effects of the supply experiments are presented by Barnett and Lowry.[7] Their findings were that there appear to have been no market effects—that is, the shift of the market demand equations for housing in the two experimental sites appears to have had no effect on housing rents in either market or in any submarket. This striking and unexpected finding requires elaboration.

In Brown County, 16 percent of renters received program payments in 1978, and payments equaled 7 percent of countywide rent payments. In St. Joseph County, 12 percent of renters received payments, and payments equaled 6 percent of countywide rent payments. Payments to owner-occupants were much smaller, and effects on prices are much harder to measure than effects on renters. Furthermore, low-income and minority residents are primarily renters; they were the subject of greatest program concern, and they were the groups whose housing choices were most restricted. Thus, the focus in Barnett and Lowry, and in this section, is on renters. The data just cited imply that the additions to incomes of renters from the program were substantial in both counties and that the effect on housing rents, at least in certain submarkets, might have been considerable. Whatever effect was to result had presumably materialized by 1978. Enrollments had stabilized by then, and the largest effects probably occurred in the short run, before supplies had had a chance to adjust.

Findings from the experimental sites and comparisons with national and regional trends are shown in table 1. Both nationally and regionally, rent increases accelerated steadily from 1973 to 1977. For each period for which data are available, rent inflation was less in both Brown and St. Joseph counties than in the national and regional averages. Not surprisingly, rent increases were somewhat less in St. Joseph County than in Brown County, because St. Joseph has a looser housing market.

7. C. Lance Barnett and Ira S. Lowry, *How Housing Allowances Affect Housing Prices*, R-2452-HUD (Rand Corp., September 1979).

Table 1. Comparisons of Contract Rent Increases, 1973–77

Percent

Area	Average annual increase in contract rent				
	1973	*1974*	*1975*	*1976*	*1977*
All U.S. cities	4.9	5.2	5.3	5.5	6.5
North Central cities	4.0	4.5	4.6	4.9	6.3
Brown County	. . .	3.7	4.4	4.8ᵃ	. . .
St. Joseph County	. . .	. . .	3.1ᵇ	. . .	. . .

Source: C. Lance Barnett and Ira S. Lowry, *How Housing Allowances Affect Housing Prices*, R-2452-HUD (Santa Monica: Rand Corp., September 1979), p. 25.
a. Includes 1976 and January–March 1977.
b. Includes November–December 1974 and 1975 and January–August 1976.

A couple of technical comments are in order about the data in table 1. First, the data from the two sample sites are based on a marketwide sample, not just on recipient dwellings. Second, contract rent may or may not include fuel and utility costs. The Rand Corporation carefully estimated the effect of fuel and utility costs on their sample data and concluded that if fuel and utility costs are added in cases where they are not included in contract rent (to give a total they call gross rent), then fuel and utility costs account for 66 to 70 percent of the inflation of gross rents on the two sites. Such figures are not available in such precise terms regionally or nationally. But it is clear that fuel price increases were entirely exogenous to the Experimental Housing Allowance Program, reenforcing the conclusion that the program had no measurable effect on market dwelling rents.

Barnett and Lowry present the following data for central South Bend.[8] Central South Bend is a low-income section of South Bend. Housing is of poor quality, and the vacancy rate exceeds 12 percent. One-third of renters are black. Twenty-seven percent of renter households in central South Bend enrolled in the Experimental Housing Allowance Program during the first two years of the experiment. Rent increases in central South Bend were no greater than in other parts of St. Joseph County.

Measuring housing rents is subject to error. But none of the obvious possible errors appears to have been important in the above comparisons. The Rand Corporation sample is carefully selected and pertains to identical dwellings in each year, so it is unaffected by gradual changes in characteristics of the housing stock. Restricting both the Rand and the national and regional data to rental dwellings avoids the complications

8. Ibid., pp. 27–29.

in estimating prices or imputed rents of owner-occupied dwellings. The conclusion seems inescapable that during its first three years the program caused no measurable increases in rents in the two supply experiment sites.

Explanations

Why did the supply experiment have no measurable upward effect on rents in either site? Explanations for this fall in two categories: either the income elasticity of housing demand of housing allowance recipients was small or the market housing supply equation was extremely elastic. Of course, both may be true.

Barnett and Lowry attribute the absence of market rent effects of the supply experiments to four causes: (1) program growth was gradual enough to let the supply side adjust as demand grew; (2) few housing allowance recipients increased housing demand substantially; (3) the cost of improving dwellings to meet required standards was small; and (4) increases in housing demand affected rents only slightly because of the considerations in the Rydell model.

The gradual phasing in of the allowance program must have facilitated supply-side adjustments. The supply experiment was preceded by a publicity campaign to make eligible residents aware of the program. Then applications were made and, if approved, the dwellings were inspected; next, if dwellings were disapproved, residents had to move or the dwellings had to be repaired. All these steps took time. The result was a gradual buildup of the program until peak enrollments were reached during the second year.

Mulford presents statistical estimates of income elasticities of demand from the two supply experiment sites.[9] The samples are surveys carefully designed to provide data for analyzing program results. But it is important to emphasize that Mulford's estimates are based on a marketwide sample survey, not on data for allowance recipients. Except for a small discount in central South Bend, Rand found no evidence of variation of rents within the two supply experiment sites. This finding justifies regression of expenditure on income to estimate the income elasticity of demand. As do other housing demand researchers, Mulford uses average

9. John E. Mulford, *Income Elasticity of Housing Demand*, R-2449-HUD (Rand Corp., July 1979).

Table 2. Predicted Housing Expenditure Increases Caused by Allowance Income

Site and tenure	Income increase (percent)	Income elasticity	Predicted expenditure increase (percent)
Brown County			
Owners	13	0.51	7
Renters	21	0.22	5
St. Joseph County			
Owners	16	0.40	6
Renters	43	0.15	6

Source: John E. Mulford, George D. Weiner, James L. McDowell, *Housing Consumption Adjustments by Allowance Recipients*. WD-382-HUD (Rand Corp., October 1979), p. 11.

income during the three-year period to approximate permanent income. He also includes a small set of demographic variables in the regressions. The regressions are linear in logs of variables. His findings are shown in table 2. All recent studies have found smaller income elasticities for renters than for owners. But elasticity estimates between 0.15 and 0.51 are extremely low. Careful analysis is required before such estimates can be accepted as realistic or as a basis for evaluating housing allowances as a national program.

The demand experiment has yielded similar but somewhat higher elasticity estimates. Friedman and Weinberg analyzed demand experiment data for a sample of Pittsburgh and Phoenix low-income renters whose allowances equaled a fixed percentage of their rental payments if they met the income qualifications for participation.[10] Using the same log-linear regression that Mulford used, they obtained income elasticities of 0.333 in Pittsburgh and 0.435 in Phoenix. They also used three-year average income to approximate permanent income and included a small set of demographic variables in the regressions. Thus the estimates from the demand experiments are higher than those from the supply sites but are still suspiciously low.

A subsequent Rand paper analyzed housing consumption responses specifically by allowance recipients.[11] Applying the elasticities estimated

10. Joseph Friedman and Daniel Weinberg, "Draft Report on the Demand for Rental Housing: Evidence from a Percent of Rent Housing Allowance" (Cambridge, Mass.: Abt Associates, September 1978), p. 64.

11. John E. Mulford, George D. Weiner, and James L. McDowell, *Housing Consumption Adjustments by Allowance Recipients,* WD-382-HUD (Rand Corp., October 1979).

Table 3. Recipients' Program-induced Housing Increases at Program Equilibrium
Percent

Site and tenure	Allowance going to increased recipient housing	Recipients' program-induced housing increase, by method		
		Repair	Move	Total
Brown County				
Owners	23.3	4.4	1.9	6.3
Renters	24.2	0.5	8.2	8.7
St. Joseph County				
Owners	15.6	3.0	2.3	5.3
Renters	17.5	0.9	8.0	8.9

Source: Mulford and others, *Housing Consumption Adjustments*, p. 12.

by Mulford, Mulford and others estimated housing expenditure increases by recipients, as shown in table 2. The first column shows percentage increases in recipients' incomes as a result of housing allowance payments. The second column shows the income elasticities estimated by Mulford. The final column shows the predicted percentage increases in housing expenditures obtained by multiplying entries in the first two columns together. Mulford and others then estimated actual housing expenditure increases from data for allowance recipients. Their estimates, presented in table 3, take account of the fact that not all recipients make housing adjustments immediately; however, the estimates are derived from data for recipients.

The estimates in tables 2 and 3 are broadly consistent, although estimates based on recipient data in table 3 show somewhat larger expenditure increases than those forecast by the data in table 2. The basic point is that both tables indicate only small increases in housing consumption as a result of the housing allowances.

The third reason offered by Barnett and Lowry for the small market rent increases resulting from the supply experiments is that enrollees could meet the required housing standards with only small outlays of resources. More than one-half of the allowance recipients lived in dwellings that already met standards when they enrolled. Those that did not meet standards "could have repaired them for about $60 and a few hours of unpaid labor."[12] Of those eventual recipients who did not meet standards

12. Ibid., p. 6.

Table 4. Characteristics of Rental Housing in Brown and St. Joseph Counties

Location	Average vacancy rate[a]	Average capital value (dollars)	Average gross rent per year per unit of housing (dollars)
Central South Bend	13.2	6,862	1,727
Rest of St. Joseph County	6.1	9,315	1,732
Brown County	4.2	12,316	1,764

Source: C. Peter Rydell, *Shortrun Response of Housing Markets to Demand Shifts*, R-2453-HUD (Rand Corp., September 1979), p. 3.
a. Percent of rent lost due to vacancies.

at enrollment, 99 percent of owners and 76 percent of renters made the necessary repairs; the others moved. Dwellings that did not meet standards and were not repaired would have cost about twice as much to repair as it cost for dwellings that were repaired.[13] Thus, recipients made repairs when it was inexpensive to do so and moved when repairs would have been expensive. It is difficult to believe that the standards inhibited participation of most people whose incomes made them eligible to participate. However, there probably were some people who failed to participate because of the cost either of needed repairs or of a move. Such people probably lived in the worst housing in the sites and may have been among the poorest people in the communities.

The final reason offered by Barnett and Lowry for the small market rent increases in the supply experiment sites is the highly elastic occupied supply curve.[14] As pointed out earlier, Rydell's theory of the occupied supply curve is somewhat complex; however, the estimation procedure used with the supply experiment data is very simple. The Rand Corporation's surveys yielded estimates of rent per unit of housing at each of the two sites. Since rents appeared to be a little lower in central South Bend than elsewhere in St. Joseph County, that site was divided into two submarkets. The result is the three observations on rents and vacancy rates in table 4. The remarkable characteristic of the data in table 4 is the small variation in rental rates among the markets, despite the large variation in vacancy rates. This small variation is consistent with Rydell's theory. Also consistent is that asset values respond much more to vacancy rate

13. Ibid.
14. See C. Peter Rydell, *Vacancy Duration and Housing Market Condition*, Rand/WN-10074-HUD (Rand Corp., January 1978).

differences than rental rates do. The assumption made by Rydell is that all three data points lie on the same occupied supply curve and that the three points differ by the position of the housing demand curves on them. Rydell estimated the occupied supply curve by regressing the log of the occupancy rate on the log of rent, using the three data points in table 4 as his sample. The estimated elasticity is 3.4, implying that a 3.4 percent increase in the occupancy rate leads to only a 1 percent increase in rental rates.

No one can place great confidence in regression coefficients estimated from only three data points. Nor can one extrapolate with confidence from the data points along the estimated equation. The log-linear relationship cannot hold as the occupancy rate approaches 1.0. However, the notion that increased demand in housing markets with significant vacancy rates results in substantial increases in asset values but little increase in rental rates is plausible and consistent with the carefully compiled data from the supply experiment.

The Rand Corporation's four explanations of the lack of effect on market rates from the housing allowances are plausible and supported by data collected at the site. In fact, if housing demand by the poor is as unresponsive to increases in their incomes as the Rand analysis suggests, there is little to explain. If renter income elasticities of housing demand are below 0.25, as the Rand estimates in table 2 indicate, then even much less elastic supply conditions than Rand finds would result in only moderate rent increases, and increases would be mostly temporary, receding as the stock of housing expands in the long run.

But if housing demand by the poor is so unresponsive to income increases, a housing allowance is approximately the same as a pure income transfer, and the value of housing allowances as a housing program becomes doubtful. Housing demand by recipients could be stimulated by more stringent minimum standards, but coercing the poor to spend transfers on housing when they view their most urgent needs elsewhere is hardly the way to improve conditions for the poor. Even more serious, the more stringent the standards, the lower the participation rate, especially by persons in the worst housing. More stringent standards are undesirable from any viewpoint. Thus, the key issue in evaluating the housing allowance experiments is whether the income elasticity of housing demand by recipients is really as low as the Rand Corporation and Abt Associates analysts believe. We will present new evidence on this matter later in this paper.

Recent Housing Demand Studies

During the 1970s, the quality of housing demand estimates improved greatly because of papers by de Leeuw and Polinsky.[15] These authors identified important sources of bias in earlier studies and suggested practical ways of obtaining unbiased estimates. De Leeuw estimated that the income elasticity of housing demand is 0.81 for renters and 1.34 for owners. Polinsky concluded that appropriate adjustments to remove biases from several estimates suggest an income elasticity of about 0.75. Almost everyone who estimates them separately concludes that renters have smaller income elasticities than do owner-occupants. The Experimental Housing Allowance Program estimates, made after the de Leeuw and Polinsky papers, appear not to be affected by the biases that those two authors identified.

Housing demand studies continue to appear frequently, and we cannot survey individual studies here. Our belief after extensive reading of recent literature is that the best estimates of income elasticities of housing demand are in the interval between about 0.7 and 1.0, with estimates for renters invariably less than those for owners. Most estimates outside this interval move within or close to it when biases are removed.

There is, of course, no theorem that says that the income elasticity of housing demand is constant; it almost certainly varies with something that is strongly correlated with the tenure choice. It may vary by income, by race, or by other conditions. In particular, poor people may have systematically different income elasticities than other people. Studies covering many decades and many countries have shown that income elasticities of demand for food decline systematically and smoothly as income rises. Food is the prime requirement to sustain life, whereas housing satisfies much more complex needs. But observation is widespread that low-income Americans spend 35 or 40 percent of income on housing and that the share falls to 10 or 15 percent at high-income levels. This observation is consistent with a constant housing income elasticity less than 1.0 or with an elasticity that declines as income rises.

Income elasticities as low as 0.25 cannot be typical among many

15. Frank de Leeuw, "The Demand for Housing: A Review of Cross Section Evidence," *Review of Economics and Statistics,* vol. 53 (February 1971), pp. 1–10; A. Mitchell Polinsky, "The Demand for Housing: A Study in Specification and Grouping," *Econometrica,* vol. 45 (March 1977), pp. 447–61.

groups of people or time periods. Income shares received by quintiles in the personal income distribution have changed little in the United States since World War II. Average real income per capita and the average in the lowest quintile have at least doubled since World War II. If the lowest quintile had an income elasticity of housing demand as low as 0.25, then the share of income spent on housing by the group would have fallen by 40 percent since the war.[16] That has not happened. Of course, if the relative price of housing had risen substantially at the same time, and if housing demand were price inelastic, then the increase in real income, low income elasticity, and constant housing share would be consistent. But the evidence from the consumer price index is that the relative price of housing, excluding fuel, has changed little in the postwar period, and most studies conclude that the price elasticity is not much less than 1.0.

The last two paragraphs are hardly econometric evidence. But existing econometric evidence suggests that income elasticities of housing demand can hardly be as low as 0.25 for a substantial group of residents or a substantial part of the income distribution. Estimates from data of the Experimental Housing Allowance Program must be regarded with deep suspicion.

New Empirical Results

In this section we present empirical results based on a sample of allowance recipients in Brown County. We first give estimates of equilibrium housing demand functions for both homeowners and renters. For several reasons, our analysis of homeowners ends with the demand function estimates. Our analysis of renter households continues with a stock adjustment model that estimates the rate at which households adjust to changes in their equilibrium housing quantities. We can then predict both short-run and long-run shifts in the metropolitan demand curve for rental housing. By relating these demand shifts to estimates of the supply elasticity of rental housing, we can explain the observed stability in the relative price of housing in Brown County during the first three years of the supply experiment. We are also able to predict similar stability in the rental price in the long run, given our estimates of the long-run demand-curve shift.

16. If the income elasticity is 0.25, then expenditure E is $Apy^{0.25}$ and E/y is $Apy^{-0.75}$. If $y_1 = 2y_0$, then $E_1/y_1/E_0/y_0 = 2^{-0.75} \simeq 0.60$.

Our analysis requires observations on households receiving allowance payments for at least two of the three years of the experiment's operation. From the Rand Corporation records, we developed a cross-sectional, time-series data base with three annual observations on each of 972 households. The first observation for each household is data for the year preceding the first allowance payment. The second and third observations are for years during which the first and second years of allowance payments were received. For the few households receiving allowance payments for the three full years from June 1974 to June 1977, the fourth year was omitted from the data set. Approximately half the households in our sample received their first allowance payments in 1975; their observations are for 1974, 1975, and 1976. The other half of the households received their first allowance payments in 1976; their observations are for 1975, 1976, and 1977.

Empirical Specification of Housing Demand

Our estimates of equilibrium housing demand functions are based on

(1) $$R_3 = R(I, A, S),$$

where R_3 = annual housing expenditures in year three, I = "permanent" nonallowance income, A = "permanent" allowance income, and S = household size.

There are five econometric issues associated with our specification of the housing demand function: (1) the omission of housing price as an explanatory variable, (2) the way in which the two components of income enter the function, (3) the implications of the fact that only a fraction of the sampled households can be expected to have reacted to the allowance payments during our sampling period, (4) the implications of a high correlation between the explanatory variables, and (5) the implication of the requirement that recipients live in housing that meets standards.

Our specification of the housing expenditure function omits price as an explanatory variable. The omission is justified if there is no variation in price in the data observations. There are two potential sources of price variation, neither of which occurs in our sample. First, since half of our households have R_3 equal to housing expenditures in 1976 and half have R_3 equal to housing expenditures in 1977, any change in the relative price of housing between 1976 and 1977 should be included in the analysis.

Evidence presented earlier suggests that only small changes in the relative price of housing occurred between 1976 and 1977. A second possible source of price variation is across space. Theoretical and empirical models of urban housing markets indicate that housing prices decline with distance from the city center. Such variation is, in theory, slight in small metropolitan areas like Brown County. The Rand Corporation's analysis of the Brown County housing market indicated very slight spatial variation in housing prices.[17]

A major policy concern of the supply experiment is whether allowance payments are treated in the same way as nonallowance income in housing decisions, that is, whether the marginal propensity to spend (MPS) allowance income on housing equals the MPS of nonallowance income. To test the hypothesis of equal MPSs, we enter I and A as separate explanatory variables. We therefore avoid restricting their coefficients to be equal. Our results indicate that the MPS(A) exceeds the MPS(I) by a large margin.

The third econometric issue concerns identifying households that are consuming equilibrium housing quantities. Moving costs cause households to consume nonequilibrium housing quantities until an accumulation of disequilibrium effects causes adjustment. In a sample with random variation in housing demand determinants, households consuming more than equilibrium quantities will be balanced by underconsuming households. The error term of a regression equation with such a sample will have a zero mean, and parameter estimates, in the absence of other econometric problems, will be unbiased and efficient.

Our sample includes only households that have received two years of allowance payments. Allowance payments have a positive effect on equilibrium housing demand, but in the short time our data covers only a fraction of the households found it advantageous to adjust housing quantities. Therefore, a disproportionate number of households in our sample underconsume housing. As a result, running the conventional regression equations generates biased estimates of housing demand parameters.

One strategy to solve this problem is to estimate equilibrium housing demand with a subsample of recent movers. Recent movers can be expected to consume close to their equilibrium housing quantities, and systematic deviations from equilibrium quantities are unlikely. However, use of a mover subsample introduces the possibility of selection bias: movers may not be representative of the entire sample. As a result, inferences for

17. Barnett and Lowry, *How Housing Allowances Affect Housing Prices*, p. 13.

the entire sample that are based on data for the mover subsample are subject to large error. In our sample, a disproportionate number of movers are from demographic groups with the lowest measured income elasticity. Therefore, income elasticities estimated with a mover sample are probably lower than the elasticities for the entire sample.

An additional problem associated with the use of a mover subsample is that households with small responses to the allowance program (that is, those that did not move) are excluded from the estimation of the allowance elasticity. Since only households with large responses to the allowance program are included in the subsample, selection bias will lead to upward-biased coefficient estimates.

An alternative treatment of this problem is to use both movers and nonmovers in the sample but to assume different behavioral relationships for each group. Specifically, we assume that the housing expenditures of movers and repairers (households that incurred large repair expenses) depend on I, A, and S, but that the expenditures of nonmovers (and nonrepairers) depend only on I and S.

For nonmovers, current housing expenditures do not depend on A, since reaction to changes in A (from zero to positive) must come in the form of a change in residence or large repair expenditures. We argue that current housing expenditures of nonmovers are determined by past levels of I, A, and S, when A was zero. Lacking data on past levels of permanent nonallowance income, we use as a proxy current permanent nonallowance income. Algebraically, our model is

$$(2) \qquad\qquad R_3 = R(I, \delta A, S).$$

The linear form of equation 2 is

$$(3) \qquad\qquad R_3 = \alpha_0 + \alpha_1 I + \alpha_2 \delta A + \alpha_3 S + \epsilon,$$

where $\delta = 1$ for movers and repairers and $\delta = 0$ for all other households.

The above specification assumes a nonzero elasticity of demand with respect to allowance income. Otherwise, nonmovers may simply be households with zero allowance elasticity, households whose equilibrium housing quantity does not change with allowance payments. Assuming a nonzero allowance elasticity means that nonmovers are households whose equilibrium housing quantities have increased as a result of the allowance program but whose consumption has not yet adjusted to the higher equilibrium level.

The assumption of a nonzero allowance elasticity would be less plausible if the length of the program were shorter, the allowance payments were smaller, and the moving costs faced by households were greater— that is, the total allowance payments were smaller relative to moving costs.

The supply experiment guaranteed payments to eligible households for ten years. On average, allowance payments to renter households were about 15 to 20 percent of their total incomes. Since moving costs for renters are small relative to total allowance payments, the assumption of non-zero allowance elasticity is reasonable. Therefore, α_2 (the coefficient of δA) is the long-run aggregate MPS(A); $100\alpha_2$ is the percentage of aggregate allowance payments spent on housing. In the short run, less than $100\alpha_2$ percent is spent on housing, since only a fraction of recipients have adjusted, but those who have adjusted will spend, on the average, $100\alpha_2$ percent of their allowance payments on housing.

Homeowners have significantly higher moving costs, and as a result the assumption of nonzero allowance elasticity may be unrealistic. We cannot infer that the long-run percentage of aggregate allowance payments spent on housing is $100\alpha_2$, since a large number of owners will not react to the allowance program. For owners, estimation of the program's long-run impact must include both the coefficient α_2 and a measure of household movement.

A nonzero allowance elasticity is not sufficient to guarantee unbiased coefficient estimates. In our procedure, households with small responses to the allowance program are excluded from the estimation of MPS(A). As a result, our coefficients are biased.

Some method must be used to distinguish between households that are consuming equilibrium housing quantities and households that are in disequilibrium. Both the dummy-variable method and the mover-subsample method generate biased coefficients. We believe that the dummy-variable method is superior, since it exploits the entire sample of recipient households to estimate the nonallowance income elasticity of demand.

A fourth econometric issue concerns the correlation between the explanatory variables I, A, and S. Allowance payments in year t are computed as follows:

$$(4) \qquad A_t = C_t^*(S_t) - .25(I_t - D_t),$$

where A_t = allowance payments in year t; S_t = household size in year t; C_t^* = the cost of adequate housing, which is a nonlinear function of S_t; I_t = nonallowance income in year t; and D_t = deductions in year t.

If we were to use as explanatory variables annual observations on A_t,

S_t, and $(I_t - D_t)$, it would be logically impossible to determine the separate effects of the explanatory variables. Since A_t is a nonlinear function of S_t, a linear specification would not suffer from perfect collinearity, but assessing the individual effects of explanatory variables would be impossible.

We are able to separate the effects of variables and to estimate equations that do not suffer from multicollinearity for two reasons. First, we use a three-year average of nonallowance income and a two-year average of allowance income in our equations. This introduces random variation among household values of I and A: households with equal I and S have different A if the time paths of I_t differ. As a result, we can assess the cross-sectional effect of small changes in A, holding constant the other explanatory variable.

The second, and more important, reason that we can separate the effects of our explanatory variables is that we use an income variable that differs from that used to compute allowance payments. We use a three-year average of total nonallowance income, while allowance payments are computed with total nonallowance income less deductions that vary among households. These deductions are for age, disability, number of secondary workers in the household, number of dependents, occupational expenses, alimony payments, and child support payments. Random variation in deductions among recipient households diminishes the correlation between I, A, and S and allows us to separate the effects of the individual variables.

We believe that the appropriate income variable is total, not adjusted, income. Most studies of housing demand have used total income, so that comparability requires that we use a similar income variable. In addition, the deductions used for calculating adjusted income are arbitrary in kind and amount, as far as housing demand is concerned.

The fifth econometric problem is that requiring recipients to live in housing that meets standards pushes recipients off their demand curves. In fact, as has been indicated, the standards were not sufficiently stringent to have had much effect. Such effects as did occur were of two kinds. To receive the allowance, some people might be induced by the standards to consume more housing than they want. Others may decide that the payments are not worth the bother and expense needed to qualify. Both behaviors mean that demand estimates from recipient data are inaccurate. But there is nothing we can do about the problem except to rely on the judgment that the effect is small.

Definition of Variables

For owner-occupants, R_3 (annual housing expenses) equals 12 percent of the market value of the home in year three, plus imputed repair expenses for year three. As pointed out by de Leeuw, using a fixed fraction of market value involves measurement error, since the fraction (housing costs/market value) is a decreasing function of market value. In our sample of low-income households, we have a tight distribution of market values and small measurement errors from using a fixed fraction of market value. Imputed repair expenses in year three equal one-fifth of the sum of repair expenses incurred in years one through three, a measure that includes imputed labor costs if the repairs were done by the occupants.[18] We transform reported repair expenses into a stream of expenses by spreading the one-time expenditures over five years. The average imputed repair expense for year three for owner-occupants was $43, approximately 2.2 percent of annual housing expenses. For renters, R_3 equals contract rent plus imputed repair expenses incurred by the tenant in year three. Repair expenses incurred by the landlord were excluded. The average imputed repair expense was $2.36, about 0.14 percent of annual housing expenditures.

A is permanent allowance income:

$$(5) \qquad\qquad A = \frac{1}{2} \sum_{t=2}^{3} A_t,$$

where A_t is allowance payment received in year t. For all households, $A_1 = 0$, since the first observation for each is for the year preceding receipt of the first allowance payment.

I is permanent nonallowance income:

$$(6) \qquad\qquad I = \frac{1}{3} \sum_{t=1}^{3} I_t,$$

where I_t is nonallowance income in year t. For owner-occupants, I_t includes imputed rental income from ownership, computed as 6 percent of equity in the home. For renters, I_t is reported nonallowance income.

---

18. Katharine Bradbury pointed out to us that the correct measure of imputed repair expenses is one-third of the same, not one-fifth. We have been unable to make the correction, but it consists only of multiplying our estimate by a constant. The effect on the estimated coefficients is certainly negligible.

Y is permanent total income:

(7) $$Y = I + A.$$

Estimation of Equilibrium Housing Demand Functions

In this subsection, we present estimates of equilibrium housing expenditure functions for both homeowners and renters. We estimate two expenditure equations:

(8) $$R_3 = \alpha_0 + \alpha_1 I + \alpha_2 \delta A + \alpha_3 S_3 + \epsilon,$$

(9) $$\ln R_3 = \beta_0 + \beta_1 \ln Y_d + \beta_2 \left(\frac{\delta A}{Y_d}\right) \ln Y_d + \epsilon,$$

where $\delta = 1$ for movers and households that incurred imputed repair expenses greater than \$300 over the three-year period and $\delta = 0$ for all other households, and S_3 is household size in the third period.

(10) $$Y_d = I + \delta A;$$

(11) $$\beta_1 + \beta_2 \frac{\delta A}{Y_d}$$

equals the income elasticity for equation 9.

If nonmovers and nonrepairers are households with zero (or extremely low) allowance elasticities rather than households with lagged adjustment to the allowance program, then this specification generates biased coefficient estimates. For such households, δ should equal 1.0, not 0. An alternative estimation procedure is to use a subsample of households that recently moved. If some of the excluded nonmover households had allowance elasticities close to zero, this procedure would generate biased coefficients as well. Exclusion of nonmovers would introduce selection bias; the subsample would include only households with large responses to the program, ignoring those that responded without moving.

As discussed above, the use of the dummy variable for allowance income assumes that housing expenditures of nonmovers do not depend on allowance payments. The measured total income (Y_d) for nonmovers is I; for movers and repairers it is $(I + A)$.

The estimated housing expenditure functions are listed in table 5. In the owner-occupant sample, 4 percent of the households moved during the three-year period, and 9.5 percent incurred significant repair ex-

Table 5. Equilibrium Housing Expenditure Functions

Sample	Equation	R^2	Equation[a]	Implied elasticity (η)
All owners	8	0.11	$R_3 = 1076 + 0.169\,I + 0.402\,\delta A - 48.2\,S_3$ (8.1) (5.6) (2.5) (−1.7)	$\eta(R_3, I) = 0.502$[b] $\eta(R_3, A) = 0.120$[e] $\eta(R_3, Y) = 0.622$[d]
All owners	9	0.14	$\ln R_3 = 2.37 + 0.601 \ln/Y_a + 0.129\,(\delta A/Y_d) \ln Y_d - 0.0028\,S_3$ (3.3) (7.0) (2.0) (−2.0)	$\eta(R_3, Y) = 0.613$[e]
All renters	8	0.33	$R_3 = 963 + 0.096\,I + 0.436\,\delta A + 34.5\,S_3$ (16.1) (5.3) (9.4) (1.9)	$\eta(R_3, I) = 0.253$[b] $\eta(R_3, A) = 0.098$[e] $\eta(R_3, Y) = 0.351$[d]
All renters	9	0.30	$\ln R_3 = 4.2 + 0.355 \ln Y_d + 0.122\,(\delta A/Y_d) \ln Y_d + 0.023\,S_3$ (9.8) (6.6) (6.7) (1.8)	$\eta(R_3, Y) = 0.359$[e]

Source: Authors' calculations.
a. The numbers in parentheses are t-statistics.
b. Computed at mean value of (I/R_3).
c. Computed at mean value of $(\delta A/R_3)$.
d. Computed with MPS (Y_d) as weighted average of I and δA and total-income elasticity equal to MPS (Y_d) times the mean value of (Y_d/R_3).
e. Computed at mean value of $(\delta A/Y_d)$.

penses, for a total of 13.5 percent of the sample in the mover-repairer classification. In the renter sample, 43 percent moved during the period, and no nonmover household incurred large enough repair expenses to be classified as a repairing household.

Two conclusions from table 5 are as follows: (1) The marginal propensity to spend allowance income on housing exceeds the MPS of nonallowance income. For owners, MPS(A) = 0.402 and MPS(I) = 0.169; for renters, MPS(A) = 0.436, and MPS(I) = 0.096. (2) The total income elasticity is an increasing function of the ratio of $\delta A/Y_d$. The result is demonstrated in the second and fourth equations, with a significant and positive coefficient on $(\delta A/Y_d)\ln Y_d$.

It is important to emphasize that the equations in table 5 are estimates of equilibrium housing expenditure functions. Based on cross-sectional data, their parameters indicate the responsiveness of equilibrium housing demand to changes in income and household size. We do not expect each recipient household immediately to spend 40.2 percent (owners) or 43.6 percent (renters) of its allowance payment on additional housing, since it takes time to adjust to the greater equilibrium housing demand.

Dynamics of the Rental Housing Market

In this subsection we will estimate the dynamic response of housing demands of recipients to changes in allowance and nonallowance income. Our analysis concerns only renter households. We will use time-series data on contract rent paid by recipient households, an accurate measure of housing expenditures. No accurate time-series measure of housing expenditures for owner-occupants exists in our data set, since the time-series observations of market value are determined by assessed value, and few of the homes were reassessed during the three-year period.

We have presented estimates of permanent income elasticities based on cross-sectional data. The computed elasticities in table 5 are the relevant elasticities for individual households in the long run; they are measures of the responsiveness of equilibrium housing demand to changes in allowance and nonallowance income. Housing consumption differs from equilibrium consumption if households do not adjust housing quantities to changes in income; moving costs cause such a divergence in the short run. We expected that most households in our sample consumed less than their equilibrium housing quantities, because only two years had passed since the start of allowance payments. We will estimate the rate at which

Table 6. Dynamic Adjustment Equations

Years	R^2	Equation[a]
1–2	0.66	$R_2 = 0.24\,(R_2^* - R_1) + 1.04\,R_1$
		$\quad\quad\;(10.1) \quad\quad\quad\quad (107.6)$
2–3	0.80	$R_3 = 0.14\,(R_3^* - R_2) + 1.03\,R_2$
		$\quad\quad\;(\;7.1) \quad\quad\quad\quad (161.6)$
1–3	0.60	$R_3 = 0.30\,(R_3^* - R_1) + 1.08\,R_1$
		$\quad\quad\;(11.0) \quad\quad\quad\quad (98.1)$

Source: Authors' calculations.
a. The numbers in parentheses are *t*-statistics.

recipient households adjust housing consumption to the equilibrium demand resulting from allowance payments.

The model we use to estimate the dynamic adjustment of recipient households is one used by Hanushek and Quigley[19]:

$$(12) \qquad\qquad R_{t+1} = \lambda_1(R_{t+1}^* - R_t) + \lambda_2 R_t,$$

where R_t is rental expenditure in period t; R_t^* is equilibrium rental expenditure, the amount that would occur in the absence of moving costs; λ_1 is the percentage of households adjusting during period t to changes in R_t^*; and λ_2 is a measure of housing price inflation between t and $t + 1$.

To compute R_t^* for renter households, we used the following equation, derived by estimating equation 8 for the entire renter sample:

$$(13) \qquad\qquad R_t^* = 963 + 0.096\,I_t + 0.436\,A_t + 34.5\,S_t.$$

Table 6 lists the estimates of equation 12 for the renter sample. Between periods one and two, 24 percent of households adjusted to their equilibrium housing quantities; between periods two and three, the adjustment rate was 14 percent. The third equation indicates a two-year adjustment rate of 30 percent. The λ_2 coefficients indicate a slightly lower inflation rate than reported by the Rand Corporation (4 percent).

We are interested in the cumulative adjustment rate over the two-year period. The third equation measures it directly as 30 percent. An alternative measure can be calculated from the λ_1 coefficients of the first two equations. The bulk of changes in equilibrium housing demand occurred between periods one and two, as allowances increased from zero to about

19. Eric A. Hanushek and John M. Quigley, "The Dynamics of the Housing Market: A Stock Adjustment Model of Housing Consumption," *Journal of Urban Economics*, vol. 6 (January 1979), p. 92.

Table 7. Actual and Predicted Aggregate Rental Expenditures

Year	Actual expenditures (dollars)	Predicted expenditures (dollars)	Error (percent)
1	745,703	728,819	2.26
3	899,861	874,572	2.81

Source: Authors' calculations.

15 percent of total income. Small changes in allowance payments occurred between periods two and three, meaning that $R_3^* - R_2^*$ was relatively small for most households. As a result, we can interpret the λ_1 coefficients in the first two equations as follows: in the first year, 24 percent of households adjusted to their equilibrium housing quantities; in the second year, 14 percent of the remaining households adjusted to their higher equilibrium housing demand, a second-year adjustment rate of 10.6 percent ($0.76 \cdot 0.14$) and a cumulative adjustment rate of 34.6 percent (24 percent + 10.6 percent).

The adjustment coefficients λ_1 indicate significant differences between the short-run and long-run responses of recipient households to allowance payments. The two-year adjustment rate is between 30 and 35 percent, indicating a long-run response roughly three times the short-run response. When all households adjust to their income changes, the demand stimulus will be roughly three times the demand stimulus following two years of allowance payments.

Simulation of the Rental Housing Market

We will now present estimates of short-run and long-run impacts of the housing allowance program on aggregate demand for housing by recipient households. We will use equation 13 to predict equilibrium housing demand for individual recipient households and a two-year adjustment speed of 35 percent to compute aggregate demand in the recipient submarket for different periods.

Table 7 lists the actual and predicted aggregate rental expenditures in the recipient submarket, as defined by our data, for years one and three. The predicted expenditures for year one were computed by assuming that all households consumed their equilibrium housing quantities as defined by equation 13. The predicted expenditure falls short of the actual by only 2.26 percent. The predicted aggregate expenditure for year three

Table 8. Simulated Rental Market[a]

Percent

Increase in aggregate rental payments, year 1 to year 3	Short run[b]	Long run[c]
Allowance induced	8.22	23.49
Nonallowance induced	1.21	3.47
Real total	9.45	26.96
Inflation[a]	10.55	12.19
Nominal total	20.00	39.15
Actual total	20.70	...

Source: Authors' calculations.

a. The assumed annual inflation rate is 4.8 percent. The percentage contribution of inflation exceeds twice the annual rate because real demand is growing.

b. Thirty-five percent of households adjusting to consume equilibrium housing quantities.

c. One hundred percent of households adjusting to consume equilibrium housing quantities.

was computed by assuming that 35 percent of households consumed their equilibrium housing quantities in year three. An annual inflation rate of 4.8 percent is assumed. Again, the predicted expenditure level falls short of the actual by a small amount (2.81 percent).

Table 8 lists our simulation results for percentage change in aggregate expenditures, assuming a 35 percent adjustment rate and 4.8 percent annual inflation rate. The short-run response was computed by assuming that 35 percent of recipient households adjusted to their equilibrium housing level in year three. The long-run response is computed by assuming that all households consumed their equilibrium housing quantities in both years one and three. Conclusions to be drawn from table 8 are as follows:

1. Our predicted nominal short-run demand response is close to the actual increase (20.0 versus 20.7 percent).

2. A slight positive trend in nonallowance income or household size is responsible for a small part of the demand increase.

3. The long-run real increase in aggregate demand is 2.85 times the short-run response (26.96 versus 9.45 percent).

4. The predicted long-run real demand increase resulting from the allowance program is 23.49 percent; the predicted short-run real increase is only 8.22 percent.

Market Effects of the Program

The housing allowance program affects the metropolitan housing market by shifting the market demand curve to the right. A major policy concern is the effect of this demand increase on the equilibrium housing price. Given the demand increase, the critical determinant of price effects is the price elasticity of supply: an inelastic supply would lead to price increases that would prevent allowance recipients from increasing their housing consumption. An elastic supply would lead to small price increases, and recipients would increase their housing consumption, not simply their housing expenditures.

In 1978, 16 percent of Brown County renter households received allowance payments. Therefore, an upper bound on the recipients' share of the metropolitan housing market is 16 percent. The actual share is less than 16 percent for two reasons. First, low-income households, including allowance recipients, consumed less than the average quantity of housing. Second, some of the households that received payments cannot be regarded as long-term participants; some received payments for only one or two years, when they experienced temporary decreases in nonallowance income. It is too early to tell whether or not program dropouts will return after a short absence and should therefore be considered long-term participants. Nonetheless, the allowance program establishes a minimum income for ten years, and low-income households, whether participating in a particular year or not, base their housing decisions on that minimum income.

The shift in the metropolitan demand curve is computed as the shift in the recipient submarket times the recipients' share of the metropolitan market. The short-run demand shift (in real terms) implied by our figures is between 0.95 percent (assuming that long-term recipients make up 10 percent of the market) and 1.52 percent (assuming a 16 percent market share).

A shift in the demand curve of 1 to 2 percent causes a significant price increase only if the supply elasticity is very low. For reasonable values of the short-run supply elasticity, such a small demand increase does not result in a price increase. It is not surprising, therefore, that data presented in this paper showed slight changes in the relative price of housing in Brown County.

The long-run real aggregate demand increase among recipients that we predicted in table 8 is 26.96 percent. This implies a long-run, metropolitanwide demand increase of between 2.7 percent (assuming that recipients make up 10 percent of the metropolitan market) and 4.31 percent (assuming that recipients make up 16 percent of the metropolitan market). Since this metropolitan demand increase is small, and since it occurs gradually, significant increases in the housing prices are unlikely in the long run; given time to adjust, supply will be sufficiently responsive to prevent price increases.

The above calculations of metropolitan housing demand increases assume that recipients are not concentrated in a submarket. Two potential sources of market segmentation are racial discrimination and land-use zoning applied to low-income housing. If a large number of recipients were concentrated in a submarket, the computed demand-curve shift would be larger, since the share of the submarket held by recipients would be greater. For a given supply elasticity, the more heavily concentrated recipients are in a submarket, then the more likely price increases are in that submarket.

The only clear case of market segmentation in the two supply experiment sites is the concentration of recipients and blacks in central South Bend. Twenty-seven percent of the renters in that area received allowance payments, and a large number may have faced barriers to housing consumption outside the area. As mentioned earlier, increases in rents were small in central South Bend. The Rydell analysis provides a convincing explanation of the small rent increases in central South Bend.

Conclusions

Our conclusions can be stated simply. The housing allowance supply experiment caused no measurable increase in rents in the relevant housing markets. The Rand Corporation explanations are plausible and well documented. But we believe that the main reason for the small increases in housing demand by recipients has to do with the dynamics of housing demand adjustment, not with the extremely low income elasticities of housing demand that Rand estimates.

Comments by A. Thomas King[20]

Mills and Sullivan have provided a fine guide to thinking about the market effects of the Experimental Housing Allowance Program. They review the aspects of housing supply and demand that determine market

20. These comments do not necessarily reflect the position or policy of the Federal Home Loan Bank Board.

effects, summarize the major findings from the Abt Associates and the Rand Corporation research, and consider the explanations offered in that research for why the program seems to have had no discernible market effects.

With respect to market effects, the central finding of the program is that there were no effects, even in the short run. Over a long period this result would have been less surprising because long-run housing supply is widely believed to be sufficiently elastic to avoid significant price increases. As Mills and Sullivan observe, the explanations for this finding are either low income elasticities or high short-run supply elasticities for housing. Research by Abt Associates and the Rand Corporation supports both explanations. Mills and Sullivan seem to accept Rydell's explanations for a high short-run elasticity of supply, but they are skeptical about the findings that income elasticities are much lower than the currently accepted range of 0.7 to 1.0. Their paper is basically an empirical study of housing demand, using previously unexploited program data to see whether the low elasticities found in other program analyses will be found again. In a second empirical section they examine the dynamics of household adjustment to allowance income to see whether slow rates of adjustment could be the reason for modest increases in market demand.

Abt Associates and the Rand Corporation both found income elasticities for housing to be low, perhaps as low as 0.2 for renters and 0.4 to 0.5 for owners. Mills and Sullivan consider the program elasticities to be "suspiciously low," not only because they are so much lower than other recent econometric studies suggest but also because they seem inconsistent with the post–World War II experience. Over the past thirty-five years the real income of the lowest quintile in the income distribution has at least doubled, yet the share of income spent on housing has remained roughly constant, suggesting an income elasticity of about unity. After considering some of the econometric problems that might have biased the program estimates downward, Mills and Sullivan conclude that these are not the explanation.

Since the previous work had no obvious downward biases, Mills and Sullivan used new data from the supply experiment to see whether these also support low elasticities. Their findings in table 5 show that elasticities with respect to permanent nonallowance income in the new sample are very close to what the previous program studies have reported—0.5 for owners and less than 0.3 for renters. Obviously, these figures are too low to account for the historical constancy of the budget share of housing for

the poor, and they are well below the currently accepted range of 0.7 to
1.0. The unexpectedly low response therefore appears to be a genuine
characteristic, and the conflict with historical experience remains.

In addition to elasticities for nonallowance income, *I*, and allowance
income, *A*, table 5 reports elasticities for the sum of these, which Mills
and Sullivan call total income, *Y*. The latter are higher than the others,
yet still low relative to the currently accepted range. Although it would
seem natural to use these total income elasticities to assess the market
effect of the allowance program, in my opinion their interpretation is uncertain, and they should be used cautiously or not at all. Certainly, if
one's interest is in reconciling the long-run constancy of share of housing
with observed program results, it is the elasticity with respect to *I* that is
relevant, since the historical patterns reflect changes in *I*, not in *A* or *Y*.

Mills and Sullivan conclude that persons will respond differently to
changes in allowance and nonallowance income, and the estimates support this. But if so, one can no longer speak of *the* income elasticity, because income elasticity will depend on which component of income has
changed. That point may not be sufficiently clear from the elasticity for
Y shown in table 5, which is calculated on the basis of an overall average
of allowance and nonallowance income; the sensitivity of the elasticity to
the composition of total income is not shown. In the case of owner-
occupants, the average composition for total income appears to be about
$0.90 of regular income and $0.10 of allowance income. Therefore, the
precise interpretation of the elasticity is that at the mean ratio of *Y* to
housing expenditure, a $1.00 increment to income, consisting of $0.90
regular income and $0.10 allowance income, would cause a change in ex-
penditure such that the elasticity would be 0.622.

With this interpretation in mind, one can see that the elasticity with
respect to *Y* has two problems. First, for any individual it should not be
the case that both allowance and nonallowance income could increase
simultaneously, since the two are supposed to be inversely related by the
formula for calculating the allowance. Thus, the circumstance in which
this elasticity would be relevant may not exist. It would seem to be more
meaningful to calculate a total income elasticity on the supposition that
one kind of income increases while the other simultaneously declines.
Second, the elasticity at the mean will depend on which income component is changing. For example, assuming that the entire change in income
were in allowance income, the elasticity in table 5 would be 1.3 instead of
0.6; if it were in nonallowance income, it would be 0.55. For these rea-

sons, I think it would be best to ignore the elasticities reported for Y in table 5.[21]

An issue related to the income elasticity but somewhat different is this: Mills and Sullivan estimate that 40 to 50 percent of allowance payments are spent on housing, yet previous program analyses concluded that recipients "allocate only small portions of their added incomes to housing expenditures." Only 25 percent, or even much less, was said to be spent on additional housing.[22] It would be interesting to understand the reasons for these different results. Is it just a matter of different samples and methods of analysis, or are there fundamental differences in behavior? Do some household types spend little or none of the allowance on housing, while others spend most of it? Or is the proportion spent uniform and moderate? Answers to these questions would help explain the effect of the Experimental Housing Allowance Program.

Many previous studies of housing have found the income elasticities to be lower for renters than for owners. I had expected that this might not be true in the Experimental Housing Allowance Program population. Presumably, many of the low-income owners bought their homes in earlier years, when their incomes were higher. If so, their current housing consumption would seem to be a function of their "permanent" income at the time the house was purchased rather than a function of their present lower income. In that sense, present housing consumption is too high with respect to income. The allowance income would not seem to be a reason

21. At the conference several persons were concerned that the elasticity for Y was the exact sum of the allowance and nonallowance elasticities. Intuitively, it seemed as though the elasticity for the sum should be a weighted average of the elasticities for the components. That problem can be resolved as follows: in table 5 the elasticity with respect to $Y(\eta_y)$ is defined as

$$(14) \qquad \left[\alpha \frac{\partial R}{\partial I} + (1 - \alpha) \frac{\partial R}{\partial A} \right] \frac{Y}{R},$$

where α is the proportion of Y from nonallowance income. This immediately simplifies to

$$(15) \qquad \frac{\partial R}{\partial I} \frac{I}{R} + \frac{\partial R}{\partial A} \frac{A}{R} \text{ or } \eta_I + \eta_A.$$

However, the intuition was not wrong either; η_y is a weighted average of elasticities in the sense that the elasticity reported for Y (0.62) lies between the elasticity calculated for an income increase solely in allowance income (1.3) and the elasticity for an income increase solely in nonallowance income (0.55).

22. U.S. Department of Housing and Urban Development, *Experimental Housing Allowance Program: A 1979 Report of Findings* (Government Printing Office, 1979), pp. 10–11.

for buying more house for owners who bought on the basis of a higher past permanent income and whose present permanent income is lower or for owners whose present income is temporarily depressed below the permanent income that was the basis for buying the house. Yet Mills and Sullivan and other Experimental Housing Allowance Program studies of housing demand have all found higher income elasticities for owners than for renters. I believe, therefore, it would be useful to know more about these low-income owners. For example, how and when were they able to purchase their homes before the Experimental Housing Allowance Program? How uniform is the owner response to the program payment? Do only some kinds of owners respond, and, if so, which kinds?

My suspicion is that the major obstacle to understanding the impact of allowance payments is that the variations in housing consumption are not well studied at the time of enrollment in the program. It seems reasonable that a family whose housing consumption is constrained by, for example, housing codes and therefore is not in equilibrium relative to income and other characteristics will respond differently to allowances than would a family whose consumption was in equilibrium. Combining the two groups in the same analysis may obscure the real impact of allowances.

In the second part of the empirical analysis, Mills and Sullivan examine the rate of adjustment to new equilibrium housing expenditures by allowance recipients.[23] The equation they estimate is

$$(12) \qquad R_{t+1} = \lambda_1(R_{t+1}^* - R_t) + \lambda_2 R_t,$$

where R_t is the family's rental expenditure in period t, R_t^* is equilibrium rental expenditure, and λ_2 is a measure of the housing price inflation between t and $t + 1$; λ_1 is defined as the percentage of households adjusting during period t to changes in R_t^*.

One question to ask about this equation is whether or not it is an appropriate description of the dynamic adjustment process. A second question is whether or not the equation accurately represents the authors' intentions. Taking the first question, I believe that there are two aspects to the adjustment process: (1) the proportion of households that adjust to the new equilibrium level during each year, and (2) the completeness of the adjustment for each household that does adjust. These are very different aspects. In the standard stock adjustment model, the assumption is that *all* units adjust, but only partially, to the new equilibrium. In contrast,

23. I am grateful to Katharine Bradbury for her perceptive questions, which helped me improve the comments in this section.

because of moving and other transaction costs, the most reasonable assumption about adjustment in the housing market is that only *some* households adjust to the new equilibrium, but they adjust completely. This distinction is worthy of note. It is easy to devise examples where the aggregate market effects are different, for example, when 24 percent of all households adjust fully to their new equilibrium consumption as compared to when all households adjust by 24 percent of the difference between their new equilibrium consumption and their old actual consumption.

These two aspects of adjustment are not properly distinguished in the equation. The definition of λ_1 implies that the equation is concerned with the *proportion* of households that adjust, not with the amount of adjustment. But when carefully examined, the equation will not bear this interpretation. Since the equation is assumed to describe the behavior of individual households, λ_1 must be the proportion of the difference between the new equilibrium and actual last period consumption that is adjusted in period $t + 1$, not the percentage of households that adjust.

The implication of defining λ_1 as the amount of adjustment is that λ_1 will have a different value for each household, depending on the amount of adjustment. In the extreme, if households that adjust do so completely, λ_1 should be 1.0, but λ_1 should be zero for those households that do not adjust. The specification of the equation, however, implies that λ_1 has a single value that is appropriate for all households. Since this is incorrect, I would be more comfortable with results derived from a two-stage model: in the first, the probability of some adjustment would be estimated; in the second, the amount of adjustment would be estimated, considering only those that did adjust.

Despite the misspecification of individual household behavior, the estimated λ_1 *may* give the authors what they want—the proportion of households that did adjust. In that sense, λ_1 may not misrepresent their intentions. The estimated λ_1 will be a weighted average of the amount of adjustment by all households in the sample. If the household adjusts fully, if it adjusts at all, λ_1 will be either 1.0 or zero; the estimated coefficient will represent a weighted average of these, making it the proportion that adjusts, just as Mills and Sullivan propose.

The problem is that interpreting λ_1 as the proportion that adjusts depends on the assumption that the real measure of adjustment is either zero or 1.0. If households that adjust, adjust only partially, λ_1 will not measure the proportion that adjusts. Given the costs of frequent adjustments, it does seem likely that adjustment will be essentially complete, but this hypothesis needs to be tested.

A different question to raise about the effort to estimate the proportion of households that adjust is why it was necessary to rely on such an equation at all. In the data set used, the proportion of households that adjust can be determined directly, by inspection. In the first empirical section the authors did just that to assign a value to δ. If it is argued that adjustment may be incomplete so that one cannot dichotomize the sample, λ_1, for reasons given previously, will not be a true measure of the proportion that adjusts. Therefore, one wonders what was gained by the more elaborate econometric procedure.

These issues may seem unimportant for practical purposes. Certainly, they do not detract from the central point that Mills and Sullivan make: complete adjustment to a program of allowances will take many years. Because of the slow buildup of demand from an allowance program, supply should be elastic and housing prices should not rise significantly.

To conclude, let me summarize what I think this paper and other program analyses say about the market impact of a program of housing allowances. In a word, the impact is probably *small*. The evidence is that income elasticities are low. Moreover, a large fraction of eligibles choose not to participate. Nonparticipation is likely to diminish over time, but the long adjustment period and the low elasticities mean that a program would not create a huge swell of demand.

Do low income elasticities mean that housing allowances are a bad program? I agree with Mills and Sullivan that the answer is no. Much of the appeal of allowances is the opportunity for greater consumer sovereignty, including personal decisions on how much to spend for housing and where to live; allowances provide this freedom regardless of elasticities. Low elasticities might seem troubling if we suppose that housing consumption has a particular claim as a merit good or because of strong external effects. But before we become too concerned, we should consider the meaning of "bad housing." In my opinion this is a very interesting question raised by the Experimental Housing Allowance Program. Consider these two findings. (1) Many occupants of "bad housing" seem to prefer their housing. They would not enroll in the allowance program if it required moving to a "better" dwelling, even though the costs incurred would be reimbursed. (2) The difference between "bad housing" and "standard housing" is sometimes so subtle that "it takes a trained inspector to detect defects," and deficiencies "often go unnoticed by renters, landlords, and homeowners."[24] If these statements are true, how meaningful is our definition of "bad housing" and how important is it that the allowance program induce recipients to purchase "better housing"? If the housing problem is not that persons are badly housed but that they must spend too large a fraction of their meager incomes on housing, then a program of allowances is an answer.

24. HUD, *A 1979 Report of Findings,* p. 11.

DAVID N. KERSHAW

ROBERTON C. WILLIAMS, JR.

Administrative Lessons

The concept of the administrative agency experiment is a significant innovation in the planning and conduct of social science experiments and demonstrations. Previous projects have treated administrative findings as by-products of the main experiment, but it is now recognized that such findings were among the most important results of the several income maintenance experiments. Only now, several years after the release of the central research findings, is a major administrative test being performed.[1]

Administrative practices often determine significant issues of program cost and effectiveness. For example, in the case of income maintenance, one cannot estimate the effects of a given combination of tax rates and guarantee levels without knowing how payment will be delivered, how income will be calculated, how often eligibility will be checked, and so forth. These variables greatly influence key behavioral considerations measured by the experiments. In the housing assistance supply experiment the responses of landlords, tenants, and homeowners are being measured in the context of *one* administrative system. We submit that even if strong, unambiguous findings emerge from the supply experiment, the introduction of a *different* administrative system in either another experiment or a national program could limit the usefulness of the experiment's results.[2]

The authors acknowledge the valuable comments on early versions of this paper from Marc Bendick, Jr., Tony Downs, Jerry J. Fitts, William L. Hamilton, G. Thomas Kingsley, David O. Porter, and James P. Zais.

1. Alan M. Hershey and Robert G. Williams, "Improving the Administration of Public Welfare Through Monthly Reporting," *The MPR Policy Newsletter* (Princeton, N.J.: Mathematica Policy Research, Spring 1979), pp. 1–3.

2. This assertion is strongly supported by evidence from the income maintenance experiments. For an illustration of the effects of that administrative system on the primary behavioral measures, see David Kershaw and Jerilyn Fair, *The New Jersey Income-Maintenance Experiment*, vol. 1: *Operations, Surveys, and Administration*, Institute for Research on Poverty Monograph Series (Academic Press, 1976), pp. 75–94.

Given the importance we attribute to explicit administrative experimentation, we credit the early planners of the housing experiments at the Department of Housing and Urban Development (HUD) for fielding an administrative test along with tests of behavioral issues important to a housing allowance program. We believe that such administrative tests should be included in all future social experiments and demonstrations.

In the first section, we define an administrative system as containing a set of seventeen general functions. Although this typology was developed expressly for this paper, it could be used in designing and assessing other administrative systems. Although many such typologies have been suggested,[3] we feel that our system provides a comprehensive framework for examining any redistributive program.

In the next section, we review the administrative findings from both the administrative agency and the supply experiments. On the basis of the Experimental Housing Allowance Program findings to date, we provide a more general assessment of housing program administration, using the administrative typology we developed. This approach reveals that there is still little or no information on almost half of these functions.

We then review the administrative agency experiment and discuss why data are missing. We argue that the problems result directly from serious design flaws imposed by initial HUD constraints, the most important being the failure to use any controlled variations to measure administrative variables. A review of data and methodological problems follows that discussion.

We conclude with a revised administrative agency experiment design illustrating our approach to administrative research. This redesigned experiment could have been conducted *within* the supply experiment. We therefore suggest that the administrative agency experiment, as designed, should not have been attempted and that the supply experiment would have yielded superior administrative findings at less cost to HUD.

Administrative Functions: A Proposed Typology

All public programs that transfer money, goods, or services require certain administrative functions. Although programs may differ greatly

3. See, for example, D. Gowler and K. Legge, "The Evaluation of Planned Organizational Change: The Necessary Art of the Possible," *Journal of Enterprise Management*, vol. 1 (1978), pp. 201–13.

in benefits supplied or population served, all programs must perform the functions outlined below. In this section we define each function in general terms. Where relevant, we specifically relate a function to a housing allowance program and offer examples of how other transfer programs would require similar activities.

1. *Administrative organization.* Determine staff size, organizational functioning, reporting, financial organization, and extent of use of existing agencies.

2. *Agency start-up.* Select staff; determine timing of hiring; conduct training; reorganize existing agencies and establish networks for communication with related agencies.

3. *Outreach.* Start initial, one-time, public information campaign; continue to analyze participation in the program; identify potential beneficiaries; direct information to missed populations.

4. *Eligibility determination.* Receive applications; screen applicants for eligibility.

5. *Enrollment.* Explain the program, including rules and regulations, participant rights and responsibilities, and procedures in which the participant might be involved; execute contract between participant and agency.

6. *Certification/recertification.* Assure that program criteria are satisfied via a signed statement by the participant or documentary evidence; certify income, household size, and other characteristics; process and verify beneficiary-initiated changes in eligibility.

7. *Distribution of primary benefits.* Deliver benefits to program participants.

8. *Distribution of adjunct benefits.* Deliver social, legal, economic, and educational benefits to assist recipients of primary benefits.

9. *Standards and conditions associated with benefits.* Satisfy certain requirements for use of program benefits (for example, requirements that the participant live in adequate housing, that the allowance be spent entirely for housing, or that the political jurisdiction in which the participant lives actively promotes integration of both neighborhoods and schools).

10. *Hearings and adjudication of appeals.* Establish and operate appeal process for decisions adverse to participant interests.

11. *Management and quality control.* Manage range of administrative activities, including budgeting, record keeping, and review procedures, as well as administrative control over the organizational structure of the agency.

12. *Auditing.* Provide for external verification of proper program management.

13. *Termination.* End benefits, which may include counseling and/or aid in transition to other programs.

14. *Interaction with other programs.* Share administrative functions, operational coordination, and/or program communication.

15. *Interaction with the general community.* Conduct public relations activities to provide an understanding of program objectives, eligibility, and probable impact.

16. *Interaction with the affected community.* Conduct public relations activities aimed toward nonbeneficiaries who are directly affected.

17. *Ongoing program assessment.* Set up monitoring procedures to measure performance regularly (may include compilation of data describing program operations and periodic field surveys of participants).

The functions outlined above provide a general description of the operations of any agency charged with administering a transfer program. Some, such as agency start-up and administrative organization, occur only at the beginning of a program's life. Others, such as outreach, management and quality control, and program assessment, are continuous. Still others, such as enrollment, termination, and hearings and adjudication of appeals, are performed only when called for by individual cases. Success of a transfer program depends on the proper handling of all these functions. An assessment of the administrative efficacy of a social program should be structured so that it will be easy to measure variations in functions that would be expected a priori to have the greatest impact on program cost or operations.

A Review of Administrative Findings from the Experimental Housing Allowance Program

Examinations of administrative functions were conducted for two parts of the Experimental Housing Allowance Program: the administrative agency experiment and the housing assistance supply experiment.[4]

---

4. The demand experiment also involved administration, but its design was such that the administrative experience could not yield insights into the administration of an active program.

Summary of Findings

The administrative agency experiment was designed to evaluate alternative procedures for administering a housing allowance program.[5] Eight existing housing agencies were selected to administer prototype allowance programs; each agency was required to perform various tasks, such as participant selection, eligibility certification, and benefit payment, but great latitude was given as to the methods for carrying out those tasks. The experiment ran for three years, during which time participants were enrolled, paid benefits according to a prescribed formula for a maximum of twenty-four months, and then transferred to other housing assistance programs. Abt Associates evaluated administrative procedures by analyzing agency records, survey data, and logs kept by observers stationed in each administering agency.

The administrative agency experiment results are detailed in more than a dozen volumes and can be summarized easily. Supply experiment results are not as well documented and are only preliminary, but they generally corroborate the administrative agency experiment findings.[6] Where possible, we intersperse supply experiment results with administrative agency experiment results. In the administrative agency experiment, the four functions of outreach, supporting services (adjunct benefits), inspection (standards and conditions), and certification were singled out for attention because of their impact on program participation, benefit targeting, improvement in housing conditions, and costs. Attempts were made to estimate administrative costs through monitoring agency activities and through computer simulation.

---

5. For full descriptions of the programs, see Abt Associates, *Third Annual Report of the Administrative Agency Experiment Evaluation—October 1974–October 1975* (Cambridge, Mass.: Abt, August 1976); and W. L. Hamilton, David W. Budding, and W. L. Holshouser, Jr., *Administrative Procedures in a Housing Allowance Program: The Administrative Agency Experiment* (Abt, March 1977).

6. The two most comprehensive sources for administrative findings in the administrative agency experiment are Hamilton and others, *Administrative Procedures*, and William L. Hamilton, *A Social Experiment in Program Administration: The Housing Allowance Administrative Agency Experiment* (Cambridge, Mass.: Abt Books, 1979). The supply experiment findings are described in Rand Corporation, *Fourth Annual Report of the Housing Assistance Supply Experiment*, R-2302-HUD (Santa Monica: Rand, May 1978), pp. 142–79. Our discussion is based primarily on these three documents.

OUTREACH. Outreach activities substantially affected the number of applications received, although lack of data and controlled variation made it impossible to determine which types were most effective. Low-intensity methods designed to attract applicants without unrealistically raising hopes about benefits produced relatively few applications. Efforts of higher intensity, which could be measured only in terms of increased expenditures, resulted in more applications. Increased use of the media seemed to be particularly effective in this regard, both in the administrative agency and supply experiments, but quantitative evidence is unavailable. The supply experiment did find, however, that half of all applicants learned about the program from media advertising, a particularly effective method for reaching elderly households.

An important need in outreach is the ability to reach the eligible population. The administrative agency experiment found that some types of households (welfare, minorities, female-headed families) were more likely to apply for benefits than were others (working poor, higher income, elderly) and that special methods are therefore necessary to reach underrepresented groups. Evidence from the experiment indicates that emphasis on media outreach can increase applications from the working poor and that personal contact with elderly households makes them more likely to apply, but nothing worked well enough to attract a demographically balanced applicant pool. Two forms of outreach were attempted to make application easier. Mail-in procedures in Bismarck, North Dakota, seemed to increase applications from outlying areas, but branch offices that were opened in other sites specifically to receive applications had little or no effect. In general, it was found that outreach is necessary to attract applicants and to achieve a balance among eligible groups; however, more research is needed to determine which methods are most effective.

SUPPORTIVE SERVICES. These services were provided in the administrative agency experiment primarily to help applicants find adequate housing and qualify for benefits. Services were either formal, offered to all applicants when they were accepted into the program, or responsive, offered only after individuals had been unable to qualify for the program on their own. The effectiveness of services varied with the characteristics of housing markets and program applicants. In loose housing markets (defined primarily by high vacancy rates), services made little or no difference in the success of applicants in becoming beneficiaries. In tight housing markets, minority households and households that had to move

Table 1. Percentage of Enrollees Becoming Recipients under Various Service and Housing Market Conditions, by Race and Moving Plans

Market conditions and level of service	Total	Moving		Staying	
		Black	White	Black	White
Tight					
High	70	65	63	77	77
Low	51	26	54	53	76
Loose					
High	86	82	84	84	88
Low	85	78	81	85	89
Total	71	47	69	71	84

Source: W. L. Hamilton, David W. Budding, and W. L. Holshouser, Jr., *Administrative Procedures in a Housing Allowance Program: The Administrative Agency Experiment* (Cambridge, Mass.: Abt Associates, March 1977), p. 15.

to satisfy housing quality criteria were significantly more successful in qualifying for benefits when a high level of services was offered (see table 1). The supply experiment, however, found that 80 percent of all enrollees were able to qualify for benefits without special counseling, and thus concluded that formal services were unwarranted. Further study is under way to determine why 20 percent of households failed to qualify and what services might be offered to help those households qualify.

The cost of supportive services in the administrative agency experiment was high (37 percent of all direct intake costs), so the potential for savings by reducing or eliminating these services is great. On the other hand, the cost of attrition because of the inability of applicants to find adequate housing was also high. Intake costs estimated at $133 per applicant were incurred for households that enrolled in the program but never qualified for benefits. Such costs returned no benefits. To the extent that services reduce this attrition, they may produce a decrease in total program costs per beneficiary; but even if savings are not realized, services may prove cost-effective because they increase the success of potential recipients in qualifying for allowance payments. Because services are of greatest value when made available in specific circumstances, targeted responsive services are probably best.

INSPECTIONS. Conditions were imposed to ensure that housing allowances were used to improve housing. Recipients had to reside in standard quality housing according to locally determined criteria, and the rent had to be at least as great as the housing allowance received. Although different methods were used to verify that the latter condition was met (such as checking directly with landlords or issuing allowance checks made payable to the recipient and landlord jointly), no method appeared to have a discernible effect on whether or not the allowance was used to pay rent. However, the procedure used to ensure that recipients were living in standard housing did have an impact on both cost and effectiveness. All agencies required that housing be inspected, but different kinds of inspectors were used.[7] Although evaluation of housing conditions is at best an inexact science, the administrative agency experiment evidence indicates that professional inspectors and agency employees were more effective in identifying substandard housing than were participants who evaluated their own housing.[8] Part of the difference clearly resulted from the relative experience of inspectors. Furthermore, professionals tended to be more objective. Agency inspectors who might have had an interest in passing units so that enrollees could qualify for benefits appeared to be more willing to overlook some deficiencies, and agency employees reviewing participant inspection forms may have done the same. Such discretionary action seemed to occur more when standards were so strict relative to average housing conditions that many units would have failed. When staff decisions were reviewed by superiors, there was less of a problem with discretion.

Three conclusions can be drawn. First, strict enforcement of housing criteria is probably unattainable if only participant inspections are used, although some training and more detailed inspection checklists might improve this. Second, strict enforcement is unlikely to be cost-effective unless the general condition of the housing stock is poor and the standards for acceptable housing are high. Under other circumstances, most units will be adequate and the cost of professional inspection is unwar-

7. The supply experiment used only professional inspectors and thus provides no data on inspection methods.

8. The administrative agency experiment evaluation contractor used its own inspectors to obtain an independent assessment of housing conditions, but even these inspection results are suspect. Multiple inspections of the same unit by different inspectors showed a correlation coefficient of 0.45 on the final decision about whether a unit was standard. While this does not provide complete information about inspection reliability, it does imply that different inspectors agreed in their bottom line evaluations no more than 72 percent of the time. (The 72 percent figure applies if exactly half of the housing stock were rated standard; if 60 percent were standard, agreement on condition would have occurred in only half of all cases.) It should be noted, however, that the multiple inspections were conducted six months apart, during which time the unit's condition might have changed.

ranted.[9] Finally, de facto relaxation of standards is likely when the effect is disqualification of a large share of the housing stock. The use of professional inspectors or review by superiors may reduce this problem, but a better solution might be a formal relaxation of standards to make satisfaction of housing criteria easier and less discretionary. It is clear that the entire issue of inspection cannot be resolved without some decision on the importance of enforcing housing quality.

CERTIFICATION. Determination of eligibility and benefit payment requires certification of both household size and income. The administrative agency experiment sheds no light on how household size can be certified since there were no basic variations in agency procedures. Three methods of determining income were used, however: self-declaration, documentation, and third-party verification.[10] Although it is impossible to assess accurately the relative effectiveness of the techniques without an external audit of income, a comparison of information from applications with information received during certification indicates that some verification produces greater accuracy than does self-declaration. Documentation or third-party verification resulted in some change in 54 to 82 percent of all cases, whereas changes were recorded in only 35 percent of those cases using self-declaration.[11] On the other hand, although verification may result in more accurate income measurement and subsequent benefit payments, the income certification method used made virtually no net difference in transfer costs of the program. Because the method does not result in cost savings, the only justification for such verification is to reduce errors and increase equity among recipients. One alternative suggested by the experiment is selective verification for households whose incomes are most likely to change. The experiment indicates that changes occur most frequently for those households receiving welfare or other grant income, those with multiple jobs, those with the lowest income, or those with male heads; the incomes of elderly households change only rarely. Certification of income of the former groups might thus be justi-

9. This conclusion does not follow if the criterion that beneficiaries live in standard housing is considered to be of paramount importance. We feel that this should not be the case and would prefer instead to allow some discretion for beneficiaries.

10. The supply experiment required either documentation or third-party verification of "critical information." It was concluded that both methods were "quite accurate" but little quantitative information is available. See Rand Corp., *Fourth Annual Report*, p. 165.

11. Donald E. Dickson, *Certification: Determining Eligibility and Setting Payment Levels in the Administrative Agency Experiment* (Abt, March 1977), p. D-54.

fied. It is also important to note that there were only small differences in cost between the different options: third-party verification cost only $6 more per recipient than self-declaration. Because there were no variations among agencies, nothing could be concluded concerning frequency of income certification.[12]

ADMINISTRATIVE COSTS. Based on the Experimental Housing Allowance Program, the final issue that can be addressed in detail is administrative costs and their variation under alternative procedures. In the administrative agency experiment, actual costs in 1976 dollars for enrolling participants (intake) varied across sites from $178 to $534 per recipient (with a median of $253), while maintenance costs ranged from $129 to $322 per recipient year (with a median of $205).[13] The supply experiment had intake costs averaging $249 and maintenance costs averaging $133 per recipient year.[14] Assuming a five-year average for program participation, total annual administrative costs per recipient in the administrative agency experiment ranged from $165 to $429 (with a median of $252), while total annual administrative costs in the supply experiment were $183.[15] Although precisely comparable figures are not available, these costs compare favorably with administrative costs of the section 8 housing program, with direct intake costs similar but administrative agency and supply experiment maintenance costs markedly lower.[16]

Costs varied considerably under alternative methods of handling administrative functions in the administrative agency experiment. As table 2 shows, the difference between high-cost and low-cost procedures was about 50 percent overall, although major cost differences occurred only for supportive services and housing inspection. The small variation for other functions means that procedures in those areas can be chosen al-

12. The supply experiment required semiannual income recertification, but nothing is reported on the cost or effectiveness of this procedure. All administrative agency experiment agencies recertified income annually.

13. U.S. Department of Housing and Urban Development, *Experimental Housing Allowance Program: A 1979 Report of Findings* (Government Printing Office, April 1979), p. 66.

14. Rand Corporation, *Fourth Annual Report*, p. 148.

15. This figure is adjusted from published data to account for the five-year amortization of intake costs. See HUD, *A 1979 Report of Findings*, p. 66.

16. Only direct costs are available for this comparison. For intake, administrative agency experiment costs were $116 per participant versus $131 in section 8, while the maintenance cost comparison was $69 versus $192. Comparable data are unavailable for the supply experiment. (It should be noted that the costs for section 8 are rough estimates and may not be fully accurate.) Hamilton, *Social Experiment*, p. 221.

Table 2. Variations in Administrative Costs
Dollars

Function[a]	Administrative agency experiment[b]			Supply experiment (average between two sites)
	Least-cost procedures	Benchmark procedures[c]	High-cost procedures	
Intake costs per new recipient				
Outreach	39.06	36.68	39.03	62.20
Screening	30.39	25.06	31.32	21.30
Certification	17.45	15.14	14.37	
Enrollment	33.72	27.80	29.95	97.99
Services	31.96	51.62	91.37	8.77
Inspection	12.42	49.46	46.95	58.56
Total	165.01	205.76	252.99	248.82
Maintenance costs per recipient year				
Payment operations	36.37	38.47	38.25	21.37
Eligibility recertification	6.37	10.50	9.96	77.79
Services	48.47	53.94	64.47	4.12
Reinspection	8.65	38.08	36.14	29.85
Total	99.85	140.98	148.83	133.13

Sources: Hamilton and others, *Administrative Procedures*, pp. 67, 69, 72; Rand Corporation, *Fourth Annual Report of the Housing Assistance Supply Experiment*, R-2302-HUD (Santa Monica: Rand, May 1978), p. 148. Figures are rounded.

a. Functions are approximately comparable between the administrative agency experiment and the supply experiment. Major differences are due in part to the emphasis of each experiment.

b. Total administrative agency experiment costs are obtained by multiplying estimated direct costs by a fixed factor to account for indirect costs. Because this factor varies by whether procedure is least-cost (2.62), benchmark (2.16), or high-cost (2.05), total costs may not always be consistent with least-cost or high-cost designations.

c. Benchmark assumes use of more stringent certification and inspection because of effectiveness, average costs for outreach and services, and least cost for other functions.

most entirely on the basis of effectiveness. The choices for inspection and services are more complicated. For inspection, the question is whether possible improvement of housing and the potential for reduced participation levels justify the added expense of professional or agency inspections, which cost five times as much as participant inspections. As to services, a balance must be found between costs and participation rates. Neither of these questions can be resolved through experimentation; they must be answered by policy makers.

Two other cost issues were addressed in the experiment. First, indirect costs were found to vary with direct costs, although the former rose more slowly. This implies that economies of scale exist in agency work load and that larger rather than smaller agencies should be used. Furthermore, using the common assumption that indirect costs are a fixed proportion of direct costs might lead to large errors in extrapolating experimental results to a national scale. Second, 36 percent of all intake expenditures were for attrition costs of applicants who did not become recipients. These costs can be reduced to the extent that administrative procedures can cut the attrition rate. Administrative agency experiment results indicate that increased supportive services or relaxation of housing inspection criteria would reduce the likelihood of attrition, particularly at the enrollee stage, when attrition cost savings are greatest. Because supportive services do not result in a reduction in housing improvement and may yield overall cost savings in particular cases, selectively increasing their use appears to be the best weapon to combat attrition.

Three general cost lessons were learned from the experiment. First, a housing allowance program can be administered at a reasonable cost, comparable to other transfer programs. Second, administrative procedures do make a difference, both in cost and effectiveness. More research is required to ascertain the exact trade-offs involved, but choices about what costs are justified for what results must be left to policy makers. Finally, some procedures appear to be clearly superior, at least for particular groups in particular circumstances, whereas some functions can be performed equally well by different methods at about the same cost. In the latter case, administering agencies can be given freedom to select procedures, but the former case will require procedural requirements.

Administration of Housing Programs

Although it may be unreasonable to expect that these experiments provide conclusions on an exhaustive set of functions, measuring the reported results against our typology seems to be the best method for summarizing what we know *in general* about running housing programs and where the focus of additional research should be.

Table 3 summarizes the housing allowance administration findings within our administrative framework. The table is based only on published reports and may be incomplete in terms of findings that have not yet been published. For example, agency case studies exist only in HUD files, and conclusions based on them are therefore unavailable. It is our hope that table 3 will point out gaps in generally accessible administrative findings and will indicate the findings that have been published concerning program administration.

Table 3. Summary of Housing Program Administrative Findings

Administrative function	General information
1. Administrative organization	No performance differences are evident in *types* of organizations.
	Possible scale economies may mean that larger agencies will show reduced indirect costs.
	Separation of *inspection* responsibility from other agency functions yields more objective inspections.
2. Agency start-up	Structured training sessions using job simulations may improve subsequent administrative performance.
3. Outreach	Rate of application increases with rate of outreach expenditure.
	Effectiveness of outreach procedures varies by demographic group (mass media for the working poor; personal direct contact for the elderly; social service agency referral for welfare clients).
	Targeted outreach, necessary to reach certain recipient groups, substantially increases outreach costs.
	Permitting applications by mail may be an effective method for outreach with rural populations.
	Opening neighborhood offices to encourage applications did not prove effective.
	Average direct cost of attracting an eligible applicant was about $6, but varied by location from less than $2 to more than $30.
4. Eligibility determination	Preapplication screening may result in fewer ineligible applicants but incurs greater costs. (Data do not allow estimation of cost-effectiveness.)
5. Enrollment	Costs varied by enrollment method and were least expensive for group enrollment and most expensive for a mixed method (although the direct cost differences between the two methods were only about $1 per enrollee).
6. Certification/recertification	Accuracy of income reporting is substantially improved when certified through documentation or third-party contact.
	Accuracy of household size reporting is unaffected by certification.
	Certification of income had little effect on total transfer costs, although it may still be warranted on grounds of equity and "program image."
	Selective certification may be warranted for certain population subgroups (e.g., welfare recipients, households with more than one income source, very low income households).

Table 3 (continued)

Administrative function	General information
	Selective certification may also be warranted after household composition changes and for households where there is a time lag between application and enrollment.
7. Distribution of primary benefits	Computerized payment procedures are half as expensive as manual procedures.
8. Distribution of adjunct benefits	In tight housing markets, minorities and people who move are better able to qualify for program benefits if provided with extensive supportive services.
	Provision of extensive supportive services may raise program administrative costs by as much as $32 per recipient at intake.
	By reducing attrition, services provided to minorities in tight housing markets actually reduce intake costs per recipient.
	Many applicants did not need any services to qualify for benefits; therefore, adjunct benefits in the program should be either voluntary (responsive) or targeted.
	The potential for administrative cost savings resulting from improving the delivery of adjunct benefits is great, since these costs amounted to 37 percent of direct intake costs.
9. Standards and conditions associated with benefits	No single method of ensuring that rent payments exceeded allowance benefits proved any more effective than others.
	Professional housing inspectors were more able to identify substandard units than agency employees, who in turn were more effective than participants.
	Professional or agency inspections cost approximately $35 per inspection, compared with $5 for self-inspection.
	The program objective of ensuring that participants live in standard housing is best met if professional inspectors are used, *except* when the bulk of the housing stock in a given area is known to be standard.
	If agency inspectors are used, a review by superiors is needed to ensure consistency and objectivity.
	Self-inspections may be improved if more detailed forms are introduced and better training is provided.

Table 3 (continued)

Administrative function	General information
10. Hearings and adjudication of appeals	There is no information with respect to procedures, number of appeals (if any), or outcome results of administrative or judicial appeals or proceedings.
11. Management and quality control	Computerized quality control and editing of enrollment forms produced few improvements in the quality of the forms.
	Most client misreporting is inadvertent.
	Independent audits and quality control checks indicate that data gathered during client interviews are accurate.
	Clients do not seem to resent audit and quality control checking.
	Formal error control procedures can substantially reduce the likelihood of errors, consequently reducing net overpayments.
12. Auditing	Independent audits conducted in the supply experiment showed some errors in reported income, household composition, and housing expenses, but in amounts that were negligible.
	There is no evidence that independent audits were conducted in the other experiments.
13. Termination	There does not appear to be any information with respect to methods of termination of individuals during the program, or assistance or referrals to other programs at the end of the administrative agency experiment.
14. Interaction with other programs	Because of overlapping client rosters, effective relationships with other agencies are important.
	There is no discussion of methods or techniques of interaction or specific agency relationships.
15. Interaction with the general community	There is no information about methods of communicating with the general public in the administrative agency experiment.
	There is considerable mention in the supply experiment of the importance of community relations and the image of the program, including the use of community presentations, press releases, appearances on news and public affairs programs, but no discussion of relative effectiveness of any method.

Table 3 (continued)

Administrative function	General information
16. Interaction with the affected community	In the administrative agency experiment, there was considerable contact with landlords, but no information about what methods seemed useful. Considerable attention in the supply experiment was paid to relations with community leaders, landlords, lending institutions, and other important market intermediaries, but nothing has been written regarding that experience.
17. Ongoing program assessment	There are no recommendations about monitoring or evaluating subsequent programs.

In our view, the most dramatic increase in general knowledge is in estimating administrative costs. Despite considerable variation across sites, functions, and experiments, the work in both the administrative agency experiment and the supply experiment dramatically reduced the degree of uncertainty over the resources required to perform most of the important administrative functions. The extent of disaggregation of the estimates also may allow cost estimates to be reformulated for some functions not actually performed or examined in the experiments. Persons familiar with the vast disagreement among experts in recent welfare reform and health insurance policy debates on potential administrative costs will appreciate this contribution.

Table 3 shows that the emphasis in the experiment was on four administrative functions: outreach, certification, adjunct benefits (supportive services), and standards and conditions (primarily inspections). As with costs, the treatment of these functions was extensive, and we know much more about them as a result of the experiments.

Two other administrative functions were largely ignored by the administrative agency experiment but received effective treatment by the supply experiment analysts. These are management and quality control and auditing, both of which were treated in a special paper under the topic of error control.[17] Within the limits of the supply experiment administrative system (which had no controlled variations), this is a thorough review of error control techniques inside and outside the agency. An analysis done in the context of variations in frequency of payments, degree of documentation, enrollment techniques, and so forth would

17. Paul E. Tebbets, *Controlling Errors in Allowance Program Administration*, Rand/N-1145-HUD (Rand Corp., August 1979).

have been desirable, but the analysis represents the results of considerable trial-and-error research by housing allowance program staff. Of the remaining eleven administrative functions, five received virtually no mention at all, and six received such light treatment that we know little more than we knew before these experiments began.

The five omitted functions begin with administrative organization, which appeared to be the one area where systematic variation was mandated from the start. We hope that some subsequent publication will discuss the relative efficacy and functioning between selected types and levels of government. If HUD is indifferent about its administrative agent, that would be an interesting finding in itself. Except for some information from the Rand Corporation on the effects of staff training, analysis of agency start-up, which should provide important information about techniques for organizing a new agency, staffing, and developing important procedures, is ignored. For the functions of distribution of benefits and hearings and appeals, we have received virtually no guidance to help us improve administration in current and future housing programs. A series of important options on how payments are distributed—regarding method, frequency, and technique—could have significant and tangible effects on the way housing programs function. The final omission is ongoing program assessment. A valuable product of the experiments would be a thoughtful, helpful design for effectively monitoring a housing allowance program, using essentially administrative data sources. Functions not sufficiently examined in the experiment should be designed into the assessment system.

Of the six functions that receive slight mention in the current Experimental Housing Allowance Program literature, three include the interactions of the housing allowance program with other programs, with the general community, and with the special, affected community (for example, landlords and lending institutions). We suspect that much has been learned about these three important functions, and perhaps some expertise has been passed on orally to HUD; however, little exists in writing to help program managers design and implement more effective housing administrative systems in the future. Finally, the table tells us something about group versus individual enrollment methods; it shows that preapplication screening may result in fewer ineligible applicants (but this was tested only in small, rural Bismarck); but it tells us virtually nothing about the costs or procedural options for terminating individuals in the program and/or referring them to other programs.

Part of the charge to the evaluator in the administrative agency experiment was "to develop a model of an agency with the appropriate characteristics for administering a housing allowance program."[18] This implies a discussion of all functions to be handled by an agency and the selection of procedures that will best meet the goals of an allowance program. The constraints imposed on the experiment by restrictive program design make this a difficult assignment. Nonetheless, the valuable conclusions that came out of the experiment could have been drawn together into a coherent and readily accessible description of a *model agency*. Such a description, followed by a brief discussion of the weaker areas of the analysis and their implications for agency design, would have provided a concise summary of experiment results to be used by federal administrators and legislators who do not have time to read the volumes of administrative agency experiment results. Although the *Administrative Procedures* report tries to summarize the major conclusions, no real "bottom line" is drawn. Some attempt is made to discuss implications for a national housing allowance program, but that discussion is brief and not well focused.[19]

Evaluation of the Administrative Agency Experiment

We have reviewed what was and was not learned in the administrative agency experiment. It is clear from our discussion that potentially useful administrative information is missing, primarily because early design decisions constrained the experiment, making it impossible to analyze certain administrative functions. In the first part of this section, we discuss the design flaws of the experiment. We then turn to methodological problems that limited the results obtained within the design constraints. On the whole, we feel that the contractor performed well and that the general success of the experiment must be credited to that performance.

Constraints Imposed by the Program Design

THE "NATURALISTIC" APPROACH AND THE LACK OF CONTROLLED VARIATION. The *Agency Program Manual* detailed ninety-two specific functions to be performed by administering agencies, but it generally left

18. Abt Associates, *Agency Program Manual: Experimental Housing Allowance Program* (Abt, March 1973), p. 2.3.
19. Hamilton and others, *Administrative Procedures*, pp. 81–89.

the choice of method to each agency.[20] Thus, no attempt was made to impose controlled variation of administrative procedures or even to ensure that there would be any variation across agencies. "The controlled variation approach was rejected . . . because it would have limited the opportunity to observe agencies innovating and adapting to real-world conditions."[21] Yet granting agency autonomy meant that any variation in methods would occur purely by chance and that some potentially effective techniques would not be used and therefore could not be observed. Variation did occur for most of the functions dealing directly with participants and, not surprisingly, much of the analysis is concentrated on those functions. Nonetheless, options were missed and, consequently, the analysis suffers. "For several functions . . . there were no major variations in procedures."[22] "Most . . . agencies chose not to verify household size. This lack of significant variation prevents any conclusions about whether some methods might have been more effective than others."[23] Thus, although allowing agencies to select their own methods may have resulted in techniques that otherwise would not have been used, it is clear that more consistent and complete variation would have occurred if systematic variation had been incorporated into the program design.

On the other hand, one view of the experiment would hold that learning which procedures the existing agencies would select is worthwhile in its own right. The fact that no agency attempted to verify household size, for example, means that agencies either did not feel that such verification was necessary to ensure accurate reporting or that they could find no acceptable way to certify household size. While not conclusive, this finding indicates that it might be impractical to impose a verification requirement on agencies since they might be unwilling to comply. It might be argued, however, that the only way to test the latter hypothesis would be to impose a requirement and observe the degree of compliance. This would call once again for planned variation in administrative procedures in the experiment.

Probably even more important is the lack of *controlled* variation brought about by allowing agency autonomy. Evaluation reports note that this lack merely made the administrative agency experiment a "naturalistic experiment," requiring "evaluation of both the significant adminis-

20. Abt Associates, *Agency Program Manual*, chap. 4.
21. Hamilton and others, *Administrative Procedures*, p. 2.
22. Ibid., p. iv.
23. Dickson, *Certification*, p. 57.

trative variations among agencies and the consequent differences in their operations and results."[24] Yet without controlling the variation in factors other than the one under consideration, it is difficult, if not impossible, to separate the effects of alternative administrative procedures from those resulting from the uncontrolled variation of those other factors. The administrative agency experiment reports note that lack of experimental controls resulted in imprecise cost estimates.[25] Further, cost-effectiveness of alternative methods could not always be assessed: "Firm cost-effectiveness conclusions require research in which these variables are systematically altered."[26] If particular techniques had been assigned to individual agencies or if agencies had been required to use different administrative methods for different client segments, variations in costs and effectiveness could have been more accurately determined. As it was, experimental results were incomplete and have limited validity.

Given these problems, why was the "naturalistic" approach chosen for the administrative agency experiment? A number of explanations can be offered. Perhaps foremost is that serious doubt existed about whether existing housing agencies could administer an allowance program well and at reasonable cost. Only through the use of existing agencies could this question be answered, and the answer was a clear "yes." Further, the designers felt that choice of alternative techniques would be difficult; leaving agencies free to select those which they felt were best and which would therefore be most acceptable in an active program would solve that problem. In fact, there seems to have been a great deal of concern about the problems involved in imposing rigid procedural requirements on administering agencies. On the other hand, given this attitude, it is unclear why a desired result of the experiment would then be to develop an agency model using the "best" procedures. If such a model could not be imposed on existing agencies, why have one at all?

Along similar lines, there was concern that an experiment with strictly controlled variation would yield results that could not be duplicated in a real-world program, either because the controls would bias the results or because the quality of personnel required to run a complicated experiment

24. Abt Associates, *Third Annual Report*, p. 3.

25. Abt Associates, *Administrative Costs of Alternative Procedures: A Compendium of Analyses of Direct Costs in the Administrative Agency Experiment* (Abt, March 1977), p. 6.

26. Jean MacMillan and William L. Hamilton, *Outreach: Generating Applications in the Administrative Agency Experiment* (Abt, February 1977).

would not be representative of people in an agency. The essence of this argument is, "It may work fine in the laboratory but we could never make it work on the production line." These are valid concerns, but we feel that proper administration of the experiment itself would have minimized these problems. In any case, it is more important to obtain the definitive results yielded by a controlled experiment, even if they have to be adjusted to apply to a permanent program, than to find that little or nothing can be ascertained with precision.

ENROLLMENT LIMITATIONS. Each agency was instructed to enroll no more than 900 households.[27] Because this meant that not all potentially eligible households could become participants, publicity was to be kept at a "low profile" to avoid raising hopes unrealistically. In practice, these conditions had three main effects.[28] First, outreach activities were geared to the enrollment target levels rather than to complete coverage of the eligible population. This generally meant that outreach was conducted at low intensity unless it became clear that such methods would not succeed in obtaining enough participants. The latter situation led to crash outreach programs as agencies attempted to meet enrollment goals within prescribed time limits. Neither experience is comparable to the outreach approach that would be used in a large-scale program, and estimated costs are therefore inapplicable. Evidence from the supply experiment indicates that outreach costs per applicant do rise as enrollment target levels are increased.[29] It may be argued that the administrative agency experiment experience was identical to what would be encountered in a program of limited scale. While this may be true, it is still important to learn which outreach methods would be needed to reach the entire population in order to target outreach to particular groups. Giving benefits to those most easily attracted to the program may reduce costs, but it does so at potentially high equity costs. One likely alternative would be legislative targeting of benefits to specific groups. Again, however, accurate cost estimation would require either that enrollment quotas be imposed in the administrative agency experiment or that outreach be conducted at whatever level is needed to attract all groups. The former would be the preferred alternative, but in its absence the latter is demanded.

A second effect of enrollment limits involved attrition and the estima-

27. Bismarck was limited to 400 and Durham, North Carolina, to 500. Hamilton and others, *Administrative Procedures*, p. 4.
28. Other effects are noted in ibid., pp. 86–87, but they are relatively minor.
29. Rand Corporation, *Fourth Annual Report*, p. 153.

tion of administrative costs per recipient. The limits meant that not all applicants could be accepted into the program, and in fact one-fourth of eligible applicants were not selected as participants simply because of enrollment constraints.[30] Some intake costs were incurred for those not selected, thus presenting problems in accurately calculating enrollment costs per recipient. This, combined with the outreach effects, means that intake costs probably cannot be accurately extrapolated to evaluate a more comprehensive program.

A third impact of constraints on program size involved indirect costs and economies of scale. Because a complete administrative structure must be developed regardless of the size of the program, one would expect that indirect costs would exhibit economies of scale and would decline per participant as the number of participants increased. Because all sites had programs of about the same magnitude, such effects were impossible to observe. Evidence from the supply experiment indicates that scale differences probably exist, although the results are preliminary and may well involve other factors.[31] If the size of the program does affect indirect costs per recipient, estimates of those costs cannot be extended to a larger-scale program without further research on how the scale economies operate.

TIME LIMITATION. Agencies were allowed to enroll participants only during an initial seven-month period, and benefits could be paid for no more than twenty-four months, yielding a total program life of about three years.[32] This limit would be expected to affect experimental results in three ways. First, the limited enrollment period, combined with target participation levels, would probably result in the use of outreach techniques different from those used in an ongoing program. Agencies, striving for rapid enrollment, might well use methods effective in drawing applicants but politically infeasible on other than an experimental basis.[33] This bias, which is opposite to that evolving from enrollment limits,[34] has

---

30. Charles M. Maloy and others, *Administrative Costs in a Housing Allowance Program: Two-Year Costs in the Administrative Agency Experiment* (Abt, February 1977), p. 48.

31. Rand Corporation, *Fourth Annual Report*, p. 148.

32. Abt Associates, *Agency Program Manual*, pp. 4.30, 4.31. A second enrollment period was allowed for Jacksonville because recipient targets were missed badly in the initial period. See William L. Holshouser, Jr., *Report on Selected Aspects of the Jacksonville Housing Allowance Experiment* (Abt, May 1976).

33. Negative reaction to media advertising of the Experimental Housing Allowance Program was encountered in Green Bay, Wisconsin, in the supply experiment. See Rand Corporation, *Fourth Annual Report*, p. 154.

34. Although the opposing biases would tend to offset one another, there is no way to estimate the net effect, and the results would still be inaccurate.

two consequences. It will tend to overstate outreach costs relative to a program which has no time limits on enrollment. More important, it becomes difficult to assess the effectiveness of less extensive outreach methods. Sites not needing extensive outreach to meet program targets would be unable to determine the long-run effects since they would have enrolled the most accessible segment of the eligible population. Agencies resorting to more extensive techniques would have problems disentangling the effects of different outreach methods. In any case, measurement of outreach cost and effectiveness, both short- and long-run, are made more difficult by the enrollment time constraint.[35]

The two-year limit on housing allowance payments is likely to have given a severe selectivity bias to the program, the effect of which was probably transmitted to the conclusions on cost and effectiveness. Applicants selected for the program were told that benefits would be paid for no more than twenty-four months. For applicants whose current housing satisfied program standards, the time limit should have had no effect on their becoming participants since they could do so without moving. For applicants who needed either to move to a new home or to undertake substantial repairs to their current unit in order to qualify for benefits, the limited program duration might have been a disincentive to enroll, particularly if the potential benefits were small.[36] This bias could affect administrative costs in several areas. Outreach costs might be higher because more intensive efforts would be required to attain the participation targets. Other intake costs would also be higher because some functions would be performed for applicants who eventually would elect not to participate. Although these cost differences might be small, depending on how early in the intake process attrition occurs, there will nevertheless be some bias to the evaluation of administrative procedures.

The limitation on total program life further compounded the problems of assessing administrative costs and effectiveness. Few functions could be conducted over a long enough period to allow operations to settle into long-term patterns. Much learning-by-doing and ad hoc adaptation would be expected to take place in the start-up phase of any program. Assessment of the effectiveness of a given method and accurate measurement of costs must take place *after* the initial phase. The short life of the admin-

35. These issues are addressed briefly in MacMillan and Hamilton, *Outreach,* pp. 41–42.

36. This appears to have been the case, since those who planned to move were much less successful in becoming recipients. See Abt Associates, *Third Annual Report,* p. 29.

istrative agency experiment probably resulted in overestimates of costs and underestimates of effectiveness.

Methodological Issues

DATA QUALITY. Most of the data collection for the administrative agency experiment was done by the administering agencies in the form of record-keeping requirements.[37] Although the evaluation contractor took great pains to review all agency-collected data through item-by-item editing and comparison with independent sources, it is clear that major data errors were encountered. Data on the number of housing inspections performed were obviously inaccurate, as indicated by reports of fewer inspections than there were program participants, despite the requirement that all participants have some form of inspection.[38] This problem required that the number of inspections be estimated, which reduced the credibility of cost and effectiveness estimates for that function.[39] Similar but less extreme data inadequacies exist for verification of allowance use, the composition of services offered to beneficiaries, and the use of outreach methods.[40] These problems would appear to stem from two sources: inadequate procedures for data collection and initial nonrequirement of some data items. Although neither kind of problem could have been completely solved by contractor action, early recognition of the shortcomings and prompt corrective action might have ameliorated later analysis difficulties. A further problem involved the lack of direct audits of experimental data. Experiment reports indicate that few data items were independently corroborated, which left their validity open to question. Data audits should have been standard procedure in an experiment of this sort. It is recognized, however, that cost considerations might have influenced the decision not to audit data more completely.

MEASUREMENT OF OUTPUTS. A major difficulty that occurs throughout the analysis is the inability to measure accurately the output of any given administrative function. For example, although all agencies were required to ensure that recipients were living in adequate housing and minimum standards were imposed by HUD, the precise standards

37. Abt Associates, *Agency Program Manual,* pp. 4.65–4.70.

38. David W. Budding, *Inspection: Implementing Housing Quality Requirements in the Administrative Agency Experiment* (Abt, February 1977), p. C-36.

39. Ibid., p. C-9.

40. Hamilton and others, *Administrative Procedures,* pp. 39, 93; MacMillan and Hamilton, *Outreach,* p. 41.

and the means of determining whether those standards were met were left up to the agency. In practice, one agency might have had strict standards that were rigorously enforced while another agency might have been lax on both counts. Yet output of the inspection function was measured primarily by the number of inspections conducted and whether the inspection was conducted by the participant or by the agency, with no consideration of other factors.[41] The wide variation in estimated inspection costs across agencies indicates that output measurement was probably a problem, yet there was no apparent attempt to discuss the issue or resolve it.[42] Similar problems were encountered in the outreach and supportive service functions, again without any resolution.[43] In fairness, it should be noted that measurement problems have long plagued research in the social sciences. There often are no solutions, so not to have found one is not necessarily a fault. What is a fault, however, is the failure to point out the difficulty of and implications for interpreting reported results.

MEASUREMENT OF DIRECT COSTS. Much of the administrative agency experiment analysis is devoted to estimating the cost of performing the various administrative functions to provide some idea of administrative expenses in a larger-scale program. As discussed earlier, program design constraints would probably have rendered such estimates inexact. Yet even within those constraints, better cost estimates might have been obtained had two issues been considered. First, the effects on costs of interactions among the different functions were virtually ignored despite the potential for sizable impacts.[44] For example, more extensive supportive services might result in participants being more able to conduct complete and accurate self-inspections of housing units, which would make such inspections more effective and reduce inspection costs. That these interactions were not considered could be attributed to the small sample size; with only eight possible combinations of functions, observing meaningful interactive effects is difficult. On the other hand, more comments on the potential interactions were called for, based either on the limited

41. Some attempt was made to use independent evaluators to assess the reliability of different forms of inspection. Because of problems inherent in inspections, these results are of questionable validity. See Budding, *Inspection*, app. B.

42. Ibid., pp. C-6, C-14, C-16.

43. Abt Associates, *Alternative Procedures*, pp. 21–22; William L. Holshouser, Jr., *Supportive Services in the Administrative Agency Experiment* (Abt, February 1977), pp. v–vii, 43–64.

44. Abt Associates, *Alternative Procedures*, p. 14.

range of observed methods or on a priori expectations. A fully controlled experiment would have made an analysis of interactive effects straightforward.

A second problem with the reported cost estimates is that they are not always based on actual full costs. In practice, this occurred for two reasons. First, data sometimes did not allow accurate allocation of incurred costs to the different functions. For example, the Tulsa agency subcontracted a large part of the program administration, which confused costs among functions and the division between direct and indirect costs.[45] The second difficulty in fully measuring costs involved the use by agencies of donated services. All agencies received some donated services, most of which were in the outreach function but which also included such things as free computer services.[46] Although some of these services might be donated in an active program, there is no guarantee that this would happen. Some attempt was made to get around these problems by omitting the Tulsa, Oklahoma, case from many cost estimates and by using an extensive simulation model to predict costs in the absence of donated services. To the extent that the model calibration was able to avoid the data shortcomings, these difficulties would appear to be minor in terms of their influence on experimental results.

MEASUREMENT OF INDIRECT COSTS. Another set of analytical problems involves indirect costs—the costs involving general administrative functions that do not provide specific services to individual households. Two basic problems are encountered in the analysis. First, because some agencies allocated indirect costs to the direct function being served or subcontracted functions involving both direct and indirect activities,[47] it is not possible to measure total indirect costs accurately. Thus, reported costs are of questionable validity. A second problem involves the estimation of indirect costs, which the analysis assumes are primarily a function of direct costs.[48] The reports note that indirect costs were probably influenced by scale effects that were operative across the experiment sites. However, estimation of such scale effects and their incorporation into cost estimates were severely limited by the lack of variation in agency size. The analysis concludes that indirect costs are probably beyond the reach of policy control,[49] and therefore little can be done to influence

45. Maloy and others, *Administrative Costs*, p. 39.
46. Ibid.
47. Ibid., p. 38; Abt Associates, *Alternative Procedures*, p. 161.
48. Maloy and others, *Administrative Costs*, p. 38.
49. Ibid., pp. 40–41, 60.

their level. It would appear that more could have been learned about this subject during the experiment.

ASSESSMENT OF COST-EFFECTIVENESS. The problems of cost estimation and the inability to measure adequately the degree to which a function is performed make it impossible to assess adequately the cost-effectiveness of different administrative procedures. For some functions, such as outreach, the evaluators did not examine the issue of cost-effectiveness because data were inadequate.[50] For others, including supportive services, limitations on input and output measurement meant that conclusions were not clear-cut, although some attempt was made to gauge the relative effectiveness of various options.[51] Because a major goal of the administrative agency experiment was to determine which procedures were most cost-effective and which should be incorporated into a full-scale program, more consistent and complete handling of this issue was called for.[52] It may once again be the case, however, that the evaluator was limited by the design constraints of the experiment and that nothing more could have been accomplished.

In conclusion, it is worthwhile to remember that no social research project is complete in the sense that it answers all questions fully. Because of constraints on time or funding or because of the requirements imposed by sponsors, some issues are highlighted to the exclusion of others and particular methodologies are chosen. That the administrative agency experiment was no exception should be clear from our discussion. However, many of the shortcomings of the experiment are the result of unavoidable trade-offs. One might argue that the wrong options were selected and that interesting questions were left unanswered. Yet in spite of the problems and omissions, the experiment did provide a great deal of useful information about the administration of housing assistance programs.

Redesign of an Administrative Experiment

This section will illustrate how the administrative agency experiment should have been designed and will develop a concrete model for subsequent administrative tests. We have identified three major design flaws in the administrative agency experiment: lack of controlled variation, en-

50. Abt Associates, *Alternative Procedures*, p. 62.
51. Ibid., pp. 152–54.
52. Abt Associates, *Agency Program Manual*, p. 2-3.

rollment limitations, and time limitations. Because of budgetary constraints, a satisfactory resolution of the controlled variation or enrollment limitation problems was never possible—there were simply too few sites with too few participants for many varying treatments. With modest additional expense, the time limitation issue possibly could have been improved.

Given the constraints inherent in the administrative agency experiment, however, it seems clear that the designers of the administrative tests passed up an excellent opportunity when they did not utilize the supply experiment to measure administrative functions. This was a large entitlement-type demonstration, scheduled to last for ten years, in which HUD and the researchers had ultimate control over the administrative structure and procedures. This experiment provided a rare opportunity to measure important administrative variables in a controlled and scientific way. To satisfy those who were worried that an administrative structure staffed and managed by the Rand Corporation would be atypically competent, energetic, and flexible (and thus make eventual generalization to government agencies and replication difficult), one could have retained one or more administrative agency experiment agencies for real-world comparisons.

The administrative design proposed here seeks to provide sound measurement of all seventeen administrative functions. It does not suggest controlled variation of all, or even most, variables, but the design does provide separate assessment methods corresponding to the nature of each function. The experiment we propose would provide information missing from the administrative agency experiment results and would largely remedy the methodological flaws, at a cost saving to HUD.

In the supply experiment, how should the seventeen functions be handled to provide information of greatest value to a full-scale allowance program? Most of the functions do not lend themselves to meaningful variation. These should be considered "try-out" cases in which just one technique is used, refined, and reported in detail. Other functions can be varied, but distinctions among alternative methods are not clear-cut and thus cannot be readily quantified for analysis. The experiment should try different ways of handling these functions, but conclusions will be relatively subjective. Finally, five functions could be performed using alternative procedures, any of which might be used in an ongoing program. The formal part of the experiment should focus on these functions. Table 4 summarizes how each function could be treated.

Table 4. Research Treatment of Administrative Functions[a]

Function	Research treatment
1. Administrative organization	Specify at outset—change based on experience
2. Agency start-up	Specify at outset—no variation
3. Outreach	Vary during course of experiment
4. Eligibility determination	Controlled variation (interact with 5, 6, 8) Mail In person
5. Enrollment	Controlled variation (interact with 4, 6, 8) Mail In person (individual and group)
6. Certification (frequency)	Controlled variation (interact with 4, 5, 8) Monthly Annually
Certification (documentation)	Controlled variation (interact with 4, 5, 8) Light (or none) Heavy
7. Distribution of primary benefits	No variation
8. Distribution of adjunct benefits	Controlled variation (interact with 4, 5, 6) None Reactive Assertive
9. Standards and conditions associated with benefits	Controlled variation (independent) Self-inspection Conditional self-inspection Agency inspection
10. Hearings and adjudication of appeals	Try out and modify during experiment
11. Management and quality control	Try out and modify during experiment
12. Auditing	No variation
13. Termination	Vary during course of experiment
14. Interaction with other programs	Try out and modify during experiment
15. Interaction with the general community	Try out and modify during experiment
16. Interaction with the affected community	Try out and modify during experiment
17. Ongoing program assessment	Design specified at end of experiment

a. Regardless of research treatment, all functions would be carefully measured and reported in detail.

Functions to Be "Tried Out"

Two of the functions, administrative organization and agency start-up, are performed only once, at the beginning of an allowance program. These functions are therefore difficult to handle in alternate ways in an experiment. Instead, a "best try" should be made to carry out these functions, and reports should detail how the procedures succeeded or failed.

Based on the trial experience, improvements and optimal methods should be suggested. Some results for these functions will come from the analysis of others; for example, the degree of autonomy that can be allowed in program regulations will depend on the need for particular methods for performing individual activities. How systematic agency start-up should be will hinge on similar factors, but because of the nature of the program, agencies must be closely controlled in the experiment.

The functions involving interactions with other programs, the affected community, and the general community are also issues to be tried out because they involve establishing communications channels and conducting public relations campaigns. These are matters of trial and error in that the agency acts and then adjusts to the problems. Again, it is important that reports discuss completely what did and did not work, so that potential pitfalls are marked to guide future administrators.

Four other functions do not appear to offer practical alternatives. Although distribution of primary benefits could involve manual benefit calculation or participants having to pick up their checks in person, mailing of computer-calculated and printed checks is probably the best method. One question might be how many beneficiaries could be handled by one payment center, but no experiment would be scaled large enough to evaluate this issue. Testing the appeals function requires setting up a system and ironing out the problems; a key here is independence, but no obvious variation is apparent. The functions of management and quality control and auditing are similar: they should be performed as rigorously as possible and their effects analyzed to determine areas most in need of controls. Record keeping must be thorough, and the experiment again involves only adjusting methods to correct problem areas.

None of the nine functions discussed so far requires more than trial, adjustment, and reporting of findings.

Two functions do lend themselves to variation, but the inputs are hard to measure and the effects may not be clear. Outreach can be conducted through a variety of media and with different degrees of intensity, but the latter is difficult to quantify meaningfully and the impact of various methods must be systematically evaluated. The use of as many alternative techniques as possible and careful observation of results are probably the best methods available, but more could probably be learned about outreach from brief consultation with any Madison Avenue advertising firm than from such an experiment. The termination function is similar. Dropping households from the program when they are no longer eligible may or may not be accompanied by counseling, but assessing the impact of counseling is subjective. Do people cope better if they are counseled? How can you tell? Even subjective assessment is valuable, however, because the program should be concerned with improving people's housing both while they are enrolled and in the future.

Finally, active program assessment cannot be evaluated within an experimental context. Rather, the experiment itself is an assessment and should yield conclusions about meaningful measures of program success. The experiment should provide the design for a procedure that could be used to monitor a permanent program. Relevant variables should be identified and reporting forms should be developed to collect data on a continuing basis. Standards should be constructed against which performance could be gauged. For this function the experiment is developmental in nature.

Functions to Be Systematically Varied

The remaining five functions are interesting from an experimental point of view in that they present clear-cut alternatives that would be expected to have substantial impacts on program costs or effectiveness. Although not all conceivable options for each function will be considered, the alternatives selected seem to be the best for use in a full-scale program.

1. *Eligibility determination and enrollment.* These two functions can be handled either by mail with minimum personal contact or in person at agency offices. The first approach is cheaper and will result in less staff involvement, but the attention given to applicants in agency offices increases participation rates and does more to improve housing conditions.

2. *Certification: frequency.* Although any number of certifications is possible, we propose that only two be tried—monthly and annually. The chief eligibility requirement for certification is income, but household size should be verified at each certification as well. Other experiments have shown that monthly certification is more accurate and effective but may cost more.

3. *Certification: documentation.* Certification can require that participants provide documentation of all or nearly all pertinent information supplied or that only a few items be documented. The first requirement

would cost more and might reduce program participation but should be more effective in ensuring accuracy of information and in reducing fraud.

4. *Adjunct benefits.* There are three options for providing adjunct benefits, which include counseling, legal services, housing education, and assistance in locating housing. First, no benefits may be provided, leaving the participant alone to deal with problems beyond the cash allowance. Second, the agency could provide services only when requested by participants. Finally, the agency could be assertive, requiring attendance at training seminars or offering to help enrollees with their housing problems. Clearly, these approaches would result in different costs; a more interesting issue is how they would affect participants' abilities to cope with the housing market and satisfy program requirements.

5. *Standards and conditions.* The most important condition to be satisfied before the allowance can be paid is that the participant live in standard quality housing. This can be verified in three ways: self-inspection, agency inspection, or conditional self-inspection. In the first option, the individual surveys his or her own dwelling and completes an evaluation form that is reviewed by agency staff. The second option requires that all inspections be performed by agency staff trained for the task. The conditional participant inspection combines the first two options. As in the first option, the individual would complete an evaluation form that would be reviewed at the agency. If the unit clearly passed or failed, that process would constitute the full inspection; if the unit were marginal (which should be construed broadly), the agency would perform an on-site inspection. Self-inspections are cheaper, agency inspections are more accurate, and conditional self-inspections provide a compromise in cost and accuracy.

The options outlined for the five functions discussed above could be combined into seventy-two distinct treatments. However, much of the variation obtained in a completely interactive network is uninteresting, and the number of treatments can be reduced substantially. It is unlikely that the method used to enforce housing standards would affect any of the other functions. However, the first four functions could well exhibit interactive effects, and it is difficult to dismiss a priori any combination of procedures. This means that each of the twenty-four treatments shown in table 5 should be tested, ranging from the arm's length approach of the first to the highly involved methods of the last. In the supply experiment, this requires assigning the applicants to twenty-four distinct groups and establishing an administrative structure for dealing with the inherent com-

Table 5. Potential Experimental Treatments[a]

Treatment	Eligibility/ enrollment	Certification (frequency)	Certification (documentation)	Adjunct benefits
1	By mail	Annual	Light	None
2	By mail	Annual	Light	Reactive
3	By mail	Annual	Light	Assertive
4	By mail	Annual	Heavy	None
5	By mail	Annual	Heavy	Reactive
6	By mail	Annual	Heavy	Assertive
7	By mail	Monthly	Light	None
8	By mail	Monthly	Light	Reactive
9	By mail	Monthly	Light	Assertive
10	By mail	Monthly	Heavy	None
11	By mail	Monthly	Heavy	Reactive
12	By mail	Monthly	Heavy	Assertive
13	In person	Annual	Light	None
14	In person	Annual	Light	Reactive
15	In person	Annual	Light	Assertive
16	In person	Annual	Heavy	None
17	In person	Annual	Heavy	Reactive
18	In person	Annual	Heavy	Assertive
19	In person	Monthly	Light	None
20	In person	Monthly	Light	Reactive
21	In person	Monthly	Light	Assertive
22	In person	Monthly	Heavy	None
23	In person	Monthly	Heavy	Reactive
24	In person	Monthly	Heavy	Assertive

a. The three ways of checking standards and conditions—self-inspection, conditional self-inspection, and agency inspection—are to be varied independently.

plexities. Although this would not be simple, such designs have been used in other social experiments and do not present insurmountable difficulties.[53]

Sample Sizes and Costs

Of great interest is how well the experiment could discriminate the effects of different treatments. From a statistical point of view, the significance of a given difference between responses to two methods depends on both the sample size and the variance of the responses being measured.

53. See Kershaw and Fair, *New Jersey Income-Maintenance Experiment*, vol. 1.

Green Bay, the smaller of the supply experiment sites, would yield about 125 participants for each of the twenty-four treatments. Unfortunately, however, we cannot estimate in advance the variance of any of the possible performance measures that might be used to evaluate an allowance program. Preliminary analysis using rough guesses about sample variance indicates that the Green Bay sample size would be large enough to allow observations of differences on the order of 10 percent, but that a more complete assessment should be made before an experiment is conducted. If sample size turned out to be a potential problem, somewhat larger sites could be used with consequent increases in program costs, or, alternatively, some treatment methods might be discarded and fewer cases tested.

We believe that the costs of this proposed experiment would be relatively modest, since it could be grafted onto the existing supply experiment. Additional administrative staff and procedures would have to be added to the supply experiment to permit within-program variation, and additional resources would have to be provided for new research. Based on similar activities in other experiments, an estimate of the cost of adding this administrative experiment to the supply experiment would range from $3 million to $5 million. The administrative agency experiment cost $20 million, although half of this was for payments to beneficiaries and thus offset other government transfer costs. Thus, $10 million was spent to obtain a limited amount of administrative information. Our calculations show that this expenditure could have been cut roughly in half had the supply experiment been used as the context for the administrative test; in addition, we would have been able to isolate many of the most important administrative considerations, which the design constraints in the administrative agency experiment prevent us from doing.

Limitations of the Design

There are limitations to the experimental design proposed above. First, it may be argued that it would be impossible to provide twenty-four different combinations of administrative procedures simply because of the management difficulties involved. However, this could be managed by having agency staff members who specialize in particular techniques supervised by a coordinator who would route applicants to the appropriate staff person. A larger problem might be the impact on measured costs of so many administrative procedures. If the coordination problem can be overcome, the issue becomes whether results of a social experiment are applicable to the real world or whether the experiment itself cannot help but bias the results.

The final concern involves whether the assessment of administrative procedures would affect the supply experiment results on housing market adjustment to an allowance program. The supply experiment was designed primarily to measure the supply effects of allowance-induced demand changes. To the extent that our proposed use of multiple procedures would result in a different demand response than occurred in the supply experiment, the measured supply changes would also be different. However, it is unclear which would provide a more accurate picture of what would happen in a nonexperimental program. What was desired was a demand increase comparable to that which a real allowance program would induce; this would occur only if the experiment were an exact copy of the real program. While it is possible that multiple treatments would result in a smaller demand change than occurred in the supply experiment, it would seem equally likely that the change would be greater, and that neither approach would yield better results a priori. In our opinion, combining the administrative agency experiment and the supply experiment would probably not have biased the supply findings.

Summary of the Design

In our judgment, the administrative agency experiment should have been part of the supply experiment, run in two sites with unlimited enrollment over a ten-year period with perhaps one or two additional sites administered by existing agencies. Five functions should have been varied systematically through the use of different techniques, with twenty-four distinct treatment groups for eligibility screening, enrollment, certification, and adjunct benefit functions, overlaid with different methods of handling housing inspections. Controlled variation for these five functions should allow full and statistically significant analysis of costs and effectiveness. Alternative techniques of performing the outreach and termination functions also should be tried, but less precise conclusions should be expected. The remaining functions should be considered as "try-out" cases in which a single procedure is used and adjusted and evaluations are primarily descriptions of problems, solutions, and suggested techniques for use in a full-scale program. Methods of evaluating the performance of a housing allowance program should evolve that would provide for a continuing assessment of whether or not goals are being met.

Comments by David O. Porter[54]

The housing allowance program was conceived in the hope of alleviating some of the frustration citizens feel in the face of a growing yet seemingly unresponsive public sector. The "mixed economy" approach to the housing problems of low-income households was aimed at being more responsive and flexible, offering participants more choice, and reducing more administrative overhead and red tape than was possible under direct public provision of housing.

But even a mixed-economy housing allowance program requires administering. Eligible households must be found and certified; some recipients need help in finding and renting an appropriate unit; housing must be inspected to ensure that it meets program standards; and allowance payments must be made.

The prevailing theories of administration in the public sector focus on hierarchy and the management of single organizations. The analysis of the administrative agency experiment was grounded in this type of administrative theory. However, single organizations do not implement mixed-economy programs such as housing allowances; tasks are carried out by professionals who adjust to the needs of individuals in specific local settings. Strategies for investigating administration in such conditions must be able to cope with multiorganizational and discretionary implementation processes. These comments suggest concepts that can better cope with these conditions than the prevailing theories of social experimentation and public administration.

In the first section of these comments I discuss the analyses of administration completed or proposed in the administrative agency experiment. I question the methodological assumptions of Kershaw and Williams, who, along with the research contractors (Abt Associates and the Urban Institute), seem to adopt a fairly restricted methodology for experimentation from the natural sciences. In the second section, I propose an alternative approach. The discussion draws from the administrative literature in product (or responsibility) center and matrix management, adapting it

54. I am indebted to James A. Schwab, Jr., of the School of Social Work and the School of Business, University of Texas, for assistance with statistical analysis and for a thorough discussion of the basic arguments in these comments. Britton F. Hall, a graduate assistant, contributed substantially to the formulations and writing. Jesse Burkhead of Syracuse University read early drafts of these comments and helped clarify and reformulate. Responsibility for any errors in fact, interpretation, or conceptualization remains with the author.

to the requirements of programs implemented through a mixed-economy approach. Management through responsibility centers emerged to cope with situations requiring local discretion and decentralization to local divisions.[55] Matrix management was designed to administer programs through two or more legitimate sources of authority.[56] I believe an administrative framework derived from this literature is more appropriate for a housing allowance program than the framework implicit in the administrative agency experiment evaluation.

Closed versus Open Organization Research

Kershaw and Williams claim that the experimental design of the administrative agency experiment was fundamentally flawed. A "naturalistic" approach allowed the eight agencies to adopt administrative practices as they each saw fit. Kershaw and Williams argue there should have been controlled variations in the performance of seventeen program functions in the smaller and more controlled housing assistance supply experiment. I strongly disagree with this conclusion. Too little would be learned about how a program is adapted to local environments in a highly controlled two-site experiment. Research in administration and organization theory has shown beyond dispute that the implementation of a human service program is greatly affected by its environment.

Debate on how to study administration and organizations stretches back at least seventy-five years. Early studies by Frederick W. Taylor[57] and the early experiments at the Hawthorne plant of Western Electric[58] used methodologies similar to the closed system methodologies suggested by Kershaw and Williams and carried out in the experiment evaluation by Abt Associates.[59]

55. Alfred D. Chandler, Jr., *Strategy and Structure: Chapters in the History of the Industrial Enterprise* (MIT Press, 1969); Alfred D. Chandler, Jr., *The Visible Hand: The Managerial Revolution in American Business* (Harvard University Press, 1977); Oliver E. Williamson, *Corporate Control and Business Behavior: An Inquiry into the Effects of Organization Form on Enterprise Behavior* (Prentice-Hall, 1970).

56. Stanley M. Davis and Paul R. Lawrence, "Problems of Matrix Organizations," *Harvard Business Review,* vol. 56 (May–June 1978), pp. 131–42; Jay R. Galbraith, "Matrix Organization Designs: How to Combine Functional and Project Forms," *Business Horizons,* vol. 14 (February 1971), pp. 29–40.

57. Frederick Winslow Taylor, *The Principles of Scientific Management* (Harper and Brothers, 1916).

58. Fritz Jules Roethlisberger and William John Dickson, *Management and the Worker* (Harvard University Press, 1939).

59. For an excellent summary of Taylor and the Hawthorne experiments, see Bertram M. Gross, *The Managing of Organizations: The Administrative Struggle,* vol. 1 (Free Press, 1964), pp. 121–28, 160–71.

One of the important findings of the later Hawthorne experiments was the impact of informal and nonorganizational factors on employee performance. Informal practices among workers at specific sites had to be understood and taken into account, or manipulated, along with the formal organizational rules and incentives. A general conclusion from this and later research is that evaluations of organizations and their performance cannot ignore informal relations and organization environments.[60]

Strategies have been developed to study both the open and closed aspects of organizations.[61] A compromise of sorts between closed and open system strategies is emerging in contingency theory. Contingency theorists suggest there are situations where one or the other approach is more appropriate.[62] Closed system strategies require situations where goals are clear, technologies are known, and problems are conceptualized and acted upon in clear-cut segments. In such cases, alternative ways of providing the service can be evaluated according to efficiency criteria, and the best method can then be selected. Because the goals of a housing allowance program are relatively ambiguous, and its technologies are uncertain, I believe there is a need for a localized, experimental approach to implementation. An open systems approach is more appropriate.[63]

One alternative to a deterministic methodology for experimentation in

60. See Howard Aldrich, "Resource Dependence and Interorganizational Relations: Local Employment Service Office and Social Services Sector Organizations," *Administration and Society,* vol. 7 (February 1976), pp. 419–54; J. Kenneth Benson, "The Interorganizational Network as a Political Economy," *Administrative Science Quarterly,* vol. 20 (June 1975), pp. 229–49; Peter M. Blau and Marshall W. Meyer, *Bureaucracy in Modern Society* (Random House, 1956); Richard Hammond Hall, *Organizations: Structure and Process* (Prentice-Hall, 1972); Sol Levine and Paul E. White, "Exchange as a Conceptual Framework for the Study of Interorganizational Relationships," *Administrative Science Quarterly,* vol. 5 (March 1961), pp. 583–601; James D. Thompson, *Organizations in Action: Social Science Bases of Administrative Theory* (McGraw-Hill, 1967).

61. Thompson, *Organizations in Action.*

62. Fred Luthans, *Introduction to Management: A Contingency Approach* (McGraw-Hill, 1976).

63. See especially Thompson, *Organizations in Action,* pp. 132–38. See also Martin Landau and Russell Stout, Jr., "To Manage Is Not to Control: Or the Folly of Type II Errors," *Public Administration Review,* vol. 39 (March-April 1979), pp. 148–56; Richard B. McKenzie, "The Non-Rational Domain and the Limits of Economic Analysis," *Southern Economic Journal,* vol. 46 (July 1979), pp. 145–57; Michael J. Piore, "Qualitative Research Techniques in Economics," *Administrative Science Quarterly,* vol. 24 (December 1979), pp. 560–69; and Arthur L. Stinchcombe, "Bureaucratic and Craft Administration of Production: A Comparative Study," *Administrative Science Quarterly,* vol. 4 (1959–60), pp. 168–87.

public policy is found in the strategy for reform advocated by the institutional economist John R. Commons.[64] Commons abhorred rationalistic reforms as utopian and unworkable. Instead of contriving artificial experimental situations, Commons looked for the best existing practice of a going concern. He selected these best practices through empirical investigation. Such practices could be put in place elsewhere through persuasion and "collective action." These practices would not be the "best" in any absolute sense, but "reasonable" in the sense that a court uses that term. He felt that reasonable, active people could understand such reform and implement it.

The original design for the administrative agency experiment fit much of Commons's prescription for research on reform. Former HUD Secretary George Romney, a very practical man, insisted that the administrative agency experiment be part of the experiment. Eight real-life agencies were enlisted to implement the program according to their best practices. Within guidelines set by HUD, these agencies were given their head to deal with the vagaries of the program, the technologies of administration, and their local environments.

Viewed from the perspective of Commons's guidelines, the problem with the administrative agency experiment was more with the evaluation of these agencies than with the original design of the experiment. The evaluation followed rationalistic canons and failed to keep the data in their environmental context. The contractors repeatedly expressed regret that there were not more "controlled variations." The reports of the on-site observers, who spent up to eighteen months living at the eight sites and recording what was happening, were never systematically worked into the analysis. Their observations appeared in the reports primarily as descriptive anecdotes; descriptive reports on each site were not published.

REFORMS IN POLICY EXPERIMENTATION. For future administrative experiments, I suggest an evaluation/demonstration/experiment

64. John R. Commons, *Institutional Economics: Its Place in Political Economy* (University of Wisconsin Press, 1961). For a succinct review of Commons's approach to social and administrative reform, see William M. Dugger, "The Reform Method of John R. Commons," *Journal of Economic Issues,* vol. 13 (June 1979), pp. 369–81. A more fully developed theoretical rationalizaton of a similar approach may be found in Severyn Ten Haut Bruyn, *The Human Perspective in Sociology: The Methodology of Participant Observation* (Prentice-Hall, 1966). See also Francis D. Wormuth, "Matched-Dependent Behavioralism: The Cargo Cult in Political Science," *Western Political Quarterly,* vol. 20 (December 1967), pp. 809–40, for a searing yet compelling discussion of the pitfalls of thoughtlessly using quantitative methods in the social sciences.

sequence following the approach of Commons. As described below, evaluation would be carried out as a continuing process at the local, regional, and national levels of a program implementation structure.[65] Demonstrations and studies of "best practices" would be undertaken by giving supplemental funds to selected agencies, drawing from the 1 to 2 percent of funds commonly set aside for evaluation in many appropriations. Workable results of these demonstrations could then be introduced into the practices of other agencies. Experiments would probably be best designed and monitored from the national level, still drawing from the 1 to 2 percent set-aside funds. Existing agencies would be selected to experiment with essentially new practices to improve program performance. These experiments could then be extended to demonstrations and finally to generalized practice.

For three reasons, an evaluation/demonstration/experiment sequence seems preferable to a single experiment with controlled variations. First, a controlled experiment is appropriate only where the problems can be dealt with through single national standards or rules, where alternatives are relatively clear and uncontested, and where technologies are understood.[66]

Second, policy time, research time, and phenomena time are all different,[67] and the evaluation/demonstration/experiment approach allows more overlap than does the "pure" experiment. The policy time of a program is the period in which the political climate is conducive to adopting it; research time is the period needed to set up a demonstration or experiment and report results; and phenomena time is the period in which the social and economic impacts of the planned changes work themselves through.

Third, the number of functions and variables that can reasonably be varied is too large for a single experiment to cope with effectively.[68]

65. "Implementation structure" refers to the clusters of public and private organizations that implement programs. This concept is developed later in the paper. See Benny Hjern and David O. Porter, "Implementation Structures: A New Unit of Administrative Analysis," *Organizational Studies* (forthcoming), for a definition of implementation structures and a rationalization of their use as units for administrative analysis.

66. See the paper by Harold W. Watts in this volume.

67. I am indebted to Michael Springer of the Urban Institute and the Department of the Treasury for this idea.

68. See Bruce L. Gates, "576,000 Ways to Integrate Human Services," paper presented at a conference of the American Society for Public Administration, April

Whether or not there are exactly seventeen administrative functions, as identified by Kershaw and Williams, is debatable. The identification of administrative functions has a long history, beginning with Henri Fayol, passing through Gulick's famous POSDCORB (planning, organizing, staffing, directing, coordinating, reporting, budgeting), to the more generic version by Gowler and Legge.[69] Even if we remain with just twenty-four controlled variations among selected functions as suggested by Kershaw and Williams, I doubt that the controlled experiment they suggested would demonstrate much because the situation would be so contrived that practicing administrators would not take the results seriously.

INTERACTIVE EFFECTS AMONG FUNCTIONS AND SITES MISSED. Serious oversights in interpreting the findings of the administrative agency experiment occurred because of the methodologies used. The analyses by the contractors focused on administrative functions, thereby underanalyzing many of the interactions among functions and the impact of site-related factors.

As shown in table 6, there were substantial variations in expenditures on each function and among the eight sites. It seems to me it was unwise, given the wide ranges and large standard deviations in expenditures for many of the variables, to have assumed (as was apparently done) that site effects were random. I suggest that a methodological error was made. Instead of an analysis of variations in expenditures by function (that is, down the columns on table 6), more resources should have been devoted to analyzing interactions among functions and site-related factors (that is, analyzing the rows on table 6). Local factors such as differences in political environments, eligible populations, and supply and quality of the housing stock were considered. But because each function was analyzed

---

1978, p. 1. Gates considers the problem of determining how many possible ways there are to implement a program. He notes, "In a very *small* community, four levels of government, 10 service providing agencies, 12 funding sources, 10 distinct client groups, 20 distinct service programs, and 6 different methods for achieving interorganizational linkages represent 576,000 different possible relationships among different organizational entities." (Emphasis in original.)

69. Henri Fayol, *General and Industrial Management* (London: Pitman, 1916); Luther Gulick, "Notes on the Theory of Organization, with Special Reference to the Government of the United States," in Luther Gulick and L. Urwick, eds., *Papers on the Science of Administration* (Columbia University, Institute of Public Administration, 1937; August M. Kelley, 1969); D. Gowler and K. Legge, "The Evaluation of Planned Organizational Change: The Necessary Art of the Possible," *Journal of Enterprise Management*, vol. 1 (1978), pp. 201–13.

Table 6. Administrative Costs in Eight Administrative Agency Experiment Sites
1976 dollars

Site	Direct intake costs per recipient[a]						Total intake costs per new recipient[d]
	Outreach	Screen-ing	Certifi-cation	Enroll-ment[c]	Services	Inspec-tion	
Bismarck, North Dakota	8 (13)	8 (13)	5 (8)	12 (20)	24 (40)	3 (5)	179
Durham, North Carolina	3 (3)	25 (23)	10 (9)	13 (12)	40 (36)	19 (17)	258
Jacksonville, Florida	15 (7)	48 (22)	31 (14)	40 (18)	59 (26)	30 (13)	534
Peoria, Illinois	15 (22)	12 (17)	9 (13)	8 (12)	10 (14)	15 (22)	178
Salem, Oregon	15 (20)	14 (18)	12 (16)	16 (21)	17 (22)	2 (3)	186
San Bernardino, California	9 (8)	21 (19)	6 (6)	26 (24)	31 (29)	15 (14)	271
Springfield, Massachusetts	28 (22)	8 (6)	6 (5)	13 (10)	64 (50)	8 (6)	248
Tulsa, Oklahoma	66 (35)	12 (6)	6 (3)	31 (16)	45 (24)	30 (16)	300
Experiment median	15 (15)	13 (13)	8 (8)	14 (14)	36 (36)	15 (15)	253

Sources: Charles M. Maloy and others, *Administrative Costs in a Housing Allowance Program: Two-Year Cost in the Administrative Agency Experiment* (Abt, February 1977), pp. 32–33, 93; HUD, *Experimental Housing Allowance Program: A 1979 Report of Findings* (GPO, 1979), p. 66.
* Less than 50 cents.
a. The numbers in parentheses are percents of total direct intake costs.
b. The numbers in parentheses are percents of total direct maintenance costs.

separately, important interactive effects among functions and among local environmental factors were overlooked.[70]

70. A statistical analysis of the effects of site-related factors and the interactions among functions was attempted, using data from the administrative agency experiment reports. The expenditure data available in the reports were not in a form that would permit a two-way analysis of variance. Such an analysis might be feasible when the raw data from each site become available.

Direct maintenance costs per recipient[b]				Total maintenance costs per recipient year[d]	Total administrative costs amortized per recipient year[e]
Payment operations	Recertifi-cation	Reinspection	Services		
12 (12)	39 (39)	5 (5)	45 (45)	235	271
14 (16)	17 (19)	7 (8)	51 (57)	231	283
30 (25)	18 (15)	7 (6)	63 (53)	322	429
12 (24)	9 (18)	15 (30)	15 (30)	171	207
18 (41)	13 (30)	* (0)	13 (30)	129	165
12 (29)	15 (37)	3 (7)	11 (27)	178	232
21 (16)	17 (13)	10 (8)	85 (64)	267	317
10 (19)	10 (19)	10 (19)	24 (44)	144	204
13 (18)	16 (23)	7 (10)	34 (49)	205	252

c. Bismarck had a target enrollment of 400, and Durham 500; all other sites had target enrollments of 900. The actual numbers of recipients by site were as follows: Bismarck, 430; Durham, 516; Jacksonville, 339; Peoria, 935; alem, 948; San Bernardino, 822; Springfield, 851; Tulsa, 915.
d. Includes indirect costs.
e. Based on five years of participation per recipient household.

If it could be verified that local staff adjusted the practice of some functions to cope with local circumstances, it would raise a serious administrative question: how can a program be controlled from the national level when substantial local discretion is necessary for effective implementation? Overall rules for the performance of particular functions seem inappropriate under such circumstances. Rather than monitoring administrative processes, as is typical in the public sector, program administrators should then focus on indicators of program results.

Need for an Alternative Administrative Framework

The evaluation of the administrative agency experiment by Abt Associates implicitly assumed an operating housing allowance program would be implemented by state and local jurisdictions, with HUD specifying objectives, providing funds, and writing regulations on how tasks were to be performed. The evaluation by Abt Associates focused on how much a universal program would cost, based on the average costs per recipient over the eight sites and on an analysis of ten functions.

Findings from the experiment suggest that the technical and institutional constraints under which a housing program is implemented require an administrative framework that gives more recognition to the need for local discretion than the framework implicitly assumed by the research contractors. Differences from site to site in how the program is implemented are too great for all the information to be gathered and analyzed by central managers. The technologies used by housing administrators and staff are too uncertain to permit general specification of how functions should be performed.

In this section, I propose an administrative framework that takes into account the interactive adjustments occurring among functions and local environmental factors and the need for state and federal monitoring of local performance.[71]

To develop an approach to examining administrative functions in a housing allowance program, I begin with brief analyses of the agencies that implemented the administrative agency experiment, administrative imperatives inherent within the program, and organizational characteristics that affect program administration.

THE AGENCIES AND IMPERATIVES IN AN ALLOWANCE PROGRAM. The agencies chosen by HUD to implement the administrative agency experiment included two housing authorities located within city governments, two state agencies responsible for housing programs, one welfare

---

71. An early attempt to formulate such an administrative framework was made in David O. Porter, George H. McGeary, and William J. Page, Jr., *Three Options for Administering a Direct Cash Assistance Program in Housing* (Cambridge, Mass.: Abt Associates, 1975) and David O. Porter, "Federalism, Revenue Sharing, and Local Government," in Charles O. Jones and Robert D. Thomas, eds., *Public Policy Making in a Federal System* (Beverly Hills: Sage Publications, 1976), pp. 81–101.

agency located within a county government, a second welfare agency that was part of a state government, a county board of supervisors, and a housing agency within a metropolitan government. At every site the housing allowance program was only one of several programs being implemented by the organization designated to administer the experiment. A distinguishing general feature of organizations, in fact, is that they implement *parts of a number of programs*; they seldom implement an entire program. Whole programs are implemented by *parts of a number of public and private organizations*. In other research, my colleagues and I found it necessary to use the clusters of organizations that implement programs as our primary unit of analysis. We labeled this new unit of analysis an "implementation structure" to distinguish it from a single organization.[72]

For purposes of this analysis, the objective of the program will be stated as "placing eligible households in standard rental units." The housing agency can find eligible households through cooperation with a number of social service agencies or by generating its own list of applicants. In the administrative agency experiment, all the agencies augmented their own outreach efforts with referrals or direct assistance from other social service agencies.

A certification process was used to determine eligibility. At some sites of the experiment, employers, social service agencies, financial institutions, and sometimes the Internal Revenue Service verified income statements submitted by applicants. Other sites relied entirely on self-declarations by applicants, which removed the need for outside verification unless sample cases were checked for accuracy.

The process of enrollment was usually handled solely by the local agency. Following enrollment, if their current housing units failed to meet the required standards, participants searched for a standard rental unit. In doing this, they sometimes used counseling services to help them learn about the housing market or how to negotiate with a landlord. Once they obtained a unit, it was inspected to determine whether it met safety and structural standards. Some experiment sites opted for self-inspections (that is, by individual participants), but relatively large numbers of rental units at these sites failed to pass subsequent inspections conducted by inspectors from Abt Associates. Some experiment agencies hired their own inspectors. In at least one case, city-employed inspectors conducted the inspections.

72. See Hjern and Porter, "Implementation Structures," and David O. Porter and David C. Warner, "Organizations and Implementation Structures," Discussion Paper IIM/dp 79 (Berlin: International Institute of Management, 1979).

During the maintenance phase of the experiment, most of the administrative functions—payment operations, recertification, and reinspection—were performed by the agencies. There were continuing contacts with some landlords concerning problems related to maintenance or rent payment.

CONSTRAINTS ON AN ADMINISTRATIVE FRAMEWORK. From the above description of a housing allowance program, several constraints may be inferred which must be considered when choosing an administrative model.

First, a housing allowance program is not implemented by a single organization. Like most programs, it is carried out through an implementation structure. Formal hierarchical lines do not connect all the implementing organizations. Rather, agreements to participate are based on negotiations and consent.

Within each of these organizations, certain actors define their functions as following an *organizational rationale*—that is, they try to mold the resources and objectives of several programs to help the organization survive. Other members in the same organizations identify more strongly with particular programs than with their "host" organization—that is, they follow a *program rationale*. They attempt to mold the resources and objectives of their own and other organizations to satisfy the needs of a particular program. In the administrative agency experiment, such program advocates tried to get the housing authorities, cities, counties, social service agencies, and landlords to agree that the housing allowance program fitted into their respective organization rationales and to commit resources to that program.

The administrative agency experiment agencies assumed the role of advocate, coordinator, and supplier of certain key resources within the overall implementation structure. In this behavior, these agencies followed a general pattern within implementation structures. Organizations develop divisions of labor as a program is implemented. Some organizations perform coordinating functions, and others specialize in planning; some provide direct services, and others supply particular resources. These divisions of labor are seldom effectively assigned by higher authorities. They emerge as various organizations recognize the willingness and competence of certain actors to perform specific functions.

The second constraint is that patterns of relations within implementation structures vary from one locality to another. The personalities and capabilities of the potential actors in each locality are different. Central managers, as a result, often run into difficulties when they attempt to mandate interactions between the same institutions all over the country. Local administrators consider large amounts of qualitative and quantitative local information as they negotiate agreements to participate in a program. In a phrase, there is a "local knowledge" requirement.

Third, the core service in a housing allowance program must be performed at the local level. Individual households contract with individual landlords in a specific location. There is no way to centralize this process. There is, therefore, a "local presence" requirement.

Fourth, as described above, the core services of the housing allowance program are coproduced by the agencies, clients, and landlords.[73]

A fifth constraint is embedded in the composition of the staffs of housing agencies. Administrative and program specialists comprise a significant part of housing agency staffs at the local, state, and federal levels. These "professions" draw from imperfect technologies (that is, the cause and effect relationships between inputs and outputs are not well understood), deal with relatively complicated and unique situations, and depend on discretion and experience for effective practice. In programs and organizations where the core technologies are dominated by skilled craftsmen and professionals, administrative goals can sometimes be specified by central level managers. But attempts by central managers to direct the actual performance of specific tasks or functions are unrealistic.[74]

In light of the five constraints just outlined, state and federal agencies should be defined as program monitors rather than as centralized authorities making detailed decisions about program operations. By monitoring performance according to a few key indicators, the states and the federal government could set rough boundaries within which the local implementation structures should adjust their activities to the exigencies of local information and environments. The analytic staffs at the state and federal levels would have the primary responsibility for formulating these indicators, collecting the data, and providing initial analyses.

For a housing allowance program, the information upon which these indicators would be based consists of three components: profiles of the eligible population, housing surveys, and spot checks of certification and

73. For a discussion of coproduction, see Roger B. Parks, "Assessing the Influence of Organization on Performance: A Study of Police Services in Residential Neighborhoods," Report T-75 (Bloomington: Indiana University, Workshop in Political Theory and Policy Analysis, June 27, 1979).
74. Stinchcombe, "Bureaucratic and Craft Administration."

inspection. This information would be separately aggregated into two streams—one to evaluate the performance of the local implementation structures and one to evaluate the performance and impact of the program as a whole.[75]

MANAGEMENT INFORMATION FOR HOUSING ALLOWANCES. Each of the three main components of the information system was used by Abt Associates and HUD in the administrative agency experiment. Ironically, these efforts seem to have been dismissed as artifacts of the experiment and were not integrated into the administrative analyses. In the experiment, the sites were instructed to implement allowance programs to the best of their ability, adjusting to circumstances in their environments. Abt Associates and HUD monitored the activities through selected indicators and sometimes offered suggestions based on these indicators to improve local performance. Neither Abt Associates nor HUD wanted to control the local agencies or overly influence local operations. The role of Abt Associates and HUD was, rather, to set perimeters within which the experiment would be implemented.

The "bottom line" of a housing allowance program is how many eligible households are placed in standard rental units. All three components in the information system proposed in these comments center on obtaining data on this basic indicator and evaluating their administrative and programmatic meanings. To this basic indicator, the experiment added criteria on the characteristics of persons participating and the kinds of rental units they obtained.

To ensure that a representative cross section of the eligible population participated in the experiment, a profile of the eligible population at each site was compiled. Census data, aid to families with dependent children data, and some heroic estimates by agencies were used to compile these profiles. The agencies were substantially off course in their first estimates of the composition of the eligible population, but these estimates were improved later by Abt Associates.[76]

The profiles gave the total number of eligible households at each site; these totals were subdivided into several demographic categories.[77] Figure

75. Robert N. Anthony and Regina E. Herzlinger, *Management Control in Nonprofit Organizations* (Homewood, Ill.: Richard D. Irwin, 1975), pp. 80–84.

76. Jean MacMillan and William L. Hamilton, *Outreach: Generating Applications in the Administrative Agency Experiment* (Abt, February 1977), app. B.

77. MacMillan and Hamilton, *Outreach*, p. A-8; and Abt Associates, *Third Annual Report of the Administrative Agency Experiment Evaluation: October 1974–October 1975* (Abt, August 1976), p. 12.

1 shows an aggregated comparison, by demographic category, between the eligible applicants and the eligible population. During the course of the experiment, such comparisons were done on a site-by-site basis. HUD and Abt Associates were thus able to evaluate whether each site was reaching a cross section of the eligible population and to suggest site-specific adjustments in outreach practices or emphasis.

Administrative agency experiment reports available to me showed no comparisons with the eligible applicants. Site-by-site comparisons were not included in the final reports. Comparisons at each site between the eligible population and participating households at critical points in the process of implementation are an important element in the general administrative framework suggested in these comments.[78] I suggest comparisons at the outreach, certification, enrollment, and recipient stages because of the likelihood that parts of the eligible population may be missed or excluded at these points.

Such comparisons would allow managers at all program levels to evaluate the effectiveness of the program. Managers at the state and federal levels could focus attention on performance, not process. They could pinpoint areas where there should be improvements or changes, without becoming involved in decisions on how local adjustments should be made. Local administrators would have discretion on how to gear such functions as outreach, counseling, and inspection to local conditions while being accountable for the results of their choices.

The reports in the experiment provide many examples of how actors at the various sites solved problems with subgroups in their populations or problems with certain functions. But the analyses of functions in the experiment should be used as *the basis for advice* to local program structures trying to cope with their environments, *not as the basis for detailed regulations* from HUD on how each function should be carried out by all local housing programs in the United States.

The second element in the information system consists of surveys of the condition and costs of housing. These surveys should include information on the availability of rental units and their characteristics. They may reveal, for instance, shortages of rental units suitable for large families. Poor performance in placing large families may show up consistently in re-

78. An example of the data form to be used may be found in David O. Porter, "Accounting for Discretion in Social Experimentation and Program Administration: Some Proposed Alternative Conceptualizations" (Austin, Texas: Lyndon B. Johnson School of Public Affairs, University of Texas, Working Paper Series 15, 1980).

Figure 1. Comparison of the Demographic Characteristics of the Eligible Population and Eligible Applicants[a]

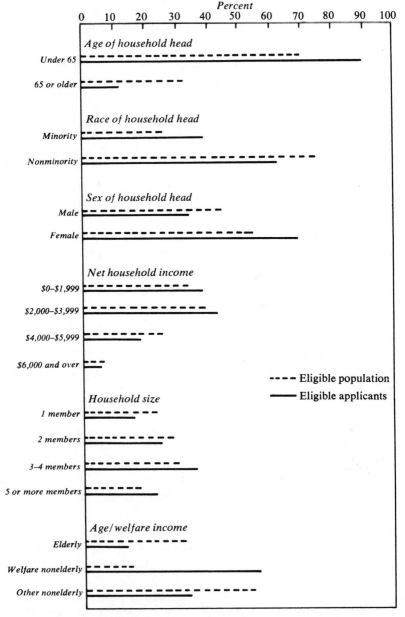

Source: Abt Associates, *Third Annual Report of the Administrative Agency Experiment Evaluation: October 1974–October 1975* (Abt, August 1976), p. 12.
a. Eligible population = 81,743; eligible applicants = 14,104, with 11 missing cases.

cipient data, but it would be hard to hold the allowance program responsible. An allowance program by itself could not solve the shortage because it relies on private markets to provide the units. The construction of more large rental units would be necessary. If large numbers of units fail at the housing inspection step of the placement process, it could also signal a need to build new units. If the housing stock in an area is in poor condition, the job of the housing allowance staff is more difficult.

The third element of the information system consists of spot checks of certification and inspection by state and HUD inspectors. Spot checks would help evaluate the effectiveness of particular functions without specifying how those functions should be performed at the local level.

With these three elements in an information system—profiles of the eligible and participating households, surveys of the condition and costs of local housing, and spot checks of certification and inspection—managers and staff at all levels could more effectively implement an allowance program. Local personnel would have information each month on how they were performing and could make timely adjustments. State and federal managers could set boundaries around the discretion necessary at the local levels, decentralizing but still retaining the capability to guide local activities.

ALLOCATING ADMINISTRATIVE SUPPORT FUNDS. The variations among sites examined in this discussion imply that a sliding scale formula to fund administrative support costs at the local level would be more appropriate than a fixed amount per recipient. Administrative support costs per recipient ranged from $165 to $429, with a site median of $252.[79] This variation resulted in part from adjustments by the agencies to local environmental factors and population characteristics. Through a sliding scale formula for administrative costs—indexed to factors such as family size and income, the condition of housing, and population density—more support funds could be targeted to areas where problems are difficult and fewer funds to areas where problems are less intense.

Data from the administrative agency experiment provide some clues about how such a formula could be indexed to sites and functions. Placing poor and/or large families seems to cost more than placing relatively better off and smaller families. The size of housing allowance payments made to a household is a rough indicator of its relative income and size. In the experiment, the average housing allowance payment per recipient

79. Maloy and others, *Administrative Costs*, pp. 21, 23.

by site is positively correlated with the average administrative cost per recipient by site.[80] An administrative cost formula could therefore be indexed in part to the size of the allowance payment. This procedure would also provide an incentive to local housing authorities to aid poorer and larger families.

But the size of the allowance payment indicates only the relative difficulty of placing eligible families. The condition of the housing stock and population density are also factors. The experiment found that when housing was in short supply or in poor condition, more effort was needed to find an acceptable rental unit.[81] An administrative cost formula should therefore include factors to adjust for population density and the condition and supply of the local housing stock.

The administrative agency experiment data suggest one other refinement in devising an administrative cost index. Some of the functions analyzed in the experiment had relatively small variations in administrative costs among sites; others varied much more.[82] A fixed amount for the functions that varied less could be included in an administrative index. A variable amount, keyed to differences in households and local environments, could be included to cover the other functions.

Conclusion

Both the paper by Kershaw and Williams and the evaluation of the administrative agency experiment by Abt Associates fail to take into account interactions of functions and local environments. When the experiment was begun, administrative theory was available that could have provided a more appropriate analytic framework. The proposals in my comments

80. Average administrative costs by site were correlated with average housing allowance payments by site, from data reported in William L. Hamilton, *A Social Experiment in Program Administration: The Housing Allowance Administrative Agency Experiment Evaluation* (Abt Books, 1979), p. 195. A Pearson correlation coefficient of 0.62 was found, with a Student's *t* measure of significance of 0.05. This finding is not conclusive. The data used in the analysis are means for which the ranges and standard deviations were not given. The number of cases was very small (eight sites). But the strength of the correlation and the relatively high level of significance for an analysis using such small numbers may indicate that these variables are highly correlated.

81. Hamilton, *A Social Experiment*, pp. 56–57, 91–99.

82. Costs for outreach, services, inspection, and enrollment varied substantially from site to site; costs for screening, certification, and payment were more uniform. Maloy and others, *Administrative Costs*, pp. 25–35.

were derived largely from that literature, augmented by findings from the experiment.

An experiment on the administration of a housing allowance program, such as the administrative agency experiment, could have been expected at a minimum to utilize existing theory in administration. In my judgment, neither the evaluations by Abt Associates and the Urban Institute nor the paper by Kershaw and Williams take into account basic materials from the administrative literature. If a broader conceptual framework had been introduced into the experiment evaluation at an early stage, the findings would have been more useful. Because it was not, important data on the effects of local environments on implementing a national program were overlooked or not reported.

JOHN F. KAIN

A Universal
Housing Allowance Program

Any discussion of how to implement a national hous-
ing allowance program must begin with two caveats. First, housing allowances need not take the form of a universal entitlement program.
Findings of the Experimental Housing Allowance Program, as well as
numerous earlier studies, strongly indicate that housing allowances or
similar demand-side strategies are a far more cost-effective means of providing low-income households with standard housing than are the costly
construction programs that federal policy has emphasized.[1] Because subsidies per assisted household are approximately half those of new construction programs, a housing allowance program would help twice as
many low-income households at each expenditure level as would
production-oriented programs such as the section 8 new construction

1. In addition to the program's clear demonstration of the cost-effectiveness and
workability of housing allowances, analyses by Stephen Mayo and others of the
comparative costs and benefits of ongoing federal low-income housing programs in
Pittsburgh and Phoenix, carried out in conjunction with the demand experiment
analyses, are especially pertinent. See Stephen Mayo and others, "Draft Report
on Housing Allowances and Other Rental Housing Assistance Programs—A Comparison Based on the Housing Allowance Demand Experiment," pt. 1: "Participation, Housing Consumption, Location, and Satisfaction"; pt. 2: "Costs and Efficiency" (Cambridge, Mass.: Abt Associates, 1979). Among the earlier studies that
support the same conclusions are Henry J. Aaron, *Shelter and Subsidies: Who
Benefits from Federal Housing Programs?* (Brookings Institution, 1972); Frank de
Leeuw, *The Cost of Leased Housing,* House Banking and Currency Committee, Subcommittee on Housing, 92 Cong. 1 sess. (Government Printing Office, 1971); Ira S.
Lowry, *Housing Assistance for Low-Income Urban Families: A Fresh Approach,*
House Committee on Banking and Currency, Subcommittee on Housing, 92 Cong.
1 sess. (GPO, 1971); Arthur P. Solomon, "Housing and Public Policy Analysis,"
Public Policy, vol. 20 (Summer 1972), pp. 443–72; U.S. Department of Housing
and Urban Development, *Housing in the Seventies* (GPO, 1974).

339

program.[2] If competing budgetary requirements make a universal entitlement plan infeasible, housing allowances would still be preferable to an inefficient new construction program that assists only half as many households.[3]

Second, the design of a national housing allowance program involves judgments that are more political than technical, such as the type of formula, benefit levels, eligibility criteria, and the nature and extent of earmarking. While analysts may advise legislators and administrators on the choice of specific program parameters, the policy makers will decide on the basis of uncertain and often conflicting technical advice, personal values, perceptions of constituents' preferences, demands by competing interests, and the benefits and costs of competing housing programs.

With these factors in mind, I consider in this paper what lessons the Experimental Housing Allowance Program offers for designing a national housing allowance program. The discussion begins with a review and critique of the Urban Institute's analyses of alternative housing allowance programs using the transfer income model. A review of recent program findings makes it clear that the transfer income model simulations substantially overpredict participation in, as well as costs of, alternative national housing allowance programs. Data from the supply experiments are used to develop alternative estimates of the number of recipients and total costs for national housing allowance programs employing different forms of earmarking. Further discussions of recent Experimental Housing Allowance Program findings emphasize the way in which housing requirements influence both participation and the fraction of allowance dollars devoted to increased housing consumption. This paper demonstrates that both participation and the extent to which housing allowances increase recipients' spending on housing can be controlled through setting other program requirements, but that these two program outcomes involve difficult trade-offs. After examining data from the supply experiment and

---

2. The section 8 existing housing program, which is similar to housing allowances in its use of existing units, also has much lower costs than the section 8 new construction program in most metropolitan areas. One difference between housing allowances and section 8 existing housing is that in the former the lease arrangements are entirely between the tenant and the landlord; under section 8 existing housing, after the recipient finds the unit and signs the lease with the landlord, the local housing authority also enters an agreement to pay a certain amount of the rent directly to the landlord.

3. A less than full entitlement program raises troublesome allocation questions. These rationing problems, however, should be less severe than in present programs, which give very large subsidies to very small fractions of eligible households.

simulation results from both the Urban Institute housing market model and the National Bureau of Economic Research urban simulation model, the final section of the paper suggests that the extent and range of possible market impacts are still uncertain.

The Urban Institute Transfer Income Model Simulations

Between December 1974 and August 1975 the Urban Institute released several reports describing use of its transfer income model to simulate a national housing allowance program. The Urban Institute work was prepared during spring and summer 1974 as backup material for an anticipated housing allowance proposal to Congress. Although prospects for some kind of a national housing allowance program seemed good at the time, the Watergate investigation immobilized the administration by fall, and interest in the proposal disappeared.

The Urban Institute prepared estimates of costs and participant characteristics for a "most likely" program, called the housing gap program center, and for several variants.[4] Urban Institute analysts identified six major program parameters: the payment formula, the payment standard, the rate at which recipient income is taxed, the income definition, the assets test, and the definition of the filing unit.

The base case used the following housing gap formula:

$$(1) \qquad\qquad P = C^* - bY.$$

The payment standard, C^*, is the standard metropolitan statistical area fair market rent used by the U.S. Department of Housing and Urban Development (HUD) in its section 8 housing program; and the tax rate, b, is a uniform 25 percent tax on all program-defined income.[5] In addition, the base case used a net income definition, no assets test, and census

4. Ronald J. Sepanik, *Variations of Selective Design Elements for Housing Allowances: Simulations Using the TRIM Model,* 216-19 (Washington, D.C.: Urban Institute, August 1975); John D. Heinberg, Joanna D. Culbertson, and James P. Zais, *The Missing Piece to the Puzzle? Housing Allowances and the Welfare System,* 216-4 (Urban Institute, December 1974); Ronald J. Sepanik, Gary Hendricks, and John D. Heinberg, *Simulations of National Housing Allowances: An Application of the TRIM Model,* 216-13 (Urban Institute, February 1975).
5. The parameter b is the fraction of income that eligible households are supposed to spend on housing. It is referred to as a tax rate because it specifies the amount the allowance payment, P, is reduced as household income increases.

households as the filing unit.[6] All program variants assumed that no household or filing unit would receive allowance payments if the estimated annual subsidy was less than $120; households headed by students or by spouses of students were also categorically excluded. Moreover, the Urban Institute modelers based their estimates on a "pessimistic" world economic state. Finally, eligible households were assumed to participate in all the allowance programs at identical rates, which were obtained from an analysis of data from the housing allowance demand experiment and the administrative agency experiment.[7]

The transfer income model simulations for the "most likely" housing allowance program indicated that in 1976 more than 11 million U.S. households would participate and receive monthly subsidies averaging $57 each, for a total annual cost of $7.6 billion. Nearly 70 percent of the participating households would have gross family incomes of less than $5,000 per year and would receive over 70 percent of the total subsidy. Households with gross annual incomes of more than $7,000 would account for 15 percent of all participants and would receive about 10 percent of the total subsidy. The average subsidy would decline as household income increased. Renters would account for 60 percent of participating households and receive two-thirds of the total subsidy amount. Persons sixty-five years or older would head about one-third of participating households, and 77 percent of participating households would be headed by whites.[8]

A major problem that the Urban Institute simulations encountered was with income transfers and in-kind services that participants receive from other programs such as aid to families with dependent children, supplemental security income, and the food stamp program. For the base case the simulations indicated that one-third of housing allowance recipients would participate in one other income-conditioned program, 15 percent would participate in two, and less than 1 percent would participate in all three. A large part of the overlap results from the fact that

6. Net income was defined as the sum of reported earnings, reported social security and railroad retirement, reported other income, simulated transfer payment, and imputed returns to equity for owner-occupants, less the sum of an allowance for work-related expenses, simulated federal income taxes, and simulated social security taxes.

7. Abt Associates, "Participation in a Direct Cash Assistance Program" (Abt, September 1974).

8. Sepanik, *Variations of Selective Design Elements,* pp. 6–10.

37 percent of housing allowance recipients would also receive food stamps, and 56 percent of this group would participate in only the housing allowance and food stamp programs. Nearly half (48.7 percent) of the base case recipients, however, would participate only in the housing allowance program.[9] Urban Institute researchers suggest that all other transfer payments should be regarded as ordinary income in the calculation of net income.[10]

The transfer income model simulations also provide estimates of participating households experiencing three different forms of deprivation—substandard conditions, overcrowding, and excess housing burden. Eighty percent of projected participants would suffer at least one form of housing deprivation, and these households would receive about 85 percent of the total subsidy. Excess burden would be by far the most prevalent condition, occurring among 66 percent of recipient households.[11] In addition, 12 percent of the projected participants would live in overcrowded conditions, and 24 percent would live in substandard dwellings. Nearly half of all recipients would experience excess housing costs as their only form of deprivation.[12]

In addition to the base case, the Urban Institute analysts evaluated four variants of the housing gap program, a rent-conditioned housing gap program, and a gross income-reference group program. The four variants maintained all features of the base case except that the payment standard was increased by 10 percent, the tax rate was increased by 10 percent of program-defined income, homeowners' equity returns were excluded from program-defined income, or an asset test was imposed ($3,000 for aged couples and $1,500 for other households). As table 1 shows, the number of participants in these eight allowance programs ranged between 8.6 and 13.0 million, while the total subsidy ranged from $5.0 billion to $9.8 billion a year in 1976 dollars. In all eight programs, households

9. Ibid., p. 13.

10. Sepanik and others, *Simulations of National Housing Allowances.*

11. A similar conclusion about the growing importance of excess housing costs was reached in a recent Congressional Budget Office study that found that in 1976 only 13 percent of all households with annual family incomes low enough to qualify for federal housing assistance lived in units needing rehabilitation. In contrast, 61 percent of renters and 39 percent of homeowners with annual family incomes below $10,000 in 1976 were paying one-fourth or more of their incomes for housing. Martin D. Levine, *Federal Housing Policy: Current Programs and Recurring Issues,* Congressional Budget Office, Background Paper (GPO, 1978), pp. 5–7, 10.

12. Sepanik, *Variations of Selective Design Elements,* p. 15.

Table 1. Estimated Number of Participants, Total Annual Cost, Average Monthly Subsidy, Percentage of Participating Households Earning Less Than $5,000, and Percentage of Subsidies Paid to Households Earning Less Than $5,000: Transfer Income Model Simulations of Alternative Plans for 1976

Plan	Number of participating households (millions)	Total annual subsidy (billions of 1976 dollars)	Average monthly subsidy (1976 dollars)	Income less than $5,000	
				Participants (percent)	Payments (percent)
Base case: housing gap program center	11.2	7.6	57	67.5	73.3
Rent-conditioned housing gap program center					
No behavioral response	8.6	5.0	49	67.1	73.3
Behavioral response	11.0	7.4	56	66.2	73.7
Gross income-reference group	10.8	8.6	67	70.5	77.8
Base case					
With 10 percent payment increase	13.0	9.8	63	61.0	68.4
With 10 percent higher tax rate	9.6	6.3	55	73.7	78.9
Excluding homeowner equity	12.3	8.5	57	65.6	72.3
With additional assets test	9.4	6.6	58	66.8	73.2

Source: Calculated from data presented in Ronald J. Sepanik, *Variations of Selective Design Elements for Housing Allowances: Simulations Using the TRIM Model*, 216–19 (Washington, D.C.: Urban Institute, August 1975), pp. 7, 18, 27, 44, 47, 49, 53, 55.

with annual incomes of less than $5,000 accounted for a minimum of 61.0 percent of all participants and received a minimum of 68.4 percent of all benefits.

The rent-conditioned housing gap formula defines the payment as a fraction (up to 100 percent) of the positive difference between the payment standard and a reasonable proportion of program-defined income:

$$(2) \qquad\qquad P = \frac{R}{C^*} (C^* - bY).$$

The first rent-conditioned housing gap program assumed no behavioral response and provided an average monthly subsidy of $49 to 8.6 million participating households; the second permitted a behavioral response and provided an average subsidy of $56 to 11 million households.[13]

The gross income-reference group program, the third variant in table 1, is identical to the base case except that gross rather than net income is used and the payment standard is based on actual rents paid by a reference group, that is, households with incomes just above the maximum for housing allowance eligibility. While these changes somewhat reduce the number of participants, they substantially increase both the total annual subsidy and the average monthly payment. Like the housing gap program and the rent-conditioned housing gap program, this variant directs most assistance to the lowest-income group and has a subsidy that decreases absolutely as income increases.

Housing Requirements and Program Participation

The Urban Institute transfer income model simulations provide valuable information about the probable costs and distributional consequences of a nationwide universal entitlement housing allowance program, as well as about the implications of changes in various program parameters. Recent Experimental Housing Allowance Program findings, however, suggest that participation rates in the transfer income model

13. The behavioral response, which assumes unitary price and income elasticities, probably somewhat overstates the response of recipients to the rent conditions. See Sepanik, *Variations of Selective Design Elements,* app. E. In their review of the Experimental Housing Allowance Program and earlier analyses of housing demand (in this volume), Hanushek and Quigley argue that the price elasticity of housing expenditures is most likely less than 0.5 in absolute value and that the income elasticity of housing expenditures is probably less than 0.5.

were much too high, implying a substantial overestimate of total program costs. Findings from the demand and supply experiments, moreover, permit a better assessment of how housing requirements and other forms of earmarking influence participation; the available data clearly indicate that the form and extent of earmarking strongly affect both participation rates and the fraction of allowance payments that recipients devote to increased housing consumption.

Using preliminary results from the administrative agency experiment, the Urban Institute estimated that 69 percent of all eligible households would participate in each of the allowance programs they investigated.[14] These experiments were, of course, limited to renters. In interpreting this participation rate, Urban Institute analysts applied it to both owners and renters and assumed it corresponded to a national program that had moderate housing standards and a maximum outreach effort. Participation rates shown in table 2 for the supply experiment, however, reveal that after 42.5 months (South Bend, Indiana) and 51 months (Green Bay, Wisconsin) of open enrollment, only 46 to 60 percent of eligible renter households and 29 to 27 percent of eligible owner-occupant households were receiving allowances. If the higher Green Bay participation rates are used, the overall national rate for owners and renters would be approximately 47 percent, suggesting that the transfer income model simulations overestimated the number of participating households by as much as 50 percent.[15] If these crude calculations are accepted for the moment, the number of participants in the base case would drop from 11.2 million to 7.6 million and the annual budgetary cost would drop from $7.6 billion to $5.2 billion in 1976 dollars.[16]

14. The transfer income model simulations used six different participation rates, varying from a low of 0.58 for elderly, white households to a high of 0.80 for white, nonelderly welfare recipients. The 69 percent estimate was obtained by a rough weighting of these rates. Sepanik, *Variations of Selective Design Elements,* p. 71.

15. The 47 percent participation rate, calculated as the ratio of current recipients to eligible households at baseline, excludes from both the numerator and the denominator some 600 Green Bay and 1,700 South Bend households who were already assisted by other federal housing programs at the time of the supply experiment. The tabulations of supply experiment records were provided by Ira S. Lowry, October 23, 1979.

16. Since participation rates tend to increase with payment size, the assumption that the decrease in total program costs is proportional to the decrease in the number of participants may understate program costs. Still, the estimate should provide a reasonable approximation of the costs of an allowance program similar to that used in the supply experiment. In commenting on the first draft of this paper, Ira S.

Table 2. Participation Rates Used in the Transfer Income Model Simulations and Estimated Participation Rates in the Demand and Supply Experiments, by City, Tenure, and Program Type

Percent

Program	Transfer income model, all, national	Demand experiment renters		Supply experiment			
				Renters		Owners	
		Pitts-burgh	Phoenix	Green Bay	South Bend	Green Bay	South Bend
Transfer income model	69	...	...	...	...	...	...
Supply experiment, minimum standards[a]	...	...	...	60	46	27	29
Demand experiment Housing gap							
Minimum standards	...	30	45	...	...	...	...
Low minimum rent	...	60	61	...	...	...	...
High minimum rent	...	42	44	...	...	...	...
Unconstrained	...	78	90	...	...	...	...
Percent of rent	...	82	87	...	...	...	...

Sources: Transfer income model percentage calculated from data in Sepanik, *Variations of Selective Design Elements*, app. C, p. 71; supply experiment percentages from a special tabulation supplied to author by Rand Corporation; demand experiment percentages from Stephen D. Kennedy and Jean MacMillan, "Draft Report on Participation Under Alternative Housing Allowance Programs: Evidence from the Housing Allowance Demand Experiment" (Cambridge, Mass.: Abt Associates, October 1979), pp. 162, 164.

a. Current recipients in September 1978 divided by baseline estimates of eligible population.

Whereas the supply experiment offered all eligible households places in a single, uniform housing allowance program, the demand experiment randomly assigned eligible households to seventeen different programs in both of its sites. The program variants tested in the demand experiment included twelve alternative housing gap programs that differed in form and extent of earmarking (physical standards, a high and low minimum rent, or no requirement), in payment level ($0.8C^*$, C^*, or $1.2C^*$), and in value of b used (0.15, 0.25, or 0.35). The five variants of the follow-

Lowry pointed out that a paper by Carlson and Heinberg contains revised estimates of the base case assuming a national participation rate of about 40 percent of all eligible households. While the paper provides virtually no information on the methods employed in making these projections, the resulting estimates of 7.2 million participants and $5.7 billion for 1976 are quite similar to the supply experiment participation rates base case estimates in table 1. David B. Carlson and John D. Heinberg, *How Housing Allowances Work: Integrated Findings from the Experimental Housing Allowance Program*, 249-3 (Urban Institute, February 1978), pp. 44–46.

ing percent of rent formula employ values of *a* ranging from 0.20 to 0.60:

(3) $P = aR.$

The statistics in table 2 illustrate that participation in the same program may vary among metropolitan areas, presumably because of differences in demographic characteristics and in the structure of local housing markets. More important, these data demonstrate that program requirements, particularly the form and extent of earmarking, strongly affect participation, implying that the participation rate can be explicitly chosen by setting the other requirements.[17]

In Pittsburgh, participation varied from a low of 30 percent for the minimum standards program to a high of 82 percent for households offered the percent of rent program. Phoenix households apparently had much less difficulty meeting the physical housing requirements of the demand experiment's minimum standards program; as a result, the Phoenix program using a high minimum rent form of earmarking had a slightly lower participation rate (44 percent) than the minimum standards program.[18] The low minimum rent program required participating households to live in units where rent levels were at least 70 percent of C^*, the cost of standard housing for the particular household. The high minimum rent program required them to live in a unit where rent was 90 percent of C^*. Ninety percent of Phoenix households eligible for the unearmarked housing gap program enrolled.[19]

Of the several variants tested, the demand experiment's minimum standards program most closely resembles the allowance program offered in the supply experiment. A comparison of participation rates, however, indicates that the demand experiment had lower participation rates in spite

17. More extensive analyses of this issue are contained in Jeanne E. Goedert, *Earmarking Housing Allowances: The Trade-off Between Housing Consumption and Program Participation,* 249-19 (Urban Institute, May 1979), especially chap. 3.

18. Stephen D. Kennedy, T. Krishna, and Glen Weisbrod, "Draft Report on Participation Under a Housing Gap Form of Housing Allowance" (Abt, May 1977); Stephen D. Kennedy and Jean MacMillan, "Draft Report on Participation Under Alternative Housing Allowance Programs: Evidence from the Housing Allowance Demand Experiment" (Abt, October 1979).

19. Further analyses of the effect of payment level for housing gap programs and for percent of rent programs of different values reveal that households receiving larger subsidies are more likely to participate than similar households offered smaller subsidies. Kennedy and MacMillan, "Draft Report on Participation," p. 21.

of more aggressive outreach techniques.[20] The principal reason appears to be that the demand experiment applied more stringent housing standards.[21] An analysis by Joseph J. Valenza shows that differences in standards accounted for a 16 percent greater failure rate in the demand experiment than in the supply experiment.[22]

Both experiments determined that households in units that pass the initial inspection are much more likely to participate than households in units that fail inspection. At the two demand experiment sites, all eligible households whose units passed the initial inspection participated, compared with only 30 percent of Pittsburgh and 44 percent of Phoenix households whose units failed the inspection at the time of enrollment.[23] Although data from the demand and supply experiments are not strictly comparable, rough estimates on eventual participation rates are nonethe-

20. The supply experiment, which sought to replicate an operational program, depended on an extensive advertising campaign, meetings with community groups, and word of mouth to inform eligible households about the program. In contrast, the demand experiment sought out a sample of eligible households and offered them an opportunity to enroll and, upon satisfying the program's housing requirements, to participate. The principal offsetting factor that would tend to induce higher participation in the supply experiment was its duration: the supply experiment offered payments for ten years, compared with three years in the demand experiment. Kennedy and MacMillan agree: "In general, [the following] discussion suggests that the participation rates estimated in the demand experiment are, if anything, higher than those that would be observed in an operating program." They add, however, that the overestimation may not be seriously misleading in terms of program outcomes. Kennedy and MacMillan, "Draft Report on Participation," p. 16.

21. The hypothesis that the minimum standards criteria used in the supply experiment were less stringent than the minimum standards criteria used in the demand experiment is supported by an independent analysis by the Urban Institute. See Joseph J. Valenza, *Comparability of Housing Standards in the Supply and Demand Experiments,* 216-9 (Urban Institute, February 1975). Jerry Fitts suggests that enrollment in the supply experiment has been selective, with disproportionate numbers of the best-housed families enrolling and disproportionate numbers of the worst-housed not bothering to enroll because of the housing requirements.

22. Joseph J. Valenza, *Program Housing Standards in the Experimental Housing Allowance Program: Analyzing Differences in the Demand and Supply Experiments,* 216-30 (Urban Institute, July 1977), pp. 19–20.

23. These participation rates are calculated for households that agreed to enroll in the program after an interview explaining the particular program to be offered. The nature of the housing requirements, of course, had some effect on enrollment rates. For example, of those offered the unconstrained program, 78 percent of Pittsburgh households and 90 percent of Phoenix households enrolled. In contrast, for households offered one of the housing gap minimum standards programs, enrollment rates were only 75 and 84 percent, respectively. Kennedy and MacMillan, "Draft Report on Participation," pp. 24, 43, 45.

Table 3. Estimated Participation Rates, Number of Participants, and Annual Budgetary Costs for National Housing Allowance Programs Involving Different Forms of Earmarking[a]

	Participation rates			Number of participants (millions)	Annual cost, 1976 (billions of dollars)
Program	Own (percent)	Rent (percent)	All (percent)		
Housing gap					
Minimum standards					
Supply	27	60	47	7.6	5.2
Demand	17	38	30	4.9	3.3
Low minimum rent	27	60	47	7.6	5.2
High minimum rent	19	43	33	5.3	3.6
Unconstrained					
A	38	84	66	10.7	7.3
B	70	84	78	12.7	8.6
Percent of rent					
A	38	84	66	10.7	4.9
B	70	84	78	12.7	5.7
Transfer income model					
base case	69	69	69	11.2	7.6

Source: Author's calculations.

a. These calculations, which assume that 40 percent of eligible households are owners and 60 percent are renters, index the average monthly subsidy payments of each program variant to the transfer income model base case on the assumption that the difference in average payment levels reflects housing market and demographic differences.

less useful. These estimates indicate that approximately 66 percent of Green Bay renters and 55 percent of South Bend renters whose units failed the initial inspection ultimately received payments.[24]

Shown in table 3 are crude calculations of the effect of different participation rates on the number of participants and the annual costs of various earmarked programs. Assuming that differences in raw participation rates primarily reflect program requirements and that homeowners and renters would respond similarly to housing requirements, the estimates suggest that although the transfer income model simulations greatly overpredicted participation in most earmarked national housing allowance programs, they probably understated the number of recipients and total costs of an unconstrained program.[25]

24. Rand Corporation, *Fourth Annual Report of the Housing Assistance Supply Experiment,* R-2302-HUD (Santa Monica: Rand, May 1978).

25. Since the demand experiment was limited to renters, homeowner participation rates for each program were estimated to be 45 percent of renters' participation rates, the ratio of owner-occupant to renter participation rates in the

The first row in table 3 repeats the revised estimate of participation and annual costs for an allowance program that uses physical standards and a payment formula similar to those in the supply experiment. These estimates were obtained by multiplying average participation rates for eligible households in Green Bay (the higher of the two supply experiment rates) times the base case national estimates of eligible renter and owner households obtained from the transfer income model simulations and times the base case average subsidies obtained from these simulations. Although the payment formula used for the simulations and both supply experiment sites was the same, average monthly payments in the supply experiment in 1976—$77 for Green Bay renters, $93 for South Bend renters, and $67 for owners in both areas[26]—were significantly higher than those obtained from the transfer income model simulations for all U.S. households. These differences could reflect higher housing costs or lower average incomes in Green Bay and South Bend, or the tendency of households eligible for larger payments to participate at higher rates. Since insufficient information is available to distinguish these effects, the calculations assume the differences are attributable to the first two factors. To the extent that this assumption is invalid, the cost of programs with lower participation rates may be somewhat understated relative to programs with higher rates.

As the second row of table 3 shows, use of the demand experiment's more stringent housing requirements reduced participation rates well below those extrapolated from supply experiment findings. These lower estimates, moreover, make no allowance for the demand experiment's more aggressive outreach techniques. In considering a national program, however, it should be noted that participation rates would increase over time as more households move to housing that satisfies program requirements; this effect is likely to be particularly important in the case of homeowners because they move much less frequently than renters. The short-term participation rates in table 3 are nonetheless appropriate for estimating the budgetary cost of a national allowance program over an initial two- to five-year period or for predicting the effects of an initial demand shock on housing markets.

The unconstrained housing gap and percent of rent programs, not

---

supply experiment. This rule of thumb was applied to all but two of the programs listed in table 3; in the unconstrained B and percent of rent B program, 70 percent of homeowners were assumed to participate.

26. Rand Corporation, *Fourth Annual Report*, p. 22.

surprisingly, have the most projected participants and the highest annual costs. Of the two sets of estimates for these program variants, the first assumes that the participation rate of owners in each program bears the same relation to that of renters as in the supply experiment; the second assumes that 70 percent of homeowners would participate in the program. The percent of rent program, the second program with very high participation rates in the demand experiment, is projected to have the same number of participants as the unconstrained program, but at two-thirds the annual cost. As with the unconstrained program, the alternative estimates reflect different assumptions about homeowner participation.

Housing Requirements and Housing Expenditures

All the allowance plans evaluated by the Experimental Housing Allowance Program permitted substantial decreases in the percentage of income that recipients spent on housing. For example, the median rent burden of Pittsburgh participants in the minimum standards program decreased from 37 percent at enrollment to 21 percent at the end of the second year.[27] Similar reductions were obtained for Phoenix households and for other allowance plans.[28] This finding reflects the tendency for recipients to spend more of their allowances on goods and services other than housing, a tendency that is especially pronounced among supply experiment households. While few individuals are likely to criticize the program's success in reducing the rent burdens of participating households, many proponents of housing subsidies are likely to be disappointed with the supply experiment's failure to increase recipients' housing consumption. Marc Bendick, Jr., and James P. Zais of the Urban Institute, for example, argue that housing allowances do not contribute significantly to HUD's policy goals, concluding that "one goal of many housing programs is to increase the quantity of housing services consumed by lower-

27. Rent burden is defined as $(R - P)/Y$, where R = monthly rent, P = monthly payment, and Y = monthly income.
28. The decrease in median rent burden for Pittsburgh households participating in other plans was from 36 to 22 percent for the low minimum rent plans, from 39 to 29 percent for the high minimum rent plans, from 32 to 21 percent for the percent of rent plans, and from 35 to 20 percent for the unconstrained plans. Joseph Friedman and Daniel Weinberg, "Draft Report on Housing Consumption Under a Constrained Income Transfer: Evidence from a Housing Gap Allowance" (Abt, April 1979), pp. 33, 68, 69; Joseph Friedman and Daniel Weinberg, "Draft Report on the Demand for Rental Housing: Evidence from a Percent of Rent Housing Allowance" (Abt, September 1978), p. 13.

income, poorly housed families . . . . Although housing allowances do offer recipients some very real benefits in terms of income maintenance, they are an ineffective means of increasing the housing consumption of lower-income households."[29]

As table 4 illustrates, however, the various demand experiment programs differ significantly in terms of how much they increase housing expenditures. While it is difficult to be certain from the analyses the Rand Corporation has provided, it appears the minimum standards program implemented in Green Bay and South Bend induced smaller increases than any of the plans tested in the demand experiment, including the unconstrained housing gap program. The *Fourth Annual Report* notes that the increase in annual rental expenditures for South Bend participants was less than 2.8 percent, while the countywide increase in rents was 3.1 percent.[30]

In contrast, all allowance plans evaluated in the demand experiment induced increases in participants' rental expenditures in excess of what would be expected without the program. Even the unconstrained plans produced increases of 2.6 percent among Pittsburgh recipients and 16 percent among Phoenix recipients.[31] Increases were substantially higher

29. Marc Bendick, Jr., and James P. Zais, *Incomes and Housing: Lessons from Experiments with Housing Allowances,* 249-9 (Urban Institute, October 1978), pp. 3, 7.

30. Rand Corporation, *Fourth Annual Report,* p. 81. Rand does not provide information on the average increase in rents paid by recipients in Green Bay. It is difficult to believe, however, that the housing allowance payments in Green Bay and South Bend failed to increase housing expenditures by at least as much as would be expected from an unrestricted allowance, that is, an amount consistent with the income elasticity of demand, estimated to be 0.45 for owners and 0.19 for renters at both sites. See John E. Mulford, *Income Elasticity of Housing Demand,* R-2449-HUD (Rand Corp., July 1979), p. vi.

Still, none of the available Rand reports or papers include an estimate of the program-induced increases in housing expenditures. The lack of control households or a model that permits baseline estimates of housing expenditures makes this determination impossible. Since the market impacts are so small, the estimated income elasticities of demand, allowing for lags, presumably provide the best estimates.

31. The increase obtained for Pittsburgh recipients is close to the simulated 1.8 percent increase Kain and Apgar estimated in their evaluation of a similar full-scale unconstrained housing allowance program for Pittsburgh households. Obtained using the National Bureau of Economic Research's housing allowance demand simulator model, this estimate is an average for both owners and renters and refers to the end of a five-year period as contrasted to the two years considered in the demand experiment analyses. John F. Kain and William C. Apgar, Jr., *Analysis of the Market Effects of Housing Allowances,* Discussion Paper D76-3 (Harvard University, Department of City and Regional Planning, October 1976), p. 8.

Table 4. Rent at Enrollment, Percentage Increase in Rents above Normal, and Earmarking Ratios for All Participating Households

	Pittsburgh			Phoenix		
Category	Rent at enrollment (dollars)	Increase above normal[a] (percent)	Ear-marking ratio[b] (percent)	Rent at enrollment (dollars)	Increase above normal[a] (percent)	Ear-marking ratio[b] (percent)
Meeting requirements after two years						
Minimum standards	119	4.3	9	135	16.2	27
Low minimum rent	115	2.8[c]	6[c]	133	15.7	25
High minimum rent	127	8.5	23	149	28.4	41
Unconstrained	107	2.6	6	135	16.0	19
Percent of rent	114	8.0	14	132	8.0	22
Meeting requirements at enrollment						
Minimum standards	125	1.1	2	150	−0.7	−2
Low minimum rent	123	2.4	6	154	−1.2	−3
High minimum rent	145	4.6	14	183	7.4	15
Not meeting require-ments at enroll-ment						
Minimum standards	114	7.5	14	128	23.6	33
Low minimum rent	93	8.7	15	101	42.0	42
High minimum rent	105	15.8	39	128	42.6	50

Sources: Joseph Friedman and Daniel Weinberg, "Draft Report on Housing Consumption Under a Constrained Income Transfer: Evidence from a Housing Gap Housing Allowance" (Abt, April 1978), pp. 28, 64, 65, 137, 139–41, 146; Joseph Friedman and Daniel Weinberg, "Draft Report on the Demand for Rental Housing: Evidence from a Percent of Rent Housing Allowance" (Abt, September 1978), pp. 8, 11.

a. This is defined as the difference between experimental households' actual housing expenditures and what they would have spent on housing in the absence of the experimental program. For the housing gap households, it is calculated according to housing expenditure functions whose parameters have been estimated by using the sample of control households. For more details, see Friedman and Weinberg, "Draft Report on Housing Consumption," chap. 4.

b. The earmarking ratio is defined as program-induced increases in housing expenditures divided by the housing allowance payment.

c. These figures adjusted by Friedman and Weinberg.

among Phoenix recipients for all plans except the percent of rent plan, which induced an estimated 8.0 percent increase in housing expenditures in both cities. Differences between the responses of Pittsburgh and Phoenix recipients presumably reflect market structure and perhaps demographic differences. One important consideration is that Phoenix households move more frequently than Pittsburgh households; both the demand and supply experiments indicate that movers spend a larger fraction of their allowances on increased housing consumption than nonmovers. Estimates for percent of rent and unconstrained housing gap

Table 5. Rent at Enrollment, Percentage Increase in Rents above Normal, and Earmarking Ratios for Movers and Nonmovers in Pittsburgh and Phoenix

	Pittsburgh			Phoenix		
Recipient	Rent at enrollment (dollars)	Increase above normal (percent)	Earmarking ratio (percent)	Rent at enrollment (dollars)	Increase above normal (percent)	Earmarking ratio (percent)
Movers						
Percent of rent	114	16	27	135	8	24
Unconstrained	109	10	15	128	15	19
Control	120	...	...	132	...	...
Nonmovers						
Percent of rent	114	2	4	127	0	2
Unconstrained	106	−1	−2	145	1	...
Control	112	...	...	125	...	...

Source: Friedman and Weinberg, "Draft Report on the Demand for Rental Housing," pp. 14, 17.

plans, shown in table 5, reveal that movers increased their housing outlays by significant amounts above normal (9 to 10 percent), while nonmovers raised their housing consumption little more than did comparable nonparticipants (1 or 2 percent).

The earmarking ratio, defined as program-induced increases in housing outlays divided by the amount of the subsidy, is a measure of each plan's effectiveness in increasing housing expenditures.[32] As table 4 indicates, the earmarking ratios for all demand experiment programs at the end of two years range from 6 percent for Pittsburgh's unconstrained housing gap plan to 41 percent for the Phoenix high minimum rent plan. Although the earmarking ratio for the supply experiment cannot be calculated from available data, it appears to be less than 5 percent.

Whether or not a household meets the housing requirements at enrollment strongly influences changes in housing expenditures. Above-normal

32. Analyses by Stephen Kennedy and Sally Merrill based on hedonic rent and value equations suggest that real changes in housing consumption were significantly smaller than expenditure changes. In the case of the percent of rent program, analysts from Abt Associates indicate that one-fifth to one-half or more of the expenditure changes represented increased spending without concomitant increases in housing services obtained. Although these analyses provide a valuable warning, they probably overstate the efficiency losses that would occur in a full-scale program because they ignore supply-side responses. Stephen D. Kennedy and Sally Merrill, "The Use of Hedonic Indices to Distinguish Real Changes in Housing from Changes in Housing Expenditures: Evidence from the Housing Allowance Demand Experiment," paper presented at the Research Conference on the Housing Choices of Low Income Families (Abt, July 1979).

percentage increases in housing outlays for households that did not meet each plan's requirements, shown in table 4, are typically several times greater than for those that did.[33] In the case of the minimum standards program, for example, Pittsburgh renters who met the program's housing requirements at enrollment increased their housing expenditures only 1.1 percent more than comparable nonparticipants, while those not meeting the standards increased their expenditures by 7.5 percent. The differences for Phoenix households are even more pronounced: −0.7 percent for households that met the standards compared with 23.6 percent for those that did not.

Table 4 also shows that program-induced increases in housing expenditures and the fraction of each subsidy dollar spent to purchase additional housing depend on the allowance formula used and the housing requirements imposed. Minimum standards and minimum rent earmarking each induce higher expenditures for housing than does an unconstrained program, with the amount of the increase depending on aggregate mobility rates and housing market conditions. The supply experiment results, however, suggest that certain physical standards may induce no or very small increases in housing expenditures, at least in some housing markets. The substantial differences in expenditure increases induced by identical programs in Pittsburgh and Phoenix, moreover, demonstrate the need for care in generalizing from the supply experiment results in Green Bay and South Bend.

Appropriate housing requirements can thus induce low-income households to increase their housing consumption. Unfortunately, these requirements exact a heavy toll in terms of lower participation rates; worse yet, they are most likely to discourage the lowest-income and largest households from enrolling. Since lower-income and large households are least likely to satisfy housing requirements at enrollment, participation of these households is adversely affected. It is therefore clear that policy makers face a real dilemma: they can undoubtedly design housing requirements that increase the fraction of each allowance dollar low-income households spend on housing, but only by reducing the participation of the neediest households.

Percent of rent programs, which combine high participation rates with relatively high earmarking ratios (14 percent in Pittsburgh and 22 per-

33. The percent of rent and unconstrained housing gap plans are not included in the bottom two panels since these plans have no housing requirements for participation.

cent in Phoenix), appear to be an attractive compromise. Their principal
drawback is that they do not ensure that recipients will correct inexpen-
sive-to-repair but hazardous conditions (such as missing or broken stair
treads and hand railings) that Rand researchers extol.[34] The discussion
thus returns to where I began: it is impossible to analyze a national housing allowance program without specifying its goals and the trade-offs
among participation rates, reductions in rent burdens, increases in housing expenditures and consumption, and elimination of specific physical
defects.

The Market Effects of a National Housing Allowance Program

A major reason for undertaking the Experimental Housing Allowance
Program—and particularly its most expensive component, the supply
experiment—was the widespread concern that a cash subsidy would dis-
rupt housing markets, fail to expand the housing supply, produce unacceptable increases in housing prices, and destabilize neighborhoods.
Although many economists were relatively unconcerned about program
impacts, believing that the supply was elastic and that anticipated transfers
would not be appreciably larger than those induced by postwar growth,
many noneconomists did not share this complacency.[35] Debates, however,
were seldom more than a restatement of most liberal noneconomists' suspicion of and hostility to unregulated markets on the one hand, and of the

34. In his paper in this volume, Henry Aaron rejects the percent of rent program
out of hand, arguing that neither it "nor the minimum rent requirement is a feasible
housing policy because each creates an incentive for collusion between tenants and
landlords; even worse, the incentive is obvious." Other critics contend that the
percent of rent program discourages recipients from shopping for bargains. I am
unpersuaded by these arguments, however. Support for the shopping effects hypothesis is based on empirical evidence from the demand experiment and ignores the
market responses that would result from a full-scale program. Competition among
suppliers would be expected to restore prices to their original levels. Similarly, the
potential for collusion and corruption exists in any program that seeks to make participants behave in ways they do not consider in their best interest. In minimum
standards programs, both property owners and allowance recipients have an interest
in influencing housing inspections. If the enforcement of building and housing codes
is any indication, the potential for abuse in this area is large.
35. I stand by my recollecton and interpretation of the posture of professional
economists on this point; others may read the historical record differently. See, for
example, C. Lance Barnett and Ira S. Lowry, *How Housing Allowances Affect
Housing Prices*, R-2452-HUD (Rand Corp., September 1979).

economists' general optimism about the responsiveness of unregulated markets on the other.

To provide persuasive evidence about the effects of housing allowances on urban housing markets, HUD contracted with the Rand Corporation to design and carry out the supply experiment. Selection of the Green Bay, (Brown County, Wisconsin) and South Bend (St. Joseph County, Indiana) metropolitan areas as sites, however, evoked considerable controversy. In particular, it was argued that market conditions in Green Bay and South Bend were qualitatively different from those found in large, old, decaying urban centers such as Detroit, Cleveland, or Newark, and that the supply experiment would simply not provide a reliable guide to program impacts in such areas.

Acknowledging these arguments, HUD and Rand countered that budgetary limitations precluded a full-scale experiment in a major metropolitan area and that the markets selected were sufficiently representative to allow generalization to larger areas. To provide an analytical backup to the supply experiment, HUD contracted with the Urban Institute and the National Bureau of Economic Research to adapt their housing market simulation models to an analysis of the probable market impacts of a full-scale housing allowance.[36] Calibrated to the Austin, Texas; Chicago, Illinois; Durham, North Carolina; Pittsburgh, Pennsylvania; Portland, Oregon; Washington, D.C.; Green Bay; and South Bend metropolitan areas, the Urban Institute model provided simulations of several allowance programs for these eight metropolitan areas as well as for several hypothetical composite areas.[37] For Green Bay and South Bend, the Urban Institute analysts attempted to replicate the program used in the supply experiment.[38]

36. Actually, HUD invited the National Bureau of Economic Research to participate in the Experimental Housing Allowance Program in January 1974 when it appeared the Nixon administration might propose a housing allowance program to Congress the following fall. HUD thus faced the prospect of having to answer questions about the probable market effects of a housing allowance some five years before the first findings of the supply experiment were expected. HUD responded by inviting the bureau to reorient its modeling activities to consider the market effects of housing allowances.

37. Frank de Leeuw and Raymond Struyk, *The Web of Urban Housing: Analyzing Policy with a Market Simulation Model* (Urban Institute, 1975); Larry Ozanne, *Simulation of Housing Allowance Policies for U.S. Cities: 1960–1970*, 216-3 (Urban Institute, December 1974).

38. Jean Vanski and Larry Ozanne, *Simulating the Housing Allowance Program in Green Bay and South Bend: A Comparison of the Urban Institute Model and the Supply Experiment*, 249-5 (Urban Institute, October 1978).

The urban simulation model of the National Bureau of Economic Research, calibrated to the Pittsburgh and Chicago metropolitan areas, provided exploratory simulations of a single full-scale housing allowance program in these two markets.[39] In addition, bureau researchers used a modified version of the model's demand sector—the housing allowance demand simulator—to evaluate the possible market effects of twelve housing allowance plans on the Pittsburgh housing market.[40]

Both the Urban Institute and National Bureau of Economic Research simulations indicated that a full-scale earmarked allowance program might cause significant rent increases for both recipients and nonrecipients, and the bureau simulations pointed out the possibility that such a program might trigger large price declines and extensive abandonment in the worst neighborhoods. Rand's current reports and papers, however, suggest that the supply experiment has resolved the question of possible market impacts. After listing the adverse outcomes predicted before the experiment, Rand analysts stated:

The evidence to date indicates that the attempts of program participants to secure acceptable housing have had virtually no effect on rents or home prices in either site. That evidence covers the period of rapid enrollment during which such effects were most likely to occur, as new enrollees got hunting licenses for better housing. It is unlikely that such effects will occur now that enrollment is leveling off.

The lack of price effects has surprised many observers who either misperceived the nature of the market stimulus that the program provides or misunderstood housing market dynamics. Some expected larger enrollments or larger increases in housing expenditures than have occurred. Few realized how easily existing dwellings could be improved to meet program standards. . . .

In short, the market stimulus has been as much as was needed to meet the program's housing objectives for about 80 percent of all enrollees. Although a program that offered larger benefits or imposed higher standards on partici-

39. John F. Kain, William C. Apgar, Jr., and J. Royce Ginn, *Simulation of the Market Effects of Housing Allowances,* vol. 1: *Description of the NBER Urban Simulation Model,* Research Report R77-2 (Harvard University, Department of City and Regional Planning, August 1976); and John F. Kain and William C. Apgar, Jr., *Simulation of the Market Effects of Housing Allowances,* vol. 2: *Baseline and Policy Simulations for Pittsburgh and Chicago,* Research Report R77-3 (Harvard University, Department of City and Regional Planning, January 1977).

40. William C. Apgar, Jr., and John F. Kain, "Effects of Housing Allowances in the Pittsburgh Housing Market," in John F. Kain, ed., *Progress Report on the Development of the NBER Urban Simulation Model and Interim Analyses of Housing Allowance Programs* (New York: National Bureau of Economic Research, December 1974); and Kain and Apgar, *Analysis of the Market Effects of Housing Allowances.*

pants' housing might press harder on the resources of the housing market, no one has seriously challenged the appropriateness of the standards of need and housing quality that were devised for the experimental program. Moreover, there is some evidence that benefits and standards would have to be increased greatly to generate such market effects.[41]

The Rand Corporation's complacency derives from the implicit view that the supply experiment tested *the* housing allowance program rather than *one* of several possible programs. Although the variant implemented in Green Bay and South Bend has considerable merit, I am not convinced that the small program-induced housing improvements are worth their administrative costs and adverse effects on participation. My personal choice would be either an unconstrained housing allowance program or a generous national income maintenance program.[42] Still, many supporters of housing subsidies are likely to object to an allowance program that fails to induce low-income consumers to increase their housing expenditures significantly.

Findings from the demand experiment indicate that appropriate earmarking criteria can induce recipients to spend more of their allowance on increased housing services. Although these analyses indicate that housing requirements also reduce participation rates, these losses can be partially or totally offset by offering larger subsidies. Finally, the demand experiment results demonstrate that either a minimum rent or a percent of rent program would probably result in higher participation and larger increases in housing expenditures, at least as compared with the supply experiment. For example, 87 percent of eligible Phoenix renters received payments in the percent of rent program and increased their housing expenditures by an average of 8 percent. Similarly, the high minimum rent variant of the housing gap program made payments to 44 percent of eligible renters in Phoenix and induced them to increase their housing expenditures by 28 percent (tables 2 and 4). Estimates of program-induced increases in housing expenditures have not been released by the supply experiment, but the available data suggest that aggregate increases in Green Bay and South Bend have been significantly smaller than increases that would result from full-scale implementation of several of the program variants tested in the demand experiment. The larger program-

---

41. Rand Corporation, *Fourth Annual Report*, pp. 99–100.
42. An unconstrained housing allowance program and a generous national income maintenance program are very similar programs. They differ principally in the emphasis given location-specific housing costs in calculating benefit payments.

induced increases in housing expenditures obtained in the demand experiment and the clear findings that larger payments can increase both participation in and magnitude of program-induced increases in housing expenditures suggest the need for caution in generalizing the supply experiment's "no market impact" finding to other urban areas and program variants.

Because the program-induced increases in housing expenditures in Green Bay and South Bend appear to have been so small, neither the supply experiment nor Rand's analysis provide much insight about the probable market impacts of allowance programs that induce larger increases in housing expenditures.[43] The argument for caution in generalizing the supply experiment's "no market impact" finding is further supported by the results of the National Bureau of Economic Research and Urban Institute simulations of programs involving larger aggregate increases in housing expenditures.

As table 6 shows, neither the Urban Institute nor bureau simulations predict a very large change in average rents following the introduction of a housing allowance program, although the Urban Institute researchers project significant increases in participants' rents for five of the six metropolitan areas they considered. While the bureau model does not provide comparable data on changes in participants' rents, it does give extensive detail on rent changes for numerous housing types in nearly 200 residence zones in each metropolitan area. These data reveal that the small (4 percent) decline in average rents for the entire region masks rather substantial price changes in various housing submarkets: increases in market rents of more than 10 percent for 20 percent of all Pittsburgh units and rent declines of more than 10 percent for 23 percent of all units. Similar results were obtained for Chicago. In both models, the percentage in-

___

43. C. Peter Rydell, *Shortrun Response of Housing Markets to Demand Shifts*, R-2453-HUD (Rand Corp., September 1979), presents some interesting and useful analyses of changes in rents and vacancies in the Green Bay and South Bend housing markets. On the basis of these analyses, Rydell argues that the negligible rent increases that apparently occurred are partially explained by the equilibrating influence of vacancies as well as by the small program-induced increase in demand for rental housing. Rydell's analysis, which considers only cases involving very small demand increases, seems less appropriate for considering the market impact of housing allowances than do studies that emphasize the quantity of housing services per unit. See Frank de Leeuw and Nkanta F. Ekanem, "Time Lags in the Rental Housing Market," *Urban Studies*, vol. 10 (February 1973), pp. 39–68. These distinctions also figure importantly in the representation of housing market dynamics in the bureau model. See Kain and others, *Simulation of Market Effects*.

Table 6. Summary Statistics for Urban Institute and National Bureau of Economic Research Housing Allowance Simulations and Supply Experiment, by City

Simulation or experiment	Average monthly subsidy (dollars)	Eligibility rate	Participation rate	Earmarking ratio	Change in participants' rent (percent)	Change in all rents (percent)
Urban Institute simulation						
Austin, Texas	53	0.34	0.79	0.64	-2	-2.0
Chicago, Illinois	33	0.24	1.00	0.66	6	0.1
Durham, North Carolina	37	0.32	0.36	0.96	17	0.1
Pittsburgh, Pennsylvania	28	0.22	0.67	0.83	19	0.2
Portland, Oregon	37	0.26	0.78	0.73	14	0.0
Washington, D.C.	54	0.20	1.00	0.49	5	-0.1
National Bureau of Economic Research simulation						
Housing allowance demand model						
Pittsburgh without earmarking	52	0.34	1.00	0.04	n.a.	n.a.
Pittsburgh with earmarking	57	0.34	0.67	0.39	n.a.	2.5 to 8.6
Full model						
Chicago	42	0.25	0.88	n.a.	n.a.	-4.0
Pittsburgh	45	0.32	0.88	n.a.	n.a.	-4.0
Supply experiment						
Green Bay, Wisconsin (1976–77)	72	0.19[a]	0.43[b]	*	*	*
South Bend, Indiana	78	0.23[a]	0.30[b]	*	*	*

Sources: Urban Institute simulations are from Larry Ozanne, *Simulations of Housing Allowance Policies for U.S. Cities: 1960–1970*, 216-3 (Urban Institute, December 1974); housing allowance demand model is from John F. Kain and William C. Apgar, Jr., *Analysis of the Market Effects of Housing Allowances*, Discussion Paper D76-3 (Harvard University, Department of City and Regional Planning, October 1976), pp. 5, 24; full model is from John F. Kain and William C. Apgar, Jr., *Simulation of the Market Effects of Housing Allowances*, vol. 2: *Baseline and Policy Simulations for Pittsburgh and Chicago*, Research Report R77-3 (Harvard University, Department of City and Regional Planning, August 1976), p. 123. For the supply experiment, average monthly subsidy and eligibility rates are from Rand Corporation, *Fourth Annual Report of the Housing Assistance Supply Experiment*, R-2302-HUD (Rand, June 1979); participation rates are from special tabulation supplied by the Rand Corporation.

n.a. Not available.

* Negligible.

a. Includes eligible households already assisted by other federal housing program; in both the numerator (eligible households) and denominator (all households) of the fraction.

b. Current recipients in September 1978 divided by baseline estimates of eligible population.

crease is relative to rents for a baseline simulation. Unless a model is developed to predict what the change in rents would have been without the allowance program, however, Rand researchers will be unable to provide comparable statistics.

In a recent paper, C. Lance Barnett and Ira S. Lowry presented a series of comparisons between the supply experiment findings and Urban Institute and bureau housing allowance simulations. They concluded that the simulation results are in error: "Contrary to predictions, the experimental evidence reveals no significant price changes attributable to the allowance program's first three years of operation in Brown County (an unsegregated market with a low vacancy rate) or its first two years in St. Joseph County (a segregated market with a high vacancy rate)."[44]

Barnett and Lowry's analyses are, at minimum, incomplete and reflect the peculiar Rand view that the program operating in Green Bay and South Bend is *the* housing allowance program. Even though the Urban Institute and the National Bureau of Economic Research evaluated programs similar to that used in the supply experiment, it is misleading to portray them as identical and incorrect to infer that the simulations are in error because they failed to replicate the supply experiment findings. The statistics in table 6 on program outcomes make it clear that the allowance programs simulated by the Urban Institute and the bureau differ from Rand's program in South Bend and Green Bay in several respects, resulting in significantly higher eligibility and participation rates and higher earmarking ratios.

Like the transfer income model simulations discussed earlier, the Urban Institute and the bureau housing market simulations used too high a participation rate. To some extent these overpredictions were by design, but they are clearly greater than at least the bureau modelers intended. The eligibility rates obtained in the bureau full model simulations were also somewhat higher, suggesting the schedule of C^* was higher than the one used in the supply experiment.[45] With the benefit of hindsight, it is also clear that the program simulations that most nearly replicate the

44. Barnett and Lowry, *How Housing Allowances Affect Housing Prices*, p. 42.
45. The schedule of C^* used in the bureau simulations was adapted from the 1974 demand experiment schedule. The housing allowance demand simulations for Pittsburgh, using $0.8C^*$ rather than C^* in the allowance formula, yielded an eligibility rate—0.24 rather than 0.34—that was much closer to that reported by the supply experiment. Kain and Apgar, *Analysis of the Market Effects of Housing Allowances*, p. 5. Use of $0.8C^*$ in the full model simulations would also more closely approximate the Urban Institute eligibility rates.

supply experiment are the bureau's housing allowance demand model simulations of an unrestricted housing allowance program; the simulations of this program produced only a small increase in demand and thus had an imperceptible impact on the Pittsburgh housing market.

The higher eligibility and participation rates and higher levels of C^* used in the bureau simulations and in most of the Urban Institute simulations partially explain the larger increase in demand. The Urban Institute model used a minimum quantity constraint that functioned like a minimum rent requirement. As a result, the earmarking ratios obtained for the Urban Institute simulations, which ranged from 0.49 to 0.96, were much larger than apparently occurred in the supply experiment. While earmarking ratios are unavailable for the bureau full model simulations, the housing allowance demand model simulations for Pittsburgh had an earmarking ratio of 39 percent.

Available Experimental Housing Allowance Program data suggest that the Urban Institute and bureau model simulations overstate the likely market impacts of a national housing allowance program. At the same time, there is no reason to believe that the effects of a national program would be as small as those induced by the supply experiment: if a national housing allowance program employed more stringent earmarking and provided deeper subsidies to low-income households, participation rates might be as high as or higher than in the supply experiment, and participants might increase their housing outlays by larger amounts. Unfortunately, because the program variant tested produced such a small increase in demand, the supply experiment itself provides almost no guidance on the nature and extent of the market impacts that might result from programs inducing larger increases in housing expenditures.

Conclusions

Analyses of Experimental Housing Allowance Program data in this paper illustrate the importance of housing requirements or other forms of earmarking in designing a national housing allowance program. Depending on the form and stringency of the earmarking, the number of participants is predicted to range from 5.4 million to 12.8 million, while the annual cost might vary from $3.2 billion to $8.4 billion annually (in 1976 dollars).

Findings from the demand and supply experiments demonstrate that particular program requirements also affect the fraction of allowance payments spent on increased housing expenditures. Somewhat surprisingly, the program evaluated in the supply experiment appears to have induced the smallest increases in housing expenditures of any of the allowance plans considered. While available analyses do not fully explain this finding, the most likely reason is the housing stock characteristics of the two markets (Green Bay has a very high quality housing stock and South Bend has an exceedingly loose housing market) and the particular housing requirements selected for the experiment. Not only did the housing requirements fail to increase recipients' housing consumption by much, but they also seem to have adversely affected participation, especially among households in greatest need.

Having induced such a small increase in demand, the supply experiment program had no perceptible impact on rents or other aspects of the Green Bay and South Bend housing markets. The experiment's findings to date are therefore of little or no help in assessing a national housing allowance program that would use a form of earmarking to induce a significant increase in housing expenditures. The Urban Institute and National Bureau of Economic Research simulations, however, indicate that such programs might lead to significant increases in rents and house values, among other market impacts. While the simulations undoubtedly overpredict participation and the magnitude of the increase in aggregate housing expenditures, we cannot ignore the possibility that an appropriately earmarked allowance program might have significant market impacts.

Because housing allowances need not take the form of a universal entitlement program, the budgetary costs of such a program are not a valid objection to housing allowances. Any of the methods currently used to limit participation in subsidy programs could also be used to ration housing allowances. Moreover, program analyses confirm the findings of earlier studies that housing allowances and similar programs that exploit the existing housing stock have subsidy costs per assisted household about half as large as conventional public housing, section 8 new construction, and similar production-oriented programs.[46] A strong argument thus emerges for the reorientation of federal policy: the Experimental Housing Allowance Program's clearest message is that housing allowances can help twice as many households as production programs can.

46. Stephen Mayo and others, "Draft Report on Housing Allowances," pt. 2.

Comments by Edgar O. Olsen

John Kain's paper has provided much information on Experimental Housing Allowance Program research, especially through its excellent synthesis of the results of the National Bureau of Economic Research and the Urban Institute simulation models. Kain correctly concludes that Experimental Housing Allowance Program research cannot possibly provide a basis for choosing a specific set of parameters for a national program, because empirical findings alone cannot have normative implications. His paper, almost exclusively an exercise in positive economics, tries to show how the outcomes of a housing allowance program change with variations in its parameters.

My comments will be devoted primarily to what I consider the major problem with the types of housing allowances tested in the program—namely, that among similarly situated families, those in the poorest housing have the lowest participation rates. Many people have mentioned this defect but most seem to regard it as an inherent problem with demand-side subsidies. Although the defect is inherent in the types of subsidies tested in the Experimental Housing Allowance Program, it is not inherent in demand-side subsidies in general. Before dealing with this issue, I would like to (1) discuss Kain's major criticism of the supply experiment research, (2) offer an opinion on the primary shortcoming of the demand experiment research, and (3) expand on his comments on the relative merits of new construction and demand-side subsidies.

I agree that the major weakness of the supply experiment research to date is its failure to predict the situation in the absence of the experiment. Since the effect of any government program is the difference between the situation in its presence and in its absence, there is considerable merit in Kain's complaint that the Rand Corporation has yet to produce estimates of many important effects of a housing allowance program—for example, its effects on housing prices. I think that the explanation for this state of affairs is that Rand has concentrated on producing evidence that is more credible to the nontechnical people involved in the policy-making process than to housing researchers. I have no doubt that results more persuasive to researchers could have been produced at a small fraction of the cost of the supply experiment. These results could have been produced with much less data and much more modeling than has occurred. However, I doubt that they would be as persuasive to people who are not researchers. Furthermore, I think the Rand Corporation's methods are adequate to show that a plausible housing allowance program will not have a large, immediate effect on the average price of housing.[47]

I would like to comment on the theory that the supply experiment results have shown the National Bureau of Economic Research and Urban Institute simulation models to be unreliable. In my opinion, the results have shown nothing of the sort. These simulation models predicted small effects on the average price of housing, and this is consistent with the Rand Corporation's conclusions. The National Bureau of Economic Research model predicted large increases for certain types of housing and decreases for other types. To the best of my knowledge, price changes for these same types of housing have not been examined using data from the supply experiment. Furthermore, the allowance programs analyzed using the simulation models differed from the supply experiment.

Having agreed that there is a major defect in the supply experiment research, fairness prompts me to offer an opinion concerning the most important shortcoming of the demand experiment research.[48] I think that the magnitudes of some crucial estimates are seriously biased because the limited duration of the experiment has not been satisfactorily taken into account. For example, I believe that a permanent housing allowance program would have greater effects on housing consumption than were estimated by Abt Associates. This belief is based on a number of puzzling findings that could be explained by the limited duration of the experiment. Let me offer two illustrations.

Estimates by Abt Associates of the price elasticity of demand for housing are below the range of previous estimates that are reasonably reliable.[49] Suppose that a typical household in Pittsburgh would increase its housing consumption by 30 percent in response to a permanent 50 percent reduction in the price of its housing. Such a large change in housing consumption is almost always accomplished by moving, which normally involves substantial out-of-pocket and other costs. If this household is offered the price reduction for only a few years, then later it would want

47. See Barnett and Lowry, *How Housing Allowances Affect Housing Prices.*

48. I hasten to add that I believe that both defects can be overcome by use of the available data.

49. See Stephen K. Mayo, "Theory and Estimation in the Economics of Housing Demand," paper presented at meetings of the American Economic Association, Chicago, Illinois, August 1978.

to occupy a dwelling similar to the one occupied in the absence of the program. Undoubtedly, some families would move to much better housing during the period that the subsidy is available and then would move to worse housing shortly after the program ends. However, many families who would occupy much better housing in response to a permanent price change would not do so in response to a temporary price change. If the limited duration of the experiment is not considered, the estimated long-run price elasticity of demand will be biased downward.

My second illustration concerns the difference in response to the housing allowance program at the two sites. Households in Phoenix improved their housing more than Pittsburgh households. It is known that households in Phoenix move more frequently than households in Pittsburgh for reasons independent of the experiment. This, together with the limited duration of the experiment, could explain the observed difference in responsiveness. For example, if a household expected to move every year, its behavior during the first two years of the demand experiment would not have been very sensitive to the duration of the experiment. The researchers at Abt Associates are aware that this is a potential problem, and they have attempted to account for it.[50] These attempts are ingenious but not conclusive. I am confident that others will try to improve upon their work.

Kain concludes his paper with some remarks on the relative merits of new construction and housing allowance programs. I agree with these remarks and would like to elaborate on them. Budgetary cost is not a valid objection to a housing allowance program because its provisions can be changed to make it have any cost desired. A housing allowance program could be designed to have the same effects on the consumption patterns of recipients as the present collection of new construction programs, and it would cost less than these programs. However, as we designed such an allowance program, we would realize that these changes in consumption patterns are far from what we want to achieve.

Let me illustrate these general remarks with some numbers from the section 8 new construction program. This program accounts for a large proportion of the newly constructed subsidized units in the United States in the past few years. The mean rent of the section 8 new units added in fiscal year 1978 was about $400 per month. From studies of other new

---

50. See, for example, Friedman and Weinberg, "Draft Report on Housing Consumption," chap. 7.

construction programs, there is good reason to believe that these units would rent for less than $400 in the unsubsidized market.[51] For the sake of argument, assume that they would rent for $350 per month. Suppose that we offer each family that would otherwise occupy a section 8 new unit a monthly payment equal to the difference between $350 and 25 percent of its income on the condition that the family spend at least $350 on housing. Each family would choose a unit renting for about $350 per month and would have 75 percent of its income to spend on other goods. (I presume that if given an equally costly unrestricted cash grant, few of these families would choose to spend this much on housing.) Therefore, this family's consumption pattern would be the same under the housing allowance program as under the new construction program, but the cost to taxpayers would be $50 less per month.

Would we seriously consider a housing allowance plan with these provisions? I doubt it, because these changes in consumption patterns involve great inequities. In 1978 the mean rent of families just above the upper-income limits of eligibility for the section 8 program was less than $200 per month. Therefore, this housing allowance program would provide low-income families with much better housing than that typical of the poorest ineligible families. Indeed, less than 10 percent of all renters spent more than $350 per month on housing in 1978.[52] Finally, I think that almost everyone would be appalled at the suggestion that we should provide housing subsidies averaging $3,200 per year to a small fraction of eligible households and deny any help to the majority of equally poor households.[53]

I believe the major shortcoming of the housing allowance schemes that have been tried is that, among equally situated families, those in the poor-

51. See U.S. Department of Housing and Urban Development, *Housing in the Seventies* (GPO, 1974), chap. 4; David M. Barton and Edgar O. Olsen, "The Benefits and Costs of Public Housing in New York City," Discussion Paper 373-76 (Institute for Research on Poverty, University of Wisconsin, October 1976); and Stephen Mayo and others, "Draft Report on Housing Allowances," pt. 2.

52. See Bureau of the Census, *Current Housing Reports,* series H-150-76, no. 76, "General Housing Characteristics for the United States and Regions: 1976" (GPO, 1977), pt. A, p. 12. This statement makes a generous allowance for inflation in rents between late 1976 and early 1978.

53. The mean subsidy for section 8 new construction in fiscal year 1978 was about $3,800. I have subtracted from this amount the cost saving due to the elimination of the production inefficiency when housing allowances replace the new construction program.

est housing have the lowest participation rates.[54] This is highly significant when we consider the reasons for offering housing subsidies to low-income families. Presumably, we offer housing subsidies because we want at least some of these families to live in better housing than they would occupy if given equally costly unrestricted cash grants. We want to achieve this change in consumption patterns because some taxpayers care about low-income families but think that some of these families undervalue housing or because better housing for these families confers tangible benefits on others.

However, it is difficult to argue for *housing* subsidies to all low-income families. There is a great variance in the housing of families having the same income and size and facing the same set of prices. Many low-income families occupy housing meeting the standards used in housing programs. Typically, this is achieved by spending a large proportion of income on housing or, more precisely, on those attributes of housing covered by the standards. Do we want these families to occupy better housing than they would choose in response to a cash grant? The often-expressed concern about excessive rent burden suggests that we do not. Most taxpayers feel that these families spend too much of their income on housing. Therefore, we want to reduce their rent burden by providing them with special incentives to consume more goods not related to housing. If we want to provide housing subsidies only to the worst-housed low-income families, then the failure to achieve high participation rates among these families is a serious deficiency of a housing program.

Why don't households in the worst housing participate in the housing allowance programs that were tested?[55] There are two major reasons for nonparticipation: (1) participation costs and (2) weak preferences for housing or, in the case of the minimum standards approach, weak preferences for the housing characteristics in the standards.

Participation costs include the loss of self-esteem associated with accepting charity and revealing personal information and the time and money spent filling out forms and submitting to housing inspections. All participating families incur such costs. Differences in these costs partially explain differences in the participation rates of different groups. How-

54. See Goedert, *Earmarking Housing Allowances,* pp. 98–99.
55. For the sake of brevity, I will limit my discussion to the minimum standards approach, but analogous arguments apply to the other types of housing allowance programs tested.

ever, there is no reason to believe that the worst-housed families have higher participation costs than other similarly situated families.

I believe that the worst-housed families have the lowest participation rates under a minimum standards housing allowance program because the design of the program ensures that families with the weakest preferences for the housing characteristics covered by the standards receive the smallest benefits. Families with the strongest preferences for these characteristics would occupy housing meeting the standards even without the program. For these families, the standards are nonbinding constraints and the housing allowances are equivalent to equally costly unrestricted cash grants. This is also the case for some of the families whose preprogram units just failed the standards. An unrestricted cash grant would induce some of these families to upgrade their housing in ways that satisfy the standards. The housing allowance is less valuable to families that would not occupy units meeting the standards if they were given an equally costly unrestricted cash grant. The standards are binding constraints for these families, and hence they prefer the cash grant to the housing allowance. In short, if participation costs are about the same for the best- and the worst-housed families having the same income and facing the same set of prices, a greater proportion of the worst-housed families would receive negative benefits from participating and their participation rates would be lower.

I have already stated my belief that the housing allowance plans tested are preferable to any new construction program because they can produce the same consumption patterns at a much lower cost. However, I also think that they fall short of achieving our goals. It is clear that we want higher participation rates among the worst-housed families and that we want to induce these families to substantially improve their housing.

To attain these goals, I propose a housing subsidy, S, that consists of a fixed payment, G, independent of housing expenditure, R, plus a fraction, K, of housing expenditure up to some maximum amount, R^*. For housing expenditure beyond this point, the subsidy could either remain constant or decline. The formulas for these two alternative subsidies are presented in the following equations:

(4)
$$S_1 = \begin{cases} G + KR & R \leq R^* \\ G + KR^* & R > R^* \end{cases}$$

(5)
$$S_2 = \begin{cases} G + KR & R \leq R^* \\ G + KR^* - C(R - R^*) & R > R^*. \end{cases}$$

Upper-income limits and other criteria for eligibility would be established to distinguish households that we want to help from those that we are unwilling to help. To avoid a notch, the fixed payment, G, and the fraction, K, should be smaller for households with higher incomes and zero at the upper-income limit for eligibility. For example, if the upper-income limit for eligibility were $10,000, G could be $500 minus 5 percent of household income and K could be 0.80 minus 0.008 percent of household income. In this case, the fixed payment to an eligible household with an annual income of $4,000 would be $300 (= $500 − 0.05 × $4,000) per year and the government would pay 48 (= 80 − 0.008 × $4,000) percent of its housing expenditure up to the maximum rent, R^*. If R^* were $2,400 per year and the household occupied a unit renting for $1,800, then it would receive a subsidy of $1,164 (= $300 + 0.48 × $1,800). Under the first alternative, a household occupying a unit renting for $2,400 or more would receive $1,452. An eligible household with an income of $8,000 would receive a fixed payment of $100, and the government would pay 16 percent of its housing expenditure up to $2,400. Such a household would receive a subsidy of $388 if it occupied a unit renting for $1,800 and a subsidy of $484 if it occupied a unit renting for $2,400 or more.

Under the proposed programs, the worst-housed families with participation costs less than the fixed payment, G, would participate. For the worst-housed families, the programs provide a special inducement to improve their housing by lowering the price to them. For the best-housed eligible families, the programs provide a subsidy with no special inducement to improve their housing (alternative 1) or with an incentive to reduce their rent burden (alternative 2). The programs contain no housing standards to deter participation by families with the worst housing before enrollment in the program. The eligibility criteria and other program provisions could be adjusted to produce any cost desired. In particular, the proposed program could have the same cost as any of the allowance plans tested but a higher participation rate by the worst-housed families.

One disadvantage of the first proposed alternative to the housing gap form of housing allowance is that it will induce some eligible households, namely those locating units renting for less than R^*, to shop less intensively for housing.[56] In effect, some of the subsidy is used to purchase leisure. Under the second alternative, less intensive search by these house-

---

56. See Friedman and Weinberg, "Draft Report on the Demand for Rental Housing," chap. 5.

holds is offset by more intensive search by households locating units renting for more than R^*. The net effect is indeterminate.

A more important potential problem is the ease with which tenants and landlords can collude to obtain the largest possible subsidy while making the subsidy equivalent to an unrestricted cash grant in its effect on consumption patterns.[57] It must be admitted, however, that such behavior has not been detected during the Experimental Housing Allowance Program.

It might be argued that many recipients would not occupy decent, safe, and sanitary housing if there were no minimum standards. It is undoubtedly true that many would not meet the standards used in the Experimental Housing Allowance Program, but is it reasonable to believe that there is a great difference in the well-being of a family living in housing that just meets or just fails to meet these standards? Decent, safe, and sanitary are relative, not absolute, concepts. Under a minimum standards housing allowance plan, many of the worst-housed families will not participate. Under the proposed program, many of these families will participate. Isn't it better to induce some improvement in the housing of these families rather than none?

57. See the paper by Henry J. Aaron in this volume.

ANTHONY DOWNS

KATHARINE L. BRADBURY

Conference Discussion

The Brookings Conference on the Experimental Housing Allowance Program revealed several remaining questions about how housing markets work and what public policies toward housing should be. Some questions appear only in the formal remarks made by official discussants for each major paper. Those formal remarks appear in this volume after each paper, and we will not deal with them further here. But many other questions arose during conference table discussions involving dozens of participants. These participants included the authors of the papers, their formal discussants, representatives of the major Experimental Housing Allowance Program contractors (the Rand Corporation, Abt Associates, and the Urban Institute), U.S. Department of Housing and Urban Development (HUD) officials, and numerous invited guests. (A complete list of participants follows this paper.)

These questions were not confined to the details of research methods or esoteric implications of the program. Many questions dealt with the fundamental implications of the Experimental Housing Allowance Program. To help clarify what the group of housing experts at the conference agreed was and was not learned from the program, we have summarized their discussion—excluding most issues addressed in the papers and formal comments.

Statements about the issues included were made at many times during the four half-day sessions; hence they did not always form a coherent, ordered discussion. However, we have grouped them into six major topics:

(1) housing standards and their policy implications;

(2) the income elasticity of housing demand;

(3) the nature and conduct of the supply experiment;

(4) the nature and conduct of the administrative agency experiment;

(5) services furnished to potential housing allowance recipients; and
(6) adoption of housing allowances.

Most statements in the summary have not been attributed to specific individuals for several reasons. Many ideas were presented by several people in slightly different forms. The sources of other ideas were not always clearly identified. Also, we often combined the comments of several people to clarify the presentation. Hence, we have attributed comments to specific individuals only when they involved ideas set forth in the major papers or when we believed knowledge of an idea's source was vital to help the reader evaluate its merits.

Housing Standards and Their Policy Implications

A central housing goal of HUD and Congress is to improve the *quality* of the nation's housing inventory by reducing the number of substandard dwellings. Therefore, a key objective of any federally funded housing subsidy, including a housing allowance, is to raise the quality of housing occupied by the households receiving the subsidy. To achieve this objective, and to measure its success, housing quality must be defined in terms of specific physical standards. However, experience gained in this program indicates that defining appropriate housing standards involves several unexpected and frustrating complications.

The Trade-off between Standards and Participation

Probably the most important complication is an apparent trade-off between the stringency of housing standards and the degree of participation in the housing allowance program. The higher the quality of housing required to qualify for subsidy payments, the lower the program participation by those living in low-quality housing. Yet occupants of low-quality housing are presumably one of the primary targets of housing subsidies with income limits, such as the housing allowance.

The evidence concerning this trade-off was clearest in the demand experiment, which involved only renter households. Some households were offered allowances without being required to live in housing of any particular quality. Very high percentages of these households accepted allowance payments. In essence, they were receiving cash income supplements in no way constrained by housing requirements. Other households were offered allowances only if they occupied housing meeting certain minimum quality standards. Much lower percentages of these households accepted such allowances. Moreover, the households least likely to accept allowances were those initially living in the lowest-quality housing units. Thus, in Pittsburgh, after two years of the program, 78 percent of households offered unconstrained cash assistance were receiving aid, whereas only 30 percent of those required to meet housing quality standards were receiving aid. In Phoenix, these percentages were 90 percent and 45 percent, respectively.[1]

It is not hard to understand why this occurred. Households not required to occupy any particular quality of housing could qualify for assistance without improving their housing or moving. In contrast, households required to occupy housing meeting certain quality standards had to upgrade their existing units or move to other ones if they initially occupied substandard units. Upgrading or moving both involve substantial costs. It was often difficult for tenants of substandard units to persuade the owners to improve the units to meet the required standards. This difficulty was probably greatest for households living in the lowest-quality units—the owners of such units would have had to incur major expenses to meet the required standards. Moving to units that met the housing standards was disruptive and often costly. Households that moved not only had to pay moving costs, but they also typically faced higher rents in their new quarters. The potential allowance payment might cover some of, all of, or more than these added costs.

This trade-off between required housing quality and program participation creates a dilemma for officials trying to design an effective housing allowance program. Insistence that all allowance recipients must occupy housing meeting high quality standards has the positive effect of pressuring potential recipients living in low-quality housing to improve their units. But such requirements also drastically reduce the percentage of households willing to participate in the program. On the other hand, lower quality standards encourage greater participation by these households but do not put much pressure on participants to upgrade their housing. The main effect of this type of housing allowance is to raise the incomes of the participants without greatly improving their housing or removing many "substandard" units from the inventory.

1. Stephen D. Kennedy and Jean MacMillan, "Draft Report on Participation Under Alternative Housing Allowance Programs: Evidence from the Housing Allowance Demand Experiment" (Cambridge, Mass.: Abt Associates, October 1979), p. 19.

Another aspect of this trade-off concerns whether the pressure to upgrade is strong under any circumstance. In the supply experiment, the housing initially occupied by most participating households was in relatively good condition. This was *not* true in the demand experiment. In fact, 43 percent of the units initially occupied by all enrolled households in Pittsburgh and Phoenix were classified as "clearly inadequate."[2] Nevertheless, comparisons in the demand experiment of households receiving unconstrained allowances and households subject to minimum standards also suggest that requiring recipients to meet quality standards did not substantially improve their housing. Although recipients subject to minimum standards were more likely to meet those standards than were unconstrained households, there was no significant difference in their probability of living in minimally adequate or clearly inadequate housing.[3] In many cases, recipients made minor changes that met requirements but did not significantly upgrade the overall nature of their dwellings. It is hard to design requirements that have that general effect of improving quality without making them too burdensome or loading them with items that seem trivial. These findings should be kept in mind when comparing a housing allowance program that contains quality requirements with either a housing allowance program without such requirements or a direct income maintenance program.

This dilemma raised several issues at the conference. The first was, would this same trade-off be as severe in a universal housing allowance program as in the small-scale demand experiment? The answer depends in part on landlords' views about that experiment. But all discussions of their views, such as those that follow, are purely speculative, since no landlords were interviewed in the demand experiment. Given the design of that experiment, only a few households in the entire metropolitan area were eligible to receive housing allowances. Moreover, the program was scheduled to last for only three years. Knowing these facts, landlords of substandard units might be reluctant to invest in major repairs, since other tenants might not be able to afford the resulting higher rents. Also, those

2. David W. Budding, "Draft Report on Housing Deprivation Among Enrollees in the Housing Allowance Demand Experiment" (Abt, November 1978), p. 26. Why the data from the two experiments concerning the initial quality of housing occupied by poor households should be so divergent is not yet clear. However, whether the poor now live in "not bad" or "very bad" housing is a crucial issue with important policy implications. Hence further research should be done on this subject.

3. See table 12 of the paper by Hanushek and Quigley in this volume.

landlords could easily find other relatively poor renters willing to occupy substandard units because housing assistance was not available to most renters.

But in a universal housing allowance program of long duration, all low-income renters would be eligible for assistance over longer periods. Hence more landlords would presumably be willing to invest in repairing substandard units because they would recognize that most households would be able to pay the resulting higher rents. And they would also fear that fewer households would be willing to continue occupying substandard units when all could receive enough assistance to afford better housing. Thus, some conference participants argued that making a housing allowance program universal would greatly reduce the dilemma posed by this trade-off.

The overall quality of the housing inventory in each community also affects this basic trade-off. The higher the quality, the smaller the initial percentage of households that live in units not meeting housing standards, which means that fewer households would have to alter their initial housing to receive allowance payments. Thus, the trade-off between imposition of housing standards and program participation would not be nearly as important in communities with high-quality housing inventories as in those with low-quality housing inventories. But this does not alter the ironic result that the greater the need for physical improvement in a community's housing inventory, the less its residents are likely to participate in a housing allowance program that includes physical standards.

One interpretation of this dilemma is that participation is directly proportional to the expected increase in each household's *nonhousing* income from the allowance program. If more of the allowance payment were needed to improve current housing, then less would be left over for nonhousing needs, decreasing a household's incentive to participate.

Relationships between Poor-Quality Housing and Household Income

A second related issue was whether any systematic relationships existed between three groups of households: (1) those occupying the poorest-quality housing as measured by program standards, (2) those with the lowest incomes, and (3) those most in need of housing assistance. The major contractors for both the demand and supply experiments stated that the poorest-quality housing units were not always occupied by the poorest households. Many very poor households occupied housing units of good quality, whereas many occupants of very low quality housing units were not poor. Hence targeting aid on households in the poorest-quality housing units is not the same as focusing aid on the poorest households, and vice versa.

Some conference participants even argued that the households in the poorest-quality units simply had low preferences for good housing. After all, taste is certainly one determinant, though hardly the only one, of the quality of housing occupied by any household. These participants asked why public policy should be concerned with the housing consumption of these households. Carrying this argument a step further, a few conference participants suggested that nonparticipation resulting from requiring households to live in higher-quality housing should be regarded as a virtue, not a drawback. Such nonparticipation greatly lowers total program costs. It also avoids paying subsidies to households who live in low-quality housing and do not place much value on occupying higher-quality housing, since they are unwilling to expend much effort to improve their units or move to better ones.

However, most conference participants rejected this view. They pointed out that most very poor households spend high proportions of their incomes on housing. Such behavior is not consistent with a low preference for higher-quality housing. Moreover, many poor households are victims of various types of discrimination that push them into the poorest-quality housing units. These conference participants regarded as a distinct disadvantage the program's apparent failure to focus assistance on households in the poorest-quality units or to induce major improvements in those units. Why should any such assistance program be considered a housing program at all? It is mainly an income-support program that helps households that already occupy higher-quality units, or could occupy such units without much effort (except for those who move, and the percentage of allowance recipients moving was not much larger than the percentage of nonrecipients moving).

Did the Program Really Test Different Housing Standards?

Still another aspect of this dispute concerned the degree to which different housing standards had actually been tested in the Experimental Housing Allowance Program. Some critics of the program's design said it had not contained enough variations in required housing quality standards to test the true sensitivity of program participation to marginal shifts in those standards. They claimed that only one housing quality standard was tested in the entire supply experiment, and only one other slightly more stringent standard was used in the demand experiment. Moreover, the effects of these two standards are difficult to compare because so many other variables differ between the two experiments. If several different levels of housing quality had been required, rather than two similar ones, much more might have been learned about the relationships between quality standards and participation.

However, other conference participants vehemently denied this contention, advancing two main counterarguments. First, since one group of households in the demand experiment had been given allowances without having to meet *any* housing quality standards, the extreme of "zero quality standards" had also been tested. The program thus produced data on the relationship between housing quality standards and participation for three different levels of standards, including the extremes of zero quality and relatively high quality. Therefore, some participants felt it would be wrong to say that this relationship was inadequately tested. The results of these tests clearly showed the great sensitivity of participation to the use of required housing quality standards.

Second, it is hard to develop reasonable housing quality standards other than those used in the Experimental Housing Allowance Program. The standards employed in both the demand and supply experiments were based on a model national housing code—the American Public Health Association–Public Health Service Recommended Housing Maintenance and Occupancy Ordinance. The program designers believed that these standards represented the most feasible set of requirements that could be imposed on housing units in any large-scale program. These codes called for housing units to meet many different interior and exterior requirements to qualify as standard-quality housing. The requirements varied greatly along several dimensions of stringency.

One such dimension is the relative ease of correcting a substandard condition. For example, it was both easy and inexpensive to remove the substandard classification resulting from the absence or poor condition of a stairway handrail. But it was both difficult and expensive to remove the substandard classification resulting from having windows smaller than the required minimum size.

Some standards also involved varying degrees of hazard to the occupants. For instance, violation of the requirement for sound, weight-bearing walls is much more serious when the whole structure is sagging and in danger of collapse than when the walls are sturdy but contain a few patches of falling plaster. Yet both violations would disqualify a housing unit, according to program standards.

Some conference participants criticized program standards for being too trivial and suggested that more stringent standards should have been used. This attack often focused on the surprisingly small average expenditure in the supply experiment necessary to qualify initially substandard units. The cost was less than $50 in the first year in both the Green Bay, Wisconsin, and South Bend, Indiana, areas.[4] Should the program designers have imposed even more detailed requirements on housing units than those currently criticized for seeming trivial? Program designers were already troubled by having to classify housing units as substandard because they had characteristics of dubious undesirability, such as windows several square inches smaller than the required minimum size. They argued that compelling housing units to meet even more trivial requirements was both impractical and undesirable. Faced by this argument, conference participants who had called for testing more stringent standards were unable to define what they meant in practical terms.

Another suggestion made by conference participants was that relationships between housing quality standards and program participation should be investigated in more detail, using data obtained in the supply experiment. This could be done by looking at participation responses of specific subgroups in the population. These could include subgroups classified by demographic traits, by the quality of housing occupied, by incomes, or by combinations of all three. The Urban Institute has already done some studies of this type, and the supply experiment contractors said they intended to pursue this approach in the future.

Should Housing Standards Be Required?

An entirely different resolution of the dilemma discussed above would be to totally eliminate housing quality requirements from any future housing allowance programs. Some conference participants suggested that this strategy would focus future housing subsidies on the lowest-income households, who presumably need assistance most. They recognized that it would in effect convert future housing allowance programs into pure in-

4. James L. McDowell, *Housing Allowances and Housing Improvement: Early Findings*, Rand/N-1198-HUD (Santa Monica: Rand Corp., September 1979), p. 37. The small average expenditure partially reflects (1) the lower likelihood of performing repairs to qualify for the program when such repairs are expensive and (2) exclusion of the value of do-it-yourself labor.

come maintenance programs. The advantages and disadvantages of this approach are discussed in the last section of this paper. However, many conference participants, particularly HUD officials, did not favor advocating an ostensibly housing-oriented program for reasons unrelated to housing. They believed that HUD-operated programs should help achieve HUD's major goal of improving the quality of the housing inventory. Hence they were unhappy with a strategy that espoused that goal rhetorically but in fact served an entirely different goal—pure redistribution of income to the poor. These participants favored income redistribution, but they also believed that any help provided by HUD should pressure the poor to spend more on improving their housing than they would if simply given more income.

This leads into the final argument concerning housing standards: should society try to impose housing quality standards on *anyone,* in the absence of a clearly established relationship between such standards and the quality of human life? Just how important is it to influence people to occupy high-quality housing rather than low-quality housing when it is so difficult to distinguish between the two? Even expert, highly trained housing inspectors did not agree on how to classify specific housing units in a few cases included in a sample classified by multiple observers. Even more important, there is almost no evidence that moving to high-quality housing units (as defined by traditional standards) improves the health, incomes, welfare, or happiness of households formerly living in low-quality or substandard units. So why should society try to force people to reside in the former housing instead of the latter, especially when programs created to do this are administratively more expensive per dollar of aid than those that only raise household incomes? Moreover, no matter what quality standards are used, there will always be many cases in which specific housing units are disqualified for what appear to be trivial reasons, such as having windows that are several square inches too small. Should society deny financial aid to poor people for such reasons?

As one person pointed out, most of the housing quality standards used in the Experimental Housing Allowance Program involved *interior* housing characteristics. But one of the two basic social rationales for requiring housing to meet any standards involves *exterior* characteristics. That rationale rests on the undesirable neighborhood effects created by housing units that are dilapidated, unpainted, or otherwise undesirable in appearance. Such units make living in their immediate neighborhod less desirable; hence they reduce the values of surrounding properties. These negative externalities justify governmental intervention to create and enforce minimum standards for the exterior appearance of housing units. But interior housing deficiencies are invisible to outsiders, and they do not create any such negative neighborhood effects. Hence public regulations mandating interior quality standards cannot be justified through this line of reasoning.

True, the second rationale for public enforcement of housing quality standards is to protect occupants from hazardous conditions, particularly those they cannot detect themselves. This rationale underlies many of the interior quality standards built into existing housing and building codes, including the standards used in the Experimental Housing Allowance Program. But some of those interior standards go far beyond the requirements of protecting people from serious hazards. Few of these standards are based on scientific analysis of the risks arising from specific deficiencies. Moreover, most consumers should be able to fend for themselves in our highly educated society; hence we should minimize the requirements imposed by governments ostensibly to protect consumers. In reality, many such requirements harm the very persons they are supposed to help by unnecessarily raising their housing costs or denying them access to financial assistance, as in the Experimental Housing Allowance Program.

Many conference participants preferred simply giving poor households money and letting them decide how to spend it, rather than requiring them to use some of it to improve their housing. Unrestricted consumer sovereignty among aid recipients is favored by most U.S. economists, and a high proportion of conference participants were economists. The most widely accepted argument against this conclusion among conference participants was not that society should require poor people to improve their housing, but that more political support could be gained for transferring resources to the poor through the *appearance* of providing housing aid than in other, more straightforward ways. This issue is discussed in the last section of this paper.

The Income Elasticity of Housing Demand

One of the program's goals was to obtain better estimates of certain basic behavioral relationships concerning housing. Two such relationships were the *income elasticity* and the *price elasticity* of housing demand. The income elasticity is a measure of how much a change in household income affects spending on housing. Specifically, it is the percentage change in housing expenditures brought about by a 1 percent increase in household income. Thus, if we observe a 10 percent rise in household income and households are found to have increased the amount they spend on housing by 4 percent, the income elasticity of housing demand is $0.04 \div 0.10 = 0.4$. Conversely, if we know the income elasticity is 0.4, we can predict that a 5 percent rise in household income will result in a 2 percent ($= 0.4 \times 0.05$) increase in spending on housing.

The price elasticity of housing expenditure is defined analogously as the percentage change in spending on housing brought about by a 1 percent increase in housing prices. A more commonly used concept is the price elasticity of housing demand, which measures the percentage change in the quantity of housing services demanded as a result of a 1 percent increase in housing prices. The price elasticity of expenditures is equal to the price elasticity of demand plus unity. For example, if a household did not move or otherwise change its housing consumption when the price of housing increased by 5 percent, its housing expenditures would rise by 5 percent. Thus quantity consumed does not change (the price elasticity of demand is zero), but expenditures must rise in proportion to the price increase (price elasticity of expenditures is equal to 1.0). Similarly, if one estimates the price elasticity of demand to be -0.3, one can predict that a 10 percent increase in housing prices will result in a 3 percent drop in housing demand and a 7 percent increase in expenditures on housing.

Elasticity estimates are extremely important in housing market analysis because they can be used to predict household responses to changes in incomes and housing prices. As one conference participant put it, reliable estimates would be "portable"—that is, they could be used to predict how households would react to many programs or shocks affecting housing markets, in addition to the specific policies tested in the Experimental Housing Allowance Program.

Very little evidence on the price elasticity of housing demand had been collected before the Experimental Housing Allowance Program. The estimates derived from demand experiment analyses are between -0.2 and -0.6, in contrast to most economists' a priori expectation of -1.0.[5] These results represent a sizable addition to knowledge and are largely unchallenged.

In contrast, there was a great deal of prior economic literature on the

5. See the paper by Hanushek and Quigley in this volume.

income elasticity of housing demand, and the demand experiment estimates are generally much lower than those reported previously. As a result, the summary of income elasticity results provided by Hanushek and Quigley and the new estimates by Mills and Sullivan based on supply experiment data provoked much discussion at the conference.

Ten years ago, before experimental data were available, economists generally believed that the permanent income elasticity of housing demand was close to unity—that is, an increase in permanent income of any given percentage would lead to an equal percentage increase in housing expenditures. Empirical investigations lent support to this belief. More recently, careful examinations of the biases inherent in previous analyses based on household cross-sectional data or aggregate time series relationships suggested that these estimates might be too high.[6] When data from the income maintenance experiments as well as the housing allowance experiments were analyzed, using different definitions and specifications, they too provided lower estimates. According to Hanushek and Quigley, the experimental data implied an income elasticity of 0.2 or 0.3 for renters and a similar income elasticity for owners. Using data from the supply experiment, Mills and Sullivan obtained estimates of 0.36 for renters and 0.6 for owners.[7]

There was some controversy over what causes income elasticity to vary. Do people of different income levels or different tenure classes have different income elasticities? Is the housing response to changes in different components of total income different? Some participants argued that the concept of income elasticity makes sense only when it is considered to be a constant across all types of households and all kinds of income. For example, analysts may underestimate the elasticity by separating owners and renters, since one way a household increases housing consumption as its income rises is to switch from tenancy to owner-occupancy of a larger unit. Until that switch, some renters may respond to income increases by increasing their savings (toward purchase of a house) rather than by renting a larger or higher-quality unit.

6. See, for example, A. Mitchell Polinsky, "The Demand for Housing: A Study in Specification and Grouping," *Econometrica*, vol. 45 (March 1977), pp. 447–61, and "The Demand for Housing: An Empirical Postscript," *Econometrica*, vol. 47 (March 1979), pp. 521–23; or A. Mitchell Polinsky and David T. Ellwood, "An Empirical Reconciliation of Micro and Grouped Estimates of the Demand for Housing," *The Review of Economics and Statistics*, vol. 61 (May 1979), 199–205.

7. See their paper in this volume.

Some conference participants thought the small size of the income elasticity estimates based on program data, including the analysis by Mills and Sullivan, might result from one or more identifiable downward biases. One potentially important source of bias is the limited duration of the experiment, which could have caused experimental reactions to be smaller than reactions to a permanent, universal program for two reasons. First, because it is costly to move or otherwise change housing consumption in response to the program, households may choose not to do so because program benefits will last only for a limited time.[8] Second, households generally do not adjust their housing consumption immediately to changes in income or other circumstances. Thus the market's full response to the experimental program cannot be observed within the short period for which data are available.

The issue regarding the speed of household responses raised broader questions about the dynamics and timing of household adjustments to allowances. Both the Mills and Sullivan analysis and the demand experiment analyses focused on two years of behavior. But small variations in response measured over these short periods, if extrapolated, become very large differences in long-run elasticity. These projections are critical to understanding the supply side of the market and the long-run impact of such a program. Yet a low elasticity observed in one year may mean two very different things over the long run. If the low elasticity results from a moderate response by only a few participating households while the remaining households delay their full response, then the long-term effect of the program may be a significant increase in housing consumption. But if the low one-year elasticity results from an immediate small, individual response by all participants with no deferral of action, the long-term effect will be much lower. Both studies provided some support for the former view. Mills and Sullivan investigated what fraction of households would adjust to the program each year in order to project the full-scale adjustment to a universal permanent program. They estimated about 30 percent of renter households responded in the first two years (although earlier in the paper they reported that 43 percent of renters moved during that period). In demand experiment analyses, Friedman and Weinberg obtained

8. Benefits in the administrative agency experiment were provided for only two years, with transition to other housing programs at the end. The demand experiment lasted for three years, with a similar promise of transition. The supply experiment pays benefits to recipients for ten years.

slightly higher estimates of the income elasticity when they accounted for the dynamics of adjustment behavior than when they did not.[9]

Furthermore, other participants pointed out that within the experimental period, many households' incomes changed enough to alter their eligibility for the program. For these households, the full response was observed within the experimental period, but not only during the years in which they received benefits. Although households received no benefits in some years, their housing consumption would be protected by potential program income in lean years. This was also true for households not even entering the program during the experimental period. For this reason, it is inappropriate to analyze only the responses of recipients in judging the total effects of the program.

All three of these duration issues suggest that use of experimental data on recipients will result in underestimates of the effect of a permanent universal program. However, the demand experiment analysts from Abt Associates pointed out that their estimates were largely derived from cross-sectional analysis of patterns of housing consumption *at enrollment*. Similarly, John Mulford of Rand examined marketwide patterns in the supply sites.[10] Neither of these approaches is tainted by the duration of the experiment or other experimental factors.

A potential source of upward bias was pointed out by Yinger in his comments on the Hanushek-Quigley paper: if landlords have market power, they may raise prices when a subsidy is made available to their tenants, even if they do not improve the quality of the housing unit. In this case, the expenditure change resulting from the program does not reflect a desire by the tenant to consume more housing but rather a change in the price at which housing is available. However, when analysts attempt to estimate the responsiveness of tenant demand to a change in program income, they cannot exclude the effects of the price change; hence they overestimate the income elasticity of demand.

Another source of bias is omission of a variable measuring the price of housing services from the estimated demand equation. The direction of this bias is unknown a priori; it depends on the correlation of price with the variables of interest included in the equation—income or the price

9. See Joseph Friedman and Daniel Weinberg, "Draft Report on the Demand for Rental Housing: Evidence from a Percent of Rent Housing Allowance" (Abt, September 1978).

10. John E. Mulford, *Income Elasticity of Housing Demand*, R-2449-HUD (Rand Corp., July 1979).

subsidy rate. However, the contractors analyzing the demand experiment data have attempted to account for any correlation between explanatory variables and price in their estimating equations.

Regarding the Mills and Sullivan analysis, there was considerable concern about the built-in relationship between allowance income and two other variables in the estimating equations—nonallowance income and family size. The relationship derives from the benefit formula that defines allowance income as a nonlinear function of adjusted income and family size. Although the correlation was not strong enough to make estimation impossible, some conference participants were not confident that the estimating procedure could properly sort out the independent relationships.

Other conference participants believed that the household sample used by Mills and Sullivan to obtain elasticity estimates was not representative of all eligible households. Either of two selection principles they used could yield a sample *more* responsive to housing aid than the general eligible population. First, their sample contained only recipient households—those eligibles who had chosen to participate in the supply experiment. This selection assumes that the required quality standards did not discourage the participation of a disproportionately high fraction of households less likely to spend increased income on housing. Second, among recipients, Mills and Sullivan estimated the response to allowance income using only those households that moved or spent more than a certain amount on repairs. Again, this selection seemed likely to introduce a bias by omitting a disproportionately high fraction of households that did not want to use the added income for improving their housing.

This latter selection, which is equivalent to estimating an income elasticity *separately* for allowance and nonallowance income, drew criticism on other grounds as well. Demand experiment analyses tested for such differences and failed to find any. It was argued that the procedure used by Mills and Sullivan statistically forced *any* difference between movers or those making substantial repairs and other households to appear through the estimated coefficient on the allowance income variable. But the correct estimate would reflect *only* the mover group's revealed response to allowance income, isolated from all other factors.

A vote was taken at the conference to see if there was a consensus on the size of the income elasticity of housing demand. However, the results are not reported here because there was less consensus on that issue than on the belief that such parameters should not be determined by vote, particularly in light of the biases brought to the vote by conference participants. Nevertheless, it is clear that at the Conference the numerical center of the debate about the true value of the income elasticity of housing demand shifted from near unity to a point below 0.5.

The Supply Experiment

Most conference participants agreed that the supply experiment had produced two surprising results. One was the low degree of participation by eligible households in the program. As in the demand experiment, about 60 percent of the households that might have received payments failed to do so. Many simply did not enroll. Others enrolled but were initially living in substandard units and failed to change to standard-quality units by either upgrading or moving. The second surprising result was the almost complete lack of market effects from metropolitan-area-wide application of a housing allowance. Neither rents nor housing prices rose significantly. There was not much improvement in the physical quality of the housing inventory nor much increase in new housing construction in either area.

These results provoked several controversies at the conference. Some are dealt with in the papers and comments, but many were also subjects of lively discussions around the conference table. These are summarized below.

One participant, John Kain, asserted that these seemingly unexpected results would not have been surprising to him or to "most economists" if they had known beforehand that the particular allowance program tested in the supply experiment would induce virtually no increase in housing expenditures. He readily admitted one error made in his own simulation model and in other models that had analyzed housing allowances before the Experimental Housing Allowance Program: these models all overestimated participation. However, he also argued that use of an income gap method of calculating the allowance payment, plus what he considered not very stringent requirements for defining standard housing, virtually ensured that nearly all the allowance payments would be spent for nonhousing goods and services. These factors created little incentive for allowance recipients to devote their added purchasing power to improving their housing. All households already living in standard-quality units could receive allowances without spending any more money on housing. Moreover, because the requirements used to define standard-quality housing were not very stringent, a significant percentage of all low-income households were living in such units at the outset. Many who were not could make their units standard with only small improvements. Even a marketwide housing allowance defined in this manner would not produce any large stimulus to housing demand, and therefore would not produce any market effects. This outcome aggravated the reduced market impact caused by unexpectedly low participation rates.

According to Kain, this result could have been anticipated, and in fact was, by almost any economist who knew in advance how the supply experiment had been designed. Kain proposed two alternatives to the existing supply experiment. The first was an earmarked housing allowance that would generate increased housing expenditures. Larger subsidies would offset the drop in participation rates induced by the earmarking effect, so this form of housing allowance would create a larger demand shock on the market than the form tested in the supply experiment. The second alternative was to eliminate the supply experiment entirely. Some of the money thus saved could have been used to test a richer and more varied set of housing allowance forms in the demand experiment.

Kain's reasoning was disputed by many conference participants. Most present believed that nearly all economists who had written about housing allowances before the Experimental Housing Allowance Program—including Kain and many others present at the conference—had predicted substantial price increases in at least some parts of the housing market. Frank de Leeuw, one of the authors of the other major model (the Urban Institute housing model) used to simulate housing allowances before the experiments, stated that his model had incorrectly predicted substantial price increases in one of the two supply experiment cities as a result of marketwide application of a housing allowance. His model did so primarily because it overestimated participation in the program as compared with the program's actual results. Hence he concurred with representatives of the Rand Corporation that the supply experiment produced unexpected results that added greatly to our knowledge.

There was also widespread agreement that no matter what economists' simulation models forecast in advance, the legislators who would have to approve or disapprove of any allowance program would never accept the validity of such purely theoretical results. Since they want evidence based on actual experience in the field, it was worthwhile to conduct something like a full-scale supply experiment to produce such evidence.

These responses did not alter Kain's insistence that he and other economists knew all along that the supply experiment as conducted would produce no significant market effects. He claimed that his model and other models had forecast big price increases partly because, for some simulations, they assumed different forms of housing allowance from that used in the supply experiment. The models assumed participating households either had to spend a certain dollar amount on rent or receive subsidies equaling certain percentages of their rents. If the supply experiment had used those forms of housing allowance, said Kain, there would have been a much larger increase in total housing demand from both higher participation and greater spending on housing per participating household. Therefore, some significant market effects might have appeared.

He then advanced another controversial conclusion: the supply experiment had not really tested what would happen if a housing allowance requiring heavy housing spending per recipient household were put into effect across an entire market. Since the form of allowance used in the supply experiment did not produce much demand shock, no one really knows what some other form that would create such a shock would do to market conditions. Therefore, the supply experiment does not provide much information about the likely effects of a strong universal housing allowance program on housing prices and rents.

Again, Kain's assertions produced spirited dissent. One Rand staff member stated that the form of housing allowance used in the supply experiment had in fact increased demand notably, by about 11 percent at each site. However, subsequent clarification revealed this figure applied only to standard-quality rental units. The marketwide increase in housing expenditures by all renters was only about 1.2 percent, not a very large demand shock. Nevertheless, this person believed the absence of market effects was caused by two other factors not anticipated by any previous simulation models. One was that the demand shock occurred gradually as the program was introduced and expanded, not all at once. The other was that the supply side of the market was sufficiently elastic to absorb that gradual increase in demand through changes in vacancy rates, rehabilitation, and some expansion of the total supply—without any significant rise in prices or rents. Thus, the supply experiment taught us unexpected things about how housing markets work, and these lessons are highly relevant to deciding whether to adopt such an instrument nationally.

Another reply to Kain's attack on the form of allowance used in the supply experiment involved denial that the kind of allowance he thought should be tested could ever be used in practice. Both Henry Aaron and HUD's representatives claimed that Congress would never pass a percent of rent form of allowance because it was too susceptible to collusive fraud by tenants and landlords. Landlords could agree to raise tenants' rents without improving their housing substantially, which would increase their own incomes and enable tenants to collect larger allowance payments. Even if such fraud were not widespread, the possibility of at least a few horrible examples would make such an approach politically unpalatable. Neither Kain nor others who agreed with him that another form of allowance should have been tested in the supply experiment were able to suggest alternative forms not subject to the same political drawbacks.

Moreover, the forms they advocated might have increased spending on housing but would not necessarily have improved housing quality. Instead, such programs might have induced landlords to raise rents without investing in any significant physical upgrading. More stringent physical standards would not solve this problem either. As discussed in our section on housing quality standards, it is hard to conceive of a reasonable housing allowance program with more stringent physical standards than were used in the experiments. Even if more stringent standards were possible, the resulting lower participation in the program would offset to some degree any added overall market effects caused by tougher standards. A final defense of the form of housing allowance used in the supply experiment was the insistence by Rand staff that it was the form that seemed at the time most likely to be incorporated into a nationwide program.

Some conference participants argued that none of the supply experiment's findings regarding invididual household behavior were scientifically valid. This was true because control groups had not been used. Hence it was impossible to know which outcomes resulted from housing allowances and which were caused by other factors. The Rand Corporation's representatives agreed that there were no control groups but pointed out that control groups cannot be used in a marketwide test that must enroll every eligible household willing to participate. They argued that this inherent limitation of any marketwide experiment should not imply that nothing useful could be learned from such a test. On the contrary, many useful things had been learned about household behavior despite the absence of control groups, and those things should certainly not be ignored or overlooked for that reason.

Rand personnel further pointed out that the supply experiment was not originally designed to study individual household behavior but to measure overall market impacts. Only after implementation of this initial, limited design had begun did the emphasis shift to analyzing individual household behavior as well. That shift occurred primarily because initial market effects were so small that there appeared to be less value in studying them than had originally been supposed. But this change in emphasis occurred so late in the supply experiment that the researchers' ability to track and analyze individual household decisions and behavior was then limited by data collection programs initially designed for different purposes.

A final criticism of the supply experiment was its confinement to only two sites—both relatively small metropolitan areas that some people regarded as atypical of American urban areas. Proponents of this view thought that many more sites should have been used. More sites would have increased the scientific validity of the findings (assuming enough sites were used) by allowing comparisons of more combinations of background variables. It might also have allowed using control sites to compare with the experimental sites, using entire markets as individual observations. Moreover, use of more sites would have enhanced the political credibility of the results.

Defenders of the supply experiment answered this attack with three points. First, use of a market saturation approach, which was essential to measure market effects, was too expensive to be tried in more sites or in sites much larger than the two chosen. Second, the sites selected had been chosen through a careful process designed to achieve as much variation along key dimensions as was possible in only two sites. Thus, the South Bend, Indiana, area had a relatively loose housing market, slow overall population growth, and a high proportion of minority group citizens. In contrast, the Green Bay, Wisconsin, area had a tight housing market, rapid overall growth, and a low proportion of minority group citizens. Hence these two areas were indeed representative of conditions found in many other U.S. metropolitan areas. This fact allowed analysts to estimate the likely range of variation but not to attribute different responses to specific local characteristics. Third, achievement of greater geographic dispersion and diversity than was possible in two sites was a goal of *all three* housing allowance experiments considered as a whole. Thus, twelve different cities were represented in the demand, supply, and administrative agency experiments, although no behavioral data were obtained from the last experiment. Moreover, these cities were picked because they were located in all the major regions of the country. Therefore, the Experimental Housing Allowance Program had been sensitive to the need to achieve political acceptance through geographic diversity but could not do so within the supply experiment alone because that would have been too costly.

At the end of the conference, opinion was divided on whether or not the supply experiment had been properly designed. Some participants thought more varieties of allowance forms should have been tested, although they had difficulty specifying just what other forms could have been used in practice. Others thought the demand experiment should have been conducted first, and on a much larger scale, because its findings might have led to abandoning the supply experiment and saving a lot of money. This view ignores the initial desire of HUD and Congress to conduct a marketwide test as well as to study individual household behavior. A third group thought the supply experiment had been as well designed as possible at the time, given what was known about housing markets. And a majority agreed that the supply experiment had produced both unexpected and significant findings relevant to future housing policy decisions.

The Administrative Agency Experiment

The key controversies concerning the administrative agency experiment are presented in the major paper on that subject by Williams and Kershaw and the comments by Porter. However, since this subject was also discussed at length during the conference, a brief summary has been included here.

The first issue was whether the administrative agency experiment should have been based on carefully controlled variations of the elements to be tested or on the natural variation approach actually followed. Kershaw and Williams argued that permitting each agency to administer the program in whatever way it wanted precluded deriving scientifically valid results. Variations in outcomes could not be attributed to variations in only one key administrative or program element, since there were many other differences in the ways sites conducted their programs. Hence it was impossible to isolate the impacts of particular methods, as could have been done if a controlled variation approach had been used.

This argument evoked comments from several conference participants. Some HUD officials argued there was variation concerning the *types of agencies* used, just as there would be in a national housing allowance program. The designers chose two local housing agencies, two state housing and community development agencies, two general purpose county and metropolitan governments, and two welfare agencies to conduct the administrative agency experiment. Moreover, when the experiment was designed, there was little consensus on what specific variations in administrative methods should be tested. Hence HUD felt that more would be learned by observing what agencies did in the field than by imposing a priori conceptions on them.

But the most severe counterattack against controlled variation came from some HUD officials who said it is impossible to get local agencies to behave the way you want them to under any circumstances. Experience shows they ignore many legally binding HUD instructions and regulations, including those given as part of experiments. The belief that anyone could get them to engage in precisely controlled variations in behavior is an academic fantasy. This contention reinforced the necessity of using some type of case study approach.

However, this issue also called into question the need for a separate administrative agency experiment. If no predictable relationships between program specifications and administrative agency behavior could be expected, why carefully choose several different types of agencies to carry out housing allowances? Those who had made this observation about agency behavior gave three answers to this question. First, it was by no means certain that any of these types of agencies would be able to administer such a program at all. There was concern that the social service tradition of these housing agencies would make it impossible for them to implement a cash-oriented allowance program. The fact that all eight agencies did operate the program effectively provided useful new knowledge. In addition, observing how they went about it, what problems they encountered, and how they solved them would provide guidance to other agencies entrusted with similar responsibilities in the future. Also, implementation in a natural setting provided credible cost estimates for possible national implementation later.

A second major criticism of the administrative agency experiment was that it could have been incorporated into the supply experiment—which would have saved a great deal of money. If different participants in the supply experiment were handled through controlled variations in administrative methods, no separate administrative agency experiment would have been necessary.

This contention was denied by those who believed it would have been politically impractical to treat households differently in an open-ended marketwide program. Households receiving different treatment would have compared their experiences, and the resulting outcries would probably have reduced the acceptance of the program among consumers and local politicians. This could have adversely influenced participation. Moreover, incorporating the administrative agency experiment into the supply experiment would have precluded testing the ability of different types of local agencies to conduct a housing allowance program. Yet that key objective of the administrative agency experiment was actually achieved.

A final criticism of the administrative agency experiment was its failure to describe a model agency and how it ought to carry out a housing allowance. Such a prototype description was called for in the initial work program but was never produced. Two responses were made to this criticism. One was that local conditions varied so greatly that no single prototype would have been applicable to even a majority of places where a housing allowance might be carried out. The other response was that the quality of records kept by the agencies conducting this experiment was so variable and often so poor that there was not enough basis for constructing an idealized model agency. This point reinforced the difficulty of getting agencies in the field to conform to any set of prescribed procedures that would be required to achieve true controlled variations. Even so, it was argued, there could have been more thorough reporting of findings and a better explanation of how they might relate to future housing allowance programs.

What Services Should Be Furnished to Potential Allowance Recipients?

As noted earlier, requiring housing allowance recipients to occupy units that meet certain minimum standards reduces participation in the program. One possible reason is that low-income households that initially occupy substandard units may have difficulty either in persuading their landlords to improve those units or in moving to standard units. Perhaps providing such households with various services related to housing, in addition to allowance payments, might help more of them participate in the program. This could be done without eliminating one of the major advantages a housing allowance program has over other direct housing subsidies: the empowerment of consumers to pursue their own interests in the marketplace. In fact, these services might increase the effectiveness of at least some such consumer sovereignty.

This hypothesis was advanced by some conference participants in discussions of the administrative agency experiment. Since other participants disputed the usefulness of at least some of these services, this was one of the controversial issues that emerged from the conference.

Advocates of providing services had several types in mind. One was extensive outreach activities advertising the availability of allowance payments, with special emphasis on informing households that might not otherwise be aware of the program (such as the elderly and very low income groups). Such outreach activities, including heavy media advertising and many staff presentations to local groups, were used extensively in the supply experiment. Outreach was mainly responsible for the fact that within one year after such publicity began, 80 percent of the household heads in the Green Bay area and 87 percent of those in the South Bend area had at least heard of the Experimental Housing Allowance Program.[11] The analysts of the administrative agency experiment also found that intensive outreach activity produced applications. In addition, the kind of outreach affected the type of people who applied. Hence there was little dispute among conference participants that a significant investment of administrative funds in outreach activities was desirable in any large-scale housing allowance program.

Some people also advocated services to enrollees to help them become recipients. These services included (1) assistance in looking for standard-quality housing in the community, (2) counseling on how to make repairs on substandard units to qualify them for inclusion in the program, (3) advice on how to obtain financing for rehabilitation of such units, and (4) general financial and budgetary counseling.

Advocates of such services were accused of unrealistic thinking by several conference participants who had operated the supply experiment. These critics argued that most eligible households would not accept or use such services, even if offered at no cost. When free instruction sessions were provided to potential allowance recipients in the supply sites and administrative agency sites, very few people attended. This was true of lectures concerning how to repair housing, how to search for better

---

11. Phyllis L. Ellickson and David E. Kanouse, *Public Perceptions of Housing Allowances: The First Two Years,* Rand/WN-9817-HUD (Rand Corp., January 1978), p. 67.

units, and how to obtain financing. Sessions on program information preceded the mandatory enrollment interview at one site, so attendance was high. Other than that, only one such service—distribution of lists of available local housing units compiled from newspaper advertisements—was popular. Whether or not the lists affected housing choices is unknown. Therefore, many present argued that providing most of these kinds of services wasted time and money.

Three positions between the extremes of providing many services or none emerged from the discussion. One participant thought that such services should not be made generally available but should be focused on categories of eligible households with the lowest participation rates. Another participant felt that most potential allowance recipients could fend for themselves without such services but that some small fraction had such low levels of experience, competence, energy, or skill that they needed help in coping with local housing market conditions. He based this conclusion on direct observation of consumer behavior in the administrative offices of the supply experiment and on conversations with staff personnel there. However, he did not believe providing such services would noticeably raise participation rates in the program. A third participant said many potential recipients appreciated receiving help in performing specific steps in the program with which they were having difficulties. Hence it would be desirable to provide some "on demand" services in response to requests, rather than furnishing predesignated services that the program administrators believed in advance would be useful. In fact, the administrative agency experiment analysts found that ad hoc services were especially helpful in tight housing markets.

One other viewpoint was that provision of such services might be combined with a housing allowance that did not impose quality standards. The person espousing this possibility thought these services might persuade quite a few allowance recipients to spend significant fractions of their payments on improving their housing, even though they would not have to do so. However, this belief did not receive widespread support among other conference participants.

Should Society Adopt Housing Allowances Rather Than Alternative Forms of Assistance?

This fundamental question is analyzed at length in Henry Aaron's paper on policy implications of the Experimental Housing Allowance Program. Because it also was a central focus of discussion at the conference, it forms the concluding issue in this chapter.

As Aaron points out, the desirability of a housing allowance depends upon the alternatives with which it is compared. If given a choice between using a certain amount of federal funding for a housing allowance or for direct income maintenance, most of the conference participants would probably have favored the latter. As many said, since most of the money spent on housing allowances is used for nonhousing purposes anyway, why not devote it to expanding current income maintenance programs? Doing so would reduce overall administrative costs and maximize the welfare of the recipients by removing constraints compelling them to spend more than they wanted on housing. There seems little point in forcing households to live in standard housing units rather than substandard ones if they really do not want to. There is no strong evidence that living in standard housing improves their health, happiness, or other aspects of their well-being. Furthermore, the program shows that housing markets apparently can respond to increased demands for housing caused by housing allowances without large price increases or other major imperfections requiring direct public policy intervention. One exception involves racial discrimination and segregation in the market, but their undesirable effects are not lessened by imposing quality requirements on households receiving aid. So why not just raise the incomes of poor households directly and let them decide how much of that added purchasing power, if any, to use in improving their housing?

Many of the same people who supported this viewpoint also argued that housing allowances were preferable to construction-related housing subsidies, if the real policy choice was between these two alternatives. In their eyes, the Experimental Housing Allowance Program demonstrated that housing allowances produced about the same results as construction-related housing subsidies, in terms of increased spending on housing and improved housing quality, but at *half the cost* per household aided. This is an extremely important result that makes the program well worth its cost—*if* the relevant authorities and the public will pay attention to it.

Nevertheless, other conference participants argued against this supposed superiority of housing allowances over construction-related subsidies. Some contended that Congress would never pass the form of housing allowance that would produce the same results as construction-related subsidies at half the cost per household. Doing so (though only on a much larger total scale than present construction-related subsidies) would provide housing quality that would be too high for the nation's low-income households—higher than the quality of housing occupied by renter households with incomes just over the eligibility limits. Many low-income households occupying housing created by construction-related subsidies already occupy good-quality housing. But there are far fewer such subsidized households than there would be under a universal housing allowance program.

A second view was that the Experimental Housing Allowance Program has shown housing allowances to have fewer and weaker virtues than originally were claimed for it in comparison with construction-related subsidies. In the early 1970s, HUD first suggested substituting a housing allowance for construction-related subsidies for several reasons. One was that a housing allowance would achieve much greater horizontal equity; it would provide aid for *all* low-income households, not for just the small fraction assisted under construction-related subsidies. In fact, a housing allowance achieves *complete* horizontal equity in terms of aid *offered,* since every low-income household gets such an offer. In contrast, very few are offered aid under construction-related subsidies because of closed-end financing. But the Experimental Housing Allowance program has shown that a housing allowance program would be much less than universal in terms of aid *actually received.* In fact, as many as half of all eligible households might not participate. Such participation would still be several times as large as the percentage of all eligible households currently receiving construction-related housing subsidies. Nevertheless, this finding somewhat weakens the superiority of a housing allowance over construction-related subsidies concerning horizontal equity of aid actually delivered.

Another supposed virtue of a housing allowance was that it would concentrate more federal aid on the lowest-income households than the particular construction-related subsidies predominant in the early 1970s. Those subsidies included many aimed at moderate-income households. But program experience indicates that many households occupying the poorest-quality housing units, including many very poor households, do not participate in a housing allowance program. Hence a housing allowance program does not concentrate aid on the neediest households as intensively as was initially assumed. This weakens its second presumed superiority over construction-related subsidies.

A third claim for such superiority was that housing allowances would allow more recipient households to move out of economically and racially segregated neighborhoods into more integrated ones than had been achieved by construction-related subsidies. But such dispersion and upgrading occurred to only a limited degree in the Experimental Housing Allowance Program; hence this supposed virtue was also weaker than advertised. However, it is true that the neighborhoods in which housing allowance recipients lived were less racially segregated than most public housing projects.

The fourth claimed virtue was that housing allowances would focus financial aid on improving the existing housing inventory, rather than adding new units. That would presumably conserve resources and help upgrade older cities, rather than undermining older neighborhoods by creating new units competitive with them. But the program produced relatively minor improvements in the existing inventory, since most funds were spent on nonhousing goods and services. As expected, the program did not stimulate new building competitive with older existing units; however, the program did not live up to its supposed effectiveness in greatly upgrading the existing inventory, although it did shift some units from substandard to standard condition.

In fact, the only anticipated superiority of a housing allowance program that emerges undiminished from the experience of the Experimental Housing Allowance Program is its lower cost per household. Diminished superiority is still superiority, even though it is smaller than that claimed by the original proponents of housing allowances. Against this remaining superiority must be weighed its disadvantages in comparison with construction-related subsidies. The latter can add more to the total supply of housing *if* these subsidies are aimed at low-income households and financed by governments rather than by conventional mortgages (otherwise the new subsidized units will be offset by declines in the production of new unsubsidized ones).[12] However, construction-related subsidies probably do not increase the supply of decent housing units any more than housing allowances, which cause upgrading of many units from substandard to standard quality. But construction-related subsidies can stimulate more employment in the home-building industry, insofar as the units they finance do not merely displace new unsubsidized units.

The last point leads into the principal argument advanced at the conference in favor of construction-related subsidies *or* a housing allowance

---

12. Michael P. Murray, "Subsidized and Unsubsidized Housing Starts: 1961–1977," Working Paper (Duke University, Center for the Study of Policy Analysis, June 1980).

rather than direct income maintenance. Both these housing-oriented forms of assistance might be politically supported by a coalition of home builders, construction unions, mortgage bankers, realtors, savings and loan associations, and building material suppliers and producers. Experience shows that coalitions of specific producer groups can be rallied in support of specialized forms of aid more effectively than broad political support can be organized for general income maintenance or job creation. Such coalitions are built around the suppliers of particular goods or services involved in the specialized forms of aid. These suppliers believe such aid will increase the demand for their products so long as the aid is somehow tied to requirements for greater consumption of those products. Examples are the suppliers of food supporting food stamps, the suppliers of health care supporting medicare and medicaid, and the suppliers of housing supporting housing subsidies. Advocates of a housing allowance without any quality requirements pointed out that the food stamp program had been modified so extensively from its original form that it was now in effect a pure income maintenance program. Yet it still receives major support from agricultural interests who believe it increases food consumption. Similarly, home builders and other real estate interests would support housing allowance funding more vigorously than pure income maintenance funding—even if the particular form of housing allowance adopted was just like an income maintenance program.

This strategy was supported by many conference participants who in theory greatly preferred general income maintenance and job creation to housing-tied subsidies for reasons set forth in Aaron's paper. They believed that such a coalition might produce far more support for redistributing additional resources toward the poor through these housing-oriented programs than any comparable coalition would produce for doing so through direct income maintenance. After all, the only obvious immediate gainers from more direct income maintenance are the poor themselves. No single clearly identifiable set of producers benefits by that form of redistribution, whereas the set described above benefits from housing-oriented subsidies—*if* those subsidies in fact increase the amount of money spent on housing. Moreover, the coalition described above will support such subsidies if they believe that to be the case, even if it is not.

As noted above, the potential political power of this housing coalition persuaded many conference participants that in reality, as opposed to theory, advocating added spending via a housing allowance would provide larger increases in welfare for the poor than advocating additional direct income maintenance. However, several participants pointed out that this coalition might reject a housing allowance in favor of construction-oriented subsidies, once its members realized how little of the money in a housing allowance program was actually devoted to housing. In fact, the housing coalition has long been wary of a housing allowance for precisely that reason. One participant countered this argument by pointing out that very little of the subsidies devoted to construction-related subsidies were ultimately spent on housing either. He contended that most of the new units thus stimulated merely displaced other new units the private sector would have built anyway, so there was little net increase in housing construction. If the housing coalition ever realized that fact, it might cease supporting *any* direct housing subsidy programs. However, few participants believed the housing coalition was likely to reach that conclusion about construction-oriented subsidies.

Clearly, the conference did not arrive at any simple or unanimous answer to the question, "Should society adopt a housing allowance program?" However, we hope the discussions of controversial issues presented in this paper will help readers arrive at their own answers in a more enlightened manner than was possible before the Experimental Housing Allowance Program.

Conference Participants

with their affiliations at the time of the conference

Henry J. Aaron *Brookings Institution*

Garland E. Allen *U.S. Department of Housing and Urban Development*

Jodie T. Allen *U.S. Department of Labor*

James S. Arisman *U.S. Commission on Civil Rights*

Pat Arnaudo *U.S. Department of Housing and Urban Development*

Helen E. Bakeman *Abt Associates*

C. Lance Barnett *Rand Corporation*

Barbara Becnel *AFL-CIO*

Marc Bendick, Jr. *Urban Institute*

Elizabeth Bernsten *Maryland State Department of Economic and Community Development*

Katharine L. Bradbury *Brookings Institution*

William Cammack *National Association for the Advancement of Colored People*

David B. Carlson *Urban Institute*

Grace Carter *Rand Corporation*

Terry Connell *U.S. Department of Housing and Urban Development*

Francis J. Cronin *Urban Institute*

Frank de Leeuw *U.S. Department of Commerce*

Cushing N. Dolbeare *National Low Income Housing Coalition*

Anthony Downs *Brookings Institution*

Jerry J. Fitts *U.S. Department of Housing and Urban Development*

Joseph Friedman *Abt Associates*

Evelyn S. Glatt *U.S. Department of Housing and Urban Development*

John L. Goodman, Jr. *Urban Institute*

William L. Hamilton *Abt Associates*

Howard Hammerman *U.S. Department of Housing and Urban Development*

Eric A. Hanushek *University of Rochester*

Larry Helbers *Rand Corporation*

Morton Isler *Urban Institute*

Franklin James *U.S. Department of Housing and Urban Development*

John F. Kain *Harvard University*

Valerie Karn *Urban Institute*

Stephen D. Kennedy *Abt Associates*

A. Thomas King *Federal Home Loan Bank Board*

G. Thomas Kingsley *Rand Corporation*

Kenneth Kraft *Appropriations Committee Counsel to Congressman Lawrence Coughlin*

Wilhelmina Leigh *National Urban League*

Martin D. Levine *Congressional Budget Office*

Ira S. Lowry *Rand Corporation*

David Lyon *Rand Corporation*

James Lyons *National Housing Conference*

Jean MacMillan *Abt Associates*

Robert E. Malakoff *Senate Banking Committee Staff*

Shirley Mansfield *Abt Associates*

Stephen K. Mayo *Abt Associates*

Sally R. Merrill *Abt Associates*

Edwin S. Mills *Princeton University*

Philip I. Moss *U.S. Department of Labor*

John E. Mulford *Rand Corporation*

Michael P. Murray *Duke University*

Edgar O. Olsen *University of Virginia*

Larry L. Orr *U.S. Department of Health, Education, and Welfare*

Larry J. Ozanne *Urban Institute*

Richard Peach *National Association of Realtors*

Joseph A. Pechman *Brookings Institution*

Wayne Perry *Rand Corporation*

David O. Porter *University of Texas*

John M. Quigley *Yale University*

Alice M. Rivlin *Congressional Budget Office*

Peter H. Rossi *University of Massachusetts*

C. Peter Rydell *Rand Corporation*

Barbara Sampson *Abt Associates*

Ann B. Schnare *Urban Systems Research and Engineering*

Morton J. Schussheim *Congressional Research Service*

Donna E. Shalala *U.S. Department of Housing and Urban Development*

Anne Squire *Urban Institute*

Michael Stegman *U.S. Department of Housing and Urban Development*

Nancy Stegman *U.S. Department of Housing and Urban Development*

Walter Stellwagen *Abt Associates*

Mahlon R. Straszheim *University of Maryland*

Jennifer Stucker *U.S. Department of Housing and Urban Development*

Arthur Sullivan *Princeton University*

James E. Wallace *Abt Associates*

Harold W. Watts *Columbia University*

Daniel Weinberg *Abt Associates*

Harold Williams *U.S. Department of Housing and Urban Development*

Roberton C. Williams, Jr. *Williams College*

Louis Winnick *Ford Foundation*

Ronald E. Wood *General Accounting Office*

Mark Wynn *U.S. Department of Housing and Urban Development*

John Yinger *Harvard University*

James P. Zais *Urban Institute*

Heidi Zukoski *House Budget Committee Staff*

Selected Bibliography

Abt Associates. *Agency Program Manual: Experimental Housing Allowance Program.* Cambridge, Mass.: Abt Associates, March 1973.

————. *Third Annual Report of the Administrative Agency Experiment Evaluation: October 1974–October 1975.* Cambridge, Mass.: Abt Associates, August 1976.

Atkinson, Reilly, William Hamilton, and Dowell Myers. "Draft Report on Economic and Racial/Ethnic Concentration in the Housing Allowance Demand Experiment." Cambridge, Mass.: Abt Associates, January 1979.

Bakeman, Helen E., Carol Ann Dalto, and Charles S. White, Sr. "Draft Report on Minimum Standards Requirements in the Housing Allowance Demand Experiment." Cambridge, Mass.: Abt Associates, February 1979.

Bakeman, Helen E., Stephen D. Kennedy, and James Wallace. *Fourth Annual Report of the Demand Experiment.* Cambridge, Mass.: Abt Associates, December 1977.

Barnett, C. Lance, and Ira S. Lowry. *How Housing Allowances Affect Housing Prices.* R-2452-HUD. Santa Monica: Rand Corporation, September 1979.

Bendick, Marc, Jr., and James P. Zais. *Incomes and Housing: Lessons from Experiments with Housing Allowances.* 249-9. Washington, D.C.: Urban Institute, October 1978.

Budding, David W. "Draft Report on Housing Deprivation Among Enrollees in the Housing Allowance Demand Experiment." Cambridge, Mass.: Abt Associates, November 1978.

————. *Inspection: Implementing Housing Quality Requirements in the Administrative Agency Experiment.* Cambridge, Mass.: Abt Associates, February 1977.

Carlson, David B., and John D. Heinberg. *How Housing Allowances Work: Integrated Findings from the Experimental Housing Allowance Program.* 249-3. Washington, D.C.: Urban Institute, February 1978.

Dickson, Donald E. *Certification: Determining Eligibility and Setting Payment Levels in the Administrative Agency Experiment.* Cambridge, Mass.: Abt Associates, March 1977.

Ellickson, Phyllis L., and David E. Kanouse. *Public Perceptions of Housing Allowances: The First Two Years.* Rand/WN-9817-HUD. Santa Monica: Rand Corporation, January 1978.

409

Friedman, Joseph, and Daniel Weinberg. "Draft Report on the Demand for Rental Housing: Evidence from a Percent of Rent Housing Allowance." Cambridge, Mass.: Abt Associates, September 1978.

————. "Draft Report on Housing Consumption Under a Constrained Income Transfer: Evidence from a Housing Gap Housing Allowance." Cambridge, Mass.: Abt Associates, April 1979.

Goedert, Jeanne E. *Earmarking Housing Allowances: The Trade-off Between Housing Consumption and Program Participation.* 249-19. Washington, D.C.: Urban Institute, May 1979.

————. *Generalizing from the Experimental Housing Allowance Program: An Assessment of Site Characteristics.* 249-6. Washington, D.C.: Urban Institute, June 1978.

Hamilton, W. L., David W. Budding, and W. L. Holshouser, Jr. *Administrative Procedures in a Housing Allowance Program: The Administrative Agency Experiment.* Cambridge, Mass.: Abt Associates, March 1977.

Hamilton, William L., and Jean MacMillan. *Outreach: Generating Applications in the Administrative Agency Experiment.* Cambridge, Mass.: Abt Associates, February 1977.

Heinberg, John D., Joanne D. Culbertson, and James P. Zais. *The Missing Piece to the Puzzle? Housing Allowances and the Welfare System.* 216-4. Washington, D.C.: Urban Institute, December 1974.

Heinberg, John D., Peggy W. Spohn, and Grace M. Taher. *Housing Allowances in Kansas City and Wilmington: An Appraisal.* 210-5. Washington, D.C.: Urban Institute, May 1975.

Holshouser, William L., Jr. *Report on Selected Aspects of the Jacksonville Housing Allowance Experiment.* Cambridge, Mass.: Abt Associates, May 1976.

————. *Supportive Services in the Administrative Agency Experiment.* Cambridge, Mass.: Abt Associates, February 1977.

Kennedy, Stephen D. *Final Report of the Housing Allowance Demand Experiment.* Cambridge, Mass.: Abt Associates, May 1980.

————, and Jean MacMillan. "Draft Report on Participation Under Alternative Housing Allowance Programs: Evidence from the Housing Allowance Demand Experiment." Cambridge, Mass.: Abt Associates, October 1979.

Kozimor, Lawrence W. *Eligibility and Enrollment in the Housing Allowance Program: Brown and St. Joseph Counties through Year Two.* Rand/WN-9816-HUD. Santa Monica: Rand Corporation, August 1978.

Lamar, Bruce W., and Ira S. Lowry. *Client Responses to Housing Requirements: The First Two Years.* Rand/WN-9814-HUD. Santa Monica: Rand Corporation, February 1979.

Levine, Martin D. *Federal Housing Policy: Current Programs and Recurring Issues.* Congressional Budget Office, Background Paper. Washington, D.C.: Government Printing Office, 1978.

Lowry, Ira S. *A Topical Guide to HASE Research.* Rand/N-1215-HUD. Santa Monica: Rand Corporation, June 1979.

————, ed. *The Design of the Housing Assistance Supply Experiment.* R-2360-HUD. Santa Monica: Rand Corporation, June 1980.

MacMillan, Jean. "Draft Report on Mobility in the Housing Allowance Demand Experiment." Cambridge, Mass.: Abt Associates, June 1978.

Maloy, Charles M., J. Patrick Madden, David Budding, and William L. Hamilton. *Administrative Costs in a Housing Allowance Program: Two-Year Costs in the Administrative Agency Experiment.* Cambridge, Mass.: Abt Associates, February 1977.

Mayo, Stephen, Shirley Mansfield, David Warner, and Richard Zwetchkenbaum. "Draft Report on Housing Allowances and Other Rental Housing Assistance Programs—A Comparison Based on the Housing Allowance Demand Experiment," pt. 1: "Participation, Housing Consumption, Location, and Satisfaction." Cambridge, Mass.: Abt Associates, November 1979.

———. "Draft Report on Housing Allowances and Other Rental Housing Assistance Programs—A Comparison Based on the Housing Allowance Demand Experiment," pt. 2: Costs and Efficiency." Cambridge, Mass.: Abt Associates, August 1979.

McCarthy, Kevin F. *Housing Choices and Residential Mobility in Site I at Baseline.* Rand/N-1091-HUD. Santa Monica: Rand Corporation, October 1979.

———. *Housing Choices and Residential Mobility in Site II at Baseline.* Rand/N-1119-HUD. Santa Monica: Rand Corporation, October 1979.

———. *Housing Search and Mobility.* R-2451-HUD. Santa Monica: Rand Corporation, September 1979.

McDowell, James L. *Housing Allowances and Housing Improvement: Early Findings.* Rand/N-1198-HUD. Santa Monica: Rand Corporation, September 1979.

Menchik, Mark David. *Residential Mobility of Housing Allowance Recipients.* Rand/N-1144-HUD. Santa Monica: Rand Corporation, October 1979.

Merrill, Sally R. "Draft Report on Hedonic Indices as a Measure of Housing Quality." Cambridge, Mass.: Abt Associates, December 1977.

———, and Catherine A. Joseph. "Draft Report on Housing Improvements and Upgrading in the Housing Allowance Demand Experiment." Cambridge, Mass.: Abt Associates, February 1979.

Mulford, John E. *Income Elasticity of Housing Demand.* R-2449-HUD. Santa Monica: Rand Corporation, July 1979.

———, George D. Weiner, and James L. McDowell. *How Allowance Recipients Adjust Housing Consumption.* N-1456-HUD. Santa Monica: Rand Corporation, August 1980.

Ohls, James C., and Cynthia Thomas. "The Effects of the Seattle and Denver Income Maintenance Experiments on Housing Consumption, Ownership, and Mobility." Draft Report. Denver: Mathematica Policy Research, January 1979.

Ozanne, Larry, and Raymond J. Struyk. *Housing from the Existing Stock: Comparative Economic Analyses of Owner-Occupants and Landlords.* 221-10. Washington, D.C.: Urban Institute, May 1976.

Rand Corporation. *Fourth Annual Report of the Housing Assistance Supply Experiment: October 1976–September 1977.* R-2302-HUD. Santa Monica: Rand Corporation, May 1978.

————. *Fifth Annual Report of the Housing Assistance Supply Experiment: October 1977–September 1978.* R-2434-HUD. Santa Monica: Rand Corporation, June 1979.

————. *Sixth Annual Report of the Housing Assistance Supply Experiment: October 1978–September 1979.* R-2544-HUD. Santa Monica: Rand Corporation, May 1980.

Rydell, C. Peter. *Shortrun Response of Housing Markets to Demand Shifts.* R-2453-HUD. Santa Monica: Rand Corporation, September 1979.

————. *Vacancy Duration and Housing Market Condition.* Rand/WN-10074-HUD. Santa Monica: Rand Corporation, January 1978.

Sepanik, Ronald J. *Variations of Selective Design Elements for Housing Allowances: Simulations Using the TRIM Model.* 216-19. Washington, D.C.: Urban Institute, August 1975.

————, Gary Hendricks, and John D. Heinberg. *Simulations of National Housing Allowances: An Application of the TRIM Model.* 216-13. Washington, D.C.: Urban Institute, February 1975.

Tebbets, Paul E. *Controlling Errors in Allowance Program Administration.* Rand/N-1145-HUD. Santa Monica: Rand Corporation, August 1979.

U.S. Department of Housing and Urban Development. *Experimental Housing Allowance Program: Conclusions, the 1980 Report.* Washington, D.C.: Government Printing Office, 1980.

————. *Experimental Housing Allowance Program: A 1979 Report of Findings.* Washington, D.C.: Government Printing Office, 1979.

————. *Housing Allowances: The 1976 Report to Congress.* Washington, D.C.: Government Printing Office, 1976.

————. *A Summary Report of Current Findings from the Experimental Housing Allowance Program.* Washington, D.C.: Government Printing Office, 1978.

Valenza, Joseph J. *Program Housing Standards in the Experimental Housing Allowance Program: Analyzing Differences in the Demand and Supply Experiments.* 216-30. Washington, D.C.: Urban Institute, July 1977.

Vanski, Jean, and Larry Ozanne. *Simulating the Housing Allowance Program in Green Bay and South Bend: A Comparison of the Urban Institute Housing Model and the Supply Experiment.* 249-5. Washington, D.C.: Urban Institute, October 1978.

Vidal, Avis. "Draft Report on the Search Behavior of Black Households in Pittsburgh in the Housing Allowance Demand Experiment." Cambridge, Mass.: Abt Associates, July 1978.

Note: The draft reports published by Abt Associates are now available in final form. Their publication date is June 1980.

Index

Aaron, Henry J., 68n, 339n, 393
Abt Associates, 4n, 6n, 8n, 9n, 16n, 17n, 18n, 67n, 76n, 126n, 142n, 166, 188, 248, 260, 289, 302n, 303n, 304n, 306n, 307n, 308n, 309n, 310n, 311n, 321, 328, 329, 332–33, 336–37, 342n, 355n, 367–68, 388
Administrative agency experiment: administration of, 328–30, 332–33; administrative cost index, 335–36; benefits, 97; certification, 97, 287, 293–94, 315–16; costs, 291, 294–96, 306–11, 318, 325, 335–36; criticism of, 302–12, 320–21, 323, 325–28, 333, 337, 395–97; data collection, 308; description, 34, 289; design, 14, 16–17, 20, 38–39, 302–05; evaluation/demonstration/experiment approach, 323–24; evaluative techniques, 17–18, 46, 308–09; function interaction, 325–28; inspections, 291–96, 308, 309, 316, 329; management information system, 332–33, 335; methodology, 308–11, 320–28; mobility, 175, 180; model proposal, 311–19; naturalistic approach, 302–05; operations, 18–20; outcomes, 289–96, 300–02; outreach, 287, 290, 305, 307, 309, 311, 314, 398; participation, 20, 143, 175, 223, 290–91, 296, 305–08, 329, 332–33, 346; site interactions, 325–27; support services, 144, 290–91, 294–96, 309, 311, 316, 397–99
Administrative systems: costs, 30, 83–87, 97, 294–96; function typology, 286–88; housing allowances and, 296, 300–02, 330–32; monthly reporting, 97, 98. *See also* Administrative agency experiment
Aid to families with dependent children (AFDC), 83–84, 86, 136, 137, 142
Aldrich, Howard, 322n

Alonso, William, 156n
American Public Health Association, 166
Anthony, Robert N., 332n
Apgar, William C., Jr., 353n, 359n, 361n, 363n
Atkinson, Reilly, 28n, 74n, 170, 182
Audits, 308

Baer, William C., 215n
Bailey, Martin J., 68n
Bakeman, Helen E., 6n, 21n
Barnett, C. Lance, 67n, 113n, 185n, 213, 242n, 254–56, 258–59, 264, 357n, 363, 367n
Barton, David M., 369n
Bayne, John, 67n
Beaton, W. Patrick, 174n
Bendick, Marc, Jr., 33n, 67n, 99n, 113n, 131n, 142n, 185n, 285n, 352–53
Benson, J. Kenneth, 322n
Bernsten, Elizabeth, 67n
Birch, David, 116, 118
Blackwell, Roger D., 174n
Blau, Peter M., 322n
Bradbury, Katharine L., 33n, 67n, 113n, 185n, 268n, 280n
Bruyn, Severyn Ten Haut, 323n
Buchanan, Garth, 76n
Budding, David W., 21n, 69n, 118n, 120n, 127n, 215, 216, 289n, 308n, 309n, 378n
Burtless, Gary, 224n

Carlson, David B., 3n, 29n, 30n, 80n, 83n, 86n, 142n, 347n
Carter, Grace E., 135n
Carter, Jimmy, 84
Cash assistance programs, 94, 104, 400; costs, 78, 83–85; criticism of, 186; demand behavior and, 208; growth of, 135–37; housing expenditure effects,

413